African Histories and Modernities

Series Editors
Toyin Falola
The University of Texas at Austin
Austin, TX, USA

Matthew M. Heaton
Virginia Tech
Blacksburg, VA, USA

This book series serves as a scholarly forum on African contributions to and negotiations of diverse modernities over time and space, with a particular emphasis on historical developments. Specifically, it aims to refute the hegemonic conception of a singular modernity, Western in origin, spreading out to encompass the globe over the last several decades. Indeed, rather than reinforcing conceptual boundaries or parameters, the series instead looks to receive and respond to changing perspectives on an important but inherently nebulous idea, deliberately creating a space in which multiple modernities can interact, overlap, and conflict. While privileging works that emphasize historical change over time, the series will also feature scholarship that blurs the lines between the historical and the contemporary, recognizing the ways in which our changing understandings of modernity in the present have the capacity to affect the way we think about African and global histories.

More information about this series at
http://www.palgrave.com/gp/series/14758

William J. Mpofu

Robert Mugabe and the Will to Power in an African Postcolony

palgrave
macmillan

William J. Mpofu
Wits Centre for Diversity Studies
University of the Witwatersrand
Johannesburg, South Africa

African Histories and Modernities
ISBN 978-3-030-47878-0   ISBN 978-3-030-47879-7   (eBook)
https://doi.org/10.1007/978-3-030-47879-7

This Palgrave Macmillan imprint is published by the registered company Springer Nature Switzerland AG.
The registered company address is: Gewerbestrasse 11, 6330 Cham, Switzerland

To the memory of Joseph William Mpofu, a father, teacher and priest.

Acknowledgements

I acknowledge the support of Professor Melissa Steyn, Dr Haley McEwen and the entire Wits Centre for Diversity Studies team whose collegiality is always intellectually nourishing. Professor Sabelo Ndlovu-Gatsheni, *Umdala wami*, Professor Morgan Ndlovu, Professor Siphamandla Zondi, Dr Blessed Ngwenya, Dr Brian Sibanda and the entire Africa Decolonial Research Network (ADERN) were monumentally supportive. Professor Tawana Kupe, Professor Mucha Musemwa, Professor Garth Stevens and Professor Ruksana Osman were encouraging and supportive of my efforts.

I must thank my friend Julius Joshua Kivuna for his interest in my work and vast knowledge of Africa and the world. The staff at Barcelos restaurant in Sunnyside, Pretoria, kept up with a strange man that insisted on colonising the tables at the corner with his books, and for watching over my table while I took walking and pipe-smoking breaks, pondering Mugabe, sometimes very late into the South African nights.

My many friends and family were pillars of support. Kagame Mbiko, Mkhosana Mathobela, Siphosami Mazanemvula, Bathabile, Simphiwe and Langalami Dinizulu endured my absences in peace. Cetshwayo Babongiwe gave me hearty good wishes. John Mbongeni Mpofu stood in for me where I could not avail myself. Mavusani Mpofu kept me on my toes and read some of my drafts.

CONTENTS

1   The Birth of the Symptom in the Postcolony   1

2   The Will to Power in the Postcolony   53

3   The Inventions of Robert Mugabe   113

4   When the Monsters Go Marching In: Mugabe the Production and Its Spectacles   171

5   A Career of Madness: Performances of the Will to Power   225

6   The Return of the Symptom in the Postcolony   305

References   345

Index   361

CHAPTER 1

The Birth of the Symptom in the Postcolony

Beware that, when fighting monsters, you yourself do not become a monster ... for when you gaze long into the abyss, the abyss gazes also into you.
—*Friedrich Nietzsche (1968: 112)*
The crisis consists precisely in the fact that the old is dying and the new cannot be born; in this interregnum a great variety of morbid symptoms appear.
—*Antonio Gramsci (1971: 275–276)*
It should be borne in mind that there is nothing more difficult to manage, or more doubtful of success, or more dangerous to handle than to take the lead in introducing a new order of things. For the innovator has enemies in all those who are doing well under the old order, and he has lukewarm defenders in all those who would do well under the new order.
—*Niccolo Machiavelli (2003a: 25)*

That the story of Robert Mugabe and his will to power will continue to arrest the attention of the world, long after his loss of power and death, cannot be doubted. What can be doubted is if the true meaning of Mugabe will be established. In life and in death, in political intrigue and spectacle, Mugabe stole the attention of the world. In his time Mugabe did not only become one of the oldest leaders in the world but also one of the most watched political actors. Whether he was lyrically pronouncing forgiveness

© The Author(s) 2021
W. J. Mpofu, *Robert Mugabe and the Will to Power in an African Postcolony*, African Histories and Modernities,
https://doi.org/10.1007/978-3-030-47879-7_1

for white Rhodesians at Zimbabwe's independence or declaring war on the political opposition Mugabe was a spectacle. Journalists, scholars and movie makers are still to feed fat on the story of the life and times of Robert Mugabe the Zimbabwean strongman whose ultimate strength finally became his defeating weakness. Mugabe filled the Zimbabwean political landscape with spectacular political performances that made the country a historical site for intriguing political spectacles and all sorts of alarming experiments. Perceptive journalists such as Heidi Holland (2008) have understood and circulated the Mugabe tale as "the untold story of a freedom fighter who became a tyrant." Similarly, committed human rights activists and liberals such as Michael Auret (2009) have lamented the transition of Mugabe from "liberator to dictator." Self-confessed adventure seekers and bored travel writers such as Douglass Rogers (2019) have treated the story of Mugabe and his fall from the graces of power as an entertaining thriller of plots and conspiracies by some brave securocrats, patriotic exiles and angry veterans of Zimbabwe's war of liberation from colonialism. In this book I lament the untruth that has widely and much misleadingly been circulated by some journalists and scholars. The falsehood that there was ever a hero and liberator in Mugabe conceals the original political desires and fears that drove Mugabe's will to power. "The Man" as Mugabe frequently referred to himself (Matyszak 2015) became possessed of a spirited will to power that was a combination of fears of weakness and desires for power. The love for power combined with a fear of weakness makes a man mad. Mugabe's will to power, that made him the ultimate political animal, a tyrant, was always concealed behind myths of gallant nationalism, pretences to undying Pan-Africanism and dramatisations of liberation heroism. In this book I attempt to separate the Mugabe of veracity, the thing itself, from Mugabe the actor and performer of things heroic, gallant and great. I seek to recover the true Mugabe from the debris of the many myths, shadows and performances of himself that he scattered around. From a socially vulnerable young boy to the strongman who built a reputation for muscular anti-imperialism and robust Africanism Mugabe spiritedly sought, found and kept power by any means necessary and some means truly unnecessary as I demonstrate in this book.

In Zimbabwe, Mugabe is remembered by the larger part of the population as a genocidist tyrant that reduced a "jewel of Africa" to a failed state that produced the country into a skunk of the world. Yet, thanks to his anti-colonial slogans and long harangues of speeches against western imperialism in Africa, Mugabe is largely held by the rest of the African continent, both the leaders and masses of the population, as a decolonial African hero of unquestionable standing. In the same way in which Ali Mazrui (1997: 125) famously found Kwame Nkrumah to be a great African statesman but a terrible Ghanaian, I find that Mugabe was a notable African and a terrible Zimbabwean leader. The Nkrumah that Mazrui condemned spoke of grand ideals of African unity while in Ghana he had more political prisoners than apartheid South Africa. To most Zimbabweans Mugabe was as good and as bad as any other colonial leader while in the rest of Africa he was and is still hailed as a gallant African liberator who spoke truth to Empire at the United Nations and other world political platforms. The African liberation heroism that Mugabe performed before African and international audiences was not the genocidal monstrosity that Zimbabweans came to know of the man. There are such African writers as Lucky Asuelime and Blessing Simurai (2013: 51) that see in Mugabe the political excellence of a "successful life president" that must be admired and emulated by the youth of Africa. As a subject of critique, political commentary and narrative Mugabe became divisible and divisive. He became many things to different people and disagreements about him were emphatic.

I note how Mugabe effectively took his place amongst the tyrants and dictators of the world that Christopher Hope (2003) has called "brothers under the skin"; whether they are white like Ian Smith or black like Idi Amin, in essence they remain the same power mongers and merchants of death. Those that go into battle against monsters, Nietzsche (1968) warned, must guard against the temptation to be converted into monsters themselves. In the fight against the monstrosity of white settler colonialism in Rhodesia, Mugabe failed to overcome the temptation to be a colonising monster in his own right. Instead of being true to the role of the freedom fighter and liberator, Mugabe was infected by the hate, anger and evil of the same colonialism that he sought to dethrone. Under the tyranny and monstrous rule of Mugabe Zimbabwe became what Achille Mbembe (1992) has described as a "postcolony," a time and a place where the violent ghosts of colonialism are refusing to be put to burial and keep returning to haunt the country. In the postcolony that Mbembe describes colonial modes of politics remain vivid when colonialism is supposed to be dead and buried.

Under Mugabe's rule Zimbabwe became a true postcolony that suffered a debilitating hangover of Rhodesia. The colonial politics of yesterday that privileged rule by coercion remained at large. Instead of emerging as a free and liberated country with a bright future, under Mugabe Zimbabwe remained captured in a forbidding political interregnum. In a typical interregnum, Antonio Gramsci (1971) noted that "the old is dying and the new cannot be born," which created a historical political stalemate that Zimbabwe still suffers today. Where colonialism and all its monstrosities were supposed to be dead and be buried in Zimbabwe, freedom itself refused to be born, creating a historical gap for political morbidities and obscenities such as the Gukurahundi Genocide that immediately followed what was supposed to be the independence of the country.

Far from becoming the gallant freedom fighter and liberator of Zimbabweans, Mugabe became a morbid symptom of enduring colonialism that refused to die. With all his vaunted education and political grandiosity, Mugabe joined those men of post-independence Africa that, dressed in their suits and ties, brought the devil of colonialism back to life in the continent. In the classic novel *Devil on the Cross*, Ngugi wa Thiongo (1987: 13) describes how African black masses, "dressed in rags," and poor like the blacks in Rhodesia, bravely fought and crucified the devil of colonialism on the cross. Just when they thought colonialism was dead and gone: "after three days, there came others dressed in suits and ties, who keeping close to the wall of darkness, lifted the Devil down from the cross, and they knelt before him, and they prayed in loud voices, beseeching him to give them a portion of his robes of cunning." Many Zimbabweans, Africans and others in the world believed that the raising of a new flag, singing of a new melodious national anthem and arrival of a besuited and bespectacled black Prime Minister in the shape of Robert Mugabe on the 18th of April 1980 meant that colonialism was dead and gone when it had only changed skin colour and name. Mugabe was to recharge and reproduce colonialism in Zimbabwe. The analytical courage to observe and name the tyranny and evil of an African post-independence leader as, not just comparable to the colonisers, but as a coloniser par excellence is what might lead observers to the true essence of such leaders as Mugabe. Inquiry into the political thought and practice of Mugabe is a journey into the systemic way in which colonialism as a system of domination was fought by black African leaders, not to replace it with liberation, but to reproduce it as a form of post-colonial domination of Africans by a political elite of new black colonisers. In this book I volunteer to join that small choir of decolonial African tragic optimists that are willing to make visible the colonialism of some black African leaders in the continent. When Mugabe (1997a) himself referred to his political leadership as the "conquest of conquest" he unwittingly described how he participated in the defeat of white settler colonialism in order to replace it with his own nativist colonisation of Zimbabwe.

After fighting colonialism, together with other Zimbabwean nationalist leaders, and achieving political power, Mugabe failed to introduce a new order of politics and power that was alternative to colonialism. The colonial order of things, in Rhodesia like in apartheid South Africa, was an overpowering universe that turned some of its opponents into its accessories and functionaries. Classically, Niccolo Machiavelli (2003b: 25) noted the difficulty, the doubt and the many dangers that confront those that aspire to introduce a new order of things after tyrannical regimes and colonial dispensations. Contrary to pretensions and myths otherwise, Mugabe did not have the mental stamina of a freedom fighter or the spiritual and emotional gravitas of a liberator that could introduce a new political order that could produce a liberated Zimbabwe. He simply imitated, amplified and tragically reproduced the colonial disorder of things that Ian Smith had been advancing in Rhodesia.

After a spectacular political career that began on the 20th of July 1960, when he formally joined anti-colonial politics, and ended on the 21st of November 2017 when he was deposed in a coup, Mugabe's political rule can be described as what Samantha Power (2008: 1) correctly called "the art of how to kill a country." On the one side a dilapidated infrastructure, many mass graves and a population of poor and second-hand people that wear second-hand clothes from far away countries are what Mugabe and his rule left behind in Zimbabwe. On the other side, much like in the colonial order of things, Mugabe ruled Zimbabwe by an iron fist and a cruel exercise of power that Mbembe (1992: 5) calls the "commandment," which mixes true tyranny with terror, evil and spectacle. Tragically for Zimbabwe, some years after Mugabe was removed from power and some months after his death, those that removed him from power are outdoing Mugabe in Mugabeism. Abductions and torture of political activists, shooting by the military of unarmed civilians and poisonings of the political rivals of powerful politicians of the ruling party are the order of the day in the Zimbabwean postcolony. Instead of becoming a living testimony of Zimbabwean liberation Mugabe, in the fullness of his time, became a symptom of the enduring malady of coloniality in Zimbabwe.

THE ANTI-COLONIAL SPECTACLES OF THE SYMPTOM

Mugabe has taught us that anti-colonialism in all its radical opposition to colonialism can be nothing more than the other side of the bloody order of colonialism, its hatred, anger and readiness for evil. In his life, and except in performances and pretences, Mugabe was never a freedom fighter or a liberator but a die-hard anti-colonialist that became entrapped in coloniality. Anti-colonialism can stumble and fall, and get entangled with colonialism. Anti-colonialism may defeat colonialism but only to institute, as Mugabe did in Zimbabwe, a venal nativist colonisation of the country. What misled many commentators, including Heidi Holland and Michael Auret, into believing that there was ever a freedom fighter and liberator in Mugabe is the long years he spent in the colonial prison, his leadership of the guerrilla war and performances of conciliatory rhetoric at Zimbabwe's independence that eventually became a pipe dream that it still is today. The limit of anti-colonialism is its imbrications in colonialism and coloniality. In his observation of what he called "Mugabeism" Sabelo Ndlovu-Gatsheni notes that Mugabe's politics was anti-colonialism that did not mature into decoloniality:

> Mugabe's politics have always been anti-colonial rather than decolonial. This is why his post-colonial practice of governance is not very different from that of colonialists at many levels. Mugabeism has embraced violence as a pillar of governance. Racism has continued despite Mugabe's earlier pronunciation of a policy of reconciliation at independence in 1980. Tribalism became normalised and exacerbated to the extent that Mugabe's regime unleashed ethnic violence on the minority Ndebele speaking people of Matabeleland and the Midlands regions. (Ndlovu-Gatsheni 2015: 2)

In the true Nietzschean political dilemma of those that fight monsters and gaze so deeply into the abyss of monstrosity and end up becoming monsters in their own right, Mugabe failed to avoid being contaminated by and reproducing the colonialism that he fought. Anti-colonialism alone is not decolonial or is it sufficient to lead to liberation; in fact, it easily degenerates to the same domination and coloniality that it seeks to dethrone. In other words Mugabe fought the negative fight, against colonialism, and did not go on to fight the positive fight, for liberation. In that way Mugabe became a negation, first to Rhodesian colonialism and next to the Zimbabwean postcolony. Ndlovu-Gatsheni insists that:

Anti-colonialism gestured towards taking over power by black elites from white colonialists. Anti-colonialism enabled black elites to inherit the colonial state. Once the black elites inherited the colonial state, they never bothered to radically transform it. Deracialisation became conflated with decolonization of state institutions. Africanisation degenerated into nativism, xenophobia, retribalization, chauvinism and racism. Therefore, anti-colonialism must not be confused with decoloniality. (Ndlovu-Gatsheni 2015: 1)

Those that saw a freedom fighter and liberator in Mugabe had confused anti-colonialism for decoloniality and liberation. For Mugabe, as I demonstrate in this book, colonialism and the cruelty that it visited on him and others turned into a school that taught and produced him into a coloniser. Instead of fighting colonial power and the colonial system in order to replace it with liberation, Mugabe turned to admire the colonial technology and infrastructure of power and, after independence in Zimbabwe, reproduced and even escalated it for his own power and dominance. The reproduction of colonial political systems and paradigms of power by black leaders that fought colonialism is a major way in which political decolonisation did not lead to liberation in the African continent. Thus, in supposedly independent Zimbabwe, Joshua Nkomo (1984: 3), a freedom fighter and opposition political leader, could mourn that the liberation movement under Mugabe had replaced colonial rule with another form of colonialism. The new colonialism of the postcolony this time was championed by those black politicians that had fought colonial rule, and that publicly demanded heroism and veneration for their liberation war sacrifices. Mugabe made much political stock and capital of his personal suffering and sacrifices in the liberation struggle, to the extent of attempting, tragically, to personalise the nation and create a family dynasty that would rule Zimbabwe in perpetuity. Mugabe has left behind veterans of the war of liberation and securocrats that believe that they own the country and are entitled to its resources and power forever.

Such writers as Sue Onslow and Martin Plaut (2018: 13) simplify Mugabe's problem in Zimbabwe to a problem of an otherwise good leader whose "tragedy was that he stayed in office as leader of the country and head of his party, ZANU-PF, for far too long," until "his achievements had long since faded from public consciousness." The problematic of Mugabe's longevity in power that Onslow and Plaut circulate is not new. Such students of Zimbabwean history and politics as Norma Kriger (2003:

307) also hold the view that Mugabe simply became "another too long serving African ruler." In this book I erect and hold the observation that it was a mistake from the start for Zimbabweans, Africa and the world to have taken Mugabe to be anyone that was charged to deliver liberation, peace and progress. His longevity in power only served to allow time, the father of all truth, to unmask Mugabe as the tyrant and dictator that he always was. Zimbabwean anti-colonialism and its anti-colonialists, exemplified in Mugabe, were always loaded and charged with colonial politics and its violences.

As early in the life of independent Africa as 1963, Frantz Fanon observed the underside and "pitfalls of national consciousness" amongst African leaders who inherited power from colonial regimes. In its anti-colonialism, African nationalist consciousness that drove such leaders as Mugabe quickly degenerated, Fanon noted, into chauvinism, racism, nativism, tribalism and xenophobia, all of which are colonial political tendencies in the very first place. Politically, anti-colonial ideologies very easily returned to the same colonial tendencies of power that they set down to fight. All because of their "intellectual laziness, and political unpreparedness" African post-independence political leaders such as Mugabe in this case, Fanon (2001: 148) argues, became "these heads of government" that "are the true traitors in Africa for they sell their country to the most terrifying of all its enemies: stupidity." The Gukurahundi Genocide of 1982 to 1987 in Zimbabwe happened too early in the history of the country and took too long for any discerning writer to dwell on an earlier Mugabe that was a freedom fighter and a liberator. Mugabe took the country, rather too quickly, from a colonial era to a genocidal moment. The Rhodesian settler colonialism of Ian Smith, at Zimbabwe's independence, only led to the nativist colonialism of Mugabe.

Mugabe personified the intellectual laziness, political unpreparedness and philosophical stupidity of the African elite that took power from colonial regimes which Fanon refers to. The tribalism that led to the Gukurahundi Genocide, the simplistic way in which land redistribution was conducted all point to some political stupidity in Mugabe's anti-colonial politicking. Even as old age dogged him and fresh ideas were no longer his property Mugabe possessed some anti-colonial entitlement to power that approached the stupid and the ridiculous in proportion. Notably, at some point, "addressing concerns now routinely voiced about her husband's advanced age, First Lady Grace Mugabe assured the nation that if Mugabe secured another term as president, he would even be wheeled to the swearing-in ceremony if necessary" and not only that "to ensure continuity in the event of his death, Grace had gone so far as to assure the shocked nation that her husband would continue to serve as president even from the confines of his tomb at the National Heroes Acre"(Nyarota 2018: 85). Mugabe, his family and other supporters had truly begun to live in a fool's paradise that was insulated from the real world, especially the world of power politics and the comity of modern democratic nations. One of the misleading and dangerous beliefs that Mugabe held about himself and his leadership was that he was a divine messenger or special agent of God himself (Matyszak 2015) whose right to rule in perpetuity was cast in stone.

If Mugabe's political stupidity had become alarming his political denialism became spectacular. He began not only to challenge but also to deny nature itself. Delusions of his invincibility and irreplaceability in power grew to become not only spectacular but also pathetic. Geoff Nyarota tells only part of the spectacular and pathetic performances of Mugabe's anti-colonial ego: "As Mugabe continued to age in office, his growing incapacitation became clear to see. He lost the ability to walk unaided; he succumbed to extended bouts of sleep, even in public; and he was rumoured even to have soiled himself" (Nyarota 2018: 117). All these spectacular and pathetic farces of a denialist anti-colonial ego happened as Mugabe publicly denied allegations of his failing health, and this with the help of clever spokespersons and learned spin-doctors. That at the age of ninety something that Mugabe had reached, everyone becomes officially and clinically unwell missed Mugabe who continued to pretend to perfect health and suitability for office.

The formations and performances of the anti-colonial ego that are embodied in Africa's post-independence leaders are of interest to this book. It is the limits, fragilities and vulnerabilities of anti-colonial mindsets and sensibilities that made anti-colonial politics incapable of being a durable alternative to colonialism. Peter Ekeh (1975) importantly explains that the class of intellectuals and political activists in Africa that replaced colonial administrators had become in itself a colonial class that shared nothing with their own people but had begun to compete with white colonial administrators for contempt for black people and pretensions to modernity and coloniality. Anti-colonial intellectual and political sensibility became fundamentally colonial and also racist. As colonialism seemed to die it was actually getting born in the hearts and minds of black African leaders that were fighting colonialism. They came to understand and know no other politics and mode of power besides the colonial, and so did they become more than ready to reproduce coloniality and become new black colonisers. Colonialism swallowed and absorbed them into its universe and they in turn swallowed it and internalised it into their own psychological and emotional make-up; it became them and they became it. It is perhaps for that reason that Fanon insisted that the unconscious but real ambition of those that were oppressed by colonialism was to become new colonial oppressors in their own right. In the Zimbabwean postcolony Mugabe spectacularly performed the dark role of a leader who fought and later tragically turned around to become a coloniser.

The state and country that Mugabe inherited from the Rhodesian regime were not even in the least reformed to suit what could be experienced and called independence. In his important book about "violence in Zimbabwe" as an "institutionalised" phenomenon, Lloyd Sachikonye (2011) describes how colonial violence structurally and psychologically produced post-colonial violence. In violently reacting to colonial violence, the individuals and organisations that fought the Zimbabwean liberation struggle became part of the culture and political system of violence as an instrument of dehumanisation. The state that Mugabe headed proved what happens "when a state turns on its citizens" (Sachikonye 2011). Zimbabwe as what Mbembe called the "postcolony," specifically in reference to Cameroon, became a chaotic site of morbid political symptoms where colonialism combined with anti-colonialism to occasion a kind of hell on earth. Those, like Mugabe, that had fought the monstrosity of colonialism had in a true Nietzschean sense become monsters. They had become incapable of bringing to life a new political order of things. They did not only maintain the colonial order of things but they also magnified and multiplied it through a violent impunity that Horace Campbell (2003: 75) called "executive lawlessness" where Mugabe became a hooligan in chief that permitted festivals of cruelty and perpetrated a genocide on part of the population.

Perhaps, a clearer understanding of how anti-colonialism failed to successfully overthrow colonialism requires another understanding of colonialism that allows a view into how it co-opted its opponents and converted them into its perpetrators. How exactly those who went out to fight colonialism ended up, not becoming freedom fighters and liberators, but symptoms of colonialism that became evidence of its continuity after independence is important to the present book. Once again Peter Ekeh's understanding of colonialism is helpful. To Peter Ekeh (1983: 1) the motives of colonisers were to take control of or create states so that they could gain access to resources and economies in Africa, and this colonial motive was sold to nationalist and Marxist leaders that fought colonialism; their focus became state power and the monopolisation of resources and economies. In that way, colonialism and the reaction to it in Africa belonged to the same political and economic agenda. Colonialism became "a social movement of epochal dimensions" (Ekeh 1983: 4). As such, colonialism shaped and produced political identities and sensibilities of both the colonisers and the colonised. Those like Mugabe that were fighting colonialism came to do so using its language, political ideologies, culture and sensibility. Anti-colonialism conducted a struggle against colonialism from within colonial perimeters and logic. Mugabe and others fought colonialism not from outside its systems and structures but from within and so could they not possibly overcome it and build political cultures and systems that were alternative to it; they could only duplicate it.

As an anti-colonialist that took over power from Ian Smith in 1980 Mugabe became much admired in Africa and especially in the West. In his early days in power, Mugabe exuded striking peace and reconciliation rhetoric. In fact, "Mugabe's rhetoric of reconciliation and nation building, which was so striking to both the suspicious white population and the international community" (Onslow and Plaut 2018: 15) was only that, rhetoric. It was a well-performed rhetoric that for some time earned him an international following. For some time "Mugabe's status as a hero of Zimbabwe's liberation was reinforced, while he became a political leader of repute, being wined and dined in western capitals, where he was showered with accolades" (Nyarota 2018: 32). Even after the Gukurahundi Genocide, in 1994, Mugabe was knighted by the Queen of England. Countless honorary doctorates from many western universities became his to receive in pomp and ceremony. Mugabe's pretences to exemplary politics of good leadership were spectacular performances that fooled not only Zimbabweans but Africa and the world. It is in the post-political nature of anti-colonialism that it creates all the euphoria but delivers treachery and tragedy. In a strong way, Mugabe became a spectacular post-political anti-colonial mistake that Zimbabwe might not easily recover from.

A BLACK AND WHITE MISTAKE IN ZIMBABWE

The tyrant proper is not only a monster but also a salesman that markets hope and circulates mesmerising promises. He begins by captivating the population with visions of a bright future and dreams of peace and prosperity. As a good anti-colonialist Mugabe performed all the promises of a new order of things to come. True to Machiavelli's concerns about the difficulty of bringing about a new order of things, Mugabe wanted to please whites that were otherwise happy under colonialism and suspicious, if not fearful, of a post-independence era. At the same time Mugabe was keen to impress blacks that were pessimistic or else rather too optimistic about the new post-colonial order. Mugabe had to pull out effective performances and presences to please a divided political audience. People were bound to be fooled. In other words, against Amilcar Cabral's proverbial warning to African leaders, Mugabe told lies and claimed easy victories in conveniently promising both blacks and whites a paradisal future in Zimbabwe.

Mugabe's pretences to great leadership and spectacular performances of exemplary politics did not only fool the naïve and the politically uncircumcised but also the critical and the enlightened amongst blacks and whites in Zimbabwe and outside. To illustrate the potency of Mugabe's post-political and anti-colonial performances of greatness that concealed his evil and had some of the sharpest minds taken in, one may need an example. Before that, it is important to state that most people's failure to understand Mugabe for what he truly was became a failure that was based on people failing to understand themselves, their fears and political interests in the very first place. Before correctly understanding the fears and desires that drive our interests and choices we may not get into anyone's shoes to correctly decipher their own fears, desires, interests and fragilities. Perhaps Slavoj Zizek (2017: 178) is correct that "people often ask themselves if a person can really imagine what it is to be another person; what a psychoanalyst would add is that we also cannot imagine what it is to be ourselves"; we are blind to our own fears and interests that make some of our dreams and wishes appear to be reality. Most people and organisation that got invested in the heroism of Mugabe are entities that were in love with their dreams and interests. Mugabe as a freedom fighter and heroic liberator was more of an imagined personality than a real person; the people's hero can be a true figment of the optimistic imagination of the followers.

In a way, Mugabe did not simply fool many Zimbabweans and the world into believing in his non-existent heroism. Many fooled themselves and Mugabe became an object of their wishful dreams, a god of their imaginations. Michael Auret wrote an entire book that battles with the question of how Mugabe as a "liberator" turned into a "dictator." Indeed, the burden of the book was to attempt a solution to the mystery:

> Part of the reason for writing this book was for me to gain some understanding of how so many of us so gravely misconstrued the situation in Zimbabwe once independence had been achieved. How was it possible that so serious an error of judgement could have been made by so many people, in the world not only in Zimbabwe? (Auret 2009: viii)

Many black and white Zimbabweans ask themselves this same question. Just how Mugabe wormed himself into international heroism and fooled the world into it might be a mystery to many up to today. The present book is only surprised that many were actually surprised that Mugabe turned out not to be a freedom fighter or liberator of many people's dreams and wishes. The answer to Michael Auret's troubling question is not so hidden as it is found only in the next paragraph from the question that he poses. In answering his own question, he says that his and other white people's "white thinking" had misled him. As whites, he notes that:

> In 1980 we hoped that the black Zimbabweans would forgive and forget the contempt in which we held them for so long, the indignities we had heaped on them, the lack of respect we had for the culture and customs of the people. We hoped that perhaps, against all that, they would weigh the development, the health and education, the communication facilities and the expertise we had brought, and find it at least pragmatic to allow us to stay, and most of all to allow us to keep the land we had occupied over the 90 years of the existence of the colony. (Auret 2009: vii)

White thinking, white wishes and white interests that were driven by the fear of black revenge after the sins of colonialism demanded that blacks should forgive and forget even when no one apologised. The damages of long years of colonialism were not undone in the postcolony. But the former colonisers post-politically felt entitled to forgiveness and the gift of reconciliation from the black people they had exploited for decades. There was also a very colonial and racist reasoning that was also naïve, the reason that blacks should be grateful for the development and modernisation that colonialism with all its evils had brought them. This rather simplistic colonialist thinking argues as if it is the law of nature that people should suffer enslavement and colonialism in order for them to develop and modernise.

Mugabe's anti-colonial and post-political performances of the rhetoric of reconciliation were aimed at white ears and white colonial and racist thinking. It was a trap and a pretence that whites fell for. It was a performance to a fearful, self-interested and wishful audience that wanted reconciliation without justice after colonialism. They wanted to keep the land and other benefits of conquest and colonialism and still benefit from black generosity, reconciliation, peace and love. They wanted to eat twice, from colonial Rhodesia and post-colonial Zimbabwe. They were not in awe of Mugabe the freedom fighter and the liberator but they worshiped their dreams and wishes of post-political reconciliation and enduring benefits from colonialism. More than simple white political naiveté was involved here; even mean white racist selfishness was involved in elevating Mugabe to a hero. For his own personal political interests, Mugabe performed mesmerising rhetoric of reconciliation. Some whites did not love and follow Mugabe the hero; they loved and followed their fears and interests, as privileged beneficiaries of colonialism and anti-colonialism. Mugabe became a true white mistake that fed on white political fears and interests; first he promised them paradisal forgiveness and reconciliation and later, during the Fast Track Land Reform Programme, he unleashed on them diabolic violence. Trusting Mugabe with heroism and unbridled power became a post-political game that was bound to end very badly. White thinking and white expectations did not help to illuminate but worked to fog the real Mugabe, a power monger.

Michael Auret was not an everyday white Zimbabwean or a racist and a bigot. He was a respected human rights activist and trusted Catholic missionary. His thoughts and words are weighty and meaningful. As he confesses himself, his words represent well-meaning but true and selfish "white thinking" and wishes about the Zimbabwean postcolony. A reflection of how black Zimbabweans were also taken in by Mugabe's pretensions to heroism is found in the writing of Trevor Ncube, a prominent publisher in the Zimbabwean and South African independent media. What troubles Trevor Ncube (2009: ix) is that "from a liberation war hero, Robert Mugabe has effectively transformed himself into one of the most despicable dictators Africa has ever known, Mugabe has so tarnished his legacy that history will certainly judge him harshly." The mistake that Ncube and other blacks made was ever to see a liberation hero in Mugabe.

In Mugabe, an illusion sold itself as such and was mistakenly bought as reality. From the beginning, except in pretence, dramatic performance and the imagination of supporters, Mugabe did not create any legacy of liberation that can be tarnished or judged harshly by any history. The elections of 1980 that inserted Mugabe into power in Zimbabwe were preceded by political violence that Joshua Nkomo (1984) compared to "terror." General Peter Walls, a senior Rhodesian army official, wrote to the British government pleading that the elections be nullified for their violence and fraud. Soon enough Mugabe decorated his questionable and discredited electoral victory with the Gukurahundi Genocide. Mugabe's legacy was from the start a legacy of violence and electoral fraud that was ignored by a black population that was hungry for a hero and white people that were too grateful for the promises of forgiveness and reconciliation that Mugabe performed. In essence the man was no freedom fighter, liberator or hero but a tyrant waiting to happen. And Mugabe happened to disastrous consequences for the Zimbabwean postcolony.

Cunning politicians especially those of the tyrannical and evil type know how and when to capitalise on the fears and desires of their populations. Mugabe forcefully circulated fictions and illusions of himself as a solution to the political problems of blacks and whites in Zimbabwe. He effectively performed heroism and the performances did not fool only novices and simpletons but discerning and sophisticated thinkers. Most of these complex minds did not know at the time that in Mugabe's performances they did not fall in love with any reality but their own imaginations, desires and wishes. Most heroes and saints, especially in politics, are creatures of the imagination. Ncube recounts his fascination with Mugabe the actor:

> Just like Mike Auret, I was taken in by Mugabe. In fact, I can confess that Robert Mugabe used to be my hero. At University, when I was vice-president of the Students Representative Council, I remember how proud I was when he came to visit us. I lined up to shake his hand in the Senior Common Room, and it was a moment I cherished. (Ncube 2009: xi)

The Mugabe who mesmerised Ncube was not a person of reality but an artefact of performance and a figment of Ncube's good wishes. Ncube and many others needed a hero and an impersonator of a hero took the place; it became a black and white mistake to take a stage character for a person. Actors, be it in the movies, on the theatre stage or in the political arena cannot be solely blamed for circulating falsehoods but spectators who take figs for facts and receive fiction as history are responsible and must be accountable. Partly, populations and the political followership became gullible and accepted personas for persons. Mugabe the hero was a persona. Behind the persona hid a tyrant that was bidding time to explode into a true monstrosity.

How Trevor Ncube and others were taken in by Mugabe can be a story that is rich in sadness. It was to be a true comedy of errors if it did not lead to much death, poverty and suffering in the once promising country. Ncube is able to relate how not only him but, in my view, the masses of black Zimbabweans were swindled by the Mugabe act:

> In fact, were it not for my mother's influence, my natural instincts were to support Robert Mugabe instead of Joshua Nkomo, a man adored by my politically active mother. To me, Mugabe had the qualities of a modern African leader. I admired the way he spoke, his manner of thought, his vision. I looked forward to when he addressed the nation, and marveled at how he fired such strong sentiments of patriotism and nationalism. As I travelled the world, I was proud to be Zimbabwean, and especially proud that Mugabe was my president. He had restored the dignity that the race-based policies of Ian Smith had taken away from black Zimbabweans. Zimbabwe was African, independent and free, Mugabe was my man, and I never missed an opportunity to gloat. (Ncube 2009: xii)

Black Zimbabweans needed their lives and pride back after a history of colonial humiliation and dehumanisation. Their thirst for liberation led them to fall for a political confidence trickster who said all the right things and said them the right way. Mugabe, like any other good actor, had a practiced and polished manner of speaking that is designed to capture and sweep away audiences.

Before and during his time in power, Mugabe used the potent weapon of oratory to construct himself as an irreplaceable spokesperson and hero. The same weapon of oratory that he used in 1960 to recommend himself to the leaders of the National Democratic Party and the poor masses of Zimbabweans he continued to deploy. In many ways Mugabe spoke and performed himself into power. Frequently he spoke himself into a trance-like state, especially when he was berating some enemy. Petina Gappah partly but effectively captures the rhetorical force and convincing performance of Mugabe in speech, the theatrical delivery that bit Trevor Ncube and many others, black and blue:

Among Mugabe's most effective instruments, and one that he deployed frequently, was his extra-ordinary voice. It may seem odd to outsiders, but Mugabe's speeches were one of the ways he held sway over his country. They contained sweeping phrases invoking Zimbabwe's fifteen liberation struggle against the Rhodesian settler regime of Ian Smith. He employed literary devices that made his words weapons ... he speaks like no one else. (Gappah 2017: 1)

What Mugabe's optimistic audience missed is that speaking eloquently of heroism and about liberation struggles does not make one a liberator or a hero; one might after all be the proverbial devil reciting the gospel. Ncube explains how exactly Mugabe's speeches to the nation and the world made Zimbabweans feel proud of being Zimbabwean and of having such a leader and spokesperson. No doubt Mugabe also knew this and employed and deployed his speechcraft to impress. But it was exactly that, a performance and dramatisation of what was an absence. After long years of the liberation struggle, finally, blacks thought they had found, in Mugabe, a hero that was going to prove to the world that Zimbabweans were also human beings and possessed some excellence. Martha Nussbaum (1998: 273) is correct that tyrants are not just political animals but are also lucky animals. Mugabe had the luck to pull his impressive act when the Zimbabwean black and white population was a willing audience that fooled itself before the clown arrived, and believed the unbelievable. Mugabe pulled out bewitching performances that hypnotised populations and put even thoughtful opinion leaders under a spell. Black and white Zimbabweans were at the time a political audience that was ready to be fooled and anything that looked like a hero and a deliverer was welcomed. Those like Ncube's mother that were not fooled became a sorry minority. Tyrants are exactly that, convincing performers. If such learned and enlightened thought-leaders such as Ncube and Auret were fooled by the convincing performance, masses of ordinary people were totally beguiled.

The black African men in suits and ties, that Ngugi describes, the ones that brought the devil of colonialism back from death and down from the cross did so with impressive and convincing performances. The besuited pretenders did not only fool peasants or gullible plebeians but also fine and sophisticated black and white thought leaders. In hindsight, after Mugabe had come out as the monster that he was and that he kept artfully hidden behind the rhetoric of peace and reconciliation, Michael Auret, in perplexity, could only ask the troubling questions: "Was Mugabe a man of peace and reconciliation, or violence and vengeance? Was he ever a man of peace and democracy? If not how did we err so seriously in our judgement of him?" (Auret 2009: xviii). Ncube who was earlier totally enchanted by Mugabe and felt black humanity and dignity had found an international ambassador in Mugabe and his leadership could only make the dark observation that many Zimbabweans came to hold:

> Mugabe has assaulted and poisoned our national pride and psyche, and it will take us a long time to get back to where we were in 1980. He has turned our hope into despair. The great expectations that political freedom held out in 1980 have been turned into a long nightmare. We have lost our pride and dignity as a people. Our hope and dreams as a nation have been held hostage to Mugabe's steely determination to stay in power until he drops dead. (Ncube 2009: xii)

The tyrant, behind impressive performances of such grand national and human ideals as peace and reconciliation, remains what he is, a thief of the dignity and hopes of the people. He turns what were dreams into nightmares. It is for that reason that all politicians must ordinarily be put under suspicion and watched no matter what their public pretences and performances are. While in criminal justice a person should be presumed innocent until proven guilty, in political reason they should be assumed guilty until proven innocent. The need for critical political pessimism about heroes and leaders is a telling lesson that Mugabe has left Zimbabweans.

Mugabe: The Thing Itself

A key attempt in this book is to locate and name the Mugabe of essence that has remained concealed behind rhetorics and performances. I intend to get hold of the Mugabe of veracity beyond the persona. In his much debated *Seventh Letter*, Plato (1952: 13) clarifies the difference between illusions, fictions, falsehoods, myths and "the thing itself which is known and truly exists" in veracity. A capital part of my observation and argument in the present book is that many illusions, fictions, falsehoods and myths about and by Mugabe himself are made to conceal the true Mugabe. Beyond the personas, the "thing itself" and the essence of the man can be established. Behind spectacular performance of grandeur and rehearsal of grandiosity there was "the thing itself" that was "Mugabe" who "despite his early reputation was never great, he was always a frightened little man" as Doris Lessing (2013: 1) insists. In this part of this chapter I seek to pay attention to Mugabe the thing itself as a type of frightened little people that have haunted human history with tragedies and catastrophes: the tyrants. An esteemed member of this infamous tribe of scared men is Augusto Pinochet that, as recalled by Roger Burbach (2003), lived his entire life in fear of unknown and nameless enemies that he believed he had to get before they got him. In a sinister way, the tyrant carries out advance revenge where he harms innocent people on the basis of a fear that in future they are going to be enemies, and this has led to many massacres of the innocent in world history. The Gukurahundi Genocide for instance, is a genocide that Mugabe committed in fear of Joshua Nkomo and the political opposition that were popular with Zimbabweans and were likely to win the elections in the near future; such a prospect is life threatening to a tyrant.

Saddam Hussein, another little, terrified and terrifying little man in the world, for instance, lived with what he believed to be the truth that he repeated continuously "I know that there are scores of people plotting to kill me, however I am far more clever than they are, I know they are conspiring to kill me before they actually start planning to do it, this enables me to get them before they have the faintest chance of striking at me" (Karsh and Rautsi 1991: 2), and in that way many innocent Iraqis perished because Saddam feared they would conspire to kill him in some future, and so was he afraid, "If I ever fall you won't find this much (little finger) of my body left, people will cut it to pieces," he repeatedly sang. The fear of defeat, punishment and powerlessness haunts the typical tyrant and leads him to commit insane atrocities. So frequently did Mugabe threaten to overthrow those that planned to overthrow him well before they had a chance to even think of it (Meredith 2002a, b: 17). That tragic belief that he can tell future conspirators and assassins in the present makes the tyrant a dangerous person, more so if like Mugabe was, he controls militias, police, secret security services and an army that had been naturalised into a partisan and personal force of the president. The typical tyrant is a scared and insane personage that is insulated from reality.

In his pursuit of real and imagined enemies Mugabe had many of his political opponents arrested and charged with attempts to assassinate him. A list of "opposition party leaders such as Muzorewa, Ndabaningi Sithole and Tsvangirai were each charged with plotting to assassinate Mugabe in 1980, 1997, and 2002 respectively" (Tendi 2016: 219). Later Joice Mujuru and Emmerson Mnangagwa were to be separately but equally publicly accused of plotting to kill Mugabe. In order to justify his attack of opponents and enemies the tyrant compresses himself into the ultimate victim and presents himself as the heroic leader that is threatened by dark forces. Whenever he survived real or choreographed assassination attempts, Adolf Hitler, for example, claimed that as a chosen messenger of God "providence intends to allow me to complete my goal" (Bullock 1992: 642). God and providence are usurped by the tyrant for his personal tyrannical interests. The tyrant's opponents that are the real victims are creatively and conveniently turned into aggressors that are intending to harm him and must therefore be eliminated as part of God's plan. When Joice Mujuru, then Vice-President to Mugabe, was understood to be aspiring for the high office, it was her turn to be framed, charged and expelled from the party. Her liberation war credentials were withdrawn and the Zimbabwean population was told that she climbed through the ranks of the liberation movement by sleeping with senior army generals that included her late husband, Solomon Mujuru. To really damn her, Mujuru was accused of attempting to kill Mugabe using the dark arts of witchcraft, and spies claimed to have the proof in multiple video footages. A keen researcher on Zimbabwean politics with access to inside sources, Blessing-Miles Tendi spoke to a "key actor in the campaign against" Mujuru. The crucial actor in the stratagems described to Tendi one recording of Mujuru's alleged rituals of sorcery:

> In one of them (recordings) traditional healers are dancing around a pot of fire. There was meat in the pot and when they are finished with their rituals she was supposed to start eating that meat with them and as they eat the meat the victim (Mugabe) starts dying. We also have her squeezing … juices from her … (Private parts) … Her juices were going to be used in a concoction to help her get (political) power. After the ritual, whoever she had sex with would become loyal to her. The ultimate form of recruitment for her was to have sex with people she wanted to have in her faction. (Tendi 2016: 220)

The intimate description of rituals of witchcraft including the clear knowledge by Tendi's key informant of what the effect of the rituals was to be betrays a possible construction of facts. Allegations were concocted to take advantage of some Zimbabwean beliefs in witchcraft to eliminate Mujuru from the political race. The described footage and many others that were publicly spoken of were never shown to Zimbabweans, but

Mugabe personally and publicly, before a huge rally, accused Mujuru of practising witchcraft against him (Tendi 2016: 220). To politically finish her off, Mugabe constructed allegations of witchcraft and loose sexual morals against her, serious allegations in the traditional Zimbabwean context. The tyrant is an expert in dark allegations. He gives damning names and descriptions to his political enemies that are portrayed as assassins, conspirators, witches and bitches. After his death it publicly surfaced that whilst still alive Mugabe gave stern instructions that his body should be protected from Emmerson Mnangagwa and others that he believed might want to harvest his organs for ritual and witchcraft purposes.

In actuality, Mugabe himself was the ultimate assassin and merchant of death through various methods that can be understood as sorcery. Blessing-Miles Tendi (2016: 218) was told by a "senior figure" in the "Zimbabwean security establishment" that Mugabe's "military Intelligence made technical changes. They imported special poisons from Kazakhstan, which work on you over 2 or 3 years so that it looks like some other disease." Since Mugabe was in the helm in Zimbabwe, the assassination of political enemies through poisons that simulate symptoms of known chronic diseases such as cancer, HIV/AIDS, sugar diabetes and high blood pressure seems to be prevalent. Besides suspicious car accidents, "natural causes of death" are afoot as diseases are choreographed to eliminate opponents. Mugabe's use of spies and spooks with dark covert capabilities is an established fact. Similar to Stalin, Hitler and Hussein that had feared spy networks (Tucker 1990: 272–273) Mugabe made use of covert security networks that caused much insecurity in the country. In many ways, the typical tyrant is a spook and a competent wizard of sorts.

Not only is the tyrant a kind of wizard, but he is also mad and power drunk. In the study appropriately titled "why tyrants go too far" Betty Glad (2002: 1) investigates and reports on the tyrant as a personality with "paradoxical behaviour" that covers his fragilities and vulnerabilities behind "grandiosity, and his skills in deception, manipulation and intimidation." Tyranny as the thing itself and a definition of such personalities as Mugabe is not exhibited as such but is kept artfully concealed behind enchanting performances, impressions and appearances of grand leadership. The typical tyrant deploys "rules without laws, looks to his own advantage rather that of his subjects and uses extreme tactics-against his own people as well as others" (Aristotle 1948: 312, 158, 287). Mugabe was such a tyrant that acted always, in excesses.

Mugabe became a law unto himself in Zimbabwe. He systematically caused a political culture that Horace Campbell (2003: 75) described correctly as "executive lawlessness." The Gukurahundi Genocide, the burying and burning of entire families alive in their huts, the rape of women and cutting of body parts, and disembowelling of pregnant women were all extreme practices of cruelty that Mugabe presided over. Mugabe effectively became a political extremist and fundamentalist who hid his excesses behind rhetorical performances of good. Zimbabwe became a land of rhetoric, "the official rhetoric in Zimbabwe was worse than anywhere in Africa, so said a United Nations report, 'never has rhetoric had so little to do with what actually went on,' the ground" (Lessing 2013: 3). Mugabe himself called the Gukurahundi Genocide a "moment of madness" but continued to deny responsibility or show any accountability to the victims. That Mugabe was mad should not be used to absolve him of the culpability in mass murder and other crimes. In his book *The Hitler of History*, John Lukacs (1997: 43) warns that "to find Hitler mad is to relieve him of all responsibility for what he did." Rather, societies should not allow insane persons into corridors of power and positions where they can threaten the security of populations. Tyranny is a political madness that societies should always be on the lookout for in politicians and other leaders.

Months after he was ousted from power, a day before the first elections after the coup Mugabe was asked by Eye Witness News amongst other media houses present in a press conference, if he was going to vote for his party, ZANU-PF. His answer was, "I will not vote for those who tormented me" (Mugabe 2018: 1). Out of power Mugabe, ever the actor, cast the pathetic figure of a betrayed and persecuted messenger of great ideas. In the height and full flight of his power he had crowds around him and forceful individuals that gave him personal and organisational support. In power the tyrant is never a loner. There are always individuals and groups that out of their own opportunism choose to give tyranny popularity and thereby become complicit in its evil (Dotcherty 2016). Mugabe, in power, had many flatterers, hangers on and sycophants that surrounded him. The tyrant is practiced in renting crowds and faking popularity.

In his treatise *On Tyranny: Twenty Lessons for the Twentieth Century*, Timothy Snyder (2017) delves into the genealogies and developments of tyranny that societies should watch out for. The first warning that Snyder gives to societies is "do not obey in advance," he says, "most of the power of authoritarianism is freely given." Tyrants do coerce and clobber populations into following them and their parties but they also earn free voluntary support from opportunistic individuals that use the name and the power of the tyrant for their own benefit. Many opportunists and other chance-takers come up to volunteer support and surround the tyrant with praises and ululations and thereby blinding him to the cold and dry reality out there. To prevent tyrants from growing and to dilute their power Snyder suggests that countries should "defend institutions" by ensuring that the courts, the constitution, the media, parliament and trade unions are independent and working, they are not captured by the tyrant and his party. In Zimbabwe Mugabe was allowed to destabilise the independent media and to totally capture the public media. Even during as ghastly a genocide as the Gukurahundi one, Mugabe as the principal perpetrator had popular support from some communities, organisations and individuals in the country. Tyrants are never simple individuals; they have networks and structures that support them. A good tyrant becomes a political culture and a system that lives after he is gone. Mugabe became a political culture and a system in the Zimbabwean postcolony.

Opposition political parties have more importance than just being possible governments in waiting. They also ensure that governing parties are kept in check and their governing continuously put under scrutiny and probity. From the start Mugabe was opposed to opposition political parties and sold to the idea of a strong one-party state led by himself. In an interview that Mugabe gave early in his tenure as the prime minister of Zimbabwe, he described opposition political parties as "repugnant" and suggested that the one-party state ensures "national unity" (Onslow and Plaut 2018: 81). In his open defence of the one-party state Mugabe was fond of quoting the North Korean leader Kim II Sung whose wisdom was that "to win the revolutionary struggle there must be a strong revolutionary organisation composed of men with one idea and purpose and their ideological unity and cohesion must be guaranteed" (Mugabe 1989: 350). Mugabe believed, from the start, in one strong party under one strong leader, himself. It is no wild guess that even his interest in reconciliation with the white population and politicians immediately after independence was part of his political ploy to eliminate all political opposition to his rule and achieve multi-racial unity under his party. The "unity of the entire nation under one political party" was to him something that was "desirable" (Mugabe 1989: 351), and he concealed this tyrannical and undemocratic desire under the rhetoric of the need for national unity which he claimed was threatened by the multi-party system. The spirited desire for a one-party state under his leadership is one sign that should have warned Zimbabweans and the world about Mugabe's tyrannical ambitions.

The Gukurahundi Genocide that neutralised the opposition ZAPU political party ensured that Zimbabwe eventually became a de facto one-party state under Mugabe's leadership. As Mugabe continued to rely on political violence and fraud to force electoral victory he openly boasted that for Zimbabweans to vote the opposition MDC was a waste of time, "you can vote for them, but that would be a wasted vote, I am telling you, you would just be cheating yourself, there is no way we can allow them to rule this country" (Mugabe 2008: 1). The one-party state, Snyder (2017) warns, is one strong way in which tyrants normalise and naturalise themselves into power without responsibility. Even where opposition political parties existed in Zimbabwe, Mugabe used violence and electoral fraud to ensure that they would not rule the country because "we have a job to do, to protect our heritage. The MDC will not rule this country. It will never, ever happen. We will never allow it" (Mugabe 2008: 1). Tyrants see themselves and their parties as naturally entitled to power and they imagine themselves to be the only ones that "have a job to do" in preserving and governing nations. Most Zimbabweans may not have realised how similar to Ian Smith Mugabe had become. Smith vowed that "never in a million years" will black people rule Zimbabwe. Mugabe, the coloniser that he had become, also vowed that "never, ever, ever" will the opposition prevail in Zimbabwe. Colonial political extremism that Smith represented had become part of the logic and vocabulary of Mugabe's postcolony. Politically Mugabe had become a black and white duplicate of Smith.

The impunity with which Mugabe dismissed opposition political parties and boasted that they will never rule a country in which they were also role players and bona fide participants should have shocked the world. Such statements as "we will never allow it" that the political opposition wins elections or rule the country one day are part of the language of right-wingers, fundamentalists and other political extremists. Societies and nations, Snyder warns, "must listen to dangerous words" because they are signifiers of the dangerous internal world of the tyrant that when externalised and practiced lead to massacres and genocides. Tyrants frequently express their intentions and their volcanic speeches and volatile intonation become early warnings for approaching catastrophes and tragedies. Behind grandiose performances of power and elegant rhetoric of peace and reconciliation, Mugabe was always a "terrified little man" and a tyrant in actuality.

Tyranny and the tyrant itself are the actuality, the "thing in itself," while pretensions and performances are simulations and dissimulations that conceal the thing itself and frequently fool even discerning minds into mistaking tyrants and despots for freedom fighters and liberators. In that way, Mugabe fooled some Zimbabweans and the world. Mugabe's pretences were dramatised in how, in spite of his storied education and several university degrees, he leaves behind no intellectual legacy or archive of recorded thoughts except the rantings and other speeches. Mugabe's poverty of intellectual products and legacy was prominently laughed off by Arthur Mutambara who noted that the now-fallen president was an intellectual dwarf:

> He (Mugabe) is not an able man, but an insecure chap of average intellect. Mugabe cannot work well with individuals of superior intellect or talent, strong personality, and independent thinking. This explains the fate of Eddison Zvobgo, Edgar Tekere, Ndabaningi Sithole, Simba Makoni, Dzinashe Machingura and Enos Nkala, to mention a few names. Mugabe's shallowness, intellectual inadequacy, and lack of gravitas are best revealed by his packing order of matters he considers important: number ONE is himself, number TWO is his family, number THREE is ZANU-PF, number FOUR is the country. This means he will do things that are just good for him alone, but which negatively impact his family, and devastate his Party. The way he has handled succession in ZANU-PF is instructive. (Mutambara 2017: 1)

Mugabe concerned himself with "personal narcissist needs" and was a true practitioner of "unparalleled mediocrity and inordinate insecurity" in the view of Mutambara. Intellectually gifted members of his party and government were marginalised and in one way or another eliminated from the race to succeed him. The fear and avoidance by Mugabe to publish any treatise or record of his political philosophy was based on that he was empty of such content and was only too happy, like any other pretender, to follow the winds of power and have no single solid idea fixed on his name except opportunistic opinions and slogans. The tyrant is a competent sloganeer and a trader in catch-phrases, not a dispenser of political philosophy of any kind. What Mugabe publicly circulated of himself was only a persona and the "thing itself" remained concealed behind grandiose performances. His seven university degrees became a perfect cover that hid his poverty of thought and evil political intentions.

LIMITS OF THE POST-POLITICAL

The idolisation of Mugabe as a freedom fighter and liberator that took place in the early years of Zimbabwe's political independence was a tragic post-political mistake that has cost Zimbabwe dearly. The tyrannical rule of Mugabe did not only impoverish the country but many lives have been lost to political violence and the country will take many years to recover from the corruption and looting that Mugabe allowed to be normalised and naturalised as a national elite culture. The euphoria and hero-worship that Mugabe was surrounded with prevented the due vigilance that Zimbabweans needed to pay in preventing the growth of tyranny. What Chantal Mouffe (2005a, b) has called post-politics is a mistaken optimistic belief in the victory of the democratic, liberal and the heroic in politics. This belief in individual heroes and triumphal political dispensations is at best innocent and at worst dangerously naïve as Mugabe has taught us in the way he turned out to be a monster that ate the revolution itself and inaugurated diabolic tyranny in Zimbabwe. Politics, especially power politics, is no arena for blind faith in the good nature of human beings.

Post-political understandings of the political and readings of individual politicians, in their excitability, assume that enemies have ended and consensual politics has at last arrived at its zeitgeist (Mouffe 2005a, b: 1), when in actuality the political remains conflictual and violently antagonistic. Heidi Holland (2008: xiv) is correct that "mad Bob, Robert Mugabe is concealing significant secrets and lessons for history." One of the telling lessons that Mugabe has taught us is that in politics enmity and evil are real and societies and nations need powerful working institutions and laws to check the growth of leaders into monsters. Leaders that come up in societies should be met with suspicion and caution, not post-political excitement.

Post-political innocence and naiveté about politics misled not only a big part of the Zimbabwean population and some opinion leaders but also some scholars. If it were not for post-political inclinations Mugabe's violence and evil would not have been received with shock as all power is bound to degenerate to tyranny if left unchecked. Mugabe should not have been given room to escalate natural political antagonism into a war upon his political opponents and enemies. Political competition, under agonistic and not antagonistic political climates, legitimates political opponents and adversaries; it does not turn them into enemies to be eliminated as Mugabe did. The political proper in its agonism turns opponents into legitimate adversaries that can be preserved (Mouffe 2005a, b). Mugabe, in his anti-political politics, and under the cover of a climate of euphoria, innocence and naiveté about politics of his supporters, was allowed to grow into a political fundamentalist that turned all political opposition and competition into enmity.

The understanding of the political proper, that Mouffe advances, in opposition to the post-political, is able to make visible that, in other words, left unchecked, any politician can become what Mugabe became. Heidi Holland (2008: xiv) quotes Sir Ian Mckellen who studied political monsters such as Mugabe for more than forty years and came to the conclusion that "one of the few lessons I have learnt from studying people who do terrible things is that they are all too human, and that we are all capable of doing almost anything" equally evil or worse if left unchecked. In other words, all politics and politicians should, away from the trappings of the post-political, be understood and treated with the suspicion and fear that they can degenerate into evil any moment in history.

Writers such as Judith Todd (2007: 1) that once optimistically believed Mugabe was a great deliverer that was to bring light to post-independence Zimbabwe were shocked when he took the country "through the darkness" of political violence and genocide. Post-political enchantments about politics and politicians lead to disappointments. White journalists such as Catherine Buckle (2003) that post-politically entertained the belief that the end of colonialism in Zimbabwe was to deliver unity and political happiness were disabused of their innocence when the violence that Mugabe unleashed became tragic "beyond tears." Many other scholars, including Andrew Norman (2004a, b: 15), experienced Mugabe as a traitor of Zimbabwe because they once had the mistaken and even dangerous post-political belief that he was going to be a messianic liberator but "instead of leading his people to the promised land" Mugabe "amassed a fortune for himself, his family and followers." Beliefs in heroes and heroism that were invested in Mugabe allowed the tyrant in him to grow to a monster that visited darkness and tears upon Zimbabwe.

The promised land naiveté of post-political thinking has allowed societies to nurture tyrants and prevented them from noticing the early developments of totalitarian habits in leaders. Mugabe was not going to visit Zimbabwe with the "catastrophe" that Richard Bourne (2011: 1) describes if optimism and euphoria about the end of colonialism and reconciliation of Zimbabweans and Rhodesians had not blinded the world and scholars from thinking straight and seeing politics clearly as a dirty and dangerous game of power that it has always been. The evil of "Mugabe's killing machine" (Moorcraft 2012: 1) in the Fifth Brigade that committed the Gukurahundi Genocide and the "power, plunder and tyranny" (Meredith 2002a, b: 1) that he championed could have been avoided if post-political thinking and excitement had not taken hold of history and thought in Zimbabwe. Not only Mugabe as an individual person, but the political itself and politics, should, pragmatically, be handled as "a predictable tragedy" (Compagnon 2011: 1), a disaster that is going to befall any society if the political and the conflictual and antagonistic nature of politics and power are not tackled with durable alternatives. The will power of individuals and organisations requires vigilant pessimistic thinking and action.

The euphoria about political change and excitement about the arrival of independence from colonialism in Zimbabwe created a post-political climate and therefore anti-political thinking. Individuals and populations suspended caution. Mugabe as a monstrosity, that I describe, became a product of anti-political expectations and wrong dreams. Holland (2008: xiii) observes correctly that the international community, Rhodesian whites that were excited about reconciliation and forgiveness, and Zimbabweans that were intoxicated by dreams of the promised land helped Mugabe become the monster that he became by ignoring that he was a politician who was in politics and had all the potential to degenerate into a monstrosity as long as he was not checked. Democratic thinking and the thinking of the will to live that opposes the will to power and the fetishisation of power should be put on guard against the degeneration of liberators to dominators. Chantal Mouffe argues thus about the consequences of forgetting that politics is naturally antagonistic and potentially dangerous:

> It is my contention that envisaging the aim of democratic politics in terms of consensus and reconciliation is not only conceptually mistaken, it is also fraught with political dangers. The aspiration to a world where the we/they discrimination would have been overcome is based on flawed premises and those who share such a vision are bound to miss the real task facing democratic politics. (Mouffe 2005a, b: 2)

The dream of paradisal politics and promised land liberation from colonialism and other forms of domination leads not only to disappointments but also genocidal disasters. Democratic politics and politics of the will to live should always be in place to prevent, early enough, those who fought against domination from becoming new dominators and oppressors themselves. It is a misfortune of scholarship on politics and politicians that "democratic theory has long been informed by the belief that the inner goodness and original innocence of human beings was a necessary condition for asserting the viability of democracy" (Mouffe 2005a, b: 2). In reality, politics and, especially, the will to power in politics can always transform otherwise potential liberators into guilty perpetrators of genocide. It is a post-political mistake that "violence and hostility are seen as an archaic phenomenon, to be eliminated thanks to the progress of exchange and the establishment, through the social contract, of transparent communication, among rational participants" (Mouffe 2005a, b: 3). It is a much safer assumption, from the start, that politicians are most likely going to be monsters. Zimbabwe and the world were mistaken to invest hope of liberation and peace in dialogue and political settlements conducted by politicians and the business elites. Mugabe's pretentious rhetoric of peace and reconciliation was taken for gospel. In a setting where the naiveté and innocence of the post-political has not taken grip, "the task of democratic theorists and politicians should be to envisage the creation of a vibrant 'agonistic' public sphere of contestation where different hegemonic political projects can be confronted" (Mouffe 2005a, b: 3) and there are no pretenses that politicians can be angels and that the political arena can be a paradise.

This book aims not just to avoid naïve and innocent trappings of the post-political regime of thinking but also to avoid simplistic notions of "right and wrong" and "left and right" that Chantal Mouffe (2005a, b: 5) debunks as misleading about politics and politicians. Human beings, in politics and outside, are capable of evil and political conflicts make the possibility more real because "when channels are not available through which conflicts could take on the 'agonistic' form, those conflicts tend to emerge on the antagonistic mode" (Mouffe 2005a, b: 5). For instance, the political opposition between masses of Zimbabweans that needed land and liberation after colonialism and a minority white population that wanted to keep its colonial and racist privileges was not going to be solved through feel-good political rhetoric but social and political justice. The avoidance of social and political justice created room in the end for Mugabe to turn antagonism and violent political conflict into the commonsense of politics in Zimbabwe. Post-politics, in thought and practice, leads to the telling of lies and claiming of easy victories.

In other words, understanding of the political and the conflictual nature of politics entails that "conflicts must be provided with legitimate forms and platforms of expression" (Mouffe 2005a, b: 4) such as free and fair elections, ballots and not bullets. In that way, to quickly make Mugabe a hero and invest in him paradisal hopes for the future was to dehumanise him and to depoliticise the political; it was to prepare him for logical development and degeneration into a monster. In that way too, this book will note, simple moral registers of good and evil in evaluating politicians and assessing the political are not helpful but conceal rather than reveal political reality. To simply complain of evil is to assume rather easily that holiness was possible in politics and in politicians.

It was in post-political naiveté or innocence that Mugabe's political intimidation and "terrorism" (Meredith 2002a, b: 10) of political opponents in the very first election in Zimbabwe, the independence elections, were ignored. That people like General Peter Walls were ignored, when he wrote to the British government pleading that the first democratic Zimbabwean elections be nullified because they were violent, unfree and unfair (Meredith 2002a, b: 12), was a post-political blunder. And this book will note that Mugabe was cultivated and groomed for political monstrosity by the post-political and also anti-political climate that was allowed early in Zimbabwe. True to the will to power, politicians as political animals are susceptible to passions, energies, desires and fantasies of power (Mouffe 2005a, b: 6) that drive and pull them to excesses and extremes. It is for that reason that Mouffe regrets "for instance" that "more than half a century after Freud's death, the resistance to psychoanalysis in political theory is still very strong and its lessons about the ineradicability of antagonism have not yet been assimilated" (Mouffe 2005a, b: 3). This book, in avoidance of the negligence of post-politicalism pays attention to the tool of psychoanalysis in examining the political thought and practice of Mugabe. The psychological conditioning and formation of Mugabe cannot be avoided if he is to be understood and known, not just condemned as another tyrant from dark Africa.

This book treats Mugabe as a subject that was created and that developed, by its agency and also by social, systemic and structural conditions and circumstances. Mugabe did not just become but he was also enabled and promoted. Writing of terrorism as a monstrosity in world history and international politics, Slavoj Zizek noted that "we all know, inspite of the formal condemnation and rejection from all sides, there are forces and states that silently not only tolerate it, but help it" (Zizek 2016: 3). The most ghoulish political monstrosities are enabled and permitted by systems and structures of power. As condemned and reviled as Mugabe was after his political monstrosities, beyond post-political immaturity, this book pays attention to the fact that he was a political and historical reality that was produced and permitted in the world political system and structure that includes powerful nations and supposedly exemplary states. A discerning Zimbabwean lawyer, scholar and political commentator, Alex Magaisa (2019) provided a telling account of just how Mugabe's tyranny and that of the regime that took over from him after the coup of November 2017 were dutifully enabled by some well-meaning and other opportunistic Zimbabweans, enterprising praise-singers and some political entrepreneurs among them.

Most scholars and writers on Mugabe dwell on the tyranny, the mass murder and economic catastrophe he created and neglect the casualties and enablements that produced and permitted him, and, as Slavoj Zizek quotes Oscar Wilde on his argument on terror and terrorism, "it is much more easy to have sympathy with suffering than it is to have sympathy with thought" (Zizek 2016: 8). Besides condemning Mugabe and mourning the suffering and death he created, political scholarship and journalism should think and consider the political uninfected by effects of pain and suffering. Some analytical distance is needed in studying and understanding monsters as a dark reality that can be avoided in history. Mourning the tragedies Mugabe caused and not thinking of the casualties and enablements to his terror will only permit a repeat of another Mugabe era as the present regime in Zimbabwe appears to be.

The dream that Mugabe, without being checked and stopped, was ever going to be an alternative to what he became may have been post-political and also anti-political cowardice. Tyranny as a monstrosity is much similar to terrorism in the production of shock and large-scale suffering that it causes. Thinking politically about terror and terrorism, and the need to take a hard and pragmatic look at them, Zizek notes that:

> The dream of an alternative is a sign of theoretical cowardice: It functions as a fetish that prevents us thinking to end the deadlock of our predicament. In short, the truly courageous stance is to admit that the light at the end of the tunnel is most probably the headlight of a train approaching us from the opposite tunnel. (Zizek 2016: 108)

If Mugabe had from the start, away from post-political confusion, been understood and treated not as the bringer of light to Zimbabwe or the deliverer of Zimbabweans to the promised land, but a potential monster, the Zimbabwean catastrophe might have been avoided and the world saved from the darkness he created. There is a need to hold not only political vigilance but critical pessimism in understanding and handling politics, politicians and the political itself. In politics, good news, good feelings and celebratory moods are the good intentions that decorate the road to hell.

Vigilance and critical pessimism should include the imagination of other ways of thinking about politics and politicians. In advancing his philosophy of the will to live that is opposed to the will to power, Enrique Dussel warns that fetishism of power has corrupted political thought and practice. Like Chantal Mouffe, Dussel notes that the political entails the need for understanding the absence of innocence in politics:

> This originary corruption of the political, which I will call the fetishism of power, consists of the moment in which the political actor (the members of the political community, whether citizens or representative) believes that power affirms his or her subjectivity or the institution in which she or he functions- as a "functionary," whether it be as president, representative, judge, governor, soldier, police officer- as the centre of political power. (Dussel 2008: 3)

In Zimbabwe Mugabe practiced the corrupt fetishism of power that allowed him to centralise power in himself and his family and to personalise the nation. Understanding Mugabe outside the "originary corruption" of the political that Dussel describes may lead to the same concealments and confusions, and disappointments that have been encountered by post-political and naïve readings of and writings on Mugabe. Mugabe fought colonialism and also came to be produced and formed by its politics. He did not only become a producer of political corruption but was in the first place a product of it. It is for that reason that, in his understanding of the political, Christopher Hope (2003) believes that Mugabe and Ian Smith whom he fought were, beyond the illusion of the skin and confusion of the post-political, "brothers under the skin." Mugabe belongs to that tribe of leaders of the Global South that fought colonialism but instead of providing alternative politics to colonialism and leadership that liberates and not dominates, they became true morbid products and symptoms of coloniality.

Fighting for liberation therefore, for decolonists and humanists, may involve fighting domination and those that pretend to fight domination. In that logic, Zizek (2016: 101) states that "our axiom should be that the struggle against Western neo-colonialism as well as the struggle against fundamentalism" and "the struggle against anti-Semitism as well is as the struggle against aggressive Zionism, are parts of one and the same struggle." The thought and struggle for liberation should confront fundamentalism from the right and the left, from the east and the west, and here and now. Confronting the potential fundamentalism of our own heroes is hard but necessary. Checking the tyrannies and madnesses of our favourite leaders is democratic homework that serious societies have to do.

This book departs from that understanding that fighting colonial domination is a struggle first and foremost against the will to power as domination regardless of its personalisation by a Smith or by a Mugabe. How those who fought colonial domination systematically and structurally and then tragically came about to embody and multiply it is a critical burden that haunts this book. How the Mugabe that pretended to freedom fighting and liberation ended up being but a symptom of coloniality invites hard thinking about the fragility of freedom and the durability of tyranny in post-political climates of the African postcolony. The postcolony is that time and place of political morbidities and obscenities that Mbembe described and which Mugabe did not only occupy in Zimbabwe but actually took pride of place in it and defined its character.

Recovering the Lost Causes

Pride of place is also what Mugabe took in the list of post-independence African leaders that after the demise of administrative colonialism became colonisers to their own people. These leaders have defamed the name and historical agenda of decolonisation that they reduced to a façade. They have represented the grand ideal of decolonisation as one of those agendas that Edward Said (2012: 527) called "lost causes." Mugabe and other African tyrants have given decolonisation a bad name and exhausted its energising and inspiring potential. Such words as "revolution" and "liberation" have become not only tired and boring but also suspicious words because those leaders that have been exclaiming about revolution and liberation in Africa turned out to be monsters from whom Africa needed liberation. Peoples of the Global South, it appears, need durable liberation and stubborn liberators that resist the temptation to become colonisers.

Owing to the diabolic political record of the tyrants, tragically, the words "decolonisation" and "independence" have become dirty words that represent lost causes. Lost causes took away the power of "belief" and that of "conviction" (Said 2012) about liberation from the mass of people in the Global South that hoped that one day freedom from Empire will be achieved. Mugabe and other post-independence tyrants of Africa did not only fight colonialism and ended up as colonisers and symptoms of coloniality but are also symptoms of the resilience of Empire and its stubborn resurrections and reproductions in people and societies that are supposed to have been freed. Mugabe is but one telling proof that Empire's resilience goes beyond the simple stubbornness of colonial systems and structures of power but it reproduces and multiplies itself through those that were supposed to be warriors against it. The residues of Empire that John Saul (2008) describes are represented in leaders, systems and structures of power that colonialism left intact in its supposed demise. The critical attitude of this book is that belief and conviction in freedom should not be abandoned because certain people and organisations that claimed to fight for decolonisation and liberation became monsters that ate the same freedom that they claimed to fight for. The colonial state of affairs captured the anti-colonial leaders and their parties that in turn made the colonial state of political affairs a reality in the postcolony. Perhaps the true state capture in Africa is in how postcolonies remain captive and hostage to the colonial order of things.

In the present, that is after his loss of power and eventual death, Mugabe is condemned and denied, no one including the powerful countries that previously backed him and enabled his infamous rule are willing to own him. Correctly, Mahmood Mamdani (2009: 1) notes that "it is hard to think of a figure more reviled in the West than Robert Mugabe" in that "liberal and conservative commentators alike portray him as a brutal dictator, and blame him for Zimbabwe's descent into hyperinflation and poverty." Mamdani contends that Mugabe ruled Zimbabwe, for a long time, with a skilful combination of "consent and coercion" and thus managed to survive spirited efforts to dethrone him and passionate international opposition and sanctions. Mugabe's defiance and stubborn survivalism were not unconnected to the fact that he was a true creature and product of the present modern/colonial world system. It might be easy to see and understand Mugabe as a problem in Africa or an African problem. I hold the view in this book that Mugabe became a world problem in Africa, a symptom of the colonial and imperial sick condition onto which Empire has placed Africa and the entire Global South. The politics of life that ethics of liberation demand, as nuanced by Enrique Dussel (2008), entails an avoidance of historical simplifications and an understanding of the way the world has been globalised, organised and dominated. Mugabe, for instance, is a true colonial subject that did not only fight colonialism but also came to further it. Most tyrants of the South have been colonising colonial subjects, the victims that became victimisers.

Studying and writing on Mugabe, an individual politician in a small country of the South may look like another lost cause. Steven Friedman (2010: 163) states that "there is some embarrassment attached to devoting an analytical article to an individual politician" however influential the politician is. In this book I hold the political attitude that those that fought for freedom from colonialism and became "freedom fighters" in the sense that they fought the freedom of their own people and their own lost their individuality and became monstrosities, structures and political systems that need to be studied and understood so that they can be overcome. Mugabe might be out of power and dead in Zimbabwe but the political culture he naturalised and normalised remains intact and continues to show the morbidities of a colonialism that is refusing to die and a decolonisation that is not getting born, to benefit from Gramsci's telling observation.

Mugabe and other tyrants of the South have been studied and written of as leaders that failed their states or simple leaders of failed states. In his intellectual curiosity about "the blood of experience" in "failed states and political collapse in Africa" Ali Mazrui (1995: 28) has written of African political leadership traditions from philosopher kings who want to rule with wisdom, to warrior kings that seek to use the force of arms, up to "poet presidents" (Mazrui 1990: 13) that deploy oratory and poetry to charm audiences. The warrior tradition, philosophic kingship and poetic presidency, as this book will show, are all political traditions that in his will to power Mugabe experimented with and performed. As much as Mugabe experimented with and performed these African political traditions, this and other books still have to effectively capture and articulate what constituted Mugabeism, a question that Sabelo Ndlovu-Gatsheni (2015) has posed, and elaborately explored in a way that benefits this book. Further to that, this book is alive to the fact that the so-called states that Mugabe and other post-independence African tyrants inherited were already failed if they were not born failed. From its genealogies in the consolidation of the nation-state in 1492 the state as it is structured in Zimbabwe is an artefact of violence. Mahmood Mamdani (2004: 4–5) remind us that "thus 1492 stands as a gateway to two related endeavours: One the unification of the nation with the state and the other being the conquest of the world." Leaders of the South like Mugabe truly failed their states but to ignore that they were also failed by states that were already naturalised and normalised to conquest and tyranny would be to participate in simplification, I argue. Nation-states such as Zimbabwe carry a bold birthmark of conquest and tyranny. These states, as conditioned by colonialism and imperialism, were not designed for the success or happiness of the natives. Conquest created and imposed the nation-state in Africa. The Mugabes of Africa did not decolonise the nation-state but opportunistically weaponised it for their own political ends.

Mugabe as a phenomenon and object of study can also be looked at in the perspective of studies on "personal rule in theory and practice in Africa" (Jackson and Roseberg 1984: 421) that also justifiably focus on such forceful, prominent and survivalist rulers as Mugabe. Mugabe's longevity in power in spite of external and internal opposition became the true stuff of legend until the coup. The theme of the tyrannical "big men" in Africa that *scholars such as* Jean-Pascal Daloz (2003: 271) have investigated and written on is important in examining Mugabe and his life in power. Equally important and relevant would be such concepts as those of "patrimonial regimes" in Africa (Vine 1980: 657) that can capture and explain the political habits and historical tendencies of tyrants in Africa. While all these theoretical and conceptual perspectives may help illuminate the life and times of Mugabe in power, the warning by Sabelo Ndlovu-Gatsheni (2012a, b: 315) that scholars and journalists that wish to understand the politics of Zimbabwe and Mugabe should move "beyond Mugabe-centric narratives of the Zimbabwean crisis" is important. As this book emphasises, there is more to Mugabe than just an individual disastrous politician. There are ways in which Mugabe became an embodiment of political systems, structures and cultures that go far beyond his individuality and Zimbabwe as a single nation-state.

To understand how Mugabe participated in tragically rendering Zimbabwean decolonisation a lost cause analysis and critique need to do more than just describe and explain the individual tyrant. Besides his conditioning by colonialism and the world system, there are political ideas, ideologies, structures and historical systems that formed, shaped and produced Mugabe. Such ideologies as Pan-Africanism, nationalism and Marxism were performed by Mugabe as a fetish to mask, as this book will show, his will to power. Typical of the tyrant par excellence, Mugabe masked his drive for personal accumulation of power behind e rhetoric of some grand goals and high-minded historical agendas. The leadership and political thought and practice of Mugabe in Zimbabwe had according to

Robert Lloyd (2002: 219) become a textbook case of "the making of autocratic democracy." Even as he became a tyrant in word and deed, Mugabe always tried to mask his tyranny behind pretences to democracy by regularly holding elections which he avoided losing by use of force and fraud. Elections in Zimbabwe became an emblem that was used to cover the reality of tyranny. For the political opposition in Zimbabwe the regular elections became a true lost cause where defeat became certain as Mugabe routinely stole victory using force and fraud.

In the Zimbabwean postcolony Mugabe also participated in fortifying the loss of Africa's cause by permitting and therefore promoting corruption by some people that were closest to him. Africa's cause is lost every time leaders become what Jo-Ansie Van Wyk (2007: 3) calls "patrons and profiteers" that preside over the looting of national resources and the impoverishment of the masses. Zimbabwe's rich mineral, human and wildlife resources have been captured and isolated for the benefit of a privileged political and economic elite. In the beautiful novel of 1968, *The Beautyful Ones Are Not Yet Born*, Ayi Kwei Armah (1988) portrays bribes and corruption as a problem that became naturalised and normalised in post-independence Africa. Mugabe personified the ugly and made visible the need for the beautiful that is yet to be born in Africa. Zimbabwe under Mugabe became a Republic of corruption where being a politician, especially of the ruling ZANU-PF party, meant obscene wealth.

Towards the end of his rule in 2017, Mugabe publicly complained that US$15 billion worth of diamonds had been looted and corruptly siphoned out of Zimbabwe. This complaint might have been too little and too late, and really not enough from an entire head of a so-called post-colonial state. Mugabe had a reputation for working hard to prevent the public media from publicising the corruption of his cabinet ministers and political allies (Nyarota 2018: 41). Geoff Nyarota (2018: 42) documents how ministers that were convicted of lying and corruption were through the influence of Mugabe and his party exonerated and released from prisons, "who amongst us has not lied?" Mugabe would say as he rationalised and therefore justified corruption. Systematically and structurally, Mugabe lent his political weight to the endorsement of corruption and moral decay.

Mugabe's first wife, Sally, was imbricated in corruption and siphoning of money from Zimbabwe to other countries. Doris Lessing (2013: 2) narrates one incident when "departing the country for a trip home to Ghana" Sally "was stopped at customs with the equivalent of a million British Pounds worth of Zimbabwean money, she protested it was her money, and only laughed when she had to leave it and travel without." Sally Mugabe, contrary to prevalent opinion, "was this Mother of the Nation, corrupt, and unashamed of it" (Lessing 2013: 3) and she milked Zimbabwe dry of scarce cash and amassed massive personal wealth that she stashed overseas. Prevalent opinion in Zimbabwe post-politically holds Sally as what was a stabilising force, a humble wife to Mugabe and a polite Mother of the Nation. When Sally died Mugabe discovered that she had, in her will, left all her massive wealth to her twin sister and family in Ghana. This enraged Mugabe so much that he threw a fit of mad rampage and broke windows at State House (Holland 2008: 24). Again that may have been too little anger too late. Breaking "innocent windows" does not solve corruption. Mugabe irrigated corruption right under his nose by allowing party loyalists and those that were close to him to loot the country dry. Like another good performer, Sally on the outside styled herself as a supporter of the Zimbabwean revolution who sourced and sometimes personally sew clothes for the guerrillas (Onslow and Plaut 2018: 59). In the name of the same revolution she entitled herself to public resources, and this happened under Mugabe's watch. In Mugabe's reign, it was a well-understood truth in the party that if one did not oppose Mugabe and supported him in everything, one could get away with murder itself; "in fact, most of them," ministers and party loyalists, "knew that unless you threaten him directly Mugabe will allow you to do whatever you please with impunity- hence the mismanagement and rampant corruption" (Ncube 2009: xiii) that prevails today. After political violence that climaxed in the Gukurahundi Genocide, Mugabe's second gravest sin in Zimbabwe was the cultivation and irrigation of corruption.

The looting of national resources by politicians, senior government employees and business people connected to Mugabe and his party became a culture in Zimbabwe. Many of the military generals and ministers that benefitted from Mugabe's laxity with corruption are now, after the coup, powerful managers of the postcolony that will make it difficult for a new Zimbabwean future to emerge as corruption has been naturalised. While tyranny is a kind of political corruption on its own, it also enables other forms of corruption like the pocketing by individuals of public money. One of the safest ways of practicing corruption in the typical postcolony is just to ensure that as you loot with one hand you salute the tyrant with another, and with your mouth shout the party slogan. The idea of Africa and pride in being African lost its glory as leaders such as Mugabe did not only give the continent a bad name but also worked to tragically give respectability to colonial and racist stereotypes that circulated the view that nothing good comes out of Africa.

The forceful domination of their countries and looting of national resources by tyrants and their hangers-on have not stopped them from desperately wishing to go down in history as great heroes. Geoff Nyarota (2018: 86) believes correctly, perhaps, that one of the reasons Mugabe stayed in power for so long was the wish to one day make great achievements, get the country through some recoveries, that would erase from public memory all the wrongs he did. Legacy making is a great preoccupation of the tyrant. From Kwame Nkrumah to many African post-independence leaders that came after him, A. H. M. Kirk-Greene (1991: 163) has noted that political thought and leadership have degenerated to a strange personal search for "eternity, eccentricity and exemplarity" by tragic and comic figures. Mugabe's political journey from powerlessness to power, the evil of his power, and eventually to dethronement in a coup d'état at the end of 2017 can be the true material of tragicomedy. The comedy is in the futile attempt to defy even the impossible odds like nature, pretending to be fit when old age had set in; while the tragedy is that as Mugabe tried to do the impossible a whole national cause for freedom became a lost cause. The beautiful ones, liberating leaders that shun corruption and tyranny, urgently need to be born in Africa for such historical and political scenario as the Zimbabwean one to be avoided. A whole country can collapse while a leader tries to be God, Mugabe has taught us.

Some scholars have found Mugabe and his political thought and practice to be beyond understanding and defying conventional analysis. Sandra MacLean (2002: 513) in particular has argued that for Mugabe to stay in power that long in spite of his infamous rule that provoked spirited local and international opposition defies academic analysis. Such writers as Peter Godwin (2010) wrote of the "fear" that Mugabe created and predicted his "last days" in power, yet he prevailed beyond all adversities and predictions of his political demise. It was at the great expense to Zimbabweans that Mugabe used force and fraud to retain power by any means necessary, and in his hands power did not only become irresponsible but it also became truly ugly. The ugliness of power and evil of politics that Mugabe represented must not lead to loss of hope and giving up conviction on the great causes of liberation and the humanisation of the dehumanised people of Zimbabwe. Grand narratives of liberty and happiness need to be recovered from their loss to tyranny and treachery in Africa and everywhere. Mugabe did not become the gallant and revolutionary son of the soil that he sold himself as. He became, instead, the prodigal son of the land that ate the revolution itself and reversed all the prospects for liberation, rendering the grand cause of decolonisation a lost cause. Mugabe, as this book will note, did not only come to exercise power without responsibility but performed power without beauty in a much inglorious and genocidal way. The "courage of hopelessness" that Slavoj Zizek (2017: x1) describes is the critical endurance and stubbornness of hope to honestly acknowledge the hopelessness that such figures as Mugabe create and also evoke enough emotional and intellectual stamina to imagine bright futures of liberation and human happiness beyond the darkness created by tyranny and terror. The evil of Mugabe in Zimbabwe is as much disastrous as it is an opportunity for critical thought about more liberated Zimbabwean futures. Mugabe provides a critical opportunity for the imagination of another politics and another politician that are different from what he represented. It is the oppressive darkness that must create the necessary thirst for liberating light.

In order to participate in the recovery of the lost causes of decolonisation and liberation and to contribute to the thinking about their restoration to possibility and importance, this book handles the subject of Mugabe with a critical attitude that Robert Kaplan (2002: xxi) describes as the "pagan ethos" and "tragic thinking" of "warrior politics." This search for political hope in political hopelessness involves the understanding of politicians and politics with "constructive pessimism" and the belief that left unchecked they will commit massacres and indulge in cozenage and corruption. It was in tragic thinking and pagan ethos that American foundational politics was formed. Robert Kaplan (2002: xxi) notes that "Americans can afford optimism partly because their institutions, including the Constitution, were conceived by men who thought tragically, before the first president was sworn in the rules of impeachment were established" and the ambitions and interests of politicians were set against other ambitions and interests, because "if men were angels no government would be necessary." It is no use, in hindsight, to simply regret that Zimbabweans did not from the start treat Mugabe with constructive pessimism. What is useful is to learn that politicians should be put under suspicion and strong institutions put in place to check their excesses. Rules of control and impeachment of leaders should be in place, regardless of the popularity and apparent heroic intentions of the politicians. Euphoria about easy independence and excitement about heroes became the political manure that fertilized tyranny in the Zimbabwean postcolony. Tyranny and corruption have become a governing political culture in Zimbabwe where it can be publicly known that the president's friends and sons are manipulating the national currency, causing inflation through black marketeering, and nothing happens in terms of attempts by the state and law enforcement to bring them to accountability.

THE WILL TO POWER: GIVING A NAME TO POLITICAL EXTREMISM

Mugabe frequently went too far. In his words, decisions and actions he became a political fundamentalist. Easily he would order the genocide of a people in one region for supporting another political party and that is how he gave the world the Gukurahundi Genocide. In Mugabe's extreme world the demolition of humble dwellings of a population of the poorest of the poor because they allegedly supported the opposition MDC political party became just, that was the Operation Murambatsvina that left many people dead, others displaced and dispossessed of the tin-shacks they at least called their homes. In his own words, cited by Peta Thornycroft (2003), Mugabe claimed: "I am still the Hitler of the time. This Hitler has only one objective, justice for his own people, sovereignty for his people, recognition of the independence of his people, and their right to their resources. If that is Hitler, then let me be a Hitler tenfold. Ten times, that is what we stand for" (Mugabe 2003: 1). The extremist Hitlerism that he boastfully conducted he always justified with the name of the people, their justice, resources and liberation. In justice, Mugabe was no man of the people and in actuality he was a true tyrant and a Hitler. It is not enough in scholarship to describe the insane determinations and energies of the tyrant to conquer and dominate others and the world. There might be a need to give a name to the fantasies and passions that propel political extremism in order to achieve an analytical handle on what fundamentally makes the "tyrant go too far" as Betty Glad (2002: 1) asks. What the imperious itch is that sent Mugabe on a mad and cruel rampage against the same people he called "his people" is important to this book.

There was an incident in 2008 when South African Transport and Allied Workers Union (SATAWU) in Durban stopped its members from offloading a cargo of weapons destined for Zimbabwe from the Chinese ship *An Yue Jiang*. At the time Zimbabwe was going through a bitter and violent dispute over elections that the opposition MDC believed ZANU-PF had rigged. That determination by Mugabe to import weapons from China for the purposes of silencing an angry but unarmed population forced British philosopher Christopher Hitchens into a meditation on exactly "what went wrong" with Mugabe. Hitchens (2008: 1) considered Mugabe's decade of incarceration in a colonial prison as the cause of his anger and paranoia, the death of his wife Sally as the cause of his angry loneliness and his old-school Catholicism was the passion that got him hatefully obsessed to a point of being attracted to homosexuals. Mugabe's public hatred of gays and lesbians became a kind of obsessed love. Finally, Hitchens settled on "envy" as the power and the drive that kept Mugabe in a violent rage: "But I have a theory of my very own: I believe that Mugabe was also driven into a permanent rage by the adulation heaped internationally on Nelson Mandela, an accolade of praise and recognition that he felt was more properly due to himself. And, harboring this grievance, he decided to denude his own unhappy country of anything that might remind anybody of Mandela's legacy" (Hitchens 2008: 2). Envy as a sentiment arises from fears of personal loss and the gain of others over one. Like hatred, it is the resentment of seeing others possess and enjoy what one wishes was his and only his, be it power, material possessions or the companionship of intimate partners. In Hitchens's important observation we can note that, possibly, Mugabe became envious of anyone and anything that seemed to steal attention from him, and this anger led to hatred which drove his vengeance, violence and cruelty. Envy as a political energy and an article of the will to power can produce the tyrant into an insecure and very dangerous malcontent. Mugabe became a dangerous person to Zimbabweans and ultimately to himself.

The fear that became Mugabe's source of "envy" and hatred for even the people that he called his people and drove him to want to stay in power forever was the fear of powerlessness. Mugabe was not born powerful, although he pretended now and again to some royalty; he was born into social vulnerability and precarity of a negligent father and overbearing Christian mother. After achieving power, against many odds and because of a series of lucky incidents and opportune circumstances, Mugabe dreaded the return to the vulnerability and precarious life of powerlessness. Mugabe became determined to conquer, dominate and rule others by any means necessary and to keep it so until perpetuity. This determination came like a demonic possession in that it took hold of him as much as he took hold of it and became a spirited and insatiable appetite for power

and domination. Those that saw in Mugabe a freedom fighter and liberator did not see his possession by a spirited passion for personal power and
domination of others. If Mandela became a global icon when Mugabe
became a skunk of the world he naturally triggered Mugabe's fear and
envy, the idea of anyone more powerful and better loved than he eats into
the heart and mind of the tyrant. Mugabe's fragile ego and vulnerable
inner life would not live with any, monster or saint, called greater than he.
The coup that deposed him was partly caused by his refusal to name any
possible successor. Like the biblical Herod that went into a murderous
spree because he had a rumour that some other king had been born,
Mugabe could not live with the name or the face of anyone called the
President of Zimbabwe, besides himself.

The epigraph from Nietzsche (1968: 112) that introduces this chapter
captures importantly the political dilemma of fighting the monstrosity of
colonialism and becoming a colonial and colonising monster that Mugabe
was confronted with. In his understanding and also celebration of power
and domination Nietzsche is a useful philosopher to those that are interested in understanding the energies, fantasies and passions that drive con-
querors and tyrants anywhere in the world. This book benefits richly,
especially from Nietzsche's philosophical concept of the will to power.
Nietzsche's triumphalist celebration of the will to power helps to illuminate not just the political thought and practice of Mugabe, but also the
inner fears and loves that propel power mongers and tyrants. In a strong
way, Nietzsche answers the question "why tyrants go too far?" that Betty
Glad (2002: 1) asks. Tyrants are driven to domination and totalitarianism
not just by the sheer enjoyment of power but also by the fear of powerlessness and vulnerability. Scholars have provided multiple psychological,
philosophical, sociological and even historical explanations to the degeneration of leaders to tyranny. I find Nietzsche's will to power concept able
to tie together most of these descriptions of the drives and pulls to tyranny
that consume such leaders as Mugabe that eventually sacrifice the cause of
liberation from domination on the altar of the god of unbridled and ugly
uses of absolute power. Nietzsche, directly opposite to my aim in this
book, describes the madness of power while celebrating and not condemning it. In his philosophical celebration of power and domination,
Nietzsche drops us clues that help us understand the loves and fears of
tyrants and despots in the modern world.

Nietzsche (1968) expands the thought of Arthur Schopenhauer (1909),
who described the "world as will" in appreciation of how spirited human

ambition was the driver of history in a gloomy world. Human ambition, determination and drive are the oxygen that gives life to discovery, achievement and progress in an otherwise uncertain place that the world is. Those who drive the history of the world and that of humanity are frequently passionate and ambitious individuals that invest their all in seeking to make changes that matter and to drive societies to different and determined directions. Amongst these individuals have not only been philosophers, scientists and inventors but also the tyrants and genocidists. As rendered by Nietzsche, the will power is a violently insatiable appetite and drive for power and domination that overcomes every obstacle, and can grow in force to a point of tragedy if it is not turned into an art and a pursuit of beauty. In the gesture that power should at least be decorated by some art and beauty, Nietzsche almost rescues himself from celebrating artless tyranny. However, as observed in Mugabe, the tyrant can be an artful performer and dramatic pretender. Mugabe's benevolence and conciliatory rhetoric was an art that was always performed for the greater good of more power for himself. Where power was at stake, Mugabe abandoned all pretences to persuasion and degenerated into genocidal violence exemplified in the Gukurahundi Genocide of 1982 to 1987 in the Matabeleland and Midlands regions of Zimbabwe. In the Nietzschean sense, Mugabe became power without beauty and authority without art, and therefore tyranny undiluted. Power without art, domination that is not accompanied by persuasion and beauty, is bereft of magnificence and glory. Inglorious and maleficent has been Mugabe's political legacy.

This book shows how in pursuit of power by all means necessary, Mugabe participated in what Achille Mbembe (1992: 3–37) cinematically described of the postcolony in Africa as the "banality of power," a tendency to the obscene and the grotesque, the use of fables and clichés, the production of illicit political performances and dramatisation of power that included systematic dispensation of pain and distribution of mass suffering. All this accompanied by monumental political stupidity. Mbembe noted the normalisation of excess and lack of proportion in the use and abuse of political power by post-colonial leaders that had not only become colonisers in their own right but had become sold and bought to political hooliganism and what Horace Campbell (2003: 75) called "executive lawlessness." Mbembe and Campbell, amongst many others, are scholars that have explored the degeneration and abuse of power in post-colonial Africa where potential liberators became present oppressors. By design, this book utilises the reflections of such scholars to expand on Nietzsche's renditions on the consuming and corrupting life of power.

Mugabe rejected all pretences to law and order. He publicly boasted of having degrees in violence (Meredith 2002a, b: 76) that he could unleash on any enemy, real or imagined. In his own words and will to power, Mugabe declared that "no judicial decision will stand on our way" (Meredith 2002a, b: 18). The law as an important arm of democratic government and the courts as a central democratic state institution were dismissed with impunity by a power-mad Mugabe. As I demonstrate in this book, Mugabe's language became a symptom of the insanity about power that consumed him. Slavoj Zizek (2001: 6) notes how psychoanalysis in its readings of the "psychic life of power" and therefore the mentality and sensibility of politicians capitalises on the use of language as a site where the unconscious is revealed. The monster that lived inside Mugabe frequently betrayed its presence and menace in his rants and curses. The words that powerful leaders use cannot be innocent of their inner life and political intentions. They are either powerful words that speak liberation into existence or words of power that enact the domination and oppression of the people.

In this book I pay attention to Mugabe's language as an index into his psyche and inner monster. If the true Mugabe has been hidden, he is easily found in the way and the things that he said. Zizek (2003: 500) emphasises the need to probe "how is the human psyche really working?" and notes that "such questions are not even taken seriously in cultural studies." I carry in this book the assumption that Mugabe's political thought and practice have been studied and reported in ways that have not sufficiently benefitted from psychoanalytical efforts, hence the many misunderstandings and non-understandings of the man and the phenomenon of Mugabeism itself. Derek Matyszak (2015: 4) notes how Mugabe changed his language in a manner where he deliberately deleted himself from conversations, making himself a spokesperson of a higher power and hiding whether he was the puppet or the puppeteer in politics. By using the illeism of language in that way, Mugabe frequently escaped accountability for his actions that he explained as acts of nature and destiny. Mugabe's political performances, his accent and diction, and political vocabulary are all a dark forest in which I intend to seek and find the true Mugabe, the thing in itself.

In celebrating his own power and boasting about his violence, as a Lacanian paranoiac and Freudian narcissist that I observe him to be, Mugabe became what Slavo Zizek (1996: 145) names as the paranoiac and narcissist politician who speaks with a tragically "self-enjoying voice" that also conceals his personal fragility and fear. Mugabe, in power, possessed some narcissist self-kissing political habits that one national occasion saw him bow down to his own picture at the National Sports Stadium. The designed way in which this book supplements Nietzsche's will to power with the psychoanalytical tools of Freud Sigmund, Jacques Lacan and Slavoj Zizek, amongst others, helps this book to effect a deeper penetration of Mugabe's political subjectivity. The benefit of ideas of decolonial philosophies of liberation such as those of Dussel equips this book with an ability to read how coloniality continues to limit liberation in such settings of the Global South as Zimbabwe. It is in that way that this book also attempts to unmask the unconscious fears and loves, fantasies and passions that drove Mugabe's will to power.

Political moderation that accompanies the politics of liberation and the courts as an important arm of good governance was ignored as Mugabe put Zimbabwe and Zimbabweans through what Giorgio Agamben (2005) has popularised as the "state of exception" where the law can be replaced with executive disorder and partisan chaos. In spectacular celebrations of power, Mugabe, in state and public events, adopted Stalinist ceremonialisation that had such performances of power as frequently seen in North Korea (Meredith 2002a, b: 77) where colossal crowds are bussed in and the people in their multitudes are staged to demonstrate the leader's—however non-existent—popularity. In the psychoanalytical study of the Confucian political philosophy in China, Zizek (2011) isolates political and cultural rituals and ceremonies as sites of tyrannical performances of absolute power. The tyrant relishes public ceremonies and rituals, mass gatherings and rallies that seem to confirm his power. Mugabe had school children bussed from remote rural areas to augment the crowds in his many rallies that he wanted big and populous. Like any spectacular performer Mugabe enjoyed big audiences that demonstrated the immensity of his power.

In this book, Mugabe's will to power as a violent political paradigm is contrasted to the decolonial and humanistic "will to live" that is conceptualised and described by the philosopher of liberation Enrique Dussel as a corrective and alternative to nihilistic philosophy propagated by Friedrich Nietzsche and others; a political philosophy that valorised conquest and domination:

Since human communities have always been threatened by their vulnerability to death and extinction, such communities maintain an instinctive desire to remain alive. This desire to live of human beings in a community can be called a will. The will to live is the originary tendency of all human beings, and I offer this notion as a corrective to Schopenhauer's tragic formulation and the dominating tendency of the "will to power" of Nietzsche or Heidegger. (Dussel 2008: 13)

The will to live that Enrique Dussel adumbrates, as a philosophy of liberation, feeds from what Max Weber presented as politics, not as a domineering and personally profitable profession, but as a liberating and humanising vocation that is primarily a responsibility to others and a duty by the self to the collective (Dussel 2008: 24). Mugabe, as I observe in this book, professionalised and personally instrumentalised politics and in that way failed in the humanist and decolonial vocation of liberation. The will to live of Zimbabwe and the happiness of Zimbabweans were neglected. To preserve the life and secure the happiness of Zimbabweans is exactly what Mugabe did not concern himself with. For Mugabe power was power only when it suited and benefitted him. The decolonial and humanist political paradigm of the will to live that Dussel (2008: 26) envisages confronts that of the will to power with its proposition that those who lead and "command must command by obeying" the will of their people that is freely expressed in democratic and fair elections, the ballot, which Mugabe rejects in his valorisation of the bullet. Dussel (2008: 30) rejects as political corruption the fetishism of power that turns leaders from liberators to self-worshiping gods that can spill the blood of their own people for power. The liberation of his people that Mugabe claimed as his goal in politics does not explain the many mass graves in which he consigned multitudes of the same people.

Just a river away from Zimbabwe is Zambia where Kenneth Kaunda (1966) forcefully preached the liberating politics of "humanism" that outlawed the use of violence and fraud in politics. Mugabe did not need to look for role models in the West but closer to home in Africa. When Kaunda lost the presidential election to Frederick Chiluba he exemplarily stepped down gracefully and remained a hero of his people. But Mugabe, in his spirited will to power, could not permit himself the humility to learn anything even from exemplary neighbours. Mugabe was too mad for power to contemplate leadership that forbade the spilling of blood and causing of pain and suffering.

Nietzsche's philosophical concept of the will to power that describes the passions, fears and loves that drive ambition for power and domination helps give a name to Mugabe's madness for power. This book also benefits from such theses as that of Hannah Arendt (1955) in the "origins of totalitarianism" who studied Nazi and Soviet totalitarianisms and reflected on the fragility of freedom, the potency of propaganda, the uses to which despots put political scapegoats and how they invent enemies to create excuses for violence and war. The political ruminations of Niccolo Machiavelli (2003a) that were admired and valorised by Nietzsche (1968) are also brought into the book to evaluate the political ideas and actions of Mugabe. Machiavelli importantly reflected on how political power mongers combined force and fraud, the manly and the beastly in pursuit of a firm grip on power. The concept of the political as nuanced by Carl Schmitt (2008) is also brought in to examine how, in word and in deed, Mugabe contributed to the revaluation of the political, in how he managed political relations of "friends and enemies" in dealing with supporters and opponents. Chantal Mouffe (2005a, b), who expanded the concept of the political that Schmitt nuanced, aids this book in the attempt to understand the naturality of antagonism and enmity in politics which needs to be disciplined into agonism. In other words, the political proper always has a potential of the will to power. Democratisation of the political, therefore, entails the pragmatism of dealing with the conflictual nature of the political, where ballots in democratic elections should replace bullets that are fired in war.

In the race for power and more power, Mugabe elected the bullet as his method. In insisting on the bullet and not on the ballot as he did, Mugabe was clinging onto the will to power as opposed to the will to life. One of the capital observations I make about Mugabe is that he became an actor and a performer who hid his true colours behind rhetoric, fictions and myths. For that reason, the theories of simulation and simulacra that are advanced by Jean Baudrillard (1994), who describes the manufacture of reality by use of signs and actions, become useful to this book. With his words and deeds Mugabe manufactured and made real a certain world after his political imagination and interests. The concepts of performance and performativity advanced by Judith Butler (1990) are used to illuminate how Mugabe simulated some ideas and dissimulated others in politics, and how he performed his will to power that largely remained concealed behind pretensions of grand goals and human ideals of liberation and humanisation.

REFERENCES

Agamben, G. (2005). *State of Exception. Chicago & London*. University of Chicago Press.

Arendt, H. (1955). *The Origins of Totalitarianism*. Boston: Harcourt, Houghton Mifflin.

Aristotle. (1948). *The Politics of Aristotle* (E. Barker, Trans.). Oxford: Clarendon.

Armah, A. K. (1988). *The Beautyful Ones are not yet Born*. Oxford: Heinemann.

Asuelime, L., & Simurai, B. (2013). Robert Mugabe Against all Odds: A Historical Discourse of a Successful Life President? *African Renaissance, 10*(2), 51–56.

Auret, M. (2009). *From Liberator to Dictator: An Insider's Account of Robert Mugabe's Descent into Tyranny*. Claremont: David Philip.

Baudrillard, J. (1994). *Simulacra and Simulation*. Ann Arbor: University of Michigan Press.

Bourne, R. (2011). *Catastrophe: What Went Wrong in Zimbabwe?* London & New York: Zed Books.

Buckle, C. (2003). *Beyond Tears: Zimbabwe's Tragedy*. Cape Town: Jonathan Ball Publishers.

Bullock, A. (1992). *Hitler and Stalin: Parallel Lives*. New York: Random House.

Burbach, R. (2003). *The Pinochet Affair: State Terrorism and Global Justice*. London/New York: Zed Books.

Butler, J. (1990). Performative Acts and Gender Constitution: An Essay in Phenomenology and Feminist Theory. In S. Case (Ed.), *Performing Feminisms: Feminist Critical Theory and Theater*. Baltimore: Johns Hopkins University Press.

Campbell, H. (2003). *Reclaiming Zimbabwe: The Exhaustion of the Patriarchal Model of Liberation*. Claremont: David Philip Publishers.

Compagnon, D. (2011). *A Predictable Tragedy: Robert Mugabe and the Collapse of Zimbabwe. Philadelphia*: University of Pennsylvania Press.

Daloz, J.-P. (2003). Big Men in Sub-Saharan African Africa: How Elites Accumulate Positions and Resources. *Comparative Sociology, 2*(1), 271–285.

Dotcherty, T. (2016). *Complicity: Criticism Between Collaboration and Commitment*. London: Rowman and Littlefield.

Dussel, E. (2008). *Twenty Theses on Politics*. London/Durham: Duke University Press.

Ekeh, P. (1975). Colonialism and the Two Publics in Africa: A Theoretical Statement. *Comparative Studies in Society and History, 17*(1), 91–112.

Ekeh, P. P. (1983). Colonialism and Social Structure in Africa. In *An Inaugural Lecture*. Ibadan: Ibadan University Press.

Fanon, F. (2001). *The Wretched of the Earth*. London: Penguin Classics.

Friedman, S. (2010). Seeing Ourselves as Others See Us: Race, Technique and the Mbeki Administration. In D. Glaser (Ed.), *Mbeki and After: Reflections on the Legacy of Thabo Mbeki*. Johannesburg: Wits University Press.

Gappah, P. (2017). How Zimbabwe Freed Itself from Robert Mugabe. In *The New Yorker*. Retrieved October 5, 2018, from https://www.newyorker.com/sections/.../how-zimbabwe-freed-itself-of-robert-mugabe.

Glad, B. (2002). Why Tyrants Go Too Far: Malignant Narcissism and Absolute Power. *Political Psychology, 23*, 1–37.

Godwin, P. (2010). *The Fear: The Last Days of Robert Mugabe.* New York: Picador.

Gramsci, A. (1971). *Selections from the Prison Notebooks.* New York: International Publishers Company.

Hitchens, C. (2008). Mandela Envy: Is Robert Mugabe's Lawless Misrule Founded on Jealousy? *Fighting Words: SLATE.* Slate.comnews: Accessed 12 April 2019.

Holland, H. (2008). *Dinner with Mugabe: The Untold Story of a Freedom Fighter Who Became a Tyrant.* Johannesburg: Penguin Books.

Hope, C. (2003). *Brothers Under the Skin: Travels in Tyranny.* London: Pan Macmillan.

Jackson, H. R., & Roseberg, C. G. (1984). Personal Rule: Theory and Practice in Africa. *Comparative Politics, 16*(4), 421–442.

Kaplan, R. (2002). *Warrior Politics: Why Leadership Needs a Pagan Ethos.* New York: Vintage Books.

Karsh, E., & Rautsi, I. (1991). *Saddam Hussein: A Political Biography.* New York: Macmillan.

Kaunda, K. (1966). *A Humanist in Africa: Letters to Colin M. Morris from Kenneth Kaunda President of Zambia.* London: Longmans.

Kirk-Greene, A. H. M. (1991). His Eternity, His Eccentricity, or His Exemplarity: A Further Contribution to the Study of His Excellency the African Head of State. *African Affairs, 90*, 163–187.

Kriger, N. (2003). Robert Mugabe: Another Too-Long Serving African Ruler: A Review Essay. *Political Science Quarterly, 118*(2), 307–313.

Lessing, D. (2013, March 1). The Jewel of Africa. *The New York Review of Books*, p. 1.

Lloyd, R. B. (2002). Zimbabwe: The Making of an Autocratic "Democracy.". *Current History, 101*(655), 219–224.

Lukacs, J. (1997). *The Hitler of History.* New York: Knopf.

Machiavelli, N. (2003a). *The Prince and Other Writings.* (Wayne A. Rebhorn, Trans.). New York: Barnes and Noble Classics.

Machiavelli, N. (2003b). *The Prince.* New York: Barnes and Noble Classics.

MacLean, J. S. (2002). Mugabe at War: The Political Economy of Conflict in Zimbabwe. *Third World Quarterly, 23*(3), 513–528.

Magaisa, T. A. (2019). The Regime and its Enablers. *Big Saturday Read.* Retrieved February 5, 2020, from www.bigsr.co.uk.

Mamdani, M. (2004). *Good Muslim, Bad Muslim: America, the Cold War and the Roots of Terror.* New York: Pantheon Books.

Mamdani, M. (2009). Lessons of Zimbabwe: Mugabe in Context. *Concerned African Scholars Bulletin, 82*, 1–13.

Matyszak, D. (2015). Coup De Grace? Plots and Purges: Mugabe and ZANU-PF's 6th National People's Congress. *Research and Advocacy Unit.* Retrieved July 10, 2019, from www.researchand advocacyunit.

Mazrui, A. (1990). On Poet Presidents and Philosopher Kings. *Research in African Literature, 21*(2), 13–19.

Mazrui, A. (1995). The Blood of Experience: The Failed State and Political Collapse in Africa. *World Policy Journal, 12*(1), 28–34.

Mazrui, A. (1997). Nkrumah: The Leninist Czar. *Transition, 75*, 106–126.

Mbembe, A. (1992). Provisional Notes on the Post-colony. *Africa, 62*(1), 3–37.

Meredith, M. (2002a). *Robert Mugabe: Power, Plunder and Tyranny in Zimbabwe.* Cape Town: Jonathan Ball Publishers.

Meredith, M. (2002b). *Our Votes, Our Guns: Robert Mugabe and the Tragedy of Zimbabwe.* New York: Public Affairs Publishers.

Moorcraft, P. (2012). *Mugabe's War Machine.* Cape Town: Jonathan Ball Publishers.

Mouffe, C. (2005a). *On the Political.* Abingdon: Routledge.

Mouffe, C. (2005b). *The Return of the Political.* Verso: New York/London.

Mugabe, R. (1989). The Unity Accord: Its Promise for the Future. In Banana, C.S (ed.) *Turmoil and Tenacity: Zimbabwe 1890–1990.* Harare: College Press.

Mugabe, R. (1997a, May 11). Lets forget the Past. In *The Sunday Mail.*

Mugabe, R. (1997b, December 6). Speech on the Fast Track Land Reform Programme. In *The Herald.*

Mugabe, G. (2018). In G. Nyarota (Ed.), *The Graceless Fall of Robert Mugabe: The End of a Dictator's Reign.* Cape Town: Penguin Random House.

Mugabe, R. (2008). Campaign Speech. In Ndlovu-Gatsheni, S. "Rethinking Chimurenga and Gukurahundi in Zimbabwe: A Critique of Partisan National History." *African Studies Review 55* (3). pp. 1–26.

Mutambara, A. (2017). Zimbabwe: Mutambara-Mugabe Very Shallow, Intellectually Inadequate and Personally Insecure. Retrieved April 18, 2018, from www.allafrica.com.

Ncube, T. (2009). Foreword. In M. Auret (Ed.), *From Liberator to Dictator: An Insider's Account of Robert Mugabe's Descent into Tyranny.* Claremont: David Philip.

Ndlovu-Gatsheni, S. (2012a). Rethinking "Chimurenga" and "Gukurahundi" in Zimbabwe: A Critique of Partisan National History. *African Studies Review, 55*(3), 1–26.

Ndlovu-Gatsheni, S. (2012b). Beyond Mugabe-Centric Narratives of the Zimbabwean Crisis: Review Article. *African Affairs, 111*(443), 315–323.

Ndlovu-Gatsheni, S. (2015). *Mugabeism? History, Politics, and Power in Zimbabwe.* New York: Palgrave Macmillan.

Nietzsche, F. (1968). *The Will to Power.* New York: Vantage Books.

Nkomo, J. (1984). *The Story of My Life.* London: Methuen.

Norman, A. (2004a). *Robert Mugabe and the Betrayal of Zimbabwe.* Jefferson: McFarland and Co.

Norman, A. (2004b). *Robert Mugabe and the Betrayal of Zimbabwe.* London: McFarland & Company Publishers.

Nussbaum, M. (1998). Political Animals: Luck, Love and Dignity. *Metaphilosophy, 29*(4), 273–287.

Nyarota, G. (2018). *The Graceless Fall of Robert Mugabe: The End of a Dictator's Reign*. Cape Town: Penguin Random House.

Onslow, S., & Plaut, M. (2018). *Robert Mugabe*. Johannesburg: Jacana Media.

Plato. (1952). The Seventh Letter. In *The Great Books* (J. Harward, Trans.). Chicago: Encyclopaedia Britannica. 7, pp. 387–391.

Power, S. (2008). How to Kill a Country: Turning a Breadbasket into a Basket Case in Ten Easy Steps-the Robert Mugabe Way. *Atlantic Monthly, 292*(5), 86–101.

Rogers, D. (2019). *Two Weeks in November: The Astonishing Untold Story of the Operation that Toppled Mugabe*. Jeppestown: Jonathan Ball Publishers.

Sachikonye, L. (2011). *When a State Turns on Its Citizens: 60 Years of Violence in Zimbabwe*. Johannesburg: Jacana Media.

Schmitt, C. (2008). *The Concept of the Political: Expanded edition*. Chicago: University of Chicago Press.

Schopenhauer, A. (1909, 2012). *The World as Will and Representation*. Berlin: Courier Corporation.

Said, E. (2012). On Lost Causes. In *Reflections on Exile and other Literary and Cultural Essays*. London: Granta Books.

Saul, J. (2008). *Decolonisation and Empire: Contesting the Rhetoric and Reality of Resurbodination in Southern Africa and Beyond*. Johannesburg: Wits Press.

Snyder, T. (2017). *On Tyranny: Twenty Lessons for the Twentieth Century*. London: Bodley Head.

Tendi, B.-M. (2016). State Intelligence and the Politics of Zimbabwe's Presidential Succession. *African Affairs, 115*(459), 203–224.

Thornycroft, P. (2003). Hitler Mugabe Launches Revenge Terror Attacks. *The Telegraph*, www.telegraph.co.uk: Accessed 6 April 2019.

Todd, G. J. (2007). *Through the Darkness: A Life in Zimbabwe*. Cape Town: Struik Publishers.

Tucker, R. C. (1990). *Stalin in Power; The Revolution from Above, 1928–1941*. New York: Norton Publishers.

Vine, L. T. (1980). African Patrimonial Regimes in Comparative Perspective. *The Journal of Modern African Studies, 18*(4), 657–673.

Wa Thiongo, N. (1987). *Devil on the Cross*. Essex: African Writers Series: Heinemann.

Wyk, V. J.-A. (2007). Political Leaders in Africa: Presidents, Patrons or Profiteers? *Occasional Paper Series: Accord, 2*(1), 2–38.

Zizek, S. (1996). The Seven Veils of Paranoia, or, Why Does the Paranoiac Need Two Fathers? *Constellations, 3*(2), 139–156.

Zizek, S. (2001). What Can Lenin Tell Us About Freedom Today? *Rethinking Marxism, 13*(2), 1–9.

Zizek, S. (2003). Critical Response: I, a Symptom of What? *Critical Inquiry, 29*, 486–503.

Zizek, S. (2011). Three Notes on China: Past and Present. *Positions, 19*(3), 707–721.

Zizek, S. (2016). *Against the Double Blackmail: Refugees, Terror and Other Troubles with the Neighbours*. London: Allen Lane: Penguin Books.

Zizek, S. (2017). *The Courage of Hopelessness: Chronicles of the Year of Living Dangerously*. London: Allen Lane: Penguin Books.

CHAPTER 2

The Will to Power in the Postcolony

Our votes must go together with our guns. After all, any vote we shall
have, shall have been the product of a gun. The gun, which produces the
vote, should remain its security officer—its guarantor. The peoples' votes
and the people's guns are always inseparable twins.
—Robert Mugabe (1976: 11)
You can vote for them [MDC: opposition political party], but that
would be a wasted vote. I am telling you. You would just be cheating
yourself. There is no way we can allow them to rule this country. Never,
ever. We have a job to do, to protect our heritage. The MDC will not
rule this country. It will never, ever happen. We will never allow it.
—Robert Mugabe (2008: 1)
In so far as we believe in morality, we pass a sentence on existence …
War is another thing. I am by nature warlike. To attack is among my
instincts. To be able to be an enemy-that perhaps presupposes a strong
nature, it is in any event a condition of every strong nature.
—Friedrich Nietzsche (1979: 13)

Robert Mugabe frequently spoke with the tone of a high priest and sometimes that of a warlord and a Mafia Godfather. Before his final fall from the
graces of power in 2017, Mugabe enjoyed the reputation of "an aging
Godfather of a feuding Mafia family" that Alex Magaisa (2016: 1) so well
described. His party was in turmoil as powerful politicians and securocrats
in feuding factions jostled for the opportunity to succeed him. In his days

© The Author(s) 2021
W. J. Mpofu, *Robert Mugabe and the Will to Power in an African*
Postcolony, African Histories and Modernities,
https://doi.org/10.1007/978-3-030-47879-7_2

of glory Mugabe would have played the factions against each other and still remained the warlord to whom they all reported and pledged allegiance. He still had his iron will to power but very advanced age and disease were eating into his body. His speeches mixed what sounded like mature advice to the feuding factions with anger, frustration and not so well-concealed fear. Mugabe's entire life in politics appears to have been a life of determined anger, hatred and bitterness that concealed personal fear of defeat and failure. Not so many scholars and journalists have understood and described Mugabe as what he truly was, an "insecure" (Onslow and Plaut 2018: 61) and most times terrified person that artfully hid his fragility and vulnerability behind performances of anger, hate and threats. Concealed behind performances of courage, anger and invincibility was what Doris Lessing (2013) described as a "terrified little man" that Mugabe actually was. The source of Mugabe's evil and monstrosity was his fragility, fear and littleness of both body and mind that he concealed with a ferocious bravado and will to power that I describe in this chapter. In a paradoxical but true way Mugabe seems to have attracted what he feared most, which is being dethroned from power and rendered a vulnerable and humiliated old soul. Although the coupsters called the overthrow of Mugabe by other names, scholars such as Blessing-Miles Tendi (2019: 1) have established that it was a coup like all others that removed Mugabe from power in November 2017. Coups and assassinations, perhaps, are real occupational hazards for tyrants that use force and fraud to remain in power against the will of their people. Fear seems to beget fear as those securocrats that removed Mugabe from power seem to have done so partly in fear that he was about to punish them for their crimes. The securocrats feared that he was about to victimise them using the law (Tendi 2019: 17) when in actuality he feared their ambition to overthrow him.

That Mugabe became the venal tyrant that haunted the Zimbabwean postcolony is perhaps well understood. What has not been named and described are the kinds of political desires, fantasies and fears that shaped his spirited ambition and drive to conquer and dominate the polity. In Zimbabwe Mugabe advanced what Willard Reno (1998: 1) has described as "warlord politics" that is a radical personalisation, informalisation and militarisation of both the economy and the polity. Warlord politics does not only produce a weak state but also normalises executive hooliganism where the tyrant can openly boast about guns and political violence, in that crude way also give respectability to political killings and some crimes against humanity. Where warlord politics has taken root, as it did in

Zimbabwe, the tyrant becomes a law unto himself and can pronounce such otherwise central democratic processes as elections a nullity. In such a setting the tyrant "becomes everywhere" by colonising "time and space" so much so that even in his physical absence, Christopher Hope (2003: 8) notes, he "becomes a majority" that can hold the entire national population at ransom. The tyrant in his privileged status as his Excellency the President of the postcolony can be exactly like that, too much, in a rather small place. In Zimbabwe Mugabe became an exaggerated presence, an imperialist of time, a monopolist of place and imagination. It was as a Godfather and a warlord that Mugabe could tell Zimbabweans that the political opposition will never ever rule the country, even if they won the elections.

What Friedrich Nietzsche (1968) described as the will to power is that combination of desires, fantasies, fears and a collective of insanities that become a tragic appetite for power and domination. Tragic in that, for the despot that is possessed by the will to power, the desire for power and domination grows into a self-loving, self-worshipping and self-eating urge that can only end in comic failure. The comedy of Mugabe's failure would be true art if lives were not lost, the economy and the polity not decayed. The autoeroticism of power, such as that of Mugabe, can exhibit a multiplicity of comedies of error, unintended and also unwanted disasters.

As a kind of celebrant of power and domination, Nietzsche describes the will to power in the tone of "might is right" and scoffs at defeat, powerlessness and weakness of those that are dominated. A close examination of the will to power as a name of the triumphant spirit of conquest and domination shows that, as I illustrate in this book, it does not as much emanate from the love of power by the strong but fear of weakness by the fragile and vulnerable. The case of Mugabe in the Zimbabwean postcolony, as I argue, illustrates how behind the persona of a gallant warrior and ranting despot that Mugabe performed, there was always the vulnerable, fragile and frightened little boy that needed love and protection of the world. In his time and place, Mugabe was entangled in a true Machiavellian paradox of the prince that does not know whether he wants to be loved or feared. Where Mugabe tried to inspire love, he attracted clubs of supporters that were mainly flatterers and sycophants; they did not love or honour him but loved themselves in him; and especially what they could do with his power for their own extractive and accumulative interests. They methodically took advantage of his hunger for love, respect and worship to sing for their suppers, lunches and breakfast combined, soliciting political appointments, grovelling for business deals and the bounty of the loot in the postcolony. So many kinds of tycoons, criminals and other scoundrels sang his praises and started all sorts of religions in his name so that he could look aside from their crimes. Where Mugabe chose to inspire fear, he wantonly discharged violence with guns and such political violence that he frequently boasted of as his "degrees in violence." In that way Mugabe became a personification of excesses and disproportions that worked together to make for tragi-comedy. Mugabe was feared but also laughed at as a kind of buffoon of power.

The postcolony itself, as well exemplified in Zimbabwe, is a haunting and haunted setting of tragi-comedies that Achille Mbembe (2001: 102) correctly observes, concerning Cameroon, to be a chaotic setting, a time and place that is haunted by stubborn ghosts of colonialism and its enduring violences. It is in the postcolony that colonial extremes encounter post-colonial fundamentalisms to produce what Chairman Mao Zedong called disorder under the heavens, which is as disastrous as it can be an opportunity for inventing new liberating futures. Chaos can be an opportunity for political thought and invention.

Mbembe, in particular, notes how the postcolony is an unstable political climate that normalises the grotesque and the obscene in politics. Bitter legacies of colonialism and excesses of fragile anti-colonialism collapse together to produce a truly strange place where the tyrant is a god, it seems. The Zimbabwean postcolony became exactly that, a stage on which the tyrant performed the tragi-comedies of his life in power. The postcolony in its haunting actuality tends to be "a particularly revealing, and rather dramatic, stage on which are played out the wider problems of subjection and its corollary, discipline" (Mbembe 2001: 103). Discipline is mostly performed in the cruel punishment of offenders and losers that the tyrant and his party will never ever allow to prevail. The postcolony is a setting of insatiable grudges and encounters of Olympics of revenge. Concerning the cruelty of discipline in the ZANLA guerrilla camps, of which Mugabe eventually became leader and overseer after winning the confidence of the commanders in Mozambique, Gerald Mazarire (2011: 583) recounts the severe beatings. Offenders were detained in pits for days and were frequently thrashed until they soiled themselves, the thrashing only stopped when flies started buzzing around the smell of human waste and blood. Mugabe's political legacy came to be formed and shaped by that kind of cruelty and evil. For more than three decades, Zimbabweans knew and experienced no other leader, or model of leadership except that of Mugabe and his performances of power that became increasingly spectacular as he grew older but was determined to act young and fit for the job. The practical irony of feigning youthfulness and fitness for power made Mugabe a caricature of a caricature who appeared to mock himself with his every move. At its unbending majesty, power breaks with comic and tragic ludicrousness.

The tyrant caricatures himself the more he strives to do and to be the impossible. Fundamentally, what the tyrant wants is to be a magician. To effectively distance himself from his supporters on the one hand and opponents and victims on the other, the tyrant must construct and produce an image of himself that Friedrich Nietzsche (2003) in *Thus Spoke Zarathustra* described as a "superman." The Nietzschean superman is a magician and a god, a conqueror that is removed from the common and the ordinary; to achieve this mythical status, the tyrant of the postcolony employs bands of myth makers and fictive imaginists that circulate his name and construct his image likewise, in political mythology.

The tyrant as a magician and wizard is common figure in the African postcolony. Ngugi Wa Thiongo (2006) portrays such a mythical superman in his fictive account of the ruler of the Free Republic of Aburiria, in the novel *Wizard of the Crow*. The Ruler of Aburiria, Aburiria being an imaginary but typical postcolony, is a tyrant of note. He is as haunting to the postcolony as he is haunted, and afflicted by a strange illness. His illness is a combination of permanent anger that consumes him from the inside like a poison and the burden of hatred and curses from his enemies and victims in the postcolony. The tears of the widows and the orphans that his many massacres of the innocent have produced haunt him. The best way the population imagines him is as a practitioner of witchcraft and an accomplished devil worshipper who sits on a throne of skulls and every morning and evening strolls the inside of a dark chamber performing fiendish rituals of power in the postcolony. Similar and worse narratives are circulated about the allegedly dark ritual and magical life of Robert Mugabe in the Zimbabwean postcolony. In a way, the arts and sciences of the political hegemony of the tyrant in the postcolony are not removed from the dark arts of witchcraft itself; the tyrant is effectively a wizard. Ernest Wamba dia Wamba (1996) once complained that contrary to the true spirit of Pan-African liberation African countries and communities were falling into the hands, not of liberating leaders, but a "few sorcerers."

Much like that of the Ruler of Aburiria, Mugabe's birthday was celebrated in Zimbabwe like a kind of Christmas. The festivities became known as the 21st February Movement after the date of his birth. In Aburiria, the Ruler's birthday was debated for many long days in Parliament. As one who brings both punishment and payment the Ruler is a man full of surprises. On such chosen days as his annual birthday festival, as if to attempt to atone for his massacres, he performs spectacles of generosity. He is known to appear in his messianic magnificence to cut the cake for the multitudes that go on to publicly feed like the masses that the Christ served with five loaves and two fish. The Ruler brings death and nutriment, punishment and payment, in a way that Mbembe (2001: 24) notes as the way of the "commandment" that holds certain "types of rationality used to rule men and ensure the provision of goods and things in sub-Saharan Africa since the end of direct colonisation." The ruler of the postcolony is at once the rainmaker and the punisher in the post-colonial hell who wields the fork to fry the condemned and the spoon to feed the hungry. Mugabe's birthday celebrations were increasingly expensive and flamboyant even in the years of drought and famine in the country. As if in attempt to insulate his fragile ego from the cemeteries he has created, he practically wants to pretend that he rules over the land of milk and honey, and that of free and happy contented citizens. On the day of his birth, so much like the Ruler of Aburiria, Mugabe gave food lavishly with his right hand while with his left hand he collected big gifts from business tycoons, foreign investors and criminals seeking favours and promotions in the food chain of the postcolony.

By holding monopoly of law, he does not only hold the power to make democratic elections a nullity as Mugabe publicly boasted of. However, he also commanded "a regime of privileges and immunities" (Mbembe 2001: 24) for his chosen disciples. The elite enjoy the impunity to commit and get away with any crime in the postcolony, from theft, rape, assaults and looting to genocide itself that remains a haunting possibility if it is not already an actuality in the postcolony. A reputation for mass murder is part of the long curriculum vitae of the tyrant in the postcolony. He has mass graves and shallow unmarked graves of the multitudes under his belt, that bloody and dark legacy decorates his throne. Being feared and hated make him feel like a true superman and magician who must not fear for himself.

The haunting ruler of the postcolony does not only want his tragi-comic performances of the magical and the powerful believed by the population but he also rather idiotically and blindly believes them himself. He has faith in himself as the champion of the super-real and the metaphysical.

It was as an intoxicated magician and blind tyrant that on the 6th of October 1981 in Cairo Anwar Sadat saw his assassins break from the military parade and run for him but never believed they would actually succeed to kill him (Belfield 2005: 259). Sadat had famously vowed that Egyptians were his children and none would dare imagine his death, let alone occasion it. He saw and believed himself to be the last of the Pharaohs, the sun was his brother and the moon his sister; he was a cosmic force until the grenades and bullets rained on him. Until that rainy day of November 2017 where the Chinese-made tanks rolled down the potholed streets of Harare and cordoned off his loyal guards, Mugabe had probably seen but not believed the inevitable coup that overthrew him. Drunk and blind of his sense of the magician and the supernatural ruler, the post-colonial tyrant is rigidly invested in the eternal immaturity of the citizens who have never, and will never, be trusted to make up their minds and act independently of the ruler and his rules (Hope 2003: 89). For that reason, those who dare oppose and actually challenge the ruler are treated as traitors beyond the redemption that on behalf of God or the ancestors the ruler must help send to hell. It is perhaps the way of the postcolony and its tragi-comedies that at the end the citizens are able to fool power by penetrating its fences and ultimately expose its blinding idiocy.

What Mbembe (2001: 102) calls the "aesthetics of vulgarity," is exactly that, the strange beauty of the obscenity of power and its clumsy excesses. At the height of power, and zenith of his magical dominance, the tyrant is an idiot that can be fooled for sport and gain. The way the powerful bully the powerless and the beautiful ways in which the powerless frequently mock and expose the idiocy of power can be understood as "mutual zombification" (Mbembe 2001: 104). This is where the ruler and the ruled are enmeshed together in a network of political silliness. Zombifying the ruler and becoming a true zombie in the process is what an enterprising village spirit medium, Rotina Mavhunga, did. Her true name was Nomatter Togarira. She and her act appeared in 2007 when Zimbabwe was suffocating under the targeted sanctions that were imposed by western countries. Food, fuel and other necessities were scarce and the economy was on its knees. Mugabe's appearance on prime time TV, then, declaring that the country's fuel problems were over was true to the magic of the ruler who makes the impossible happen. Unbeknown to the world and Zimbabwean multitudes is that the venturesome spirit medium had made Mugabe believe that Zimbabwe's generous ancestors had decided to send pure diesel from down under the mountains of Maningwa in Mashonaland. In his time, Mugabe loved to hear from spirit mediums what the ancestors were saying and paid full attention to messages from God that many enterprising prophets generously delivered. The metaphysical, magical and supernatural had become the explanation and commonsense of his immense power and it separated him from common souls but also made him, effectively, a blind fool. If Mugabe was a genuine contractor to the traditions and religion of the Munhumutapa or Nehanda; he would not have been fooled by such a pretender. It is his opportunistic belief and pretended respect for the ancestors that made him a true candidate for that kind of fraud.

Mugabe sent several high-level ministerial delegations that came with the great news that for sure diesel was oozing out of the mountains and at one point, a delegation brought twenty litres of the precious liquid that was specifically meant for the presidential limousine, an ancestral gift to the ruler. The brave spirit medium was showered with farms, cars, cash, cattle and buffalo from the national herd. She became a recipient of many generous presidential gifts; her messages from the ancestors to the ruler were evidence of his otherworldly power, and for that Mugabe was grateful. His tyrannical ego was polished to shine by such ancestral recognition that he did not want to think of it as a silly but calculated ruse. For a moment in the Zimbabwean postcolony, an otherwise powerless young woman used her reputation for spirituality to gain access to some kind of political power. Seeing her power and influence on the President, several ministers, under the cover of darkness, nicodemously visited her shrine bearing gifts of all shapes and sizes. For a moment, she had become a feared presidential advisor that could tell Mugabe how to run the country in manner that would please the ancestors. No doubt, the ministers believed the President would consult with her before making appointments; they had to appease her and the ancestors she represented.

Her game fell down when she continued to make outlandish personal demands and pronounce even stranger messages from the ancestors. She had begun to enjoy her newly found power rather extravagantly. An irritated delegation of scientists and security details finally uncovered that she had industrially buried drums full of diesel on the mountain top and connected hose pipes that she triggered to carefully leak the fluid before the eyes of bemused ministerial delegations. She was eventually disgraced, tried before the courts and jailed but her act had been done; she had spectacularly fooled the President, a powerful man with exalted intellectual accomplishments that were sung by his flatters repeatedly like an anthem of the postcolony. That pure diesel could be received from the ancestors from under some rocks could only be believed and made world news by a president that was sold and bought to the magical and the miraculous, but also one who was an opportunistic pretender to the religion and traditions of the land. The imagined superiority of the superman had been his unmasking. Like the rest of us, the emperor is naked under his regal clothes. Power can be in the air in the postcolony; those that the ruler relies on for information on what God or the ancestors are thinking frequently use their positions to exercise and enjoy some power.

If Nietzsche as a celebrant of the will to power betrays the inner logic of its desires, passions and maddening drives, Mbembe exposes the rhetorics, fictions, myths and spectacular performances of power in the postcolony. Nietzsche makes visible the fantasies and imaginations of power, in theory and philosophy, and Mbembe displays the practical workings of the sensual life of power in the Cameroonian postcolony under the tyranny of Paul Biya, which postcolony in its grotesque and obscene spectacles of power mirrors Mugabe's haunted Zimbabwe.

The Pornography of Power

I refer to the pornography of power in two ways. First is the way in which power in the postcolony, as Mbembe describes it, becomes preoccupied with displays and exposures of its workings through ceremonies, rituals of party protocol and massive public rallies. In Mugabe's rallies and other public ceremonial appearances, grown men and some wartime colleagues of his would be seen kneeling before him as before some god. Mugabe relished in public displays of his authority and demonstrations of obedience. Second is the forceful way in which philosophers and theorists make public and visible what is otherwise intimate and invisible about the life of power. After all, pornography is in many ways the public practice, celebration, the making a sport, of that which is usually supposed to be concealed even if it is otherwise common. While power itself tends to publicly exhibit its obscenities, such theorists of power as Nietzsche, Machiavelli, Mbembe and others help to name and describe power and how it performs its multiple lives.

Power at its most spirited flight does not seem to see its own excesses nor does it name itself as such, power and domination. Ignorance of itself is part of the undoing of power. For that reason, it has to be observed and named, and its performances understood. Niccolo Machiavelli (2003a, b: 5) in his *The Prince* classic delves into a pornographic exposition of power politics in that he makes explicit what is essentially private and internal about domination and control. Machiavelli's success is in how he uses the case of one prince, to whom he addresses himself, to make a keyhole observation of the intimate political universes of tyrants and despots and renders their inner lives public. If Machiavelli's *The Prince* is a manual of tyranny as well as it is an intelligent mockery of despotism, in his rendition of the philosophy of the will to power, Friedrich Nietzsche (1968) in turn provides a manifesto of power and its appetites for conquest and domination. In Nietzsche's will to power exposition power finds a spokesperson through whom it airs its vaunting boasts and threats. In the will to power, Nietzsche at once gives a name and offers an elaborate description of the multiple fears, desires and passions that are the drives that propel tyranny and envelope the lifeworlds of tyrants wherever they are found.

Whilst Machiavelli appears to advocate but also lampoon technics of power and domination by princes, Nietzsche erects himself as a celebrant of conquest and domination. In his elaboration on the will to power, Nietzsche (1968) dismisses morality and elevates war and violence, much in a similar way that Mugabe (1976: 11, 2008: 1) celebrated the gun ahead of electoral votes as a means of political resolution in Zimbabwe. By so celebrating the gun and using it to threaten opponents Mugabe fashioned himself as a kind of warlord in the postcolony. In its vaunting celebrations of conquest and consumption of domination the will to power scoffs at morality in politics and laughs at the preoccupations with matters of good versus evil. As it had become to Mugabe, the attempt to contest power by democratic and electoral means tends to be a laughable exercise in futility when the tyrant insists on using gun power, war making and bloodletting as technologies of seeking and keeping power by any means necessary. Morality and fair play in politics are to the will to power "a sentence on existence" as the life of the tyrant in power depends on being by nature warlike and liking war, becoming a strong natured enemy (Nietzsche 2016: 13). In Zimbabwe, Mugabe (1976: 13) came to worship the gun as a fetish of power and decision maker in political contestations. To vote his opponents was for the people of Zimbabwe a waste of time and expenditure of life itself as the powerful tyrant "will never ever," and "will never allow it" (Mugabe 2008: 1) that the opponent wins access to power. Loss of power and its gain by the opponent is for the tyrant a kind of end of time and life that must not be permitted. Concealed behind Mugabe's pornographic boasts about guns and the personal symbol of a clenched fist, his performance of strong natured enemy, was fear of loss of power. The tyrant's obscene celebration of power and public enjoyment of its privilege thinly veils fear. The tyrant is, behind his entire act, essentially a terrified coward.

Nietzsche and Machiavelli in their different but compelling ways successfully describe the spirited desires and drives of power that consumes the tyrants. The two provide a microscopic and also critical gaze that strips power and tyranny naked before the observer. In the explication of "the aesthetics of vulgarity" that is the beautiful but also bizarre performances and consumptions of power by the "commandment" in the "postcolony" of Cameroon, Achille Mbembe (2001: 103) exposes the pornographic way in which power and domination are displayed and turned into commonsense by the tyrant and his supporters and opponents alike. Political rallies, military parades and colourful party regalia that is severally emblazoned with the head of the ruler became part of Mugabe's public display and performance of power in the Zimbabwean postcolony. For the rallies to show force attendance was boosted with villagers bussed to the capital city from remote villages. Children were forced from schools to come out and swell the crowds to create human electricity that was supposed to exhibit the glory of the ruler. Promises of lots of food and drink were used to lure hungry villagers into Mugabe's rallies; and that was besides the threats that were circulated to scare those that were determined to stay away from the gatherings.

For his belief in and practice of political violence as a means of seeking, finding and keeping power by any means necessary Mugabe became toxic (Tendi 2011: 308). In the view of Sabelo Ndlovu-Gatsheni (2009: 1139), there have been two major and contrasting readings of Mugabe's drive to power, that is, the "nationalist aligned scholars understanding it as a Pan-African redemptive ideology opposed to all forms of imperialism and colonialism" on the one hand. On the other hand, Ndlovu-Gatsheni notes "a neoliberal-inspired perspective" that "sees Mugabeism as a form of racial chauvinism and authoritarianism." Mugabe's support and opposition, even amongst scholars, tend to come in two diametric extremes, total affirmation or unnegotiable condemnation. The tyrant and tyranny itself are unknown to moderation but at home in extremes and fundamentalisms.

Both the nationalist and neoliberal readings of Mugabe's spirited desires and claims to power that Sabelo Ndlovu-Gatsheni observes are trapped in the limiting dichotomy of good versus evil, right against wrong, which are readings and understandings that can be simplistic. In his dismissal of moral inhibitions in politics, Nietzsche allows power and the political to be observed and unmasked. The inner ambitions and fears of power are exposed. With the aid of the will to power as a passionate drive to power and also insane celebration of overcoming opponents and dominating time and place, we are able to read and understand Mugabe as both a subject and an object of power. The will to power puts to rest the post-political (Mouffe 2005a, b) temptations and optimisms of seeing heroes and imagining the end of history. Post-political readings and end of history understandings of power fantasise of the end of enemies and the arrival of messiahs and heroes. Monstrosities such as Mugabe in the Zimbabwean postcolony awaken societies from their post-political slumber, remind them that enemies are still here, and are real. Away from post-political naiveté, in the will to power, a grim reading of power and politicians is allowed, and it pornographically exposes the obscene and evil passions of power. This book otherwise benefits from the explicit way in which Nietzsche, Machiavelli and Mbembe, in their different ways, graphically describe how power lives and works. Mugabe was the performer of power that helps us to read the tragedies and comedies of the will to power.

Nietzsche's will to power philosophy that emphasises philosophical and political understanding beyond the simplistic limits of good and evil allows this book to get a wider and deeper understanding of the political thought and practice of Mugabe who seems to have cast away all moral cares for a violent drive to power and domination of the postcolony. As a political drive, an ideological passion and impetus to history, "the will to power ontologically constitutes everything and all that exists, being and becoming, nature and sociality, overcoming, to master and to dominate, to grow and to expand" (Jenkins 2013: 2). In that way, the will to power is a spirited energy and overcoming drive for power and domination, a search for perpetual mastery and superiority. Possessed of the will to power, the tyrant carries himself as a magician, a miracle worker and maker of wonders that owns history in the postcolony. The will to power does not only explain the ambitions, desires and fears that possess the tyrant, but also illuminates how otherwise simple and well-meaning people can very easily become tyrants once mistaken for heroes and messiahs in such a time and a place as the postcolony where excess and obscenities are turned into commonsense. Tyrants can be the unfortunate products of the mistaken optimism of populations that after long years of struggles for liberation are understandably hungry for messiahs.

In the true flight of the will to power, the tyrant ensures that "power is maintained over the self and over others with cruelty, mastery and domination" (Nietzsche 1969: 32). In such a postcolony as Zimbabwe the ruler is feared for his cruelty and ability to command soldiers, the police and militias that are true merchants of death. Machiavelli's advice to the astute prince was exactly that:

> A Prince, therefore must have no other object or thought, or take up anything as his profession, except war and its rules and discipline, for that is the only art that befits one who commands. And it has such power that it not only maintains those who are born princes, but often enables men of private station to rise up to that rank. And one sees, on the other hand, that when princes have thought more of luxurious living than of arms, they have lost their state. (Machiavelli 2003a, b: 63)

The celebration of violence such as that of Mugabe was not just an embrace of the arts of war as a discipline and profession but also a fearful guard against loss of power and exposure to weakness. Mugabe, as the next chapter will show, rose to power from vulnerable and humble beginnings, the pain of which he never wished to return to. It is not only in the enjoyment of cruelty of the will to power that "a new prince must always inflict harm on those over whom he rules, both with his men at arms and with countless other injuries his new conquest entails" (Machiavelli 2003a, b: 10), but it is also in fear that power might anytime be lost. The tyrant is not only a violent but also a terrified monstrosity. Concealed behind his cruelty, evil and confident outbursts was always the truth that Mugabe was a terrified little man that Doris Lessing (2013) described. The evil that Mugabe carried in mind and heart was carefully covered under the attractive but misleading rhetoric of anti-colonialism with all its post-political fragilities. Loss of power is a nightmare that Mugabe lived in dread of.

As a political drive and a force of personality, the will to power is "the tyrannically inconsiderate and relentless enforcement of the claims of power" (Nietzsche 2003: 22). Nietzsche brutally describes the will to power as a political and philosophical energy to be a drive that is "essentially a process of appropriating, injuring, overpowering the alien and the weaker, oppressing, being harsh, imposing your own form, incorporating and at least, at the very least, exploiting" (Nietzsche 1968: 259) those that have been overcome and defeated. In the Zimbabwean postcolony Mugabe was at his worst when he was punishing and disciplining opponents and losers, he could not be imagined outside a climate of enmity and cruelty that fed on revenges and punishments. As if with Mugabe in mind, Mbembe (2001: 105) notes how in the postcolony "the state was embodied in a single person, the President, he alone controlled the law, and he could, on his own grant or abolish liberties" and became known for his structural and systemic dispensation of punishment and pain to opponents and challengers. In the postcolony, Mbembe describes, the tyrant and the "commandment" that he runs perform spectacular displays of power in both its brutality and magnificence through ceremonial exhibitions where domination publicly struts its stuff during state events, national holidays and political rallies.

Mugabe might not have described his political thought and practice with the brutal clarity of Nietzsche but Nietzsche's candour in the description of the drives of power, as this book will show, helps to illuminate the political life of such tyrants as Mugabe who created a reputation for infamy by being oppressive, harsh and in many ways exploitative. In other words, to this book, Mugabe enacted what Nietzsche described as the will to power, knowingly or unknowingly. In word and in deed, politically, Mugabe became Nietzschean to the extent that Steven Chan (2007: 1) could write of him as a "Nietzsche in Harare" that was battling both friends and enemies in the struggle to remain in power when his time was obviously running out. Mugabe's desperate attempt to defy old age and repeatedly overcome adversities had become a true tragi-comic performance in the Zimbabwean postcolony. While coming from one of his many overseas trips in 2015, Mugabe alighted from his jet and tried like the "old young man" that he frequently described himself as, to walk with a spring in his step but fell down. The security services tried desperately to get photographers to delete images of the falling and fallen tyrant. They failed as the photographs went viral causing worldwide laughter and pathos at the same time. The giving in of the aging body and the fall in public seemed to be nature's way of laughing at Mugabe's attempt to defy destiny. The will to power has its tragic and also comic limits. For instance, Nietzsche (1968, 1990) threatened to re-evaluate all values and to change the world by "philosophising with a hammer," a forceful attempt that ended in his insanity and eventual death. His mind tragically broke before he could tear the history of the world apart in fulfilment of his ambitious philosophical promise. The will to power provides a fitting reading and understanding tool for exploring Mugabe's beginnings in vulnerability, triumphs of power and eventual tragedies in power and outside after his overthrow in the Zimbabwean postcolony.

For that reason, I provide a justification of the will to power as a tool of reading power and its tyrannies as embodied in Mugabe in his time and place in the Zimbabwean postcolony. If Nietzsche's descriptions of the ambitions, passions and desires of power may be understood to be distant from such historical settings as Zimbabwe and personalities as Mugabe, Achille Mbembe's renditions on the African postcolony and the "commandment" of tyrants help to demonstrate, in a relevant way, how the will to power has played out in African polities. Simplistic and racist takes on tyranny in Africa seek to isolate the problem of despotism to dark Africa. However, Nietzsche helps to locate the problem of power and its excesses on the shoulders of history, humanity and the world.

The paradigm of politics as war is explored to illuminate the warlord politics that Mugabe came to embody and perform. Machiavellianism as a technic of power, control and domination is also explored before an examination of the nationalist and Marxist ideologies that Mugabe employed and deployed and that also became the fantasies and drives of his will to power. Ideologies once assumed and taken as political certainties tend to become forceful drives and pushes that turn a ruler such as Mugabe into a fundamentalist. Achille Mbembe's idea of the "postcolony" and its lives and performances of power helps me to interpret, expand and domesticate the Nietzschean idea of the will to power for purposes of effectively understanding Mugabe as a colonial and colonising subject. Before its conclusion, this chapter reflects on the "will to live." The will to live suggests another politics and philosophy of liberation that is different from the nihilist will to power. In its nihilism, the will to power in many ways leads to what Mbembe (2004) appropriately called politics in Africa as a form of human expenditure where pain must be endured and lives sacrificially lost in the gruelling wars and Olympics for power. Where the tyrant, as Mugabe did in the Zimbabwean postcolony, has vowed that his opponents will never ever prevail or gain access to power, opposing him even if legally and by democratic elections becomes the politics of human sacrifice and political martyrdom. Where the tyrant in the postcolony has taken to accompanying votes with guns and ballots with bombs politics does not only become a dirty and also painful game but it also effectively turns into a way of dying.

Intoxications of the Will to Power

Power intoxicates and maddens. In a rare moment of self-reflection, Mugabe once described the Gukurahundi Genocide that he committed using the Fifth Brigade as a "moment of madness." The will to power as a drive to conquest and domination is maddening. It suspends sober reflection and restraint and takes over the tyrant the way intoxication does the drunkard. Mugabe in many ways became a drunkard of power. It may have been out of prejudice and insecurity at the encounter with a brave African anti-imperialist leader that Ronald Reagan called Muammar Gaddafi, the late Libyan leader, a "mad dog of the Middle East." However, in his helm, Gaddafi frequently dramatised the insanities of power that I observe in Mugabe. At an Arab Summit in 2009, Gaddafi found reason to hurl insults at the Saudi King, Abdullah, and accused him of being a puppet of the USA and the UK. It is Gaddafi's description of himself that was more revealing; "I am an international leader, the Dean of the Arab rulers, the King of Kings of Africa and the Imam of Muslims, and my international status does not allow me to descend to a lower level" (Gaddafi 2009: 1). Not once but several times did Mugabe speak in such terms and such a tone, uttering such self-believing and self-worshipping statements as that "no judicial decision will stand on my way" (Meredith 2002a, b: 18), and the tyrannical vaunt, "I Robert Mugabe cannot be dragged to court by a mere settler" (Hope 2003: 252) betray the impoliteness of an insane ego of the tyrant proper. Mugabe put himself above the electoral and judicial processes of Zimbabwe, becoming a jury, prosecutor, lawyer and judge in his own trial for power. Ironically, at the height of desiring to be known and understood as a gallant fighter against racism, colonialism and imperialism, the tyrant of the postcolony does and says exactly those things that affirm rather than disrupt stereotypes of Africans as naturally given and taken to insane despotism.

Except by an understanding of the will to power as an intoxicating ambition and drive for power, a maddening passion and a demon-like possession, it is difficult to understand why otherwise such a good boy as the young Robert Mugabe grew up to be the monstrosities that he became. When tyrants such as Mugabe appear observers often understand them as tragic figures, heroes that carried so much hope for their people but fell and became traitors. Other observers understand the despots to be original villains that tried to be heroes and naturally failed as their true colours appeared from behind the performances and pretences of heroism. Both these prevalent readings and understandings of tyrants suffer from post-political limits in that they believe in easy heroes and simple villains. The prevalently simplistic readings and understandings of power and the political are invested in the end of history and the exhaustion of enmity that blinded Francis Fukuyama (1992). Fukuyama erroneously understood the end of the Cold War to be the end of ideological enmities in the world and the arrival of global friendships under the perpetual and uninterrupted rule of neoliberal politics and economics under the championship of the USA and Europe. The optimistic thinking that the end of administrative colonialism was to bring liberation and heroes, in Zimbabwe and other postcolonies, somehow produced Mugabe.

The events of 9/11 in the USA were to tragically prove that enemies existed and had to be reckoned with. Similarly tyrants happen and appear in time and in place as kinds of disasters that remind societies that heroes do not exist or have not arrived except in the optimism and imagination of populations. In many ways, heroes are imagined personalities. The will to power as theory and method of reading and understanding a tyrant and tyranny overcomes post-political naiveté and allows a grim understanding of power and the political, which departs from the cold and dry reality that evil and villainy are real. In Zimbabwe Mugabe became evidence of evil. Understanding the political as Chantal Mouffe (2005a, b) has gestured should involve appreciation of politics as naturally conflictual and productive of enemies and villains, and therefore requiring democratic institutions and systems of checking the excesses of power, and the insanities of all politicians as potential tyrants. Mugabe was not, I argue, going to be the tyrant and villain that he became, if in the very first place, Zimbabweans and the world, never mistook him to be a kind of messiah and hero of liberation. The appearance and spectacles of Mugabe in the Zimbabwean postcolony are a true 9/11 that reminds the world that tyrants and other disasters will perpetually appear and need handling in advance to avoid tragic surprises. In that way, political thinking and democratic activism in the direction of liberation from domination and its humanising project will always be a kind of critical disaster readiness, prevention and management. Tyranny does not announce its approach or arrival, and tyrants do not wait to be born; they can simply emerge from the transformation and corruption by power of otherwise trusted heroes.

In many telling ways, what Nietzsche described as the will to power appears to be exactly what Mugabe embodied and practiced in his spirited drives for power. There also seems to be a strong way in which what

Mugabe said and did politically reproduced the insanities of the will to power that Nietzsche described. In employing and deploying the philosophy of the will to power as a theoretical vantage point and looking glasses of reading the life of Mugabe and power, I hope to illuminate the otherwise largely opaque political thought and practice of the Zimbabwean "strong man" that has eluded a number of scholars and students because:

> Mugabe had it all, and maybe that's why people never saw it. Maybe there was something in his unbridled power that made it almost impossible to take seriously-until the killing started- and even then people, lots of people still could not see it. Even now, who he is and what he stands for and what he believes are mysteries. (Hope 2003: 216)

Mugabe was a slippery subject to understand. Sandra Maclean (2002: 513), for instance, complained that Mugabe in his infamy and ability to withstand opposition, to defy the odds, "defies systematic analysis" and escapes scientific understanding. In using a philosophy such as the will to power that goes beyond simple good and evil, I aim to overcome the slipperiness and elusiveness of Mugabe as a subject of study and observation. For the reason that Mugabe seemed to carry all the promise for revolutionary change and liberation in Zimbabwe, he had it all, but tragically delivered violence and tyranny, Stephen Chan (2007) correctly described him as "Nietzsche in Harare" because of the way he, like Nietzsche, believed more in war and in enmity as instruments of conquest and political dominance. For Mugabe politics became war by all means and an art of the impossible for those that opposed his rule in the Zimbabwean postcolony.

To pretend that Mugabe was anything besides a fragile individual that was from the beginning thirsty for strength, total power and dominance, as many writers have done, conceals, rather than reveals, the workings of power and the nature of the political itself. The way populations of such postcolonies as Zimbabwe make and follow heroes only leads to historical tragedies as heroes do not only not exist but in their seeming to exist keep people either excited or asleep, not prepared for approaching disasters such as the Gukurahundi Genocide that Mugabe visited upon southern Zimbabwe from 1982 to 1987. Mugabe became a god that some Zimbabweans built with their minds and after that knelt down before him as their almighty creator. The god-figure that Mugabe projected of himself was more of a theatre performance than a reality. And he was a convincing performer. Tendi (2019: 20–21) notes how the otherwise unsoldierly and even effeminate Mugabe became good at acting out "hegemonic masculinity" and military bravado.

The promise of paradisal Zimbabwe and heroic leadership that Mugabe seemed to carry and which he later betrayed and delivered the opposite was, in my view, a post-political promise that was never there. Only a post-political climate of euphoria and excitement about revolutionary change and liberation could blind observers to Mugabe's growing political absolutism, I note. After many long years of a punitive and expensive war of liberation, Zimbabweans were hungry for a hero. The Rhodesian whites were thirsty for a conciliatory hero that will guarantee their peaceful and prosperous stay in the Zimbabwean postcolony. America and Europe needed a brave leader that would be a bulwark in the struggle against the encroaching spectre of communism in Southern Africa. Mugabe sounded and appeared to be the man of the moment, everyone's hero that was going to satisfy black expectations of liberation from colonialism, address Rhodesian white fears of black revenge and punishment, and fulfil western wishes of a capitalist Zimbabwe and Africa. In a way, Mugabe pretended to be all what everyone expected of him, until he achieved absolute power and was consumed by its absolutely corrupting trappings and drives, and then the monster in him appeared. Heroism is as long and lasts as far as until that disaster when the hero naturally reveals his true political colours.

The will to power tends to use the religious and the spiritual for its affirmation and negation alike. Both Nietzsche and Mugabe, in their different histories and places, spent their early and formative years under strong religious tutelage and influence. As the next chapter will reflect, Mugabe was born of a deeply religious mother. He was brought up, educated and formed by Jesuit priests (Norman 2004a, b: 16, 35, 36, Holland 2008: 6). Frequently Mugabe admitted and boasted of being strongly formed of and influenced by the priests (Meredith 2002a, b: 19). I observe later in this book that the Jesuitical experience injected Mugabe with some delusions of political messianism and a dangerous Christ-consciousness that made him see political opponents not as legitimate interlocutors but as sinners to be sent to their damnation. Nietzsche was alike brought up by Lutheran and deeply religious parents. Nietzsche (1968) grew up to despise the Christian church and to rubbish it as moralistic and deceptive in its engrossment with matters of good and evil. Mugabe too, when the Catholic Church condemned his political violence, turned around to condemn the priests as deceptive and mischievous "jeremiahs" (Hope 2003:

105). In a way, both Mugabe and Nietzsche are children of the Christian church who grew up to know how to use and abuse the church for political and philosophical ends respectively. Mugabe as a Christian and politician that grew up to espouse a kind of political messianism began to be a Christian without Christ and that was a kind of Christ himself and wanted a church after his own image and political interests. If the church opposed his violent politics, it was a lost church that needed to repent and come back to the ways of the political messiah of the postcolony that he had come to be. The tyrant enjoys some kinds of righteousness and political holiness in the postcolony. Because of his vivid religious background, Mugabe's will to power developed, as this book will illustrate, into a political messianism that allowed him to see political opponents as kinds of Judases and other traitors and sinners that must be dispatched to hell.

In his discussion of "the violence of the fantasy" Slavoj Zizek (2003) describes how, paradoxically, the ultimate fantasy of Christians is to fulfil pagan desires and that of pagans to meet Christian demands. Mugabe, as I reflect later, came to use the dignity and cover of the Christian church, its sponsorship and education, to perform what otherwise was truly pagan politics. Similar to the South African apartheid regime dictator Hendrik Verwoerd (Hope 2003: 31) who had an "appetite for theory" and learning, Mugabe grew up studious and keen on education to the extent of gathering seven university degrees even as he was studying under the nervous conditions of a colonial prison. The passionate seeking after knowledge and love for education is also a deeply Nietzschean quality. Nietzsche (1969: 1) boasted that when he philosophised he did so "with a hammer," in reference to his intellectual gravitas. Both Nietzsche and Mugabe became cerebral thinkers and activists that are like those that Albert Camus (1953) described as political and intellectual "adults" who defend their actions with philosophical thinking as an "alibi." Intellectual and academic achievements are used in the will to power as resources to build and manage an image of suitability for power and domination. Such education and intellection ceases to be for liberation and humanisation but a weapon of domination of others. As a result, scholars such as David Moore (2015: 29) have forcefully argued that Mugabe's intellectualism largely was pretence rather than a reality. In that way, in his multiple degrees Mugabe became so informed but truly not educated and cultured for liberation. His violent and evil politics that valorised guns and bloodletting gave education and the educated a very bad name. Mugabe's life of books, big ideas and knowledge was nothing but a performance for purposes of cultivating and image he needed to bully less educated comrades in the struggle. The impressionable world came to know him as "a bibliophile" that "even as Zimbabwe's leader—Mugabe would fly incognito to London to browse the shelves of Dillon's bookshop" (Onslow and Plaut 2018: 18). If anything, books and knowledge were wasted in Mugabe that grew up to be an unpolished political hooligan.

Even as both Nietzsche and Mugabe grew to despise the church that brought them up and negated its values, they both carried themselves with some messianism and priestly demeanour. Mugabe in politics acted with a "missionary spirit" (Hope 2003: 16) and dictated his political views in the manner of a political high priest, a messiah and a deliverer of his people. After all, "the saint and the tyrant are only a prayer apart, the saint sacrifices himself to save souls and the tyrant sacrifices his people to save himself" (Hope 2003: 245). Mugabe put the country and people on the cross for power. Nietzsche's philosophy was also, according to Alain Badiou (2009: 1), dominated by the figure of the priest, and became a "variant of religion" even as it attacked religious belief. Some of Nietzsche's essays were signed off as "the crucified one" in reference to himself as a messiah and a martyr that is crucified for his ideas. In reality "Nietzsche's philosophical thought is given in a primordial network of seven names: Christ, or the crucified, Dionysus-Ariadne, Saint Paul, Socrates, Wagner" and "Nietzsche" himself (Badiou 2009: 2) as a kind of messianic and prophetic voice for his ideas. In referring to himself severally as "The Anti-Christ," Nietzsche had become not just an opponent of but also a competitor and contestant to the Christ. I reflect in the next chapter on how Mugabe came to accept from his ministers and flatterers such titles as "Son of God" and "Second Son of God" that constructed him as a kind of messiah and political Christ of sorts. In a strong way, both Mugabe and Nietzsche believed religiously in the truth of their ideas and justice of their actions; in other words the will to power is a deeply convincing and arresting political and philosophical dogma. Tyranny is fond of concealing itself behind grand ideals. Slavoj Zizek (2001: 6) states that authoritarianism and the authoritarian mind always claim and appeal to a higher power and superior good, use the name and appearance of divinity to cover fundamentally base political agendas. In the Zimbabwean postcolony Mugabe carried himself as an anointed deliverer of his people whose voice was the voice of God. Drawings of Robert Mugabe at the national Heroes Acre portray him as a towering shepherd-like figure leading the national multitudes as a flock of sheep being driven to some paradisal pastures, an imaginary promised land. Such drawings that were done with Mugabe's permission and authority betray a tyrannical mental universe that was, to a point of insanity and sickness, consumed by delusions of revolutionary messianism.

In his political representation in rallies, public gatherings and funerals of fallen comrades, Mugabe projected himself in religious symbolism. He frequently allowed ministers like one Tony Gara to say to him "you are the only one" the "Head of State, Head of Government, First Secretary of the Party, Commander in Chief of the Defence Forces, Chancellor of all Universities" and the "second son of God" (Meredith 2002a, b: 80). Such exaggerated laudations that were associated with Idi Amin the tyrant of Uganda became for Mugabe the good food of a mind that was sold and bought to fantasies of might and absolutism. As outlandish and exaggerated as the flattering praises were, Mugabe seemed to have believed them. The will to power turns the most embarrassing flattery into some gospel truth in the troubled and troubling mind of the despot. The despotic mind is a faithful mind that dutifully believes even some of the most otherworldly make-believe.

In graveside orations, Mugabe projected what Kizito Muchemwa (2010: 504) described as "nicrophilic imagination" a habit of priests to love to pontificate over dead bodies and use death as an opportunity to preach and make converts to the religion. By the side of coffins and graves, Mugabe became frequently priestly and prophetic in his orations. Frequently in these priestly funeral orations, Mugabe (2002: 77) pleaded with his enemies and opponents to "repent" of their sins of negating him and what political gospel he stood for (Meredith 2002a, b). Given that most politicians in the Zimbabwean postcolony died suspicious deaths in mysterious car accidents and fires, Mugabe's orations to his opponents to repent while he stood over the recently dead sounded like true death threats and warning to stubborn enemies that would soon face their own demise if they did not toe the line of the ruler. Death of comrades seemed to remind Mugabe of his own long life and the futility of opposing him by enemies in the opposition and adversaries in his own party.

A deep kind of Stalinist and North Korean–style memorialisation and ceremoniality accompanied Mugabe's public political performance and representation (Meredith 2002a, b: 77, Hope 2003). As I will demonstrate later, the will to power as a political and philosophical energy advances itself as a stubborn messianism, a missionary spirit and political gravitas that produce the stuff of tyrants and totalitarians who see opposition to themselves and their ideas as sinful, heretic and punishable by death. The admiration Mugabe had for Stalin, North Korean leaders and other tyrants and fascists shows the kind of will to power that drove his political ambitions. Asked why as a freedom fighter he chose to shave in a manner that made him look like Hitler Mugabe said he was just trying to irritate the prison warders (Holland 2008). He was in actuality an oppressed person that admired oppressors and envied their power. Mugabe secretly admired the figure of Hitler that he openly impersonated.

In the pursuit and construction of his philosophy of the will to power, Nietzsche confronted and contradicted philosophy as it was known and understood in Europe at the time. A number of scholars and students have as a result failed to understand Nietzsche for what he thought and what he was because:

> Nietzsche is not a philosopher; he is an anti-philosopher. This expression has a precise meaning: Nietzsche opposes, to the speculative nihilism of philosophy, the completely affirmative necessity of act. The role that Nietzsche assigns himself is not that of adding a philosophy to other philosophies instead, his role is to announce and act without precedent, an act that will in fact destroy philosophy. (Badiou 2009: 1)

Thus, in the view of Badiou, Nietzsche escapes the understanding of many because he was the anti-philosophical philosopher who sought to invent a new philosophical practice. In a way, Mugabe has been the anti-political politician who has frequently escaped the understanding of many, "over the years, people black and white, high and low—have struggled to make sense of Robert Mugabe" (Norman 2008: 161). In his description of the "Robert Mugabe phenomenon" Dinizulu Macaphulana (2017a, b: 3) noted that Mugabe "is a photocopy without an original" and a phenomenon that "cannot be repeated except by itself" because he operates differently from other politicians, predictable yet so unbelievable, but still a typical tyrant. To read Mugabe's anti-political politics using Nietzsche's anti-philosophy of the will to power justifies the approach of this book as a study of power and the political. A philosophical negation of philosophy is used to critically study a political negation of politics, and in that way, this book makes its humble contribution to both the discipline of politics and that of philosophy in their engagement with the historical travails of the postcolony in Mugabe's Zimbabwe.

The tyrannical politician like the nihilist philosopher has the ambition to change the world. Badiou (2009: 1) emphasises the point that Nietzsche himself noted that the philosopher, counting himself as one, is "the greatest of all criminals" in that he wishes to change history and the world towards an apparently perverted destination of his own imagination. Badiou follows Nietzsche's vaunting about politics and history. Nietzsche made such terse statements as that "the concept of politics has been completely dissolved in the war between spirits, all powers have been blown to bits,—there will be wars, like there have never been before;" and that, as Nietzsche, "I am strong enough to break the history of mankind into two" (Badiou 2009: 5). Nietzsche's philosophical promise or threat of war can be compared to Mugabe's political vauntings about his strengths, and threats of political violence against opponents that are summarised in his claim to possess degrees in violence (Meredith 2002a, b: 76). "Mugabe could be very unpleasant," said Sir Michael Palliser, head of the British Foreign Office, who noted also that Mugabe "had a very sharp, sometimes very aggressive, and unpleasant manner" (Meredith 2002a, b: 7) that he used in communication to frighten opponents.

International pressure had to be applied to stop him in the very first Zimbabwean election, in 1980, when Mugabe resolved to use a rifle as an election symbol (Meredith 2002a, b: 9). The symbol of a gun was to be used to signify a future of war in the newly independent country. Even though Mugabe agreed to drop the symbol of a gun for another much peaceful signification, the gun defined the Zimbabwean postcolony that was to unfold. He did not only continue to boast of guns and their power over votes and ballots but went on to use guns against the civilian population of Matabeleland in the Gukurahundi Genocide of 1981 to 1987. The true colours of the tyrant were embodied in some early fantasies and signs that Mugabe showed that included his love for the symbol of the gun, even as he was no soldier to talk about.

To scare and to frighten is the delight and the relish of the tyrant. Mugabe frequently told his followers to "strike fear in the hearts of the white man, our real enemy" (Meredith 2002a, b: 17). In the height of his anti-politics of dismissing law and order, during the violent seizure of white-owned commercial farms he could publicly say, "no judicial decision will stand on our way" (Meredith 2002a, b: 18). Such statements are politicidal statements that could come from only totalitarian and fascist anti-politics, and which can be clearly understood only by using an anti-philosophical philosophy such as the will to power that Nietzsche articulated. The will to power being political madness itself. In his madness of the will to power Mugabe could boast of his reputation for violence and evil. In a conversation with Robin Renwick in London in the sidelines of the Lancaster House Conference, Mugabe frequently said his "power springs from the barrel of a gun and I have a post-graduate degree in terrorism" (Tendi 2019: 21), a boast that displays an unashamed and insane celebration of violence and evil even.

For his anti-political political practice, Mugabe could then be compared to Julius Caesar, Hendrik Verwoerd, the North Korean Kims, Chong II and II Sung (Hope 2003: 19) who were all leaders that were possessed of an iron will to power. In his "tyranny" that was accompanied by "menace" Mugabe signified both "Hollywood and hell" with his "supernatural pretensions" and appetite for political "expansion" (Hope 2003: 19). As a missionary for power, like Nietzsche, who aimed to shape the history of mankind in a different direction, Mugabe had an iron will and a determination. In a resolved way "he was always determined, whatever he wants to do he can do, he never recognised the word no: It was not in his language" (Holland 2008: 2), nor was it in his political practice to submit to negation. At the end, "like Ian Smith, Mugabe chose the lawless tradition of leadership inherited from Cecil John Rhodes" (Holland 2008: 83) because in actuality "nothing matters to Mugabe, except staying in power" (Holland 2008: 91). The will to power, in religion, philosophy and politics, does not brook opposition, as it is a missionary spirit that has messianic pretensions. In that way, Nietzsche's descriptions and enactments of the will to power help to render visible and open the inner desires and drives that propelled Mugabe to tyranny and ultimately to tragedy.

In prevalent readings and understandings, as noted above, Mugabe initially carried a lot of optimism and promise for his people and the world but turned out to be the "freedom fighter who became a tyrant" (Holland 2008: 1). Tragic contradiction and paradox seem to be a central quality of Nietzschean nihilism as it is embodied in the concept of the will to power. The power to betray promises and hopes seems to be the true Judas spirit of the tyrant. The same promise and optimism that Mugabe built around himself and carried, he went on to squander and destroy it for the monstrosity that he eventually became. "Whatever I create and however much I love it" Nietzsche (1969: 75) said through the character of Zarathustra, "I have to oppose and my love: thus will my will have it." In its destructive and treacherous spirit, the will to power presents itself as what Henlee Barnette (1972: 9) called "extremism" of both the left and the right that holds its strong religious and political convictions as a kind of fundamentalism. In the postcolony the tyrant turns into a negation of all that which was supposed to be good and great. To overcome everything and eventually to overcome the self, and destroy what it has built, seems to be the nihilism of the will to power that is expressed by Nietzsche and seems to be enacted by Mugabe who became the anti-hero par excellence of the Zimbabwean postcolony. Correctly, Mugabe is understandable as someone that squandered what had the potential to be a great political legacy.

The philosophical paradox of destroying what one builds and loves is usable in reading the political paradox and contradiction of Mugabe. Mugabe squandered the historical opportunity and political optimism that he constructed. History will record it that Mugabe turned into hell the country he so helped liberate from formal colonialism, which country he went on to subject to a kind of colonialism of his own after what was supposed to be decolonisation in 1980. In that way, the nihilism of the will to power seems to be contradictory, paradoxical and ultimately tragic. That there was ever a promise of the good and the great in Mugabe and what he represented makes his failure tragic.

By using the philosophical paradox of Friedrich Nietzsche to read and understand the political contradictions of Mugabe, I escape what is otherwise the simplicity of such studies as that of David Lamb (1990), Robert Kaplan (1996) and Patrick Chabal and Jean-Pascal Daloz (1999). These influential studies essentialise tyranny and abuse of power as a quality of backward African despots and not a human and a world phenomenon. Without naturalising and normalising tyranny, I examine and treat power the way Christopher Hope (2003) does when he examines Mugabe, Ian Smith, Hendrik Verwoerd, Joseph Stalin and other world tyrants as "brothers under the skin." As brothers under the skin tyrants, whether black or white, in Europe or in any African postcolony, are dangerous anti-heroes.

The abuse of power and naturalisation of violence as an instrument of rule are not excesses that are a preserve of the postcolony or a unique quality of black people. Before heroes and saints are made in the postcolony, constitutional and political mechanisms should be put in place to check their inevitable degeneration to despotism. Heroes and saints either do not exist at all or are hard to come by. The vigilant thing to do in the postcolony is to treat even the smallest politician as a huge monster waiting to happen like a typical 9/11, spectacularly shocking and disastrous. Political leadership should be put on watch and checked with working legal, ethical and democratic institutions.

By first humanising Mugabe as a dictator amongst other dictators in the world, black and white, this my narrative is better able to illuminate his political inhumanity not as racial weakness but as a human tragedy driven by the drives, passions, pushes and pulls, of history, ideology and power. The deployment of Nietzsche's will to power concept allows me to see Mugabe as what Albert Camus (1953: 7) calls "an unhappy intellect" and an angry mind, "menacing and exposed to menace, driven by an entire world intoxicated with nihilism, and yet lost in loneliness" with a "knife in one hand and a lump in the throat." Mugabe in power was angry beyond repair. He seemed, even if there was no excuse, to look for a reason to be angry about something so that he could be himself. Anger had become part of his identity. The anger of the tyrant as a dangerous man changes the weather in the postcolony. His volcanic temper mirrors the moods of the climate; he is unpredictable and dangerous.

The historical moment of Mugabe in Zimbabwe was a moment of thought-out and planned crimes. It was perhaps the same world and time that Camus (1953: 1) describes as "the era of premeditation and perfect crimes, our criminals are no longer those helpless children who plead love as an excuse, on the contrary, they are adults and they have a perfect alibi: Philosophy, which can be used for anything, even for transforming murderers into judges." Mugabe thoughtfully normalised political hooliganism into a national political culture that was to be reproduced by both his supporters and opponents. The tyrant can be infectious; some respectable opposition politicians in the Zimbabwean postcolony took to unconsciously and also embarrassingly mimicking the Mugabe way of talking, dressing and walking. In that Camusian way, there is philosophical method in the madness of Mugabe. A method that systematised itself into a political culture that still envelopes Zimbabwe today. Reading Mugabe using Nietzsche's concept, therefore, becomes theoretically profitable. The will to power as a pornographic philosophical insanity, pornographic in that it makes a public display and sport of what is inside and otherwise private to power, is usable in understanding tyranny and such a despot as Mugabe.

The will to power is a drive and a passion for "domination and mastery" (Jenkins 2013: 3) as much as it is a historical and political search, a spirited quest by groups and individuals to be superior and to achieve "eternal return," perpetual "recurrence" and longevity (Heidegger 1967: 413). In other words, the will to power is a valorisation as well as it is a fetishisation of power and strength ahead of everything else. In all the historical currency and political purchase that the will to power gives to strength and dominance, it appears that it may also originate from weakness, insecurity of groups and vulnerability of their individuals. Nietzsche is not only known to have been sickly and poorly, but he admitted to his personal condition of ill-health and physical weakness. "I am a decadent" that is troubled by "my sick condition" and in the true spirit of the will to power "I took myself in hand, I myself made myself healthy again, I made out of my will to health, I ceased to be a pessimist" (Nietzsche 2004a, b: 5). Knowing his sickness, Nietzsche mentally and physically simulated health and believed himself to be healthy to a point of being "healthy again." Similarly, tyranny and domination can be imagined, constructed and believed into reality by the weak and the ambitious in search of strength. Tyranny can begin in the mind of the despot as a little confidence and positive thinking and grow into a monstrous appetite for more power. To the observer, "Mugabe at first impression seemed more cut out for the priesthood than for the leadership of a political party" (Onslow and Plaut 2018: 29) and was clearly "not a warrior" but the same angry weakling that he grew up as.

Mugabe, as I illustrate in the next chapter, grew up lonely, weak and physically fragile. He was carefully nursed and disciplined by his mother, he did not enjoy or endure physical fights, and he suffered mockery from other boys and could only promise or threaten revenge in some day to come (Holland 2008: 4). He did nurse the keen wish to be strong and powerful enough one day to be able get even with those that humiliated him. Dinizulu Macaphulana (2017a, b: 3) argues that once Mugabe the weak "Mama's baby" and a "sissy" found himself with a guerrilla army and some "rough boys from the bush" under his command he found power that he never had or dreamt of and was determined to keep and use it to the extremes. The weakling found himself in charge of an army, police, the secret service and militias that Paul Moorcraft (2012) called "Mugabe's war machine" and that was a real temptation. A temptation that he failed to resist as he used the war machinery with alarming abandon. In Mugabe political power found itself in the hands of a vengeful coward.

I argue in this book that Mugabe's will to power, his passionate love for dominance, actually emerged from the fear of weakness by an individual that like the sickly Nietzsche had known and lived fragility before. In apparent admission of fear, Mugabe once remarked, before a state banquet in 2000, that "I do not want to be overthrown and I will try to overthrow those who want to overthrow me" (Meredith 2002a, b: 17). The fear of defeat and the weakness that the loss of power brings haunt the tyrant as an ultimately terrified and terrifying personage. The concept of the will to

2 THE WILL TO POWER IN THE POSTCOLONY

power, therefore, permits me to establish the way power as domination can be connected to and somehow originate from weakness and vulnerability. The way terror can originate from fear can be understood in the way Mugabe sought to find the security that comes with power and later used that power to cause fear and insecurity in the Zimbabwean postcolony. With an army, police and spies on his side even the most damned of cowards becomes a very dangerous man. It is the terrified coward that uses power with abandon.

The Fist of the Coward

The Ndebele people of Zimbabwe have a saying that "ingqindi yegwala iyingozi" (a coward's fist is dangerous). This saying emerged from the long tradition of fistfights amongst the herd boys looking after their cattle in the forests. Older boys would, for fun and also for purposes of establishing hierarchies of power, set younger boys against each other in often-bloody brawls. That boy who defeated all others would become *ingqwele*, a kind of leader with a lot of powers and privileges in the forests. Not everyone could win, some bloody losses were registered and some boys became servants of others in the veld. Cowardly boys lived in fear of beatings and defeats. The cattle grazing lands became a true jungle of the survival of the fittest boys.

The weaker and cowardly boys invented their own bush technologies of escape and survival. It was frequently observed that the cowardly boy would throw one forceful punch to down his opponent, and while the opponent was down, he would make good his escape. The coward fears a neat bare-knuckled fistfight, not for him is the punchy exchange; he prefers a technical knock-out that allows good escape to the safety, often of the mothers' lap, back at home. The forests were not for sissies and some mother's milk types but for the boys with some hardihood, it was understood.

As a little boy that looked after cattle in the bushes of Kutama Mugabe never even went as far as attempting the coward's punch on rival boys; he simply fled. James Chikerema, a relative and fellow cattle herder with Mugabe, described his cowardly and escapist tendencies to Heidi Holland. "Chikerema remembered Robert simply detaching himself from the group, selecting his own beasts from the herd and driving them into the hills far away from other boys" (Holland 2008: 7), and "his standard response to criticism" and challenge "was to warn that he would get even some day." Mugabe grew up with scores to settle and he was a careful keeper of bitter grudges, that proverbial dog that was always going to have his day some time. Perhaps his day finally came when Mugabe had a war machine to unleash on opponents and enemies. Mugabe's deliberate and designed absence in the fistfights of the bush did not stop the political development where his personal symbol has been the raised clenched fist. Before and after every speech he was known to raise the tightly clenched fist high and utter such a chilling slogan as "pasi *naMabhunu*" (down with white people), literally signifying how the opponents of the moment should be floored with a well-placed and forceful blow.

Mugabe's postcolony, like all other postcolonies, became a dramatic setting where illusions frequently overtake reality and establish themselves as the truth. Few opponents and supporters of Mugabe understand that the raised fist is exactly that, a symbol and not a blow that has floored any real opponent. Mugabe was the coward that did not like losing a good fight. He would rather escape to avoid or postpone the fight. Power and victory were, in his imagination, his "territory" about which he warned opponents in 2001, "no matter what force you have, this is my territory and that which is mine I cling unto death" (Holland 2008: 202). There is no doubt that it was his deep cowardice accompanied by a love for power and victory that led him to deploy soldiers and their guns against voters and political opponents during elections.

A former ally of Mugabe who became a fierce opponent and critic, Margaret Dongo (2016: 1) questioned Mugabe's war and fighting credentials, arguing that the feared ruler "cannot even fire a pistol," was a simple "war prisoner," not a true war veteran, and that is why, she said, Mugabe had no war name. Much like Nietzsche who wrote passionately about war and demanded endless wars but was not a warrior but a philosopher in his closet library and university office, Mugabe spoke of guns and war that he in actuality did not directly get involved with. A war-time comrade and government colleague of Mugabe's for a long time, Edgar Tekere (2007: 141) describes how Mugabe did not only fear being physically attacked, but other comrades feared for him too when time came for brawls. After Tekere came close to walloping him in one incident, Maurice Nyagumbo, a comrade, came to his protection. Mugabe sheepishly said, "I am sorry Eddie Tekere, I did not know I was irritating you" (Tekere 2007: 141). Even as a Prime Minister with an army of bodyguards Mugabe lived in the fear that one of his ministers might one day punch him. In his life Mugabe feared places, events, incidents and people that might have in any way created a possibility of a "punch-up" (Holland 2008: 30–31). In the 2013 election Mugabe's raised and tightly clenched fist was canonised by ZANU-PF youths in campaign posters as "The Fist of Fury," symbolising the political gravitas of the leader and his party. Behind the evident fury of the fist, however, was always the fear of the coward, all the way since Mugabe was a toddler.

Mugabe's war and violence were delegated and deployed; he relied on others to physically execute the needed violence. In building his war machine that he delegated to unleash violence Mugabe often turned around to befriend even opponents whose brute force he needed. The war veterans he used to displace white commercial farmers and to bludgeon the opposition began as opponents demanding compensation for war injuries and losses, accusing Mugabe of being a sell-out. Mugabe quickly printed money, paid them and turned them into his own militia, even as the Zimbabwean economy came to its knees as a result. In the contested 2008 elections that the opposition is believed to have won, Mugabe resorted to the war veterans and their guns, and he boasted of it:

> The war veterans came to me and said, "President, we can never accept that our country which we won through the barrel of the gun can be taken merely by an 'X' made by a ballpoint pen." *Zvino ballpoint pen icharwisana ne AK?* (Will the pen fight the AK rifle?) Is there going to be a struggle between the two? Do not argue with a gun. (Mugabe 2008: 1)

As commander in chief and now head of state, he could not escape to the hills or at least throw the infamous fist of the coward; he could rely on hired muscle and rented guns. State instruments of coercion were now at his disposal. The Zimbabwean economy still has not recovered from the billions and trillions of Zimbabwean dollars Mugabe simply printed to bribe war veterans to his political side when his hold on power was threatened. In that way the postcolony becomes a vivid site of cruel paradoxes. The feared tyrant who orders the use of guns and celebrates spectacles of bloodletting, including massacres and genocides, is himself a cold coward who cannot stand the sight of a drop of blood, or contemplate a drop of his own. For power Mugabe shed the blood of many people, turned many others into murderers and bled the Zimbabwean economy to death in the process.

In that way the tyrant participates in a double evil. He does not only occasion killings, he makes sure that others carry out the killings, he creates both victims and victimisers, only the power and the dominance that arise from the violence becomes his to own and keep. The will to power, in that way, becomes immorality. Nietzsche (1968: 10) boldly stated that "in so far as we believe in morality we pass a sentence on existence." For absolute power the tyrant must be prepared to be evil. What Mugabe did not have in physical ability to fight a good fight he covered up with the evil that enabled him to produce both the killers and those that are killed in the postcolony. The dear price of power that Mugabe became willing to pay was capacity for evil. Nietzsche (1968: 37) noted that "there is nothing to life that has value except the degree of power, assuming that life itself is the will to power" and nothing else. When power has become everything to the tyrant, nothing else is of value, and the cowardly tyrant understands that "everything done in weakness fails" (Nietzsche 1968: 28). The true coward must throw a killer blow to escape a return blow and to ensure survival and the power that remains with it. In the search for domination, Nietzsche noted, "waste, decay, elimination need not be condemned, they are necessary consequences of life." Mugabe had to brave a soiled name and a reputation for evil, witness the decay of the polity and the economy of the country, and consign multitudes of Zimbabweans to mass graves, for power. It is in that way that the will to power can present itself as a demonic possession and a satanic intoxication, a seizure that compels even the legendary coward to throw a killer blow. Mugabe's violence was the violence of a coward and a weakling who sought to reap the benefits of terror but was never prepared to participate directly even in the smallest scale of the crime. The "degrees in violence" that Mugabe frequently boasted of were at the same time an expression of his degree of evil and also his intention to conceal personal fragility, vulnerability and cowardice. A reputation for being evil and dangerous in the postcolony conceals that the ruler is not only an ordinary bread eater and water drinker, but also that he might be a frightened and fearful coward.

In that way, Mugabe's roaring and chilling speeches were at once a display and a concealment. The way Mugabe spoke to rallies, he spoke like the commander and leader that Nietzsche (1968: 129) described as the powerful man of history that must get those that are weaker than himself to obey or risk punishment and total elimination. Mugabe spoke with the impunity of the "superman" that Nietzsche's spokesperson, Zarathustra, described (Heidegger 1967: 413), a powerful individual that becomes a law unto himself, someone that seemed to have access to higher reality above and beyond the forces and the masses that he commanded. Mugabe desperately wanted a reputation as a warrior, and, like Nietzsche, he wanted to be known as one who could change the history of the world and that of mankind. That whole bravado and performance of gravitas, however, does not conceal the fist of the coward and the fact that he was, even as an old man, a fragile little boy looking for love and protection in the rough world.

The Paradigm of War

The reputation of a warrior is a reputation that Mugabe did not only relish but vigorously performed and acted. War and what Ali Mazrui has canonically called the "warrior tradition" is one important way in which the African postcolony has appeared not only to imitate but effectively reproduce the colonial order. Importantly, Achille Mbembe (2001: 25) has reflected on three major modes of violence that the colonial order deployed: violence for conquest, legitimation and authentication. An order of power violently conquers space, time and a people. Because violence alone does not ethically legitimise a regime of power further violence is deployed to force legitimacy. As a result, violence keeps being employed and discharged by the political establishment to authenticate and normalise an order of power and domination as natural, normal and, above all else, punitive. In the struggle against the colonial order of things, the postcolony, Zimbabwean one included, seems to have failed to overcome and survive war and violence as paradigms of making resolutions on power, seeking control and domination. Anti-colonial politics, as represented by Mugabe and other despots in Africa, repeated violent tendencies of colonial politics and duplicated colonial modes of domination. For that reason, philosophers and theorists of liberation have had to spend much time engaged with the problem of the paradigm of war in the Global South.

In celebrating the gun and frequently using it to neutralize political opponents and enemies Mugabe became a true practitioner of the modern and colonial paradigm of politics as war. A central part of the "philosophy of liberation" that was expounded by Enrique Dussel (1985) is the opposition to violence and antagonism to war as languages of politics and power. Centrally and forcefully Dussel diagnosed the historical and political problem of the modern world as the political uses of war:

> From Heraclitus to Karl Von Clausewitz and Henry Kissinger, "war is everything" if by everything one understands the order or system that world

dominators control by their power and armies. We are at war—a cold war for those who wage it, a hot war for those who suffer it, a peaceful core existence for those who manufacture arms, a bloody existence for those obliged to buy and use them. (Dussel 1985: 1)

In the modern colonial world system, and such pockets as the Zimbabwean postcolony, those who engineer war and throw clenched fists into the air in encouragement to and celebration of violence and war do not exactly experience the heat of the war; they don't suffer it and its bloody businesses. Importantly, Dussel finds that the powers that dominate the world economically and politically have done so through the use of war and punishment for the weak and the dominated. Politics as war and violence has, in the world, graduated into a powerful paradigm that leaders of nation-states such as Mugabe have adopted and deployed to seek, find and keep political power by any means, even unnecessary means.

In their discussion of what they described as "Mugabeism," Busani Mpofu and Sabelo Ndlovu-Gatsheni (2015: 121) noted Mugabe to be entangled in word and in deed in "the crisis of the will to power and the paradigm of war" where violence has become his language of politics and rule. To this observation I add that for leaders such as Mugabe who seem to have defined power as conquest and domination, force and fraud become the rule rather than the exception. Martin Rupiya (2005) noted that Mugabe governs by military operations and declarations of war. In the absence of just causes and reasons for war in the postcolony the ruler and his party imagine and invent enemies upon whom war must be declared and carried out. The will to power feeds on enmity and war. Power and domination in the postcolony require that new enemies and new victims continue to be perpetually produced so that they can be overcome. Notably, Mugabe was at his best when declaring operations, most articulate and vehement when he raised the fist against some enemy. He seemed lonely and pathetic when there was no enemy to shout at, and no violent operation to declare against some "elements" out there in the form of traitors, sell-outs and intruders.

In his thesis on the philosophy "against war" as elaborated in the book by the same title, Nelson-Maldonado-Torres (2008) describes the paradigm of war and condemns the Nietzschean idea that erects war in the world as a natural state of things. The notion by Nietzsche (1968: 74–75) that "you should love peace as a means to new wars—and the short peace more than the long" is found by Dussel, Maldonado-Torres and other philosophers of liberation as a decay in world politics and decline in the ethics of liberation and humanism. In defence of war as natural and as an engine of history Nietzsche noted that:

> The valuation that today is applied to the different forms of society is entirely identical with that which assigns a higher value to peace than to war: but this judgement is anti-biological, is itself a fruit of the decadence of life. Life is a consequence of war, society itself is a means to war. (Nietzsche 1968: 33)

For Nietzsche peace is anti-life and war is a natural part of navigating the world and negotiating power. In the modern world "with war being connected to everything else and everything else being connected to war, explaining war and tracing its development in relation to human development in general almost amounts to a theory and history of everything" (Gat 2008: xi). This observation and argument presents an indication that war and politics as a violent and a dirty game have been, to a great extent, naturalised and normalised. In the African historical and political context Ali Mazrui (1977) described the presence of "the warrior tradition" where to lead and govern meant to dispense war as a political language and violence as a technology of domination and control. Mazrui's detection of a domineering warrior tradition in the history of African political thought and practice helps me here to expand and translate Nietzsche's theory of the will to power to the Zimbabwean and African settings of the postcolony. In the postcolony the residues of the warrior tradition combine with the will to power of the colonial order to produce political chaos and anarchy. The will to power as political nihilism is not simply a European philosophical and political pathology, nor is it an African political decadence but a human weakness of power; in that way, this book contributes to decoloniality by unmasking stereotypical simplifications and political generalisations, by putting power and its corruption in focus. I resist modernist temptations of only isolating evil and degeneration to Africans and blacks when it is a human and world problem. As a coward and also a monster, Mugabe is a child of the world and of humanity; he can appear anywhere under the sun covered in any colour of the skin, any time and called by any other name.

For this book, it will be interesting to observe the political production and conditioning of Mugabe by the African warrior tradition. It will also be enriching to note his conditioning by the paradigm of war that was part of the colonial politics of conquest in Africa that in a strong way formed

him. Both the warrior tradition and the colonial paradigm of war are combined to show the nihilism of politics that adopts and is adopted by certain
philosophers and politicians in the world at large. Enslavers and colonisers
called their war on natives and victims a civilising and modernising mission; Mugabe and other rulers in postcolonies have named theirs anti-
colonialism, anti-imperialism and even wars of liberation. Whenever
violence has been used to conquer and dominate one by the other it has
been a perpetuation of the paradigm of war that is evil and dehumanises
both the perpetrators and the victims. The will to power itself as an unhygienic appetite for power and domination does not call and describe itself
as such, but it is circulated as the truth, and as human deliverance, it is
powerfully and deliberately blind to its own actuality.

Violent and racist colonial conquest, for instance, is celebrated by
Nietzsche (1968: 93, 127) who boasts that "a master race is either on
top" by any means necessary "or it is destroyed," and as masters the colonisers had to colonise and govern with iron and blood to impose Empire
on those who found themselves on the underside of modernity. The tragedy is when those like Mugabe who led struggles against colonialism eventually became some kinds of colonisers in their own right in the way they
used violence and domination as technologies of rule. This book shows
how the violence of colonial conquest produced victims who also became
victimisers as they adopted the same colonial violence that they set out to
negate with liberation struggles. Christopher Hope (2003) compares tyranny and its violence to a perfume of power that engulfs everyone and
everything around it, including turning those who come into contact with
it, its victims, into participants in tyranny. It is, perhaps, in that way that
those like Mugabe who led anti-colonial struggles in Africa easily became
some kinds of colonisers in their own right, in the way they reproduced
coloniality and its violences.

In the canonical explication of the "concept of the political" Carl
Schmitt (1996) described the political proper as the critical management
of friend and enemy relations, where enmity is ethically reduced to bloodless rivalry that is opposed to ultimate war. In that argument of Schmitt
violence and war in politics are anti-political. When it comes to debunking
evil and its uses of war Schmitt may not be a role model but a wrong
model with his storied dalliances with Nazi politics, yet some of his submissions are usable in thinking about the politics of liberation.

Illuminatingly, Chantal Mouffe (2005a, b) expanded the concept of
the political that Schmitt submitted to explain that the project of

democratic politics is to turn the antagonism in political competition to agonism, to turn enemies into legitimate adversaries that can be conflicted but do not have to eliminate each other. In respect to the arguments of Carl Schmitt and Mouffe the "will to power" in its valorisation of war and violence is politicidal and inhuman. In his understanding of friends and enemies, and his practice of the political in the postcolony, Mugabe went for total friends and total enemies, and nothing in between. Mugabe had no political opponents or adversaries; he saw enemies and practiced politics as the Armageddon, final war between the last good and the last evil, in the postcolony. In that totalisation of enmity and friendship alike the will to power becomes a kind of political fundamentalism.

In a strong way, the political proper admits that there are enemies in politics, and democratic and ethical practice allows that those enemies are legitimated as adversaries that have to be engaged with, even defeated in political competition, but not destroyed or killed. Mugabe seemed incapable of legitimating his opponents or of understanding himself as an enemy "I don't make enemies," he denied, "others make me an enemy of theirs" (Holland 2008: 228). Putting the blame on others and awarding himself all the right allowed Mugabe the will to punish and seek to destroy others, as this book will show. Mugabe insulated himself from the blame and accountability that Schmitt suggests the political demands. Schmitt, however, as I have stated, has his own imbrications in the will to power when his support for the Nazi regime is considered. In its rejection of post-politics, this book values the weight of thoughts ahead of the moral complexion of thinkers; hence, such morally compromised thinkers as Schmitt are also engaged with and even deployed where their thoughts are found illuminating.

To Mouffe (2005a, b) in particular, communication and human dialogue are supposed to be substitutes for war. Similarly, to Schmitt (1996) elections and the political jostling and competition that go with them are a humanising substitution for war where every ballot cast stands in place for a bullet that was to be fired in war. For that reason, when Mugabe scorned the idea of votes as a replacement of bullets and elections as a substitution for war, he spoke in the true terms of the paradigm of war and the will to power in politics. In the thinking of Nietzsche and his celebration of the will to power, even communication and speech making that are supposed to be options against war have become part of war making:

In the way men make assertions in present-day society, one often hears an echo of the times when they were better skilled in arms than in anything else; sometimes they handle assertions as poised archers their weapons; sometimes one thinks he hears the whir and clatter of blades; and with some men an assertion thunders down like heavy cudgel. (Nietzsche 2004a, b: 183)

Such political demagogues as Mugabe, Adolf Hitler and others, when they made political speeches, as Nietzsche describes, they enacted war in words. As this book will show, Mugabe has been sold and bought to fiery political speeches where violence and war are not only dramatised but celebrated. Dinizulu Macaphulana (2017a, b: 5) asserts that nothing is as eloquent as Mugabe when he is cursing political enemies and scattering invective. Political communication as war has found fortification amongst some theorists of war and politics, for instance, "is not war merely another kind of writing and language for political thought? It has certainly a grammar of its own, but its logic is not peculiar to itself ... the Art of War in its highest point of view is policy, but, no doubt, a policy which fights battles instead of writing notes" (Clausewitz 1985: 402, 406). In many ways when Mugabe spoke he actually fought and symbolised war as a vocabulary of power. The raised and tightly clenched fist is a signification of battle. In that way, communication that is supposed to be a substitution for war is usurped and instrumentalised by the will to power and used as war by other means. In the will to power, dialogue is infected with violence and appropriated by war. All human resources and capacities are turned into some raw materials for fighting and war; nothing is left for peace to clutch on. Mugabe scattered hate speech and described political opponents as elements, things, objects and many different kinds of animals. Mugabe languaged his political opponents in the diction and vocabulary of hate that made them candidates for violation.

War by Other Means

In his description of the will to power as the will to existence, Nietzsche (1968: 148) noted that "life is will to power." In that understanding to live entails the demand to be powerful or die. Not only that, but even when a politician appears to speak and do good, behind the gestures of good and ethics is concealed the drive for power (Nietzsche 1968: 156). To be good and ethical in politics is only fair as a pretence and an alibi. In other terms, gestures of humanism themselves have, in the will to power, been instrumentalised for power and dominance. In the case of Mugabe, Robert Rotberg (2010: 10) observes how such ideals as peace and the political unity that, Mugabe once in a while embraced, were utilised as strategies and techniques for tyranny and domination. As this book will later show, Mugabe at certain episodes gave inspirational speeches for peace, unity and reconciliation that he later negated by resorting to diabolic and genocidal violence. The politician that has taken hostage of, or been captured by the will to power, becomes a pretender whose word cannot be taken, who does not mean what he says. The tyrannical desire for a one-party state under his leadership in the Zimbabwean postcolony was covered by Mugabe (1989a, b: 336) under the tantalising grand goal of national unity and purpose. Those who for very good reasons opposed the one-party state were easily labelled as enemies of the nation and its great unity. Mugabe always clothed himself and covered his deeper designs with the name of some good.

In the discussion of "the tyranny of unity in Zimbabwe" Rotberg (2010: 11) demonstrates how Mugabe used the languages of peace and unity to conceal his continuing spirited drive for power and domination. After the disputed 2008 elections he brought his political opponents into a government of national unity, not to share power with them, but to use them to regain international legitimacy and credibility. Political gestures of humility, magnanimity, reconciliation and peace can, in the will to power, be opportunistically weaponised for power and domination. The will to power, in other words, knows how to pretend to peace and humanism, can actually use the language of peace and humanism to further the objectives of tyranny and domination in the same way in which scriptures can be eloquently abused by the anti-Christ, in the theological script of the Abrahamic faiths. In a way, that politician who uses the will to power or is used by the will to power that is an aggressive paradigm of politics as war tends to dominate and usurp everything including the very opposite language of peace and humanism. It is perhaps the devilish tendency of the will to power in the postcolony to take over, usurp and appropriate the scriptures of peace and harmony when its intentions are the exact opposite, to make war upon the nation.

As this book will show, underlying Mugabe's gestures of reconciliation in the early days of Zimbabwean independence, in the 1980s of political and economic optimism, was a drive to eliminate opposition by use of unity, to achieve worldwide acceptance and political legitimacy. He enacted, opportunistically, the drive to unite all parties and achieve a one-party state under his command; he was actually not in any quest for peace and democracy as was widely understood. Under the spell of the will to power or the will to power under his spell, the tyrant can dramatise peace and love for purposes of enacting violence that is used to unduly gain power and domination. In that way, perhaps, the will to power also becomes Machiavellian in the way Niccolo Machiavelli exhorted princes to make but not keep their promises, to signal to the left when they mean to turn to the right, philosophically and politically. The will to power can circulate myths and fictions of itself that work as illusions that mask its brutality and evil. It is not as a violent coward that Mugabe once became a hero of the Zimbabwean postcolony and the world; but it was as a conciliator and gallant peace-maker that embodied the hopes of former colonisers and their former victims. Mugabe fronted a face of himself as a deliverer of the people and healer of the wounded, and in that way, the tyrant is that evil monster that perfectly knows how to look good at the right time and place. The tyrant is a performer to the scripts of power, and, as such, illusions and appearances are his stock in the trade of power.

MUGABE AS A MACHIAVELLIAN

For his valorisation of war and reputation for electoral fraud, and his use of machinations and shenanigans to stay in power, Mugabe came to be understood as a Machiavellian. Machiavellianism as the art and science of power and the overcoming of adversaries, opponents and enemies is a kind of will to power. In his extensive elaboration on Machiavellianism, Louis Althusser (2010) has noted that in the classic *The Prince*, that is supposed to be an embodiment of Machiavelli's ideas of realpolitik, Machiavelli might have been writing ironically as he was a thoroughgoing republican in actuality, and not the nihilist of power that he is now widely believed to be. Althusser implies that those politicians that follow the letter and spirit of Machiavelli's *The Prince* might be suffering the problem of taking a joke seriously and practicing an irony. Even so, Machiavellianism has come to exist as the art of politics as war, deception and cunning. Deception and cunning in politics are, in the understanding of this book, a kind of will to power. Fraud and force separately or combined constitute political violence. Mugabe became infamous for fraudulently rigging elections and for deploying political violence to coerce voters. He publicly boasted that ultimately it was the gun with its bullet and not the pen and its ink that decided power in the Zimbabwean postcolony.

It is noteworthy that Nietzsche admired Machiavellianism in politics. In politics, Nietzsche (1968: 170) observed that "Machiavellianism is per-fection" and excellence. Machiavelli (2003a, b), in articulating his philoso-phy of power, counselled that princes or leaders should practice mercifulness only strategically lest they appear weak and vulnerable; he exhorted them to rather be more feared than loved: "I say that every prince should desire to be considered merciful and not cruel, nevertheless he must take care not to use his mercies badly, a prince therefore must not mind acquiring a bad reputation for cruelty in order to keep his subjects united and loyal" (Machiavelli 2003a, b: 71). The Machiavellian princes should seek a repu-tation for being good but not necessarily be good or they will perish or lose power. As argued above, as a true Machiavellian, Mugabe has sought recognition for being conciliatory and peaceful and has unleashed violence when the option of ethical politics does not guarantee success. Scholars such as John Saul and Richard Saunders (2005: 953) understood Mugabe to be an "arch-strategist and Machiavellian in the way he stood for every-thing and sometimes for nothing as long as it guaranteed power." The tyrant and the prince of the postcolony can be an empty signifier that stands for everything and nothing at all at the same time. Princes or lead-ers, Machiavelli insisted, should take war seriously. "A prince therefore," Machiavelli (2003a, b: 63) argued, "must have no other object or thought, or take up anything as his profession, except war and its rules and disci-pline for that is the only art that befits one who commands." The naturali-sation and normalisation of politics as war is central in Machiavellianism as it has been understood from *The Prince*. In his political thought and prac-tice Mugabe has demonstrated a valorisation of war and even a celebration of violence. The cowardly boy who feared violence against himself came to trust violence in dealing with enemies. The valorisation of war and cele-bration of violence, and performances of peace and reconciliation here and there as methods in politics, make Mugabe a kind of Machiavellian. A kind of technician of power whose weapon of the last resort is opportunism, he believes in everything and in nothing at the same time.

In speech, the Machiavellian princes should make promises and go on not to keep faith in their words because "one sees from experience in our times that those princes have done great things who have had little regard for keeping their word" (Machiavelli 2003a, b: 75). The Machiavellian prince is advised to know the ways of man and those of the beast in order to secure power. The keeping of power by all means necessary, including brute force, is in line with the will to power where political ethics come secondary to the keeping of power by any means necessary. In the will to power, guile and deception are central planks as they are in the Machiavellian science of power. Nietzsche (1968: 248) also advised that telling the "truth limits power" and makes a leader weak and predictable. Truth and knowledge must be manipulated or constructed in a way that they are weaponised and instrumentalised for purposes of seeking, finding and keeping power. In that respect, the uses of deception and propaganda, as understood in this book, are part of the manufacture of political consent, which is the use of epistemic violence that is still a political technology of the will to power. Mugabe's monopolisation and use of the public media as well as his control and violence against the independent private media would be understood as workings of the will to power in controlling information and knowledge in an Orwellian and Machiavellian manner. Information and communication themselves are mobilised for the manufacture of political consent and for arresting and capturing the imagination of the masses. The masses, in that context, are reduced to the tyrant's captive audience and victims who must have no alternative information to the myths and fictions about himself that the tyrant forces down their throats.

Part of the political language and performance of Mugabe as this book demonstrates has been the use of and appeals to ideals of the liberation struggle, self-determination and sovereignty of Africans and their right to their land and other resources. This language gave Mugabe a reputation in Africa for being a gallant anti-colonial and Pan-African hero. A critical observer of Zimbabwean history and a student of the political thought and practice of Mugabe in particular, David Moore (2009: 49) notes "enthusiasms" that are created by Mugabe's political pretensions, even amongst such leading scholars as Mahmood Mamdani that are supposed to see and know beyond myths and fictions of power. Mugabe's political pretensions to peace, reconciliation and revolution deceived even some gifted African minds. Invoking grand popular ideals while concealing personal and partisan political agendas is part of the Machiavellian will to power, in a way. Nietzsche explains this dissembling performance of the will to power in politics:

> Christianity, the revolution, the abolition of slavery, equal rights, philanthropy, love for peace, justice, truth: All these big words have value only in a fight, as flags, not as realities but as showy words for something quite different, indeed the opposite. (Nietzsche 1968: 50)

In other words, the will to power may assume pretences and deploy illusions to conceal its agendas. The political leader can invoke grand narratives such as Pan-Africanism, land reform and social justice in Mugabe's case. These grand narratives and ideas are used as flags and emblems that are weaponised in concealing the violent and even genocidal passions for partisan and personal power that the tyrant stands for. In the real scheme of the will to power "we see that every high degree of power involves freedom from good and evil and from the true and the false, and cannot take into account the demands for goodness" (Nietzsche 1968: 140). The despot in power, as a tyrant in the postcolony, keeps himself innocent and free of truth and fairness. In pursuit of power, a leader possessed of the will to power ignores the importance of right and wrong. Martin Jenkins (2013: 2) notes how Nietzsche thought that "might is right" and not the opposite. In valorising the bullet over the ballot, Mugabe participated in the elevation of might over right, a political gesture that sustains, rather than disturbs, nihilism, and that enacts the will to power at its political height. In letter and spirit, the will to power exudes a survival of the fittest attitude to power. The name and reputation of grand narratives and humanist ideals are adopted and deployed in the fight for power but their essence and actualisation cunningly denied and ignored. This book will pay attention to how Mugabe's own will to power can be considered to be Machiavellian or similar.

Frantz Fanon's understanding of how nationalist politics in Africa degenerated to chauvinism and violence, in a way, to a will to power of a kind and a type in the continent is an important way of looking at Mugabe's Zimbabwe. Mugabe as a political thinker and actor that once claimed nationalism and Marxism cannot be fairly and fully understood without an examination of the will to power that is embodied in these political ideologies as, in themselves, passions and drives that push and pull politicians and that are pushed and pulled by politicians at work. Ideologies, I argue, can be spirited energies and desires, and also fears that can blow the tyrant to some dizzy heights of political insanity. Ideologies as what is believed and what must be made to be understood, believed and followed religiously, can be intoxicating and specifically maddening. In that maddening way, ideologies also become convenient political religions in the name of which tyrants commit all sorts of atrocities, pretending to be furthering this and that cause of ideology. Ideologies, however false as consciousness and sensibilities, can drive leaders, people and history itself to spectacles of lunacy and evil.

IN THE NAME OF THE NATION AND MARX

There is a time in the history of Africa when being a nationalist and a Marxist was valorised. As an African intellectual and political thinker, Ali Mazrui found himself with reason to defend his belonging and loyalty to the continent. In the essay "Africa, My Conscience and I," Mazrui (1974) recalls that there was a time in Africa when not being Marxist or nationalist carried a punitive stigma. For being neither a Marxist nor a nationalist, in justice, Mazrui personally suffered stigmatisation and spirited campaigns in the African academy; there were calls that his books and other works be boycotted. That was the time when the name of the nation and that of Karl Marx were religions and not to answer to them or swear by them was, politically, considered heretic and blasphemous. That is also the time, the historical and political climate of the 1960s and the 1970s, when Mugabe was emerging as a leader in the Rhodesia that was fast shaping up into the postcolony that Zimbabwe has become. Marxism and nationalism were in vogue; to be a political leader and intellectual of note one had to exhibit competency in and love for the two ideologies. The following chapter reflects in some length, hopefully depth and width, on how Mugabe was politically formed and shaped by Marxism and nationalism. Here the objective is to thinly reflect on how the two ideologies might have become passions and drives that gave body and oxygen to Mugabe's will to power.

For the reason that Mugabe and others fought colonialism under the banner of African nationalism and Marxism, it is important for such a book as the present to explore how nationalist ideology itself and Marxist thinking had their own will to power. By the will to power, this book, here and above, refers to an underside, an excess and a toxicity that accompanies what was supposed to be liberatory tropes that turned to domination and became oppressive and exploitative in their own content and expression. In a study of the "ideological formation of the Zimbabwean ruling class" David Moore (2007: 472) uses a Gramscian perspective of hegemony as a framework to observe how the ruling elite were pushed and pulled by ideological political drives, and how they used both "persuasion and force" for power. Ideological force, in its pulls and also pushes, cannot be ignored in understanding the will to power and the way it is produced by and also produces political leaders in place and in time. During liberation struggles and after, in the African postcolony, a lot of disasters and even massacres happened in the name of ideology.

In a forceful critique of nationalist ideology that is treated at length in the next chapter, Frantz Fanon (1967: 119), in the essay "Pitfalls of National Consciousness," noted that instead of being a uniting force nationalism degenerated to a divisive and toxic ideology due to the "intellectual laziness," the "unpreparedness" of the educated class of African leaders that took over from the colonial rulers. Under this class, Fanon noted, the nation is passed over for race and the tribe is preferred for the state. African nationalist rulers frequently degenerated into nativists and chauvinists that could not build the same nations that they were supposed to have decolonised. In this book I demonstrate that the nationalist government of Mugabe in Zimbabwe committed the genocide of the Matabele tribe in the 1990s in apparent degenerated nationalist chauvinism and xenophobia. The Gukurahundi Genocide was conducted by a special force "trained by the North Korean army," centralised around the Shona tribe and was marked by "its fanatical ideological loyalty to Mugabe" (Moorcraft 2012: 105); it was "Mugabe's war machine." Mugabe, as I reflect, failed to escape, or chose to use the underside of nationalism, its racism, tribalism and xenophobia for purposes of seeking, finding and keeping power and dominance, at all costs. From his assault of the Ndebele people to his attack on white commercial farmers in the Zimbabwean postcolony, Mugabe exuded tribalism, racism and xenophobia of a true intellectually lazy African nationalist that Fanon decried. When it came to the narrow politics of tribes and clans, even as an individual that was supposed to be an intellectual and scholarly titan, Mugabe degenerated into a true bigot; he was blinded and deafened by prejudice.

The name "Gukurahundi is a Shona word to describe the rain that blows away the chaff" after the harvesting season (Moorcraft 2012: 105) and clears the land for a new season that is cleansed of the pollutants of the last season. The genocidal connotations of cleansing the land of political enemies as "chaff" cannot be missed. Sabelo Ndlovu-Gatsheni (2012a, b: 1) argues that ZANU-PF under Mugabe "deployed the ideology of *Chimurenga (the ancient Shona spirit of war)* in combination with the Gukurahundi strategy as well as politics of memorialisation to install a particular nationalist monologue of the nation." The will to power prefers monologue and monomania, obsession with one big idea, to dialogue. Power itself becomes a big idea that is believed, loved, religiously kept, and is not negotiable.

In the perpetration of the Gukurahundi Genocide, Mugabe appears to have been driving and also being driven by a toxic nationalist and chauvinist will to power that diminishes political opponents to "chaff" that must be cleansed off the land to create a new national purity and authenticity in the absence of those that are condemned as enemies. This toxic nationalist ideological push and pull is described by Slavoj Zizek (1989: 114) as "national paranoia" that is the "fear and doubt of a nation's completeness and authenticity" in the world which compels drives for purification and cleansing of the other, political drives that are essentially genocidal. When some citizens of the postcolony are seen and believed to be pollutants the grounds are set and fertilised for massacres and genocide.

In the understanding of Frantz Fanon, the degenerated nationalism of the new African ruling class turned them into the new colonialists that weaponised identity politics for the purposes of excluding other classes and populations from a share of the national cake. Speaking as a nationalist and a Marxist, Samora Machel (1996) is recorded to have said in Africa, "for the nation to live the tribe must die," a political sentiment that justified the suppression of the ethnic consciousness of minority tribes such as the Matabele in Zimbabwe. The suppression of ethnic consciousness frequently degenerates into massacres, ethnic cleansing and genocide, the elimination of certain ethnic bodies and groups that espoused other tribal identities and political sensibilities. In Marxist terms ethnic consciousness was seen as false consciousness that was unwanted and needed to be erased in one way or another. Erasing consciousness is separated by a thin line from the annihilation of bodies that embody that consciousness, in such political realities as of the postcolony. In the postcolony other ideas are beaten and killed together with the bodies that embody and carry them. The one idea of the tyrant, his political party and supporters must be the only idea; all others must die together with the people that advance them. In that way the postcolony is a garden of tyranny and also a cemetery of other ideas and their bearers.

In his critique of African nationalist and Marxist ideologies as powerful but also false, Achille Mbembe (2002a, b: 629) noted the development of "Afroradicalism" and "nativism" as political energies, pulls and pushes, that were not only limited but had a toxic and fundamentalist underside that is limited and limiting to the very liberation that they set out to seek and to find. Mugabe's political performance of Marxism, nationalism and Pan-Africanism that included the political need, he said, to "strike fear in the hearts of the white man, our real enemy" (Meredith 2002a, b: 17) became essentially radical and nativist in a politically and historically limited way that consumed the very nation and country that were supposed to be liberated and built. Marxism and nationalism, under the stewardship of tyrants, degenerated to doctrines and dogmas that were repeated, Mbembe notes, but were not permitting to the liberatory potential that they claimed. Nation and Marx, in positive essence, were left behind as the "ism" was given a front seat in politics. Ideologies became a mask for power and its many tyrannies. Mugabe championed "Afro-radicalism and nativism" that Onslow and Plaut correctly note as "Mugabe's Afroradicalism (that) was purposive as a state ideology and also a self-serving political imagination for a specific elite" of soldiers and politicians that wanted to and did milk the country dry while pretending to be liberators and revolutionaries.

Ideology became an emblem, an alibi and an excuse that was used to cover hunger for power and evil itself. "Mugabe and many of his associates," argues Daniel Compagnon (2011: 4), "saw Marxist-Leninist discourse as an idiom to power" that they could use and abuse without even believing in it; this can be extended to their instrumentalisation of nationalism for power and domination in the African post-colonial settings. Socialism, democracy, human rights and black empowerment might all have been used (Compagnon 2011: 4) as Nietzschean masks and flags to conceal the real game that is the will to power by any other name and description. Being anything and doing anything for power and domination appear to be the logic of the will to power.

In the important discussion of nations as imagined communities Benedict Anderson (1983: 144) observed patriotism as a nationalist passion to be a political energy that forces men and women to kill and be killed for the nation. In other words, nationalist ideology can be a violent ideology of othering that produces those that are not insiders to the nation into enemies that should be eliminated. Nationals as lovers and defenders of the nation become martyrs that are willing to die for man, woman and country. Nationals are required to be patriots that are willing to die and kill for the motherland. As such they easily become nativists and xenophobes as national duty and patriotic consciousness. The underside of love for the nation is hatred of those that are not nationals. It is perhaps for that reason that Samuel Johnson (1775) said "patriotism is the last refuge of the scoundrel," an ideological enclave that is usable by tyrannical leaders in punishing dissenters and opponents the way Mugabe mobilised tribalism in disciplining his Matabele opponents that he deliberately, and also deceptively, elevated to fatal and eternal enemies that deserved their death. Those that have been imagined and constructed to be outsiders to the nation, enemies, traitors and aliens are given the death treatment. Mugabe gave the Ndebele the death treatment with, perhaps, a clear national and patriotic conscience.

In the view of Ali Mazrui (1982: 22) African nationalism contributed immensely to the fight against colonialism but failed to help African leaders to build nations and it became a major contributor to the development of failed nations and failed states in the continent. Stateless nations and nationless states were created. For that reason, it will be important for this book, here and later, to examine how nationalism as a part of the will to power contributed to the evolution of the political thought and leadership of Mugabe. Sabelo Ndlovu-Gatsheni (2009: 1144) notes that African nationalism that produced such leaders as Mugabe was shaped by colonialism and failed to transcend the colonial as national leaders became schooled in colonial rule, perhaps in the same way in which Nietzsche warned that those who fight monstrosities tend to become monsters in their own right. Nationalists and Marxists in Africa did not only fight colonialism but went on to learn political bad habits from the system, habits that they went on to spectacularly reproduce, amplify and magnify, in the calamitous postcolony.

In other words, African nationalist rule failed to shake off the infection by colonial rule, to the extent that leaders such as Mugabe became products of colonial rule that led their countries with the will to power of colonisers rather than that of liberators. How opponents of colonialism and its will to power came to be produced by it and also reproduced it in ruling their people in Africa is one of the observations that this book stands to make using the case study of the political thought and leadership of Mugabe. Noteworthy is that Mugabe's will to power might be a product of a combination of personal drives, historical conditioning and production, and ideological passions and drives. Below, I delineate the will to live as the antithesis of the will to power. The will to live helps this book to flesh out a decolonial and humanist philosophy of power and politics that is alternative to the will to power in its centring of life and ethics in politics.

It appears to me that the will to power itself as a passionate and spirited political drive is a product of a combination of systemic and structural forces such as colonialism and imperialism. Structures and systems combine with the characters of individual political players to produce and reproduce tyranny. The personal inclinations of individual leaders, social conditioning and production, and ideological drives that then produce and shape such a politician as Mugabe into a kind of monstrosity of tragic proportions are all ingredients of untampered political ambition. Mugabe, in his will to power, became a politician who produced in mass, dead bodies, and occasioned "fear" (Godwin 2010). The historical and political effect of Mugabe's will to power and rule in the Zimbabwean postcolony became what Catherine Buckle (2003) described as "tragedy," pain and suffering that are "beyond tears." Mugabe, because of his will to power and the political deeds that came from it, has been read and understood in many Luciferic terms, rightly and wrongly. Mugabe's Zimbabwe was named in lists of countries of the world that were the "axis of evil" and "outposts of tyranny" in ways that fed into racist stereotypes of Africa but were unfortunately true in their description. Evil and tyranny walked on two legs and wore a hat in the Zimbabwean postcolony, proverbially speaking.

THE WILL TO LIVE AS THE POLITICS OF LIBERATION

In the political scheme of the will to power and its philosophical paradigm of politics as war, acceptability and respectability have been given to the cliché that politics is a dirty game. It does not only become forgivable but also commonsensical that a politician should be a warlord, trickster or another type of slippery and dodgy character to whom morality is not important. In the naturalisation, normalisation and acceptance of politics as a dirty game, violent force and fraud are made into the commonsense of politics. In the postcolony daily jokes and bunter do not only mock politics and politicians as dirty but in many ways give understanding and acceptance to the violent, fraudulent and corrupt in politics. The tyrant's reputation for being dangerous and slippery, in the postcolony, is turned into the very mark of his heroism as the political and politics proper are mistaken, first for a game and next for a site where even angels proverbially fear to tread. Victims of political violence and fraud are not in so many ways told to stay away from politics or muster enough dirtiness to survive in the bloody business of politics. Politicians, their supporters and opponents alike get sold and bought to the idea and practice of politics as dirty and dangerous in the catastrophic postcolony, tyranny itself is normalised.

In the more than three decades of Mugabe's rule in Zimbabwe his political violence and fraud had come to be spoken of as a kind of glory and rare political talent. An attitude of 'if you cannot defeat him join him' had begun to circulate like important political wisdom, and this unfortunately rationalised the political violence of opposition politicians and their political parties. For that reason, political violence turns into the very culture of politics in the postcolony and to be a politician and to participate in politics one must consciously cultivate a character of violence and display performances of true hooliganism to be considered a player in the game. The danger of this development in politics is that bleeding wounds, dead bodies, electoral cheating, political cozenage and massacres come to be appreciated as, what else, but politics as it naturally is. Part of the reason for Mugabe's survival and long stay in power was that he had come to be understood as the very natural cause and effect of politics as a dirty game, a rule rather than an exception of things in the postcolony. It is perhaps one of the forceful tricks of tyranny to pretend as much as possible to nature and commonsense.

The cliché dictum of politics as a dirty game is itself a dirty idea of the politics of conquest, violence and domination. The naturalisation and normalisation of cheating and dirt in politics is an artefact of the will to power that gets invested in the need for it to be widely understood and believed that force and fraud are the other name and description of politics. In this book I mobilise and deploy the idea of the philosophy and politics of liberation that hold it to be true that it is neither natural nor should it be normal that politics is dirty and bloody. To denaturalise and denormalise violence and all forms of dirt in politics is to participate in the philosophy and politics of liberation, I argue. The philosophy and politics of liberation should entail the scandalisation of immorality in politics. That politics should be a game, and a game of dirty devils and slippery tricksters, is itself a colonial idea that seeks to give respectability to violence, conquest and domination.

Chiefly, it is Enrique Dussel (1985) who in 1969 conceptualised and articulated the philosophy of liberation as a body of thought against war and domination of the poor, colonised, racialised and discriminated peoples of the world, especially the colonies and postcolonies of the Global South. In his *Twenty Theses in Politics*, Dussel (2008) provided a direct counter to the "will to power" as a paradigm of politics as war and philosophy of domination. Dussel condemned the "fetishism of power" that "defined power as domination" and was propounded by Friedrich Nietzsche, Niccolo Machiavelli and other artists and scientists of power, in preference for the "will to live" as liberation (Dussel 2008: 13). In the "will to live" as a philosophy of liberation Dussel (2008: 24) argues that politics should be liberated from its "corruption" and its reduction to a "profession" and returned to its status as a noble "vocation." In Zimbabwe

Mugabe and his party practised politics as a profession of hooligans and scoundrels. As a profession and not a vocation politics is colonised and dominated by understandings and practices of it as a dirty business occupation where profits, gains and other personal and partisan advantages become more important than ethics. The business of politics becomes only power and more power and nothing else. Politics as a profession permits all sorts of tricks, stratagems and gerrymandering that a mission and a vocation do not allow as they demand more dedication, and even sacrifice, instead of calculated opportunism.

In that missionary way, I argue, the politics and philosophy of liberation, the will to live, has its own messianic spirit. The violence of the philosophy and politics of liberation is in exactly that, exploding the myths and disturbing the practices, that seek to naturalise and normalise politics as a game first and as dirty next. That people, for instance, had to be enslaved and colonised, so that they could be civilised, modernised and Christianised, was part of the rhetoric of slavish and colonial politics and its will to power that sought to give a decent name to evil. To give slavish and colonial politics an acceptable nickname has been part of the will to power of Empire in the Global South. In opposition to Empire, ethical and liberating politics is, according to Dussel (2008), that "obediential" use of power where those who lead do so with the consent of the led, where "those who command must command by obeying" the multitudes that are commanded. Mugabe, in the Zimbabwean postcolony, did not only command by disobeying Zimbabweans but also by attacking those that questioned and challenged his leadership.

In this book; the "will to live" as a philosophy of liberation and paradigm of peace is erected as the anti-thesis of the "will to power" that is a philosophy of domination and a paradigm of war. For that reason, the political thought and leadership of Mugabe as guided by a kind of will to power will be evaluated against the gesture of the "will to live" that proposes a humanistic and ethical politics. It is in this way that this book stands to contribute to the debate and scholarship on a humanist theory and philosophy of power. Noteworthy is that while the will to power carries itself with a kind of missionary spirit as argued earlier above, so does the will to live whose philosophical inspiration is traceable to liberation theology and critical humanism of philosophers such as Dussel, Paulo Freire and, for instance, the humanism philosophy of Kenneth Kaunda of Zambia. Kenneth Kaunda (1966: 10) proposed a critical political humanism that asked political leaders "to handle power without being tainted by it," a political philosophy that condemned "leaders that have waded into power the spilt blood of their followers." For politics to be liberating and for political leaders to be humanists, Freire (1993: 26, 27) advanced a political humanism that urged the oppressed to fight for a world that will liberate both the oppressed and the oppressors so that the future world is not caught up in a toxic circle of revenge, hate and counter-hatred. Mugabe, on the other hand, seems to have espoused a politics of anger and revenge that turned what was supposed to be a liberation movement and party into a repetition and reproduction of colonialism par excellence. Joshua Nkomo, another nationalist leader and rival of Mugabe's, complained thus during the Gukurahundi Genocide:

> We accused and condemned the previous white minority government for creating a police state and yet we exceed them when we create a military state. We accused former colonisers who used detention without trial as well as torture and yet do exactly what they did, if not worse. We accused whites of discrimination on grounds of colour and yet we have discriminated on political and ethnic grounds. (Nkomo 2002: 72)

In his own way and words Nkomo was condemning the way Mugabe successfully failed to overcome colonial politics but reproduced and magnified it in the Zimbabwean postcolony. A politics of the will to power that does not espouse the "will to live" and does not take seriously the rehumanising value of liberation, for both the oppressor and the oppressed, collapses to the same coloniality and domination that it set out to dethrone. It is in that way in which Mugabe, for Heidi Holland (2008), came to embody "the untold story of a freedom fighter who became a tyrant." The will to power collapses would-be liberators into the same oppressors that they set out to dethrone and replace. Also, in possessing and being possessed by the will to power, oppressors such as Mugabe became, may pretend to be liberators. And this is when their foundational desires and drives are oppressive and colonial. The colonial politics of dirtiness and domination exists beyond the conquest, domination and oppression of natives by white settlers in the postcolony. Black bodies chanting slogans of black politics frequently embody and advance colonial politics in the African postcolony. Once in power, Edgar Tekere narrated, Mugabe became a new kind of colonial master except in skin colour. Perhaps the capital tragedy of Robert Mugabe in power became the rather efficient way in which he performed himslef as a liberator when he was the true opposite, a tyrant of the postcolony.

In pursuing and exercising what I understand as the politics of the will to power Mugabe spiritedly moved to take "authoritarian control of the political arena in Zimbabwe"; he used "violence as a cornerstone" of "political survival"; he controlled the media, annexed the judiciary, plundered the economy and created an international crisis (Compagnon 2011). In the same patriarchal bravado in which Nietzsche (2004a, b) despised women and femininity, and distasted men who did not exhibit masculine gravitas, Mugabe demanded that men be masculine. Mugabe demanded that his ministers become "Amadoda sibili (real men) "I do not want ministers who are in the habit of running away. I want those I call, Amadoda Sibili (real men), people with spine … our revolution was not fought for by cowards" (Meredith 2002a, b: 223). This demand was in spite of the fact that many women courageously fought in the Zimbabwean struggle of liberation. In its misogyny and exploitative partriachy, the politics of the will to power that Mugabe espoused reduced Zimbabwe into what Horace Campbell (2003) described as an "exhausted patriarchal model of liberation" that negates real liberation and permits toxic "executive lawlessness" and political impunity (Campbell 2003: 76). In his search for real political manhood that became political hooliganism Mugabe practiced the same phallic politics of slavish and colonial domination, the rule by the stiff penis. Achille Mbembe (2001: 13) notes how "in many ways the form of domination during both the slave trade and colonialism in Africa could be called phallic, during colonialism and its aftermath," in the postcolony "phallic domination has been all the more strategic in power relationships."

The will to power entailed that Mugabe became a man even over other men that he had kneel before him and perform other acts of submission and worship that were in many ways sexualised. For their docility and exaggerated performances of obedience, Margaret Dongo called ZANU-PF ministers "Mugabe's wives" in comparison to subdued wives and daughters-in-law of patriarchal societies. In the postcolony and its patriarchy and sexism, like in slave plantations and colonies, some men are feminised and compelled to perform femininity before the ruler and his party. Elderly men and some celebrated war types were frequently seen kneeling down in public and clapping hands before Mugabe and his wife in near religious supplications. There is a way in which Mugabe relished in making servile women out of other men in public. This was perhaps part of his violence and war making. In describing and condemning the paradigm of war Nelson Maldonado-Torres observes that:

> War however is not only about killing or enslaving; it includes a particular treatment of sexuality and femininity: Rape. Coloniality is an order of things that places people of colour within the murderous and rapist view of a vigilant ego, and primary targets of this rape are women. But men of colour are also seen through this lenses and feminised, to become fundamentally penetrable subjects for the *ego conquiro*. (Maldonado-Torres 2008: 218)

The feminisation of the powerless and the conquered belongs to the phallic ego of the conqueror. Mugabe deployed sexual violence against enemies in the Gukurahundi Genocide where soldiers raped women and the various episodes of electoral violence where opposition supporters were punished by rape. The model of politics and its bravado that Mugabe used was observed by Horace Campbell (2003) to be patriarchal, masculine and sexist in that women had no place except as powerless followers, sex objects and other victims. Powerless men, amongst supporters and opponents alike, were reduced to rapeable women. Mugabe did not only enjoy his power but he also derived a certain pleasure from the public performances of powerlessness by victims and supporters. The sissy and "Mama's baby" that Mugabe grew up as hungered to see other men and everybody performing servile sissy roles.

In its negation of liberation and denial of humanism, the politics of the will to power that Mugabe practiced seemed also to weaponise not only patriarchy and a sexist masculinity but also ageism and what Christian Potholm (1979: 31) called "gerentocracy" where old age and historical experience are mobilised as political resources and excuses for staying long in power. Mugabe forcefully tried to project himself as the inevitable great old man that was an irreplaceable asset to Zimbabwe. He imagined himself and wanted to be believed as the start and the end of Zimbabwean history, an epochal and epical hero, combined in his body and person. As I noted above, Mugabe turned his birthday, 21st February, into a national holiday where his many days on earth and long years in power were recounted and celebrated as a national gift and heritage. Now and again he publicly repeated his gratitude to God who still had work for him to do in the country. In this ceremoniality and memorialisation, not in so many words, women and youths were bludgeoned with the weight of old age, liberation war experience, long years in prison and maturity. The life of the durable and long-suffering patriarch was narrated and used to discourage women and the youths from ever aspiring for power which is located in the province of the battle-scared old men.

In the scheme of imperial politics, Edward Said (1993: 3) notes that "appeals to the past" including claims of historical experience "are among the commonest of strategies in interpretations of the present." By use of his old age, long experience and life journey Mugabe advanced politics of the will to power that sought to monopolise history for purposes of owning power and excluding others from it. The philosophy and politics of the will to live that Dussel (2008) advances as the ethics of liberation restores the human to people, including women and the young into life, and demands power that is not for domination, that is not the "fetishism of power," but is for liberation and rehumanisation, "obediential" power. The will to live does not only negate individual politicians like Mugabe in their excesses but confronts systems and structures of domination that expressed themselves not only in violence and war but also patriarchy, ageism, ableism and other intersections of oppression.

After an in-depth study of the life and times of Mugabe, interviewing his relatives, colleagues, friends and political opponents, Heidi Holland arrived at an important conclusion about his durable and overwhelming will to power. Mugabe held beliefs about his life and destiny that became a compelling script according to which, like an experienced actor, he rehearsed and performed his daily life:

> Robert Mugabe believed he was born to rule and behaved accordingly. Once the king always the king, he reckoned. In his idealised view, his loyal subjects would worship the ground he trod forever. In reality, the great majority of Zimbabwe's people supported him enthusiastically for 20years. It was only when his policies began to impoverish the country that they turned against him. Characteristically, Mugabe never forgave them. Growing ever more vengeful, he ripped down their shelters, destroyed their livelihoods and snatched the food from their mouths. Those in his court who remained loyal to him were richly rewarded with money, property and power. In death, they were buried amid extravagant fanfare at Heroes Acre, the monument to Zimbabwe's liberation on a hill outside Harare. (Holland 2008: 192)

Mugabe, in his will to power, believed power and the domination of Zimbabwe and Zimbabweans to be a God-ordained, natural and normal order of things. He daily carried himself as a chosen one of God and the ancestors. Consequently, he experienced opposition to his rule the way any messiah encounters the heresy of non-believers and sin of those that want to crucify the chosen ones of God. The Zimbabwean postcolony became a site of judgement where sinners and non-believers were isolated for punishment and damnation while faithful believers were rewarded and promoted. In pulsating graveside orations Mugabe made an example of his loyal followers, celebrating them as if to appoint a special place for them in heaven with his upper lip while with his lower lip he cursed his opponents as if to consign them to hell where they would be proverbially fried by a Lucifer with a long fork. Paradoxically and also tragically, Mugabe himself was not buried at the Heroes Acre but at his rural Zvimba home as if the loss of political power and death returned him to his true status of birth as a commoner.

REFERENCES

Althusser, L. (2010). *Machiavelli and Us* (G. Elliot, Trans.). London: Verso.

Anderson, B. (1983). *Imagined Communities: Reflections on the Origin and Spread of Nationalism*. London & New York. Verso Books.

Badiou, A. (2009). Who Is Nietzsche? In D. Hoens, S. Jöttkandt, & G. Buelens (Eds.), *The Catastrophic Imperative* (pp. 195–204). New York: Palgrave Macmillan.

Barnette, H. H. (1972). The Anatomy of Extremism: Right and Left. In E. West (Ed.), *Extremism Left and Right*. Michigan: William Eerdmans Publishing Company.

Belfield, R. (2005). *Assassination: The Killers and Their Paymaster Revealed*. London: Magpie Books.

Buckle, C. (2003). *Beyond Tears: Zimbabwe's Tragedy*. Cape Town: Jonathan Ball Publishers.

Campbell, H. (2003). *Reclaiming Zimbabwe: The Exhaustion of the Patriarchal Model of Liberation*. Claremont: David Philip Publishers.

Camus, A. (1953). *The Fastidious Assassins*. London: Penguin Books.

Chabal, P., & Daloz, J.-P. (1999). *Africa Works: Disorder as Political Instrument*. Bloomington: Indiana University Press.

Chan, S. (2007). Nietzsche in Harare. *Prospect*, May, p. 134.

Clausewitz, C. V. (1985). *On war*. Harmondsworth: Penguin.

Compagnon, D. (2011). *A Predictable Tragedy: Robert Mugabe and the Collapse of Zimbabwe*. Philadelphia: University of Pennsylvania Press.

Dongo, M. (2016, August 9). In Bulawayo24 News, *Mugabe War Credentials Questioned, War Prisoner not War Vet*.

Dussel, E. (1985). *Philosophy of Liberation*. New York: Wipf and Stock Publishers.

Dussel, E. (2008). *Twenty Theses on Politics*. London/Durham: Duke University Press.

Fanon, F. (1967). *The Wretched of the Earth*. New York: Grove Press.

Freire, P. (1993). *Pedagogy of the Oppressed*. London: Penguin Books.

Fukuyama, F. (1992). *The End of History and the Last Man*. New York: Free Press.

Gaddafi, M. (2009). Libya's Gaddafi Hurls Insults as Saudi King. Address to the Arab Summit. Retrieved September 10, 2018, from https://www.smh.com.au/world/libyas-gaddafi-hurls-insults-at-saudi-king-20141031-9h9r.html.

Gat, A. (2008). *War in Human Civilization*. Oxford: Oxford University Press.

Godwin, P. (2010). *The Fear: The Last Days of Robert Mugabe*. New York: Picador.

Heidegger, M. (1967). Who is Nietszche's Zarathustra? *Review of Metaphysics, 20*(3), 411–431.

Holland, H. (2008). *Dinner with Mugabe: The Untold Story of a Freedom Fighter Who Became a Tyrant*. Johannesburg: Penguin Books.

Hope, C. (2003). *Brothers Under the Skin: Travels in Tyranny*. London: Pan Macmillan.

Jenkins, M. (2013). Aristocratic Radicalism or Anarchy? An Examination of Nietzsche's Doctrine of Will to Power. *Pathways of Philosophy*. Retrieved July 20, 2018, from www.philosophypathways.com/fellows/jenkins.pdf.

Johnson, S. (1775). In J. Boswell (Ed.), *Life of Samuel Johnson, LL.D.* (Vol. 1, p. 478). London: Wordsworth.

Kaplan, D. R. (1996). *The Ends of the Earth: From Togo to Turkmenistan, From Iran to Cambodia: A Journey to the Frontiers of Anarchy*. New York: Vintage Books.

Kaunda, K. (1966). *A Humanist in Africa: Letters to Colin M. Morris from Kenneth Kaunda President of Zambia*. London: Longmans.

Lamb, D. (1990). *The Africans: Encounters from the Sudan to the Cape*. London: Mandarin Publishers.

Lessing, D. (2013, March 1). The Jewel of Africa. *The New York Review of Books*, p. 1.

Macaphulana, D. M. (2017a). Mnangagwa and the Theft of History. In *Bulawayo24 News*. Retrieved February 14, 2019, from https://bulawayo24.com/index-id-opinion-sc-columnist-byo-122102.html.

Macaphulana, D. M. (2017b). Robert Mugabe the Physical Man Naturally Retreats. In *Bulawayo24 News*. news: Retrieved August 4, 2017, from bulawayo24.com.

Machel, S. (1996). In Mamdani, M. Citizen and Subject: Contemporary Africa and the Legacy of Late Colonialism. *Perspectives on Political Science, 26*. 120–120.

Machiavelli, N. (2003a). *The Prince and Other Writings*. (Wayne A. Rebhorn, Trans.). New York: Barnes and Noble Classics.

Machiavelli, N. (2003b). *The Prince*. New York: Barnes and Noble Classics.

MacLean, J. S. (2002). Mugabe at War: The Political Economy of Conflict in Zimbabwe. *Third World Quarterly, 23*(3), 513–528.

Magaisa, T. A. (2016, February 26). The God Father Has Spoken- But Was It Much Ado About Nothing? In *Zimbabwe Independent*.

Maldonado-Torres, N. (2008). *Against War: Views from the Underside of Modernity*. London / Durham: Duke University Press.

Mazarire, G. C. (2011). Discipline and Punishment in ZANLA, 1964–1979. *Journal of Southern African Studies, 37*(3), 571–591.

Mazrui, A. A. (1974). Africa, My Conscience and I. *Transition, 46*, 67–71.

Mazrui, A. A. (Ed.). (1977). *The Warrior Tradition in Modern Africa* (Vol. 23). South Holland: Brill Publishers.

Mazrui, A. A. (1982). Africa Between Nationalism and Nationhood: A Political Survey. *Journal of Black Studies, 13*(1), 23–44.

Mbembe, A. (2001). *On the Postcolony*. Berkeley: University of California Press.

Mbembe, A. (2002a). On the Power of the False. *Public Culture, 14*(3), 629.

Mbembe, A. (2002b). African Modes of Self-writing. *Public Culture, 14*(1), 239–273.

Mbembe, A. (2004). An Essay on Politics as a Form of Expenditure. *Cahiers Etudes Africaines, 1*, 173–174.

Meredith, M. (2002a). *Robert Mugabe: Power, Plunder and Tyranny in Zimbabwe*. Cape Town: Jonathan Ball Publishers.

Meredith, M. (2002b). *Our Votes, Our Guns: Robert Mugabe and the Tragedy of Zimbabwe*. New York: Public Affairs Publishers.

Moorcraft, P. (2012). *Mugabe's War Machine*. Cape Town: Jonathan Ball Publishers.

Moore, D. (2007). "Intellectuals" Interpreting Zimbabwe's Primitive Accumulation: Progress to Market Civilisation? *Safundi, 8*(2), 199–222.

Moore, D. (2009). Mamdani's Enthusiasms. *Concerned African Scholars Bulletin, 82*, 49–53.

Moore, D. (2015). In S. Ndlovu-Gatsheni (Ed.), *Mugabeism? History, Politics, and Power in Zimbabwe*. New York: Palgrave Macmillan.

Mouffe, C. (2005a). *On the Political*. Abingdon: Routledge.

Mouffe, C. (2005b). *The Return of the Political*. Verso: New York/London.

Muchemwa, K. Z. (2010). Galas, Biras, State Funerals and the Necropolitan Imagination in Re-Construction of the Zimbabwean Nation, 1980–2008. *Social Dynamics, 36*(3), 504–514.

Mugabe, R. (1976). In Meredith, M. (2002). *Our Votes, Our Guns: Robert Mugabe and the Tragedy of Zimbabwe*. New York. Public Affairs Publishers.

Mugabe, R. (1989a). Struggle for Southern Africa. *Foreign Affairs, 66*(2), 311–327.

Mugabe, R. (1989b). The Unity Accord: Its Promise for the Future. In Banana, C.S (ed.) *Turmoil and Tenacity: Zimbabwe 1890–1990*. Harare: College Press.

Mugabe, R. (2002, July 2). Follow in the Footsteps of Father Zim, In *The Herald*.

Mugabe, R. (2008). Campaign Speech. In Ndlovu-Gatsheni, S. "Rethinking Chimurenga and Gukurahundi in Zimbabwe: A Critique of Partisan National History." *African Studies Review 55* (3). pp. 1–26.

Ndlovu-Gatsheni, S. (2009). Making Sense of Mugabeism in Local and Global Politics: 'So Blair, Keep Your England and Let Me Keep My Zimbabwe. *Third World Quarterly, 30*(6), 1139–1158.

Ndlovu-Gatsheni, S. (2012a). Rethinking "Chimurenga" and "Gukurahundi" in Zimbabwe: A Critique of Partisan National History. *African Studies Review, 55*(3), 1–26.

Ndlovu-Gatsheni, S. (2012b). Beyond Mugabe-Centric Narratives of the Zimbabwean Crisis: Review Article. *African Affairs, 111*(443), 315–323.

Ndlovu-Gatsheni, S. (2015). *Mugabeism? History, Politics, and Power in Zimbabwe.* New York: Palgrave Macmillan.

Nietzsche, F. (1968). *The Will to Power.* New York: Vantage Books.

Nietzsche, F. (1969). *Thus Spoke Zarathustra.* London: Penguin Books.

Nietzsche, F. (1979). *"Why I Am so Clever," in Ecce Homo.* London: Penguin Classics.

Nietzsche, F. (1990). *Twilight of the Idols/ The Anti-Christ.* New York: Penguin Books.

Nietzsche, F. (2003). *Thus Spoke Zarathustra.* London: Penguin Books.

Nietzsche, F. (2004a). *Why am I so Clever?* London: Penguin Classics.

Nietzsche, F. (2004b). *Human, All Too Human* (M. Faber and S. Lehmann, Trans.). London: Penguin.

Nietzsche, F. (2016). *Why I Am so Clever.* London: Penguin Classics.

Nkomo, J. (2002). *The New Zimbabwe.* Harare: SAPES.

Norman, A. (2004a). *Robert Mugabe and the Betrayal of Zimbabwe.* Jefferson: McFarland and Co.

Norman, A. (2004b). *Robert Mugabe and the Betrayal of Zimbabwe.* London: McFarland & Company Publishers.

Norman, A. (2008). *Mugabe: Teacher, Revolutionary, Tyrant.* Gloucestershire: History Press.

Onslow, S., & Plaut, M. (2018). *Robert Mugabe.* Johannesburg: Jacana Media.

Potholm, C. P. (1979). *The Theory and Practice of African Politics.* New Jersey: Prentice-Hall Inc Publishers.

Reno, W. (1998). *Warlord Politics and African States.* Boulder/London: Lynne Rienner Publishers.

Rotberg, R. I. (2010). Mugabe über alles: the tyranny of unity in Zimbabwe. *Foreign Affairs,* pp. 10–18.

Rupiya, M. (2005). Zimbabwe: Governance Through Military Operations. *African Security Studies, 14*(3), 116–118.

Said, E. W. (1993). *Culture and Imperialism.* New York: Vintage Books.

Saul, J. S., & Saunders, R. (2005). Mugabe, Gramsci and Zimbabwe at 25. *International Journal, 60,* 953–975.

Schmitt, C. (1996). *The Concept of the Political*. London & Chicago: University of Chicago Press.

Tekere, E. (2007). *Edgar "2boy" Zivanai Tekere: A Life Time of Struggle*. Harare: SAPES Books.

Tendi, B.-M. (2011). Robert Mugabe and Toxicity: History and Context Matter. *Representation: Journal of Representative Democracy., 47*(3), 307–318.

Tendi, B-M. (2019). The Motivations and Dynamics of Zimbabwe's 2017 Military Coup. *African Affairs*, 1–29.

Wa Thiongo, N. (2006). *The Wizard of the Crow*. London: Vintage Books.

Wamba dia Wamba, E. (1996). Pan-Africanism, Democracy, Social Movements and Mass Struggles. *African Journal of Political Science, 1*, 1–133.

Zizek, S. (1989). *The Sublime Object of Ideology*. London: Phronesis.

Zizek, S. (2001). What Can Lenin Tell Us About Freedom Today? *Rethinking Marxism, 13*(2), 1–9.

Zizek, S. (2003). Critical Response: I, a Symptom of What? *Critical Inquiry, 29*, 486–503.

CHAPTER 3

The Inventions of Robert Mugabe

*Our mother explained to us that Father O'Hea had told her that
Robert was going to be an important somebody, a leader ... Our
mother believed Father O' Hea had brought this message from God, she
took it very seriously, when the food was short, she would say give it
to Robert.*
—Donato (*2008*: 6)
*Like the abused child who risks becoming an abusive parent, the
politically oppressed have regularly turned into oppressors in countries
all over Africa. Mugabe furthered his rule with the despotic strategies
employed by the colonial settlers he so derided. His drive towards
centralised control, for example, was facilitated by Smith's 15-year
State of Emergency.*
—Heidi Holland (*2008*: 83)
*That's what my mother also used to say. I always had a book tucked here
(gestures under his arm) when I was a young boy. Yes, I liked reading,
reading, reading every little book I found. Yes, I preferred to keep to
myself than playing with others. I didn't want too many friends, one or
two only.—the chosen ones. I lived in my mind a lot. I liked talking to
myself, reciting little poems and so on; reading things aloud to myself.*
—Robert Mugabe (*2008*: 223)

Robert Mugabe's habit was always to simply look aside when ministers
and the party apparatchik publicly called him the "Son of God," and at

© The Author(s) 2021
W. J. Mpofu, *Robert Mugabe and the Will to Power in an African
Postcolony*, African Histories and Modernities,
https://doi.org/10.1007/978-3-030-47879-7_3

times the "Second Son of God." What became a culture in ZANU-PF was "outlandish sycophancy towards Mugabe by party cadres with suggestions by the faithful at the more modest of the spectrum that Mugabe is divinely appointed and, at the extreme that he is divine himself" (Matyszak 2015: 16). To Mugabe the outlandish titles and otherworldly descriptions of himself seemed commonsensical. He was also called by the names of such edible substances as Cremora, the tasty coffee creamer. In all his public naming and calling, the name of his biological father never featured in his political curriculum vitae that was prevalently sung in public by ambitious loyalists soliciting promotions. That Mugabe's father of flesh and blood was one Gabriel Matibili, a Malawian immigrant and a competent carpenter, is a truism that was kept in the dark like a family secret by the party faithful and the choir of Mugabe's praise-singers. Mugabe the political construction and the figure of the fertile imagination of his supporters was always put ahead of the man of flesh and blood. Some politicians around Mugabe knowingly fed into and ballooned Mugabe's constructions and inventions that held him as a divine personage. In all he said and did, Mugabe seemed to relish the godification.

Those around him that could have at least led him to the real world of flesh and blood made things worse with their self-interested myth-making. As a good politician who knew the right things to say, during her time as Vice-President, Joice Mujuru (2013: 1) told a rally of villagers in Mhondoro that Mugabe, at the age of ten years, was anointed by God to rule Zimbabwe. She said so as she laughed at those in the ruling party and the political opposition who thought they could depose and replace Mugabe in power. Mugabe's long stay in power, by the use of force and fraud, was explained by the loyalists in terms of the will of God who appointed him and not the will of the voters in Zimbabwe, or his electoral fraud. Before the 2008 elections when the popular opposition Movement for Democratic Change party was mounting a formidable challenge to his hold on power, Mugabe (2008: 1) publicly swore, before a meeting of local business people and some foreign investors, that "Only God who appointed me will remove me, not the MDC, not the British." Mugabe did not only believe the stories of his divine anointing but also went on to live a life of a chosen one. He did not need the friendship of mortals but a few chosen disciples and followers; living in his mind and talking to himself as a child were the early signs of the desire for self-worship and the self-loving and self-eating propensity he was to exhibit at his old age. In his helm, Mugabe became what Ken Wilber (2017: 9) called a "narcissist nihilist," a person that for the sheer love of and belief in himself can burn the whole world.

Mugabe's will to power was never, it seems, centred on any metanarrative or grand ideals but on himself and his believed divine commission, which made him a dangerous law unto himself. The name of God was always opportunistically dropped in narratives of his biography to seek to glorify what was always the development of an idolatrous and tyrannical political personality cult. With one hand the faithful of the cult saluted God and his chosen one while with the other they looted the gold and other precious resources in Zimbabwe. Supporting Mugabe became itself a business occupation for enterprising tycoons and opportunistic politicians. The tyrant's name is a talisman in the postcolony; dropping it here and there opens up the gates of fortune.

Concealed behind the idolatrous performances of his personality cult was the stubborn truism that Mugabe was a true son of Matibili and a fellow of otherwise ordinary, if not humble, birth. At the beginning of his narrative of the *Life of Castruccio Castracani of Lucca*, Niccolo Machiavelli (2007: 404) notes how after achieving power men of low birth and troubled family backgrounds do not name their fathers but attribute their birth to this and that other god. The absence of Mugabe's father in the multiplicity of narratives about his life is itself a stubborn presence that explains the many ways in which he unconsciously sought to be fathered by God and to father all other people in Zimbabwean politics. He passionately sought to be everyone's chosen one who in turn enjoys the power and privilege to choose who was to be around him. Much like the Christ who chose his disciples carefully, Mugabe developed, I demonstrate below, what I call a Christ-consciousness and a messianic sensibility.

Towards the end of his rule Mugabe was determined to turn the nation into a big political thought and practice of family, led by his household with him as a permanent father. Otherwise behind his powerful figure of a ranting deliverer of the people, a messiah of sorts and a father of the brave revolution, Mugabe, there was always a fragile little boy needing a hug and some assuring love and acceptance. Behind the iron face of the tyrant is frequently masked a pathetic toddler crying for love. At a time when ordinary Zimbabweans were symbolically a fatherless lot that could scarcely afford basic food and drink, then Information and Publicity Minister, Webster Shamu (2011: 1), could publicly call Mugabe Cremora, the coffee creamer. The metaphor of Mugabe the ruler as the tasty coffee creamer was not accidental because in the postcolony that Achille Mbembe (2001) describes, tyranny does not only punish its opponents but also generously pays and feeds its praise-singers and supplicants. The tyrant does not only come to be imagined as a messianic son of God but also as a sumptuous meal and a delicious beverage in the land of poverty and starvation such as became Zimbabwe. Singing praises to the tyrant, as loyalists like Shamu did, makes the tables at home dirty with food and drink as tyranny delivers the delicious and the creamy of supplies to the faithful. Dropping the name of God, celebrating the opportunities and privileges of eating and drinking well by the favoured of the tyrant becomes part of the method of the madness in the postcolony. Understanding how a fragile boy grew to be the messianic captain of a chaotic postcolony is, perhaps, one way of exploring not only the political but also the maddening energies of power, as well as its consuming tragi-comic idiocies.

The life of the orphaned Castruccio Castracani who grew to be the conqueror that ruled Lucca in ancient Italy is used by Machiavelli (2007) to demonstrate how tyrants are born and also made. A combination of factors of "fortune" as destiny itself and self-fashioning, and fashioning by others, incubates and conditions the despot to his bitter fruition. The development of a fragile and vulnerable child, that Mugabe was, to a true venal despot was driven by what became a burning passion and overwhelming desire for power and domination. Friedrich Nietzsche, himself a believer in the virtue of the instincts, passions and drives notes that:

> There is a time with all passions when they are merely fatalities, when they drag their victims down with the weight of their folly—and a later, very much later time when they are wedded with the spirit, when they are spiritualised. (Nietzsche 1990: 52)

Mugabe's drive from the weakness and vulnerability of his youth, like that of the orphaned Castruccio Castracani, grew into a demanding fatality that dragged him down to tragic ends as he had effectively spiritualised what was otherwise a human ambition. Mugabe turned his personal ambition for power and domination into a kind of religion. The will to power as a passion that, does not as much love power as it fears weakness, morphs into a punitive spirit that punishes as it also promotes the tyrant. It works like a demonic possession.

Psychoanalysts such as Erich Fromm (1986), Malcolm Bowie (1991), Frantz Fanon (2008) and Slavoj Zizek (2015), like Jacques Lacan and Sigmund Freud before them, have advanced arguments that leaders as personalities with psychic lives are driven by unconscious desires that appear as passions, fantasies, complexes, phobias and philias that are produced by their traumatic conditioning in society. I seek to explore the social and psychological conditioning and production of Mugabe that might have formed his political and philosophical sensibility that in turn drove his will to power. In exploring the social and psychological production of Mugabe's political and philosophical sensibility I benefit from the musing of theorists, philosophers and psychoanalysts on the formation and production of political drives. Upon what meat he fed, and what summers and winters his body melted and froze accordingly, in his life and political journey, should provide telling clues to the making of the monstrosity that Mugabe became. Tyrants are terrified and therefore terrifying personages, in the main. Understanding Mugabe's fears that became the source of his forbidding love for power aids the examination of the political and power that I make in the present account.

The journalist Heidi Holland (2008) explores how Mugabe grew up being regarded as a special child, by God's word, a child that would grow up to be a great leader. Mugabe's mother, Bona, particularly irrigated the narratives and beliefs of her son as an elected divine messenger. As Mugabe turned out to be a leader who fought colonialism and ended up being a kind of coloniser of his people who killed his country (Power 2008), the question arises as to how leaders that fought for liberation came to threaten the freedom of their countries and people. How did colonialism end up becoming a kind of school from which its very victims were to graduate as new colonisers to their own people is a question that haunts this book. The thin line between the liberator and new oppressor, the hero and the villain, does not only spell out the fragility of freedom but also that heroes do not really exist except as creatures of the imagination, imagined personalities in actuality. As noted earlier, Mugabe as a hero and liberator was more of a figment of the imagination of his supporters and opportunistic looters that used his name as political and economic capital. In negotiating big deals and threatening people, big business tycoons and politicians drop the name of the tyrant here and there in the postcolony.

What dramatised his believed chosenness is that Mugabe grew up a loner, a friendless toddler who buried his attentions on books and reading (Holland 2008: 223). His humble and lonelfy beginnings are lauded as what typically portended his great destiny. To that extent Mugabe's education and many university degrees are a subject of interest in understanding his political production and philosophical formation into a tyrannical leader. Chosen persons and chosen nations, in the world, have proven to be dangerous to others and to themselves, frequently. The ideas they acquire and which they hold and believe about themselves, humanity and the world are important. Storied education and its artefact of the book became for Robert Mugabe a fetish and a recommendation to power. Education and the book as a container of high secrets became, also, a disqualification for Mugabe's opponents who did not possess as much claim to knowledge, and he laughed them off for it. Mugabe lived his education as a kind of war for power and the book he used as a weapon to fatally disadvantage contenders to power. The way chosen nations fetishise the ancient scriptures that are supposed to predict their destinies, the chosen person clings with the energy of a fundamentalist onto those fictions and myths that suggest his higher and permanent destiny.

The question of how a political leader who grew up a Christian and a scholar turned out to possess what Richard Hofstadter (1964: 77) called an "angry mind" that is hostage to the "paranoid style" of politics is central to investigations of the political and power itself in this book. In the essay on "Making sense of Mugabeism in local and Global Politics" Sabelo Ndlovu-Gatsheni (2009: 1139) explores how Mugabe was politically produced and shaped by leftist nationalism, Afro-radicalism, nativism, patriarchal and neo-traditional political passions that turned him into a practitioner of "chauvinism and authoritarianism." Mugabe seems to have weaponised these ideologies, with all their fundamentalisms, as much as the ideologies instrumentalised and possessed him. Like Ezeulu, the Chief Priest of Ulu in Chinua Achebe's *Arrow of God*, Mugabe came to be a weapon in the hand of mighty ideologies as much as he believed himself to be a chosen hand of God whose tyranny was in actuality, as he saw it, a service to humankind.

In the study of "the ideological formation of the Zimbabwean ruling class," of which Mugabe was a large part, David Moore (1991: 472), as noted before, examines how Zimbabwean political leaders were formed by ideology into leaders that employed both "force and persuasion" as strategies of seeking, finding and keeping power. Mugabe was most likely not going to escape being a true product of the political histories and cultures that enveloped the Rhodesia and the pursuant Zimbabwe in which he found himself. He was to carry all the dust and mud of the history, political cultures and ideologies that he encountered, and which he gave body and life to. In that way Mugabe came to be fathered by history, ideas and institutions, and individuals that he came into contact with, a child of many and of none, and therefore easily given to the fatherhood of God himself. Being a weapon in the whim of so many a force and in turn weaponising so many passions made Mugabe a raging mixture of contradictions whose only continuity and purpose became power at all costs.

Following David Moore, Sabelo Ndlovu-Gatsheni and Heidi Holland, therefore, I assume that leaders such as Mugabe are not just born with certain toxic passions and violent instincts but are also produced, formed and shaped by historical conditions, social circumstances, ideologies and political influences in their life journeys. In reference to Mugabe, Blessing-Miles Tendi (2011: 308) argues that from "the beginning he was toxic" and elaborates that historical and political conditions added to and influenced the political character and philosophical personality of the leader. Besides his personality and character that may have been originally toxic, "increasing domestic and international challenges to his rule" contributed to Mugabe ending up being the unforgivable tyrant who deployed "harsh means to maintain" his largely infamous rule (Lloyd 2002: 219). In other words, his will to power and drive to keep power by any means necessary under opposition and adversity compelled Mugabe to desperate and most times violent measures of maintaining hegemonic control of Zimbabwe. The fear of returning to fatherlessness and the vulnerabilities and weaknesses it entailed charged Mugabe into a maniac for power and more power, it seems. As I will illustrate below, if one did not become a mother or a father to Mugabe one had to be his child or become an enemy to be eliminated. Ahead of the party and the state itself, for Mugabe the family with its father and mother, and children, was to become a tyrannical framework that ruled his world and beyond which he saw and knew nothing. The toddler who hungered for a father grew up to a monstrous father figure that turned the nation into his personal family and demanded due recognition as such, the one and only, fathered by God and destined to be everyone's father.

On the Formation and Production of Political Leaders

To effectively examine and reflect on the political and philosophical formation of Robert Mugabe into a leader who drove and was also driven by an aggressive will to power, an understanding should be made of some ideas on the formation of leaders. Various philosophers and students of the political have studied and written on the production and behaviour of political leaders in the world at large and in Africa specifically. In his study of post-independence African leaders, for instance, A. H. M. Kirk-Greene (1991: 163) observed how the political leaders, in an obsessed way, were driven to a search for "eternity," that was accompanied by "eccentricity" and pretensions of "exemplarity." The leaders that Kirk-Greene studied seemed to aspire to live and rule forever, displayed strange and eccentric behaviour, and pretended to be rare individuals that were different from the rest of their peers and followers. In a way that has fascinated scholars and journalists, the post-colonial African leaders came under pressure to distinguish themselves as rare breeds:

> The behaviour of independent Africa's heads of state, be they President or Prime Minister, General or once upon a time Sergeant, exercises an unusual level of fascination on a no less unusually widespread range of readership. Their characteristics and their ideologies, their excesses, their eccentricities and their example, their often conspicuous way of living and usually brutal manner of their dying, have provided data for scholarly analysis and intellectual typologising. (Kirk-Greene 1991: 163)

While Kirk-Greene simplifies the understanding of political leadership by isolating strange and excessive behaviour as an African post-colonial attribute, his observation that literature exists that points to patterns and types of leadership styles is important. It became easy for those born under colonialism to, after achieving some education and political leadership, count themselves as distinguished and extra-ordinary achievers that under none but God himself or the ancestors had triumphed against adversities. Mugabe's political thought and practice will be understood as a type and style of political leadership amongst other types and a style of the will to power, not as a simple example of degenerate African politics.

Perhaps, in a psychic way, the hardships and humiliations by colonialism itself, the humble births and upbringing of some of these leaders injected in them a hunger for exaggerated power and grandeur. Those that have been out in the rain and cold tend to exceedingly cherish the warmth of power, and particularly fear the return to the freezing winters of powerlessness. The postcolony itself might after all be that theatre of terrified leaders and anxious followers that are both trying and failing to make sense of what and who they are in violently changing times. The uncertainty and fear of the unknown, perhaps, make it easy for God and his name to be brought down as explanations and justifications of why things are what they are in the postcolony. The postcolony provides combinations of exaggerations, superstitions, excesses and lacks that the leaders of the postcolony embody and normalise. This makes the postcolony itself a true site of 'the gods must be crazy' kind of political spectacles. The postcolony is a site of drama and spectacle, otherwise.

Historical backgrounds, social conditions and political experiences, especially suffering and trauma can inject into leaders, who prevail from humble beginnings to power, an illusory sense of divine anointment and pre-destination. In reference to Castruccio Castracani the prince of Lucca, who had a humble birth and was without parents, Niccolo Machiavelli (2007: 402–403) notes that:

> Men who have accomplished great deeds and excelled above all others of their era were low in birth and obscure origins, or were tormented beyond compare, they were exposed to wild beasts, or had such lowly fathers that in shame they declared themselves to be sons of Jove or some other god. I believe the lowly origins of great men is Fortune's way of demonstrating that it is she and not Wisdom who makes men great. So that Fortune be acknowledged as supreme, she shows her powers very early in a man's life, well before wisdom could hope to play a role. (Machiavelli 2003a: 404)

For prevailing to the leadership of their people and their countries through the tribulations of colonialism, poverty, imprisonment and suffering, such as Mugabe did, some of the post-colonial African leaders might have come to believe themselves to be the children of destiny or messengers of God. To lead political parties and to become heads of states after traumatising histories of colonial violence, inferiorisation and dehumanisation that are described by Albert Memmi (1974), such African leaders as Mugabe might have arrived at a strong but illusory sense of victory and greatness that produced delusions of divinity and grandeur. That he came from God and that his rule and power were God-given is a belief that Mugabe held far much deeper and stronger than many observers and scholars have understood. It is a belief that like forbidding spectacles was to cloud his views and twist his judgements in many unfortunate directions including that his political opinions, especially opinions of himself, were divine wisdom. One may, after a reading of Mugabe, wish for the Moses effect, that is the historical scenario where those that fought for liberation do not become the ones that lead their people after political independence.

In the discussion of the influential ideas of Karl Marx and Sigmund Freud, Erich Fromm (1970) notes that Freud proves that society does stamp its signature and influence on the psyche of human beings while Marx proves that human beings, in their thoughts and actions, create systems and structures that shape society. In other words, there is a relationship of co-production between man and history in society. Political leaders such as Mugabe have through their thoughts and actions produced history while history has also produced and formed their thoughts and actions. In that way, the destiny and wisdom, wisdom as in thoughtful agency of leaders, are symbiotic in their relationship, I note. The Mugabes of history are not hapless victims of history but are also conscious and most times willing conspirators in the comedies and tragedies that define society. This is also as much as tyrants are excitable and excited puppets of their passions and drives, interested believers in the fantasies and fictions of their own construction.

For Erich Fromm as a sociologist and psychoanalyst, understanding how people think and act the way they do became of primary importance as it is for us here to understand how Mugabe came to think and act politically the way he did. For Fromm as "an only child" that had an "anxious and moody father and a depression-prone mother was enough" to spark an intellectual "interest in the strange and mysterious reasons for human reactions" (Fromm 1986: 3). To understand Mugabe's political reactions, the dispositions of his father and deportments of his mother should be scrutinised to locate influences of parentage, birth and family life on his will to power. What excesses and lacks in family become to children triggers to their drives and passions can only be important in understanding the inventions and production of such leaders as Mugabe.

Relevant to us also here are philosophical musings and political ruminations of such thinkers as Plato who aspired for the production and formation of young political leaders into philosopher kings in ancient Athens, believing earnestly that leaders are made. Plato (1993: 285) opined that those that were to be formed into philosopher kings were to be taken out of society to be educated and trained into being those rare individual leaders that came from "the company of the gods." The belief in his God-given destiny situated Mugabe in that disturbed position where he understood himself as a kind of companion of God who did not need the friendship and company of mortals. The kind of education and training that Mugabe received and that formed him into the leader that he became is an important unit of understanding as earlier argued. Further, Plato

(1993: 285) noted that some young people are driven to seek political leadership and power because of the miserable and powerless lives of their mothers that are wives to poor and powerless men. The negligence and absence of Mugabe's father that Heidi Holland (2008: 3) discusses and the misery and wishes of his pathetic mother, that made her wish for power and greatness in Mugabe, and believed him to be a kind of arrow of God, will be examined to note how they drove Mugabe to a will to power. Did perhaps the wishes of a mother that her son will grow to be a great leader and rescue her from the misery of abandonment become to Mugabe a trigger to a death drive to power by any means and all means necessary? The postcolony itself might be a setting for certain political death-drives, chaotic dreams and fantasies that tragically become nightmares from which societies must urgently wake up. As I note in this book, such despots as Mugabe are frequently driven by fear and anger. A certain void inside the tyrant drives him to want to fill the world with his presence.

Fear can manifest in the tyrant as anger, hate and aggression. Amos Elon (2006), in his introduction of Hanna Arendt's study of the passions and drives of the Nazi regime, notes how tyrants and cruel leaders are sometimes produced not by strengths and power but weakness and fear. For instance, Hannah Arendt (2006: xiii) observes that Adolf Otto Eichmann, Hitler's principal torturer and hangman, became a "bureaucrat of death" because he grew up weak, afraid, pathetic and with feelings of failure and uselessness. The possibility that Mugabe's own storied will to power arose from some strengths or weaknesses and pathos is an important question, given his troubled and desperate family life, and life in the colonial prison, and the traumatising struggle for liberation. The persecuted and oppressed of colonialism became more than ready to be persecutors in their own right.

The study of "civilisation and its discontents" led Sigmund Freud (1994: 7) to an investigation of how religion and religious beliefs originated in a child's helplessness and need for a father that is not found in the biological father and is desperately sought in the metaphysical and spiritual universe. Religion, in the understanding of Freud, also arose from hearts and minds that were haunted by fear and guilt feelings that were seeking both punishment and protection from a higher source (Freud 1994: 62). Mugabe's troubled youth, his birth of a deeply religious mother who aspired to be a nun but failed and his own tutelage by Jesuit priests that gave him a kind of strong religiosity will be explored to observe how he was produced by religious conditions and passions, into a leader with an iron will to power that had religious pretensions. The metaphysical, religious and spiritual seem to have had their own many handed grip of the octopus on the world and mind of Mugabe, whose later rejection of the Christian church might be easily read as his deluded competition with Christ, a kind of sibling rivalry, of the sons of God that Mugabe's fantasies produced.

Influentially, Niccolo Machiavelli (2003a: 25) also ruminated on how some leaders come to power by fate and fortune, that is, historical circumstances and chance can enable the production of a leader. Some leaders, Machiavelli (2003a: 33) states, come to power or are delivered to power by force and fraud and they try to invent new ways of rule or try to rule by imitating ancient or current leaders that they admire. In a strong way, as I illustrate later, in power Mugabe became a tragic imitation of Ian Smith, the colonial leader he so bitterly fought, an imitation to the point of duplication and reproduction. The production and formation of a Machiavellian leader is also an idea that I will recognise in the examination of the political production and philosophical formation of Mugabe's will to power.

Severally, Mugabe seemed to have been the right person at the right time for power, a conspiracy of circumstances and opportunities that might have most tragically fed his believed and deeply held messianism. The durability of his will to power and his longevity, against powerful odds, in power seem to suggest that there could not have been another person except Mugabe suited to rule. Yet the observation of the circumstances and opportunities that favoured Mugabe shows exactly what a mistake it has always been to trust him with power and opportunity. A kind of comedy of errors explains the coming and becoming of Mugabe in power. It is exactly for that reason that the flourish of literature on Mugabe shows that journalists and scholars alike have experienced him as a tragic figure, one who carried all the promises, but could not avoid delivering nightmares and disasters. It has also been easy to understand Mugabe as one who could not escape his inevitable self, a figure that could not defeat itself in order to deliver to promises of liberation, partly because such a figure exhausts its energies looking at and fighting enemies out there when the demons that matter are inside, in the mind and heart. That Mugabe might have been a captive of his internal and own contradictions might be confirmed by the way he was finally deposed by a military junta that he created and which created him, to ensure perpetual stay in power in the true pursuit of the eternal return and perpetual presence of the Nietzschean will to power.

The Family, Friends and Colleagues of Mugabe

It is Edward Said (1999: 3) in the observation of how his birth and family life shaped his very being and philosophical sensibility, who noted that "all families invent their parents and children, give each of them a story, character, fate and even language." Mugabe was no different; with Gabriel as his middle name that invokes the biblical angel, the messenger of a virgin birth, he was destined for greatness, he believed. The name Robert allegedly came from Robert Moffat, a British Christian missionary. As the following chapter will show, In Zimbabwean politics some flatterers called Mugabe an angel and a saint. In pursuit of power by all means necessary and some unnecessary Mugabe carried himself like a true political missionary.

Families are by their social and psychological design and nature a vivid site of reproduction and production, a field of influences and forces that determine the becoming and ultimately the being of their members. So charged with triggers for passions and drives is the family that, perhaps, all human beings carry visible and invisible birthmarks and *growthmarks* that are traceable to the familial context. Early family life, if traumatising, can give that stubborn wound that insists on gaping and bleeding every time it is healed.

From the observation that birth conditions and family life invent a thinker and an activist, I am interested in how the nature of Robert Mugabe's birth in time and place, and his parentage and family life gave him a political character and philosophical personality that in turn gave him a will to power and historical fate. Or how in turn his family life and socialisation made him an empty and also a ready vessel for certain desires, fears and other passions that formed his will to power.

In most cases those sick individuals that in turn produce sick societies are human beings that would have grown up with childhood fears and anxieties that they failed to overcome and remained bottled up in their psyche (Fromm 1986: 41). Such a psychopathology amongst individuals is usually connected to their parentage and family life as a formative site and experience. The influence that family, friends and colleagues might have had on the political character of Mugabe, how they contributed to the formation of his will to power, is a present preoccupation in this book.

THE ABSENCE OF THE FATHER

In the psychoanalytical discussion of paranoia, how it veils itself, and "why the paranoiac" individuals "need two fathers," a biological father and a powerful symbolic father that is a kind of super-ego, Slavoj Zizek (1996: 142) demonstrates how absent fathers can psychologically be replaced in a child's mind by a symbolic and psychic father that exercises tyrannical authority over the angry and lonely child, driving them to more excesses of paranoia. In his political life, as will be demonstrated later, Mugabe found symbolic fathers at school, in church where he sought to replace his biological father with Jesuit priests and God himself, in such British personalities as Lord Soames and some former Rhodesian securocrats. In other words, the presence and absence of paternal love, care and authority in a child's life may determine whether they develop into a balanced individual or a paranoiac that once in power can be tyrannical and violent. Fatherless and angry, taken over by fear, the paranoiac subject becomes a charging monster that must urgently be fathered by more powerful forces or it will violently subject, everyone and everything, under its own disastrous fatherhood.

Mugabe's father, Gabriel Matibili Mugabe, abandoned his family soon after the death of one of his sons, Michael, and went to Bulawayo, where he remarried and returned only many years later with three children from his second wife (Holland 2008: 3). As well as Mugabe carried the name of his father, Gabriel, as his middle name, he seems to have carried the wound of being abandoned as part of his very identity; he could not escape his father the way one cannot shake off their name and personal shadow. On the social media platforms in Zimbabwe, a multiplicity of jokes circulated about how Mugabe never forgave the people of Bulawayo and Matabeleland at large for the sins of that one woman who snatched his father away from his dear mother. The anger that belied Mugabe's hatred of the people of Matabeleland, and poured fuel to the Gukurahundi Genocide, might not be unconnected to the love Mugabe held for his abandoned Mother.

For the reason of abandonment by the father who did not contribute to the education and upbringing of his children Mugabe developed a "pathological hatred of his Father" (Holland 2008: 7) that he carried to his old age. Anger at being abandoned by his father and the hatred towards him might have developed into a psychic, social and political energy that Mugabe was to vent on opponents and enemies later in life. Anyone that seemed to reject Mugabe or refused to support his political drives to power and stay in political office might have suddenly become his hated negligent father, in the kind of psychologically wounded soul that he had come to be. Easily, political enemies and opponents of Mugabe became shadows of his very first negation and opponent, the father who left him to poverty and vulnerability at an early age. In his political life Mugabe seems to have grown to hate and fear rejection of any kind including the rejection by voters.

Mugabe, as earlier noted, grew up a lonely, angry and brooding boy who "seemed to have matters to think about" (Holland 2008: 6) beyond what children his age were occupied with. In the Zizekian sense that is explained above, the absence of Mugabe's father in his formative and needy years might have produced in him symptoms such as "the seven veils of paranoia" (Zizek 1996: 1390) where the individual conceals their fragility and psychological woundedness behind pretences either of being too happy, possessed with a "father of all enjoyments," living by some strict unwritten rules, being out of joint with normal society, vocalising anger and hate to supplement lacks in life, having strong desires and fantasies, and pretending or trying by all means necessary to be the "Big Other" to others. Some of these behaviours and qualities, as I will demonstrate, are evident in the political behaviours and performances of Mugabe. After being deposed in a coup, Mugabe became a true crying baby whose pathos exposed how behind the strong man that once haunted the world, there was a needy toddler that needed fatherly protection more than anything. A good father, perhaps, is what Mugabe caused all the political and historical hullaballoo looking for in the Zimbabwean postcolony. Power itself, perhaps, with the comforts and immunities that it afforded him might have become at the end of it all a father that Mugabe would cling to with emphasis. The will to power as a drive became to childish Mugabe a commanding father whose will he could not, even if he wished, oppose. Mugabe hugged onto power the way a needy child does on a protective father

THE OVER-PRESENCE OF THE MOTHER

If Mugabe suffered a wounding absence of paternity in his formative years he also endured an injurious excess of maternity. Like Adolf Hitler and Augusto Pinochet who both had mothers that adored them (Burbach 2003: 22), Mugabe grew up under a lovingly influential mother. Mothers in their attention and inattention to their children have formative influence that shapes the character and personality of their offspring. From his family life, Edward Said (1999: 7) learnt that "mothers are to be loved" as dear parents "and taken care of unconditionally," yet "because of their selfish love they can deflect children from their chosen careers" and as a result "mothers should not be allowed to get too close." There is a way in which Mugabe's mother was allowed to get too close and her selfish love conditioned the life of her son. There is a strong way in which she tried too hard to compensate for her failure to be a nun and her abandonment by the father of her children by using her maternal stamina to shape Mugabe into a kind of messiah, a messiah of her wished for virgin birth that would deliver her from her miseries. She somehow did not own the reality that she was a fallen nun and imagined her son Robert to be a holy child of a kind. In his life and political messianism of his fantasies, Mugabe does not seem to have related to the truth that unlike the biblical messiah, he was not born of a virgin conception and was a fallible bread eater whose power had to be checked.

Mugabe's mother, Bona, intended to be a nun but was seduced by Gabriel Matibili Mugabe and she became pregnant. She and Matibili got a son, Michael who died in his youth. After the death of their son, Michael, that she wished was going to be a priest; she started praying that Mugabe would be a catholic priest (Holland 2008: 3) and for some time Mugabe "became an exemplary catholic" who would become a great priest one day. Bona was an abandoned wife and a fallen nun; to her Mugabe became the son that "set about trying to restore the light in her eyes" (Holland 2008: 3). Her ambitions of greatness for her son unfortunately put the toddler and later the teenager under immense pressure. The mother generated confusingly mixed feelings and pressures on the fragile boy. For instance, the knowledge that his mother intended to be a nun and did not want to have children might have filled Mugabe with fear and anger at the possibility that he was not to be born in the first place, and also deep gratitude that through chance and failure of her mother to be a nun, he was born after all, which made him deeply love and also unconsciously fear and hate his mother. In that way, he was indeed a miracle child that was conceived and born only through the fall rather than will of the mother. The knowledge that one's birth was not intended but that one by chance and failure of the mother's intentions was born can generate unhappiness and also deep-seated anger, and some delusions that one is a miracle child who overcame a great obstacle to be born. One who was born against human design.

In her interest to shape Mugabe into a great son, or in her own drive to prepare him for what she believed was the prophecy of his greatness, Bona also gave him tough love with strict discipline which he appreciated; as a result "if his mother smacked him" Mugabe did the strange thing to "thank her for correcting him" and "he thanked her every time" so much so that "the other children used to tease him and he became lonely" (Holland 2008: 4) as a child. In her maternal, physical discipline or violence on Mugabe as a child, Bona might have been venting her anger on a child and children that were her shame and failure at becoming a nun, children of her sin and fall from grace. The gratitude Mugabe expressed after being smacked was the gratitude for the favour of being born in spite of the mother's contrary intentions.

In her holding of the belief that Mugabe was a child of destiny that was born to do great things his mother made him a "too good to be true" child that was going to be a priest. She made sure that he had something to eat ahead of other children if food was scarce (Holland 2008: 6). It seems that after her experience with a negligent and absent husband Bona wanted to make Mugabe into a wished-for perfect man. In driving himself to live up to the wishes of his mother, Mugabe might have pushed himself too far. For the reason that he became a loner and did not fight with other boys Mugabe developed a reputation for physical weakness and cowardice, and was mocked by other children (Holland 2008: 6), which gave him anger and an inferiority complex. "As he grew up, Robert got a sense of who he was from Bona, a cold, stern nun of a mother" that was keen to make him "the leader chosen by God" (Holland 2008: 7) to rule forever over other people. In a way, Mugabe was, too early in life, deprived of a social and physical life and that pushed him into metaphysical aspirations for greatness, which may have underdeveloped him or overdeveloped him into a personality with a messianic sensibility and god-complex, I note.

The growth of Mugabe between an absent father and a rather excessively present and ambitious mother possibly created psychological and social pressures that can only produce imbalances and instabilities in a person. Mugabe's mother, her pains and fears might have stamped a bold signature on his person and psyche, to the extent that he carried a part of his mother in his mannerisms and public deportment. Christopher Hope (2003: 21) observed Mugabe in a public rally and noted that "certainly, as I watched Mugabe mount the platform, there was a mincing elegance; it was more than feminine, it was distinctly dainty, when he was seated he joined his knees together and seemed to reach for an invisible skirt to cover them," a suggestion that something womanly hid in the alpha-patriarch that was Mugabe. The raging and ranting tyrant might after all be concealing, not so deep under the skin, an unhappy woman. Mugabe was so thoroughly mothered by Bona that her presence made itself visible deep in his sensibility, not much wonder that he named his own daughter Bona.

Mugabe's physical weaknesses and inferiority complex might also have planted a strong wish and drive to be strong and powerful one day, which is a wish that might have turned into a forceful will to power. Sigmund Freud (1994: 10, 43) notes that children grow up wanting to love and to be loved, lack and excess of which may lead to psychotic searches for love and passionate pursuits of compensatory gratifications and escapes from pain and loneliness. The anger and hatred that Mugabe had for his absent father he might have made up for it with love for power and domineering masculinity, a drive to be everyone's father himself, as I argue, and even to see his hated father in political opponents, challengers and enemies. In the Zizekian sense, Mugabe might have developed or underdeveloped into a paranoiac personality that pushes and hugs everything around itself in search of a father. Or that narcissist personality that wants to impose itself as a father upon everything and everyone, and gets enraged when its fatherhood is rejected. In combination, Mugabe's father and his mother, with all her outwardly good intentions, seem to have produced Mugabe into a terrific and also terrifying personality that was not grounded in any respect for other people but itself and its divine lacks and excesses. Mugabe does not seem to have been parented and socialised into one that could be a liberating leader but an ambitious and spirited power monger that would not suffer for a while the idea to be led by anyone. Great leaders, especially liberating ones, are frequently those personalities that are easily prepared and able to be led by others. Mugabe did not, by all counts, become one of those. In his own way, Mugabe became a fatherless and motherless monster.

THE WIVES OF ROBERT MUGABE

Wives, mistresses and girlfriends, like other participants in the intimate economy around an individual, can form an influential social and psychological climate that can be formative and commanding. From high school headmasters through diplomats, right up to heads of states, A. H. M. Kirk-Greene (1991: 172) argues, the impact and influence of wives on the thought and practices of leaders cannot be ignored. After observing Mugabe and the way his ministers feared and knelt before him, Margaret

Dongo, an opposition politician, accused the ministers of being "Mugabe's wives" (Gudhlanga 2013: 1). There is a strong way in which Robert Mugabe in power has been observed to have been able to emasculate other men under his leadership (Gaidzanwa 2014: 200). The political metaphor of a leader who makes himself a husband over other men in Dongo's accusation points to Mugabe as excessively patriarchal; perhaps in compensation for his absent father, the husband that was not there for his excessively present mother. Mugabe effectively styled himself as the divine anointed father of the nation and, not in so many words, demanded the respect and reverence that is given to commanding African traditional fathers before whom wives and children kneel to perform their fear and love.

Sally Hayfrod Mugabe was Mugabe's wife that he met in Ghana, in 1957, and eventually married in 1961. Sally is noted to have idolised Mugabe as a political thinker and activist that was a teaching expatriate in Kwame Nkrumah's newly independent country (Holland 2008: 11). As a wife Sally Hayfrod was supportive, patient and loyal to the extent that she waited for him all the eleven years of his detention in the colonial prison. She proverbially used to go to libraries in Europe to read books and copy notes to send to Mugabe, who was studying from prison. The industriously copied notes included some quotations from books that were banned in Rhodesia (Holland 2008: 16). In that way, Sally became a dissident in her own right, for Mugabe and his academic interests and political pursuits. Her habit of sewing and washing the military fatigues of the ZANLA guerrillas in their camps in Mozambique (Onslow and Plaut 2018: 59) was a gesture that made her appear like a true mother of the revolution to many in the party. She was a practiced performer of great deeds.

The only person that Mugabe, more than his close friends and colleagues, seems to have genuinely "trusted with his feelings and even his political problems" was Sally (Holland 2008: 21). While many Zimbabweans understand Sally to have been not only sober minded but also charitable and a stabilising force to Mugabe's leadership (Meredith 2002a, b: 96), some scholars have noted otherwise. For instance, Heidi Holland (2008: 12, 25), after studying the couple closely, concluded that she was a political animal on her own and stuck around her husband to further her own ambitions that at the end included siphoning large amounts of money from Zimbabwe to her people in Ghana. Her use, abuse and instrumentalisation of Mugabe and his power might have been carefully concealed because he seems to have trusted her totally; the otherwise grave and brooding leader is noted to have become a kind of a clown when with her in privacy (Holland 2008: 18). She managed to bring out the child in him, and around her he became the jester and the baby that was never seen in public. In public Mugabe made sure, always, to appear ceremonial and stately. Around Sally, Mugabe became the happy toddler that he never was as he clowned and laughed heartily. Sally, otherwise, effectively babied Mugabe.

Sally might have over time become another overwhelming mother figure to Mugabe who grew up under maternal tough love and authority. On Mugabe's instructions, Sally was referred to in the public media as "Amai" which means mother, and in her case it was extended to mean "Mother of the Nation" (Meredith 2002a, b: 96). For Mugabe to insist on Sally being called Mother of the Nation means that he imagined himself to be the Father of the nation, an imagination which reduces the country to his imaginary family, perhaps one family that he presided over as a present father, unlike his own absent biological father that he hated with a passion. Horace Campbell (2003) and Rudo Gaidzanwa (2014) are two scholars that have observed, prominently, the workings of patriarchy in Mugabe's political thought and practice in Zimbabwe. In a way, Mugabe, who had an absent and rather weak father, was determined to be a strong father to the nation, a strength that developed into a tyrannical will to power.

The impression from Holland's well-argued conclusion is that Sally might have been a woman who performed love and faith around Mugabe so that she could use him for self-empowerment and enrichment of herself and her family back in Ghana. The incident at the airport where she was intercepted and stopped trying to leave Zimbabwe for Ghana with an obscene amount of Zimbabwean cash (Lessing 2013) is anecdotal of her siphoning ways. Mugabe's mother, Bona, "was a devout and pious woman who taught the catechism and the Bible" (Meredith 2002a, b: 19) but had failed in her ultimate religious goal to be a nun as noted above. In wishing that Mugabe would be a priest and working on him to be that, she seems to also have tried to use her son to compensate for her spiritual failures. Abandoned by his father, used by his mother to pay her own religious and spiritual debts, and exploited by Sally Mugabe for her material gains, Mugabe appears to have been a victim, rather than a beneficiary, of parental and spousal family relations. The adoration and respect that some Zimbabweans hold for Sally might not exactly be that of appreciating her but expressing contempt for Mugabe's later wife Grace Mugabe who is understood to have been a negative influence to his political leadership.

Unlike Sally, Grace Marufu Ntombizodwa Mugabe does not seem to have successfully concealed her selfish political and social agendas; she became flamboyant and showy, much to the anger of the majority poor and suffering population of Zimbabwe. Otherwise the myth that Sally was a sobering influence on Mugabe is exactly that, a myth. Mugabe committed a whole genocide with her by his side.

Sally was still alive, but very sick, in 1987 when Mugabe started a love affair with one of his secretaries, Grace Marufu (Meredith 2002a, b: 96), apparently so that he could have children since Sally could no longer have children because of illness. Sally died in 1992. In 1996 Mugabe formally married Grace Marufu; their first child was a girl who was symbolically named Bona after Mugabe's influential and overwhelming mother. Naming his first-born daughter after his mother was Mugabe's gesture that he was keen to reproduce his mother and maintain her presence even beyond her physical demise. Mugabe seems to have carried the name and influence of his mother beyond her life.

Grace Mugabe's corruption and material greed were not so hidden as those of Sally Mugabe; her brother Reward Marufu became one of the biggest beneficiaries of the fund that was designed to compensate liberation war veterans (Meredith 2002a, b: 37). In the investigation into the character of Grace Mugabe, Heidi Holland (2008: 2, 9, 59, 148, 166, 176) uncovered many foibles and negations on her character as a First Lady that had influence over the thought and practice of Mugabe. Firstly, she was disapproved by Mugabe's family that saw her as an opportunist that had come for Mugabe's power and wealth The family doubted that she ever loved or cared about Mugabe, "a thoroughly bad influence on his character" she was described. To marry Grace Marufu, Mugabe was forced to defy Catholic Church rules because she was illegitimate and unacceptable, their wedding was considered too lavish and a mockery to poor Zimbabweans. Holland (2008) describes how Grace, in an international event that gathered African first ladies, shocked other wives of African heads of states by persistently asking them to say who exactly she resembled amongst the Spice Girls, a popular international musical band of female artistes. Grace carried herself with not so concealed pretensions of pop-celebrity and magazine cover girl illusions. She was, otherwise, not called Gucci Grace for nothing.

When Grace Mugabe looked set for greater heights in politics, the ZANU-PF political patronage and sycophancy machinery went into overdrive. In 2013 the Women's League elevated her to its leadership. She was called "the elegant First Lady, and Angel, a Queen and the nations' own Cremora in near perfect being, as well as her philanthropic disposition" in the public media (Matyszak 2015: 16). Her beauty was described in enhanced exaggerations; for instance, a newspaper stated that " her beauty left even journalists momentarily forgetting their pens and notebooks, in awe, with their eyes glued on the learned First Lady" (Matyszak 2015: 17). Flattered to such heights of illusion Grace Mugabe could not help Mugabe come down from his own delusions. She could only lead him deeper into the mythical forests of grandeur.

Socially, Grace Mugabe seems to have been another materialist and opportunist like Sally but she was of the dramatic, spectacular and explicit type who imagined herself as an international musical celebrity. Towards the overthrow of Robert Mugabe in a coup, in the years 2015 to 2017, Grace Mugabe exhibited her own political ambitions and desire to succeed Mugabe (Macaphulana 2016). Arguably, Mugabe's seeming endorsement of his wife to succeed him led to his downfall when his war-time friends and colleagues resorted to a military coup to stop the unfolding of a family dynasty. From his mother to Sally and Grace, Mugabe seems to have been surrounded by ambitious women and mother figures that loved him for what they could do with him and his power. While Grace's direct political ambitions seem to have been the cause of the coup that dethroned Mugabe, his mother in her belief that he was a gift and a messenger from God might have been the foundation of Mugabe's stubborn will to power.

In combination, Sally and Grace Mugabe appear not to have been the nuns that Bona was; the two were materialist mother figures that differently handled their materialism and political ambitions, one shy and stealth while the other was exhibitionist. Both of them could not have tempered Mugabe's will to power as they needed his absolutism for their personal designs. Before and after Mugabe's fall from power and death, there is a courageous side of Grace Mugabe that Zimbabweans seemed to admire. She had an ability to confront feared war veterans and Mugabe's loathed successor, Emmerson Mnangagwa. Part of her defiance was to deny Mnangagwa the opportunity to pontificate over Mugabe's body at the Heroes Acre by having him buried in Zvimba, a few steps away from the door of the family house, under layers and layers of concrete slabs. She eventually owned the living and the dead Mugabe, hoarding his body as political treasure.

Friends of Robert Mugabe

Politics, in the influential understanding of Carl Schmitt (2007), may after all be the art and science of critically managing friend and enemy relations in the competition for power. In that way, friends and enemies are a reality that cannot be ignored but has to be understood and worked with to avoid politics degenerating to violence and the elimination of one by the other. Interestingly, Mugabe, in his insulation from reality or purposeful denialism, denies ever having enemies:

> I feel I am just an ordinary person. I feel within me there is a charitable disposition towards others, just as I find charitable positions towards me from others. And I don't make enemies, no. Others may make me an enemy of theirs but I make no enemies. Even those who might do things against me, I don't make them enemies at all. No. (Mugabe in Holland 2008: 227)

In being involved in politics which is an essentially conflictual engagement (Mouffe 2005a, b) and denying that he makes enemies and that he has enemies Mugabe conceals, rather than reveals, the political and himself as a political animal. Interestingly, Mugabe also denied making friends at all, "I avoid, you know, a relationship that is far too close, with one or two individuals. Why should that happen?" (Meredith 2002a, b: 97), he asked. In a way Mugabe positions himself as one without friends and without enemies, except what some other people make of him. This may be revealing of a god-complex or some political righteousness that appears as a denialism that depoliticises politics and seeks to dissocialise society.

After suggesting that he was an ordinary person, Mugabe went on to seek to suggest that he is an extra-ordinary individual, a friendless and without enemies being, who might as well be godly. In truth, there should be some realities about Mugabe's friendships and enmities that he did not have the strength to admit and to face. To Holland (2008: 223) Mugabe said, "I preferred to keep to myself than playing with others," as he grew up he "didn't want too many friends, one or two only.—the chosen ones. I lived in my mind a lot. I liked talking to myself, reciting little poems and so on; reading things aloud to myself." The "chosen ones" that became Mugabe's friends were seemingly taken by him to be lucky to be favoured with his friendship and were supposed to be grateful for it, an indication of Mugabe's potential god-complex, even at an early age. In the family at home, "the Mugabes" as a family unit "had no friends" (Holland 2008:

25), perhaps as a political strategy to distance themselves, remove his person and name from ordinary mortals that he sought to rule over with a spell.

The Ndabaningi Sithole that Mugabe later replaced as leader of ZANU is widely remembered as one of the few friends Mugabe had. Geoff Hill (2003) narrates how Sithole became friends with Mugabe when they were fellow teachers at Dadaya Mission in the Midlands province of Zimbabwe. It is widely believed that Sithole became a political mentor to Mugabe. Sithole was to complain that he found Mugabe to be an "impossibly self-absorbed" individual who was charming and persuasive when he needed help from others and was stingy with what others needed from him (Hill 2003: 49). Self-absorption is another description for selfishness and narcissism. It would appear then that Mugabe as someone that had internalised ideas of himself being chosen of God and being exceptional began to see friends and mentors around him not as relations but as simple resources at his service. Helpful friends and mentors such as Sithole might have been, in Mugabe's sensibility, not legitimate individuals whose help was valued but political raw materials and ingredients to Mugabe's power, placed around him by destiny and God.

James Chikerema, a friend and also a relative of Mugabe, told Heidi Holland that Mugabe kept stubborn grudges and did not entertain ideas of reconciliation or compromise; his "response to criticism" from friends and relations "was to warn that he will get even one day" (Holland 2008: 7), meaning that he would revenge. As Lawrence Vambe states, Mugabe "was always settling scores. That was his nature, even as a child" (Holland 2008: 209). Somehow Mugabe seems not to have experienced friendships and relations, as human opportunities for society and growth, but as battlefields where he was supposed to win at all costs.

At an early age Mugabe was already shaping up as a kind of social and political gladiator with a spirited will to power, to whom life was an opportunity for a fight. This might explain better why he had no friends, except few chosen ones that were able to put up with his fighting personality. Later in life and in his term as head of state Mugabe seemed to possess more need for enemies than friends to the extent that he had to imagine and invent them if they did not exist. It is after all "only in opposition" and enmity that the will to power "become necessary" and get its justification to exist as a raging passion (Nietzsche 1990: 54).

Mugabe's mother gave him tough love and she religiously believed in him and his chosen destiny. Lawrence Vambe thought, his mother, the school and the Jesuit priests pushed Mugabe too hard and too far to the extent that he would break trying in everything in his will to be better than the rest, and to live up to expectations of greatness (Holland 2008: 6) that became a kind of pressure on him. A small child that gets parentally and educationally filled with big passions of a great destiny may explode with complexes of imaginary power. In his passionate drive to fulfil expectations of his greatness Mugabe began to see the world in enmity and opposition to his destiny and frequently needed enemies to punish and feed his anger and hatred. The mother's love and the expectations of teachers and priests gave Mugabe an insatiable will to power rather too early in his youth. He began to fancy himself as a kind messiah and divine agent.

Out of his will to power, Mugabe might have avoided friends in fear that they would, in being close to him, become like him and share in his chosen destiny. He strove to be extra-ordinary to the extent of creating distance between himself and peers. George Kahari told Heidi Holland that the school and his family committed the social mistake of conditioning Mugabe into a "too good to be true" person (Holland 2008: 7). In his drive to perform to the script of extra-ordinariness Mugabe became an unrealistic personality that took "strong positions" on everything, an extremist of a kind. The reputation, amongst other children, of being a bookish coward and a sissy (Holland 2008: 6) should also have shaped and produced Mugabe into a person with a political mentality of wanting to prove too much and to overcome and compensate for many barriers and absences in his person. Starting as determined and driven, Mugabe might have ended up pushed and crashed by pressure to be bigger, better and more powerful than a mortal can ever be.

Driven and pushed always, from a young age, to be bigger and more powerful than others, Mugabe was not just unwilling, but "was unable to make close friends" (Norman 2004: 165, 58); as a result he became a loner and solitary person. Edgar Tekere, a liberation war friend, ally and companion of Mugabe, later on described him as unwilling to take even constructive criticism (Holland 2008: 58). Tekere found Mugabe to have become a new master after the colonial masters of Rhodesia had been defeated (Norman 2004: 97) in the way in which he reproduced colonial methods of rule and power relations with the ruled. In that way what was called Mugabeism might have been a personalised political religion that was led by a kind of messiah.

Joshua Nkomo is another friend and mentor of Mugabe who later expressed his disappointment in him. When Mugabe stopped communicating with Joshua Nkomo and reneged from contesting Zimbabwe's independence election as a patriotic front in the unity of ZANU and ZAPU, Nkomo complained: "I don't understand why Robert Mugabe is doing this to me. He was my friend. We fought the war together. We have worked together. And now Robert has cut me off" (Meredith 2002a, b: 38). Nkomo was at best innocent, post-political, and at worst politically naïve to see a friend in Mugabe. For political opportunity and power, Mugabe had grown to be able to cut off and sacrifice friends and colleagues. Mugabe had proverbially come to have permanent interests in power and impermanent friends in life.

For power, Mugabe went out of his long way to turn some enemies of his into friends. For instance, Mac McGuiness was Mugabe's jailer and punisher, a strongly built prison warder and intelligence operative who had a reputation for cruelty. During prison time and after, when Mugabe was in power and in no need of favours and the mercy of the Rhodesian prison warder, he sought McGuiness out and befriended him (Holland 2008: 28), to the extent of pleading with him to stay on in Zimbabwe and serve his black government after the independence of the political country. In the process of being oppressed and persecuted by the Rhodesian regime, as a weak person who needed power, Mugabe seems to have grown to admire the Rhodesian machinery of power and violence, and, in his will to power, wished to own and control it for himself. He would befriend an enemy if he could use the enemy's power for himself, as a new master that had his own enemies to persecute. As a colonised person, and one that suffered fighting colonialism, Mugabe came to admire the coloniser's power and infrastructures of violence. He grew to love and seek to befriend the enemy. Much like a bullied child that grows up to be a bully, Mugabe developed into a coloniser of a kind, fundamentally.

Mugabe's facility for political friendships and enmity can also be understood from his relationship with Jonathan Moyo. Moyo, a political thinker and actor of courage and wit, was frequently accused by opponents and detractors of harbouring an agenda to destroy ZANU-PF from within for the reason that his resentment of the party and its violent history was well known, yet he became one of its ablest strategists and defenders. Mugabe once publicly called Moyo "the devil incarnate" and part of the "weevils" that were eating the party from inside (Matyszak 2015: 12). To the discerning Mugabe's admiration of Moyo's political gamesmanship and combative intellect was not so hidden. At that political moment Moyo became "the rat that every cat secretly admired" (Macaphulana 2014: 2) as he became a suspect that was also an asset to the party and to Mugabe himself politically.

Alongside his love for and reliance on witty and some combative political communicators such as Moyo, Mugabe fell into the trap of misleading flatterers and sycophants. In the elaboration on how princes and leaders should rule, Niccolo Machiavelli advised that "those whom princes have as secretaries" or ministers should be chosen carefully as a leader can be judged on the company he keeps (Machiavelli 2003a: 99). Added to that, Machiavelli (2003a: 101) noted "how flatterers should be avoided" because they blind a leader with false and misleading praise, and lead to his demise. In his relations, because of his sense of being extra-ordinary and destined, Mugabe seems to have failed to discourage or avoid flatters such as Minister Tony Gara who publicly described him as the "second son of God" (Meredith 2002a, b: 80). In pursuit and relish of Jonathan Moyo's artful and also combative support, Mugabe fell into the hands of some artless flatterers. In finding such exaggerated flattery as that of Tony Gara not offensive or finding it truthful Mugabe was carried away by false relations and flattery into an imaginary universe of his chosenness by God and which universe was essentially a wished-for and not the real world. In that way, the will to power and passion for extra-ordinariness may be blinding. Social and intimate relations, so far, seem to have been determined to shepherd Mugabe as much away from the real world as possible, which did not hinder but helped his escalation to delusions and illusions; he became insulated from the real and exposed to the fantastic and imaginary world.

Jesuitisation of Robert Mugabe

Mugabe was frequently noted to be an "intellectual" politician that "was shaped by his Jesuit education and Marxists beliefs" (Onslow and Plaut 2018: 18). He was known to boast of the superior discipline and quality education that he received from the Jesuit priests at Kutama Mission (Meredith 2002a, b: 19). It is a Jesuit priest who predicted that one day Mugabe would become a great leader, a prediction that Mugabe's mother held onto as a powerful prophecy, and which Mugabe also internalised as a fetish of destiny. We may not easily understand Mugabe's will to power without appreciating the influences of Jesuitism and how it impacted on him.

One of the many wisdoms that Saint Ignatius Loyola passed on to the Society of Jesus is said to be the wish that "let us hope that the Order may never be left untroubled by the hostility of the world for very long"

(Barthel 1984: 9). Foundationally as a religious and also political Order the Jesuits have as much expected hostility and trouble from the world as they are said to have troubled the world with their minds and works. Manfred Barthel (1984: 10) who took the trouble to study "the history and legend of the Society of Jesus" concluded that few organisations of people have influenced the world as much as the Jesuits, with only a few thousand men, have done "through their achievements in philosophy, science, education—or indirectly—as a result of the bitter intellectual controversies and counterattacks their activities always provoked." The figure of the Jesuit appears in religion and in politics as a figure of controversy. Barthel (1984: 10) notes Saint Ignatius Loyola's favourite verse that he quoted to his protégés from Saint Paul's Epistle to the Corinthians: "I am made all things to all men, that I might by all means save some." The Jesuit does not avoid the world but gets into it and becomes different parts of it in the hope to understand, know and then change the world. In that way are the Jesuits worldly and practical in their approach to the matters of the earthly kingdom and their pursuit of the heavenly Empire.

The approach of the Jesuit Order to the world has made the Jesuits appear as many things to different people in different societies. Barthel has observed how the Jesuits were as a result of their approach implicated in Nazism and also mentioned in the struggle against anti-Semitism. Barthel sites the historian Egon Friedel's telling description of the Jesuits:

> They were the most brilliant courtiers, the sternest ascetics, the most self-sacrificing missionaries and the sharpest traders, the most devoted footmen and the shrewdest statesmen, the wisest confessors and the greatest impresarios, the most gifted physicians and the most skilful assassins. They built churches and factories, sponsored pilgrimages and conspiracies, proved theorems in mathematics and stated propositions in church dogmatics, worked to suppress the freedom of inquiry and made a host of scientific discoveries. They were—in the broadest sense of the word truly capable of anything. (Barthel 1984: 10)

The Jesuits became the world and the best and the worst of it in their drive to change it. They exercised a will to power that demanded they have excellence on their side in every discipline and profession under the sun. Their universal competence was a design and a means to an end, to prove that theirs was the greatest faith and true knowledge and they frequently did this with dogmatic inflexibility (Barthel 1984: 10). In many ways,

Mugabe carried the gravitas and will to power of the Jesuits that became one of his influential mentors and teachers to the extent that, when power finally approached his way, he publicly promised to go and passionately pray at the grave of Father Jerome O'Hea in memory and gratitude for his mentorship and prophecy concerning his destiny. Mugabe was not just produced by the Jesuits for the world; he also reproduced, multiplied and amplified the Jesuit teachings for his own will to power.

Jesuitism is, as I use the term here and as used by Gerald Groveland Walsh (1930), the political and intellectual philosophy of the Society of Jesus, a distinct Catholic Brotherhood of Christians trained after the religious doctrines of Ignatius Loyola. Similar again to Augusto Pinochet who was formatively educated by the Catholics (Burbach 2003: 23), Mugabe's primary and formative education was under Jesuit missionaries at Kutama Mission in Mashonaland. The Kutama Jesuit Mission was founded by the Jesuit Jean-Baptiste Loubiere of French origins (Holland 2008: 4). Mugabe's Mother Bona was a worker at the same mission and a devout participant in the religious activities of the mission where she became one of the preachers (Meredith 2002a, b: 19). By his own admission and also boast, Mugabe prided himself of having been "brought up by the Jesuits" and being "most grateful" for the way he "benefited from their teaching enormously" (Meredith 2002a, b: 19). With a mother that was a religious preacher and taught by radical Jesuit priests at school, "strict disciplinarians" that they were, Mugabe was enveloped by Jesuit religious teachings and discipline at home and at school. If the argument by Sigmund Freud (1994: 7) that religious belief is founded in the child inside all human beings that helplessly seeks a mighty father in fear of fate, then we can note that in the Jesuit Mission at Kutama, Mugabe's mother had found a husband and Mugabe a father, in the absence of the biological Gabriel Matibili Mugabe who had abandoned his family. In being Jesuitised, Mugabe was fathered in a symbolic, psychic but also forceful way. For Mugabe, in a way, the Jesuit priests had become exalted earthly fathers and God a protective and assuring heavenly father, who approvingly dispensed a great destiny for him. After the death of Jean-Baptiste Loubiere, the Kutama Jesuit Mission, St Francis Xavier, was taken over by Father Jerome O'Hea, an Irish Jesuit priest that had a "realistic view of the world" and that quickly "broke down taboos"; he became responsible for "naturing Robert" like a true substitute for his father (Holland 2008: 4–5); like a true son Mugabe enjoyed "carrying his books and cleaning the blackboard" in class.

In the observation of Father Jerome O'Hea, Mugabe as a toddler exhibited "unusual Gravitas" (Holland 2008: 6) for a young boy and possessed an "exceptional mind and exceptional heart" (Hill 2003: 48). Mugabe became a good candidate for the mission and vocation that the Jesuits had in the world, the inflexible and dogmatic desire to order the world in a certain way. It became clear to Father O'Hea that Mugabe was destined for great achievements in the world; he shared this belief with Bona. Interviewed by Heidi Holland (2008: 6), Mugabe's elder brother Donato noted that their mother told them that "Robert was going to be an important somebody, a leader" and that Bona in her faith "believed that Father O' Hea had brought this message from God, she took it very seriously." Mugabe's mother "believed he was a holy child and she wanted him to become a priest" and as he grew up, Mugabe himself "believed he was born to rule and behaved accordingly, once the king always the king" (Holland 2008: 6, 192) was his political attitude.

Mugabe carried himself as such and accordingly, a chosen one, in many social ways he removed himself from the society of boys and girls his age. Clearly, Mugabe's childhood landscape was dominated by beliefs, and especially his mother's, of being a chosen one of God. So beholden did Mugabe become to the Jesuit priest that as a grown man at the Lancaster House Conference in 1979, that paved his way to power, he exclaimed that "one day he would like to pray at O, Hea's grave (Meredith 2002a, b: 22), perhaps in celebration that O'Hea's prophecy about him was getting fulfilled. Idolising those he believed to have delivered him to power and an appetite to be idolised himself seems to be a tendency that grew in Mugabe and that he grew up with, until it was weaponised into an idolatrous will to power. The desire to go and hold a fast and a prayer at the grave of his Jesuit mentor was also from Mugabe a gesture of gratitude to a great father who filled the gap made by his absent father.

Describing Jews and their belief of being the chosen people of God, for instance, Edward Said (1999) states that such a belief can turn a people into tyrants that walk the earth with impunity. As such, belief in his being a chosen one of God might have injected Mugabe with an attitude of importance and impunity that followed him all his political life. Further, "the sons of St Francis Xavier," of which Mugabe was a special one at the Jesuit Mission at Kutama, "were exhorted to save the heathens beyond the borders of their tight-knit community by becoming teachers" (Holland 2008: 4); they were charged with a missionary spirit to go out and save other lost natives, a spirit that might have made Mugabe feel like a superior teacher and saviour to others earlier and later in his political life. A spirit of knowing it all and of being an inspired and chosen political deliverer might have been the root of Mugabe's stubborn will to power.

For us to effectively understand the power of the Jesuit philosophy and the influence that it might have had on the political thought and practice of Mugabe, a brief examination of the doctrine of the Society of Jesus that scholars have engaged with (Little 1952: 34) is needed. Rene Fullop-Miller, F.S. Flint and D.F. Tait (1930) wrote of "the power and Secret of the Jesuits" as a stubborn influence in world religion and politics. Critics of the book by the three authors noted that "anyone who in our days seeks the truth about Jesuitism will find more valuable help" (Walsh 1930: 338) in reading the narrative that was considered seminal in unmasking Jesuitism. The book reveals that the teachings of "Ignatius Loyola," the founder of the Society of Jesus, "taught that even those who did not possess the supernatural illumination, could achieve perfection by their own efforts and pains" (Walsh 1930: 339). This teaching entails that an individual even without direct inspiration from God and the supernatural can achieve great power and success. In the case of Mugabe at the Jesuit Mission, Holland (2008: 8) states that the great lesson was that "from humble beginnings" with "discipline" he could "triumph over adversity" and prevail over all odds to become a "king of the castle."

After a study of Mugabe and his Jesuit background and influences, Paul Moorcroft (2012: 44) noted that the prime Jesuit principle that Mugabe internalised was that "only self-discipline can allow a person to triumph over adversity" and "self-discipline was a constant feature of Mugabe until late in life when absolute power turned his original virtue into utter self-indulgence." The unusual gravitas, exceptional mind and exceptional heart of the toddler Mugabe that Father Jerome O'Hea noted was further enhanced, disciplined and fortified into a passion for overcoming all odds and opposition, which is a will to power of a tyrannical kind.

The students and critics of Jesuitism note that central to its teachings is that "perfection could be attained in an ordinary manner by will and purpose more surely than by contemplative mysticism" (Walsh 1930: 339). In other words, with a strong will and a purpose a human being, Mugabe was taught, can achieve excellence and perfection over others. This teaching, added to his beliefs in being a chosen one of God, should have given him the superman sensibility that is described by Friedrich Nietzsche. The "secret of the Jesuits turns out to be their Pelagianism (free will and asceticism that was taught by Pelagius)" and their "power" was their

"Protestantism, their readiness for any compromise" (Walsh 1930: 339), their ability to be anything anytime in a given place. The Jesuits, Walsh argues, became a brotherhood that strived to come to terms with the world by mastering all forms of human expression from theology, natural science, philosophy, art, economics, constitutional law and jurisprudence. They aspired to be masters of the universe.

Mugabe's storied love for education that propelled him to achieve a multiplicity of university degrees might have been, after all, a passion of the will to power imparted on him by the Jesuits. The Jesuit Christian, it seems, because of the belief in free will and the agency of man, becomes a Christian that really does not need Christ as he believes in his own power to achieve and overcome. Arguing psychoanalytically of Christianity at large, Slavoj Zizek (2015: 77) suggests that while the church wears an institutional mask, and exudes a conscious performance of holiness, it has a pagan unconscious which is its true reality and drive. Zizek cites G.K. Chesterton who notes that:

> The outer ring of Christianity is a rigid guard of ethical abnegations and professional priests; but inside that inhuman guard you will find the old human life dancing like children, and drinking wine like men; for Christianity is the only frame for pagan freedom. (Chesterton 1995: 164)

Mugabe, in his will to power, came to wear the inhuman mask of the church and of Christianity and to personify its ethics and holiness, more as a performance than as an actuality. The church, like a good parent, was keen to be seen to have produced a deliverer for the people, a fulfilment of its mission. Even as Mugabe began to commit atrocities and to violate human rights, the "catholic church became a protective Father that could not admit the child's mess" (Holland 2008: 157) and continued to own him, but in his own Jesuit free will and political agency he was willing to threaten the priests who cautioned him and say that "when the church leaders start being political we regard them as political creatures—and we are vicious in that area" (Holland 2008: 147). He needed the church as long as it supported his power and not when it began to question and threaten it. The church is political by its nature and Mugabe was partly politicised in the church; he only did not want the politics of the church that was opposed to his own. He wanted a church and a religion that believed in him as an imaginary son of God. Accordingly, Mugabe used the church as a mask for his will to power and political paganism and the church used him as a flag to display its ability to supply deliverance on earth; he was later to embarrass the church and threaten it with violence; he had become a true Christian without Christ, in the Zizekian sense, a real Christian with full benefits of paganism.

Mugabe's Jesuitism that was combined with his bottled-up childhood anger and belief in chosenness developed into a will to power that was willing and ready to overcome the same church that brought him up. As Christians that also believed in the agency of the self, their critics argued, the Jesuits believed that "the end justifies the means" and were willing to "influence the masses, and know how to exploit the wildest superstitions of the people for their own purpose" (Walsh 1930: 340) as will later be narrated about Mugabe in this book. Mugabe elected "not divine norms but the human foot rule" that Walsh reports as the true drive of the Jesuit spirit.

It is acknowledged that "Mugabe's Jesuit education imbued him with a spirit of discipline" (Norman 2004: 47), but that strong discipline and steel will became usable for evil. A trusted friend and personal spiritual advisor to Mugabe, Jesuit priest and head of the mission in Harare shared with Heidi Holland the lessons that the Jesuit taught Mugabe in Kutama. Mugabe was injected with "intellectual rigour" that was accompanied by "self-consciousness" which taught an individual person to "defend his actions" and "to practice talking to oneself in meditation," to "listen to the heart, listen to the self" to have no interest in personal needs, and be efficient in what one does (Holland 2008: 143).

Intellectual rigour can easily breed intellectual snobbery and self-consciousness combined with the will always to defend one's actions can breed a feeling of righteousness which is the true substance of tyrants. Meditation as dialogue with the self, and not a prayer to a higher power, can be prayer to the self that easily can degenerate into a god-consciousness that is a tyrannical sensibility. Meditation and talking to the self are not far from self-worship which is also otherwise the desire to be worshipped by others. After his Jesuit education, socialisation and conditioning, Mugabe's religiosity became complicated, if not corrupted, it was after all:

Such-pseudo-religiosity (that) arises out of the hotchpotch of ingredients that make up Mugabe's political creed, and which might be described as Pan-African nationalism, founded upon a base of agrarian Maoism. It remains the core belief amongst Pan-African nationalists: a philosophy in which the peasant is exalted, the land is worshipped, much in the way the Nazi's revered the soil. (Hope 2003: 16)

In other words, Mugabe's religious sensibility became confused and complicated with secular ideologies and political passions that produced in him a tyrant of some extents, with a dangerous god-complex. As cited in Paul Moorcraft, Andrew Young, President Jimmy Carter's envoy in the late 1970s, remarked that "the trouble with Robert Mugabe is that when you have got a Jesuit education mixed with Marxist ideology, you have got a hell of a guy to deal with" (Moorcraft 2012: 19). Mugabe did become a true hell of a guy once in power. In power, Robert Mugabe carried himself with a "semi-religious temperament" that smelt of "communism and Christianity" but had lost the best of both beliefs and passions (Hope 2003: 75); a complicated communism and confused Christianity may become a toxic political ideology and will to power, a religio-ideologico-political fundamentalism. Jesuit philosophy is, as it appears, a stubborn philosophy of excellence and art of overcoming, surviving and conquering adversity. Depending on whose hands it is and which head drives it, in practice the philosophy can be a monstrous will to power. In Mugabe's head and hands, Jesuitism became a true monstrous philosophy of power. In Mugabe the monstrous philosophy and practice found a ready and willing vessel.

THE EDUCATION OF ROBERT MUGABE

After the above exploration of how Mugabe was Jesuitised it is important to examine his education specifically. The nature and depth of Mugabe's education, and how he used his education as a recommendation to power, are of interest to any engagement with the political and power such as this book is pursuing. In colonial and post-colonial Africa, education and educational qualifications became instrumentalised and even fetishised by black politicians as a recommendation to power. Achille Mbembe (1992: 27) notes that "the enumeration of the slightest educational achievement is one of the postcolonial codes of prestige" where leaders "cite the number of diplomas with great care, they show off their titles." In observance of the same, Thandika Mkandawire (2005: 24) states that there is a negative tendency amongst African leaders, for purposes of legitimation of their power, to pretend to be philosopher kings and most times present their gut feelings and opinions as political philosophy. Mugabe did, in tone and accent, strive to have his political opinions received as deep philosophy.

At high school, Mugabe was determined to be a teacher (Holland 2008: 11), not a philosopher or a politician. The dream to be a teacher took Mugabe to the Ghana of the 1960s that was already independent and under the leadership of Kwame Nkrumah, where, as an expatriate teacher at St Mary's College in the town of Takoradi, Mugabe experienced black euphoria and black power (Hill 2003: 52) that were being experienced and celebrated there. Being resident and working in an independent African country injected Mugabe with passionate dreams of an independent Zimbabwe. The early 1960s were the time when British Prime Minister Harold McMillan had spoken of the "winds of change" and decolonisation that were sweeping across Africa. Mugabe got intoxicated with the air of political independence in Ghana. Independent Ghana gave Mugabe a sense of the possibility and feasibility of an independent future Zimbabwe. Mugabe saw himself in Nkrumah and began to feel and see a potential Nkrumah in himself, a powerful, educated, black leader of his country. Independent Ghana filled Mugabe with envy and ambition of a kind as I note in this book.

The political uses to which Mugabe put his education are treated in some length in the next chapter. While on a visit back home in Rhodesia in 1960 on the 20th of July, as a teacher from Ghana, Mugabe was asked to address an NDP rally in Hatfield. That address became Mugabe's formal entrance into politics (Hill 2003: 53). Mugabe was introduced to the crowd of many thousands as a distinguished scholar that had travelled the world and boasted three university degrees (Meredith 2002a, b: 26–27). University education, travel, work and stay in independent Ghana became an important recommendation for Mugabe to the crowd that roared in applause as he clearly articulated issues and narrated anecdotes from independent Ghana (Hill 2003: 53). Superior education and travel became fetishised and instrumentalised by Mugabe as part of his will to power. Education was used to build a distance between Mugabe and the rest. An intellectual image, even if it was not supported by any intellectual substance, could work as serious political capital in an Africa and a Rhodesia where educational opportunities were scarcely available to black people. The few educated black Africans, at the time, were regarded as the eyes, ears and mouths of their poor and illiterate people. The scarcity of educated, travelled and well-spoken black leaders became a vacancy for Mugabe's political messianism; he became the deliverer, representative and spokesperson the people had always needed. The mass of the colonised people's hunger for messiahs and heroes created an opportunity for Mugabe. Like a good Jesuit, he feasted on the opportunity.

Not only in Africa is an intellectual image usable for power and prestige. Erich Fromm (1986: 15) describes how even Joseph Stalin, a tyrant who had no literary or scientific talents, or any intellectual aptitude for that matter, was forced by the wish to seem and sound educated to write books or have them written in his name. The drive to use education and intellection for the legitimation of leadership and power has led many political leaders, in their will to power, to resort even to plagiarism (Fromm 1986: 76). Mugabe clearly understood the potency of superior education in the pursuit of political power. Talking about his increasing number of university degrees Mugabe said, "I do it for myself and for Zimbabwe" and "I know that one day we both will need these degrees" (Norman 2004: 62). "We both" in reference to himself and Zimbabwe points to how very early Mugabe came to equate himself with the country in stature and gravity. Education had become for him part of the passion and baptism of the messiah; it was no longer education as the development of the individual but also an effort at delivering a country and its people; he had begun to conflate the nation with himself. In an appetite for power, Chilean dictator Augusto Pinochet, for instance, was pushed to embarrassing plagiarism in his political effort to be known and understood as "narrator, historian and strategist (Burbach 2003: 31). Mugabe's energetic pursuit of education was in the full knowledge of how an image as an educated leader can be an avenue to power.

Many university degrees, eloquent speech and the sojourn in Ghana made Mugabe special, especially at that time. Africans, in different countries, during colonialism, sought knowledge as an instrument of national emancipation and integrity (Nkrumah 1964: 4). Education, especially higher education in combination with Christianity, had become an important facilitator of entrance by African peoples and their leaders into modernity (Mangcu 2008: 22). Even as he was informed but not educated, not developed into a rounded and ethical human being and leader, but only had a veneer of it (Holland 2008: 47), Mugabe weaponised his many university degrees for power and used his oratory prowess to become a leader amongst other leaders and a spokesperson for the liberation movement in Rhodesia. Diploma and degree certificates became fetishes and passports to power for the black elite in colonial and post-colonial Africa.

Mugabe explained his sojourn in Ghana as an adventure: "I went as an adventurer, I wanted to see what it would be like in an independent African state" (Onslow and Plaut 2018: 41). Before he went to Ghana, Mugabe in 1949 was admitted to the University of Fort Hare, a hot pot of an intellectual space, that produced many African political leaders, some that Mugabe personally encountered there (Hill 2003: 51). It is also at the University of Fort Hare that Mugabe encountered the influential writings of Karl Marx and Friedrich Engels (Hill 2003: 51) that were a kind of revolutionary bible of African liberation movements. At that stage Mugabe began to mix his Catholic and Jesuit ideology with Marxism and African nationalism (Hill 2003: 51). Encountering radical African nationalists and political activists at Fort Hare University and also accessing Marxist literature that was largely banned in Rhodesia at the time nourished Mugabe's political ideas and ambition, and energised his growing will to power. Higher education, travel in Africa and contact with other African nationalist political activists did not only radicalise Mugabe but also, added to his superior oratory skills, gave him an edge over other political leaders, guerrillas and the black masses in Rhodesia. That was the edge that Mugabe weaponised as a will to power and a monumentalisation of his believed chosenness, and pre-destination to leadership and greatness.

The education that Mugabe received and prided himself with was, in many ways, still colonial and colonising education, which, in the case of the education of Jomo Kenyatta of Kenya, Bronislaw Malinowski (1938: ix) described as "the injury of higher education" in that it turned the colonised into colonisers of their own people. Colonially educated black leaders became some kinds of colonisers that were full of a sense of superiority and power over their own people. Mugabe's vaunted higher education became a legitimation and an energy of his will to power, turning him into a leader who fought colonialism and also became a kind of coloniser to his people that he ruled with an iron fist. The education of the colonised, especially political leaders, became part of what cemented and also troubled the relations between the coloniser and the colonised that Albert Memmi (1974: 5) discussed in depth. Education gave such political activists and leaders as Mugabe a sense of superiority compared to the mass of their people and a kind of political confidence that they could contest and replace the white colonisers as leaders. The black and educated political class became a troubling and also a troubled class that was on the spot, caught in between being true liberators of their people or proper sell-outs and conspirators with colonialism, and nothing else. In the next chapter I develop the discussion on how education was used to produce Mugabe into a performer of power that weaponised his storied education for purposes of dominating others and the country.

THE PRISON FORMATION OF ROBERT MUGABE

In many ways, the prison experience became another kind of school that formed and produced Mugabe and his will to power. Prison added to how Mugabe became a colonising colonial subject. In his observations, arguments and conclusions on "the birth of the prison" and the penal system, Michel Foucault (1977) suggests that prison was meant to discipline and punish renegades and get them to comply with dictates of the hegemonic power of the day. Prison is in that way a kind of school that disciplines, shapes and is intended to produce a certain kind of person. The prison in the argument of Foucault both punished the body and tried to reform the soul and sensibility of the imprisoned, and in many ways the jail is a formative and productive institution. Here I seek to explore how the Rhodesian colonial prison sought to discipline and punish Mugabe and also how he instrumentalised the prison experience which became suffering that contributed to his will to power. Mugabe and other Rhodesian liberation political activists were detained without trial in 1964. "Personally" Mugabe and "other old guard" nationalist leaders "had suffered severe hardship, imprisonment, exile and isolation" (Ranger 1980: 75). In prison, Mugabe suffered physically and emotionally as he was even refused permission by the Rhodesian regime to attend the funeral of his son Nhamodzenyika that died back in Ghana (Holland 2008: 27). Prison was for Mugabe and others a harrowing place that occasioned a hellish experience. Friedrich Nietzsche (1969: 233), as part of the enunciation of the concept of the will to power in Zarathustra, presented suffering as part of the wounding that is a preparation for power and overcoming of obstacles and adversity. The pain of suffering is in the scheme of the will to power a provocation to the striving for survival and power. As a Jesuit of a kind Mugabe took adversity and pain as a test of his strength, a kind of baptism of fire and his own preparation for a mission of power and rule in the postcolony.

Mugabe took the punishment and suffering in prison as a school and a qualification that gave him entitlement to power. Mac McGuiness, one of Mugabe's jailers and prison warders, told Heidi Holland (2008: 32) that over and above resenting being in prison, Mugabe "regarded it as a battleground for power, which it was, we talked about that. He saw it as a battle of wits and strategy," he said, "and believe you me, Mugabe had a first class brain for the job." In that way Mugabe instrumentalised and weaponised his stay and suffering in prison as a strategy and entitlement for power, over and above that it equipped him with the anger and bitterness that he was later to vent out on political opponents. The will to power is a passion that needs anger and enmity for its life. Mugabe said prison did not cause him personal bitterness but "you came back with the sense that you had been punished for nothing, and that you must fight for that for which you have been punished"; he insisted that "such has not come" even long after release in 1974 (Moorcraft 2012: 19). Long after the prison experience of pain, Mugabe carried the anger and urge to keep angry and fighting real and imaginary enemies; having suffered and been persecuted in prison became a permanent excuse to continue fighting whoever and whatever presented itself as an obstacle to his power.

Interestingly, the prison punishment became a reason and a prize that gave Mugabe the will to fight even those that opposed his rule. The prison injury became a permanent wound that he kept permanently and continuously bleeding so that he could talk and fight about it. During the long years in power Mugabe reminded his supporters and opponents that he and his comrades did not stay so long in prison in order to lose but to keep power. Stay and suffering in prison became a political credential and recommendation to power in post-independence Zimbabwe that no one knew how to take away from Mugabe. Those that had not gone to prison were not qualified to contest power or seek political office. The colonial prison and the war of liberation itself were made into an impossible university of life only whose graduates could participate in the leadership of the Zimbabwean postcolony. The will to power does not only mobilise for power such attainments as education but also pain and suffering are turned into talismans for power.

The use by Mugabe of his stay and suffering in prison as a kind of motivation for the will to power is expressed in how he combined prison life with education and more learning. Notably, "in prison Robert Mugabe returned to his bookish ways" (Holland 2008: 26). Mugabe exhorted his fellow inmates in prison not to "waste prison time" but to use it to study and better themselves as future leaders of the country (Hill 2003: 61). In this education while in prison strategy Mugabe led by example by showing discipline in prison life as he did outside (Meredith 2002a, b: 33). He not only read and studied himself but also taught other prisoners (Meredith 2002a, b: 34) while also, in that way, asserting his authority and superiority over them which he was to continue after prison as the most educated of them all. In many ways Mugabe's public political performance has been that of a high priest, a school headmaster and as the "chancellor of all universities in the country," the teacher of the nation, a supplier of high knowledge and superior thinking in the postcolony. Ceremonially, but politically significant, other prisoners made him the "prison headmaster" (Holland 2008: 26–27; Hill 2003: 61).

Mugabe is also remembered for making fiery political speeches in prison (Hill 2003: 61) to other prisoners, probably displaying his oratory arsenal, rehearsing for power after prison and also exhibiting his superior mind that he weaponised as a strong recommendation to power before and during his years in power. The experience of being punished and of suffering in prison, much like the persecution of any messiah, was used by Mugabe as a learning opportunity in shape of actually studying academically and also picking up lessons of punishing and causing pain which he was to reproduce in disciplining his own political opponents (Hill 2003: 61).

In Mugabe, the imprisoned was slowly internalising the prison system that he was to reproduce and use to punish his own victims in the classic way in which most of those in Africa who fought colonialism later became colonial overlords who dominated their own people. Like the school and the university college, prison became for Mugabe a site for internalising colonial sensibility and preparing himself, knowingly and unknowingly, for his role as a tyrannical and violent political leader that was to use punishment as weapon of rule. Prison gave Mugabe the much needed pain and the rage that he was to vent, reproduce and transmit in his tenure as the leader of Zimbabwe. In that way Mugabe became a permanent prisoner of colonial pain, suffering and anger—he carried the prison in him and with it he was to imprison many in Zimbabwe.

From the long and painful school of prison Mugabe does not seem to have gained and graduated in the same education as Nelson Mandela. Prison appears to have dehumanised Mugabe and humanised Mandela. This might be an indication that other personal and idiosyncratic factors might have contributed to the formation of Mugabe into a monster besides the pain and suffering of prison life and punishment. Mugabe was in jail for eleven years while Mandela was in for twenty-seven years. Reflecting on what prison did to him Mandela said:

> It was during those long and lonely years that my hunger for freedom of my people became a hunger for the freedom of all people, white and black. I

knew as well as I know anything that the oppressor must be liberated just as surely as the oppressed. A man who takes away another man's freedom is a prisoner of hatred; he is locked behind the bars of prejudice and narrow-mindedness. I am not truly free if I am taking away someone else's freedom, just as surely as I am not free when my freedom is taken from me. The oppressor and the oppressed alike are robbed of their humanity. (Mandela 1994: 611)

Mandela seems to have suffered prison not as a personal injury but as a reminder to him of the importance of human freedom and dignity. The colonial prison and its wounding sent Mugabe to the opposite direction of bitterness, anger and vengeance. Zimbabweans were supposed to be eternally grateful that he suffered for them. He became the Messiah that after crucifixion and resurrection returns to demand compensation for his pains at the political cross. Power, for Mugabe, became a religion in which those that he led were supposed to continuously pay homage to the messiah that suffered on their behalf, a messiah that daily demands praises, support and homage or else he unleashes hell itself on earth. Mandela's humanist and liberatory lesson about and from the colonial prison led Sabelo Ndlovu-Gatsheni (2016) to conclude that Mandela was possessed of decolonial humanism, especially that, unlike Mugabe as I note, Mandela saw the need for the freedom of both the oppressor and the oppressed as part of true liberation where revenge has no political place. The tyrant in the postcolony does not want to know himself or to be known as one that is attacking people but one that is carrying out operations of revenge, feeding grudges and getting even with those that previously injured him. The tyrant severally presents himself as a justifiably angry victim, not an oppressor. In a Mugabe that was charged with a tyrannical will to power, the prison experience gave the right sense of victimhood that was turned around as vengeance that became usable in oppressing those that found themselves under his domination.

The Ideological Intoxications of Robert Mugabe

Mugabe cannot be fully understood without an exploration of the ideological influences and the maddening intoxications of ideologies he toyed with and pretended to. I understand ideological belief and practice to be intoxicating and maddening because of their impassioned but also biased energies. In his description of ideology, Slavoj Zizek (2013: 4) says it is "a set of explicit and implicit, even unspoken, ethico-political and other posi-tions, decisions, choices, etc. which predetermine our perception of facts, what we tend to emphasise or ignore, how we organise facts into a consis-tent whole of a narrative," and in that way Zizek calls ideology a strong kind of bias. Here, I reflect on exactly that, the strong ideological biases that Mugabe held and which held him, how the nationalist and Marxist ideologies that fuelled the Zimbabwean and African liberation struggles might have contributed to the political and philosophical formation of Mugabe, how the ideologies became for him and others a kind of strong and blinding bias. The previous chapter briefly treated the intoxicating effects of ideology as fuel to the will to power.

Based on his study of Karl Mannheim's "ideology and Utopia" thesis, Gilbert Khadiagala has distinguished between what ideologies and utopias do differently in the progression of history in Africa. Ideologies are those ideas that both maintain and stabilise an existing order while utopias are a family of ideas that force change in the prevailing social and political order (Khadiagala 2010: 376). It is the pursuant observation of this book that the nationalist and Marxist ideologies that drove the Zimbabwean strug-gle for liberation in which Mugabe was instrumental turned out to main-tain and stabilise rather than seek to totally overthrow colonialism and coloniality, to the extent that Mugabe in power ended up being a colo-niser in a black skin to his own people. In a speech on the "struggle for Southern Africa" Mugabe (1987: 311) expresses a clear understanding of colonial and imperial domination of the Global South by the Global North, and how African countries have been reduced into "spheres of influence" of western political and economic powers. In spite of that clear understanding nationalist and Marxist sensibility seems to have limited Mugabe's ability to see and to act beyond the ideological perimeters and limits that colonialism created. Mugabe's otherwise clear understanding of the world systemic workings of colonialism did not enable him to think and act in liberatory and liberating terms. He remained stuck, somehow, in the cycles of domination.

In the critique of "the pitfalls of national consciousness" in the African liberation struggles Frantz Fanon (1961: 1) observed a problem of "unpreparedness of the educated classes, the lack of practical links between them and the mass of the people, their laziness, and let it be said their cowardice." Nationalism produced African nationalists into racists, tribal-ists, xenophobes and nativists who revived, rather than dethroned, colo-nialism and colonial domination. The Gukurahundi Genocide that the

Mugabe regime carried out in Matabeleland is understood to have been mostly driven by ethnic and tribalist hatred (Moorcraft 2012). That genocide continues to be a divisive event in Zimbabwean history and politics to the extent that genuine nation building has not taken place as secessionist movements and protests keep popping up, in the same way in which Fanon (1961) predicted in his condemnation of the toxicity of nationalism that has a tendency to be exclusionary, nativist and conflictual. Fanon warned that domineering nationalism led by majority tribes cannot build nations but produces secessionist movements and sub-nations by its domination. In a way, nationalism became inherently infected with the undemocratic and violent politics of colonialism that it rose up to fight in Africa:

> But perhaps there was something inherent in nationalism itself even before the wars and the adoption of socialism, which gave rise to authoritarianism. Maybe nationalism's emphasis on unity at all costs—its subordination of trade unions and churches and all other African organisations to its imperatives—gave rise to an intolerance of pluralism. Maybe nationalism's glorification of the leader gave rise to a post-colonial cult of personality. Maybe nationalism's commitment to modernisation, whether socialist or not, inevitably implied a 'commandist' state. (Bhebhe and Ranger 1995: 2)

Ngwabi Bhebhe and Terence Ranger note that nationalism as an ideology even before it was mixed with Marxist and socialist thinking could have had its own underside of violence and authoritarianism. The nationalist underside and its political passions of commandist leadership would have shaped and drove leaders such as Mugabe into tyranny. For that reason, Sabelo Ndlovu-Gatsheni (2003: 103) notes that what has escaped observation is that nationalist struggles of Zimbabwe did not simply become "schools of democracy" that "put people first" but they also became negative schools of despotism, authoritarianism, violence and the cult of the personality of the leader, such as became Mugabe as the leader of Zimbabwe. When Robert Mugabe infamously described himself as having "degrees in violence" he might have spoken as a graduate of the nationalist school of tyranny that Sabelo Ndlovu-Gatsheni describes. In that way, Mugabe as a nationalist leader became a product of a violent and despotic nationalist political culture that did not prepare him for democratic leadership but shaped and energised him for a toxic will to power that led to his infamous tyrannical leadership.

In his engagement with African nationalism and Marxism as ideologies that had "power" but also became "faked" philosophies, Achille Mbembe (2002a: 629) advances the idea that there was forceful falsehood in the political and liberatory claims of the two ideologies. That falsehood led to nationalism and Marxism becoming the opposite of what they proposed, advancing dominance instead of liberation, and the leaders consequentially becoming dominators and not liberators:

> I develop the idea that Marxism and nationalism, as practiced in Africa throughout the twentieth century, gave rise to two narratives on African identity: *nativism* and *Afro-radicalism*. I contend that the objective of these two discourses was not only to pronounce once and for all the "truth" on the issue of what Africa and Africans is (theory), but also to chart what might or should be the destiny of Africa and Africans in the world (praxis). I state that when analyzed closely, these two orthodoxies are revealed to be faked philosophies (*philosophies du travestissement*). As dogmas and doctrines repeated over and over again rather than methods of interrogation, they have led to a dramatic contraction and impoverishment both in the modes of conceptualizing Africa and in the terms of philosophical inquiry concerning the region. Nativism, everywhere actively lamenting the loss of purity, is a form of cultural-ism preoccupied with questions of identity and authenticity. Faced with the malaise resulting from the encounter between the West and the indigenous worlds, nativism proposes a return to an ontological and mythical "Africanness" in which the African subject might once again say "I" and express him—or herself in his or her own name. Drawing its fundamental categories from a Marxist political economy, Afro-radicalism claims to have founded a so-called revolutionary politics, which seeks to break away from imperialism and dependence. (Mbembe 2002b: 629)

Afro-radicalism and nativism that Mbembe describes make the claim but really do not make a break with coloniality but maintain it. The nativism and Afro-radicalism that led Mugabe (2002) at the Earth Summit in Johannesburg to famously and also infamously tell the then British Prime Minister Tony Blair to "keep your England and let me keep my Zimbabwe" can be limiting in that while it expels imperialists from the land it also reduces a country like Zimbabwe and its people into the property of a singular dictator. In adopting nationalism and Marxism, and also being shaped, in thought and in deed by the two ideologies, Mugabe and others were formed and produced into Afro-radicals and nativists that are as incapable of democracy and human liberation as the same colonialists that they set out to fight. Mugabe could so symbolically and politically expel Tony Blair back to England, but to go on to erect himself as the owner of the land and the people of Zimbabwe was to produce himself into an imperial overlord with the same toxic will to power and domination as the colonial settlers and Empire builders. For Mugabe the reference to "my Zimbabwe" was not a simple patriotic statement but an expression of one who thought he owned the country and was entitled to rule over its people in perpetuity. As a leader Mugabe became a true personal empire builder.

An important reflection into the workings of nationalism is provided by Benedict Anderson (1983) who notes not only how nations are imagined communities but also how nationalism produces kinds of patriotisms that get men and women to want to kill and be killed for the nation and the country. Anderson reflects how nationalism produces new enemies, insiders and outsiders and enemies and friends in progression. In the case of Mugabe and Zimbabwean nationalism, Sabelo Ndlovu-Gatsheni (2009: 1140) observes how Mugabe as a nationalist leader began to apply toxic nationalism and patriotism in Zimbabwe and on Zimbabweans:

> After 2000 and 2002 elections in which many people voted for the opposition Movement for Democratic Change (MDC) in the parliamentary and presidential elections, Mugabe began to divide Zimbabweans into traitors, puppets, sell-outs, enemies of the nation versus patriots and authentic national subjects. Those who had voted for the MDC became categorised as traitors, sell-outs, puppets and enemies of Zimbabwe. Only those who voted for and belonged to the ruling Zimbabwean African National Union-Patriotic Front (ZANU-PF) qualified as patriots and authentic national subjects. This mentality enabled a politics of exclusion of a large number of people from the nation and the authorization of violence against those who were written out of the nation. (Ndlovu-Gatsheni 2009: 1140)

Mugabe wrote many Zimbabweans out of the nation. What Sabelo Ndlovu-Gatsheni describes here are the same divisive toxicities of national consciousness that Frantz Fanon condemned and the limits of Afro-radicalism and nativism that Achille Mbembe denounced, where nationalism as an ideology of politics and power turns the nationalist leader into a divider and dominator of the nation, country and the people that he powerfully claims to represent and to liberate. David Moore (2008: 6) goes back to the history of the nationalist movement in Zimbabwe to unearth disunity, the crashing of dissent and rebellions, and uses of violence to institute hegemony of the party line and the tyranny of the person of the leader. Mugabe became a spoilt little brute of ideology.

In the thesis about "discipline and punishment in ZANLA: 1964 TO 1979," a thesis that I reflect on in the next chapter, Gerald Mazarire (2011) explores and uncovers uses of shootings and cruel torture in maintaining discipline and obedience in the nationalist movement that formed and produced Mugabe as the supreme leader who eventually became president of Zimbabwe. This history of Mugabe's nationalist and also Marxist ideological formation and political production became a history of violence and domination that could not possibly have produced a democratic but a tyrannical leader. Nationalism as an ideology that produces political passions creates what Sigmund Freud (1994: 43) called narcissism of difference in nationalist passions where those that disagree with one idea that is loved and believed are hated and must be eliminated without any compromise, understanding or sympathy. Mugabe fanatically enforced the discipline of the party line and obedience to the same through violence.

From a world systemic and decoloniality standpoint, Ramon Grosfoguel states that one of the causes of the failure of decolonisation in the Global South was that Marxist and nationalist political paradigms that were pushed by and also pushed decolonisation movements of the South were limited and incapable of delivering liberation. In that view, "the old national liberation and socialist strategies of taking power" from colonial administrations "at the level of a nation-state are not sufficient, because global coloniality is not reducible to the presence or absence of colonial administration or to the political/economic structures of power" (Grosfoguel 2011: 17). In the absence of colonial administration, politically and otherwise, nationalist leaders such as Mugabe remained behind advancing the colonial machinery of power and in a way being the new colonisers to their own people. By the foregoing, nationalism and Marxism as ideologies that Mugabe advanced and those which also propelled him as political passions seem to have formed and produced him and his political thought and practice, into a leader with a tyrannical and violent will to power. The underside of nationalism and darker side of Marxism came to be personalised in Mugabe that became a true "hell of a guy."

The Colonial Formation of Robert Mugabe

It is one of my principal observations that Mugabe fought colonialism but failed not to become a coloniser himself. Perhaps one of the central questions in understanding the political life and thought of Mugabe has been the question of how a potential liberator became a coloniser and a dominator of his own country and people. This section of the chapter delves into how colonialism as a system formed Mugabe into the political thinker and actor that he eventually became. Sigmund Freud (1994: 16), in pursuit of psychoanalytical understanding, observed that there is a way in which human beings tend to seek pleasure in those things that cause them pain. It might be possible that Mugabe found psychotic enjoyment and fulfilment in reproducing the pain and suffering that he went through. Niccolo Machiavelli (2003a: 24) also noted that there are political leaders who find it hard to introduce change and difference and tend to rule by imitation and duplication. This book stands to observe if, in the Freudians sense, Mugabe was caused so much pain and suffering by colonialism and colonial rule that he inevitably came to seek use of and happiness in the same political system, or that, in the Machiavellian sense, Mugabe came to unconsciously or consciously imitate and reproduce colonial rule as the only form of rule that he knew and had impacted on his psyche. Oppressions such as the slavish and the colonial have a way of co-opting those that fight against them.

Somehow Mugabe came to admire and love colonialism and its infrastructures and systems of power. Heidi Holland (2008: 110) notes that Mugabe's post-independence cabinet of ministers became full of Anglophiles, blacks that admired and loved the English and British way of life. Similarly, Peter Godwin (2008) observes how in dress and cultural taste Mugabe had become thoroughly British. Behind the vitriolic and venomous speeches against the Rhodesians and the British as settlers and imperialists, Christopher Hope (2003) senses in Mugabe a tragic and perplexing Anglophilia and deep admiration for the former colonisers and their political system. As this book shows, at Zimbabwe's independence, Mugabe courted the Rhodesian and British securocrats that ran the colonial administration's security and administration to remain in Zimbabwe and work with him. It is possible that as an inexperienced guerrilla leader Mugabe wanted to benefit from the administrative experience of the departing colonial regime and also to demonstrate reconciliation and forgiveness for the former enemy, for international political legitimation. It is also possible that out of his own will to power, Mugabe admired the efficiency and power of the colonial machinery of security, insecurity and domination, and wished to adopt and inherit the monstrous system for his own use and abuse against political enemies as unfolded in the Gukurahundi Genocide of 1982 to 1987. That Mugabe went on to cut secret political deals with the racist apartheid regime of South Africa behind the back of other African nationalist and liberation movements (Holland 2008: 36) may prove the later to be true, that he admired colonial and apartheid machineries of power and he wanted some for his own will to power. He came to see heroes in such strong colonial leaders as Ian Smith and the series of apartheid South African presidents.

By virtue of his education and political activism Mugabe became part of the African elite that became historically positioned to be complicit in colonialism or to challenge it and confront the white settlers. This class of Africans that Frantz Fanon (1961) accuses of treachery and laziness was a product of colonialism as much as it acted out challenges to colonialism. Peter Ekeh notes thus:

> In the course of colonization a new bourgeois class emerged in Africa composed of Africans who acquired western education in the hands of the colonizers, and their missionary collaborators, and who accordingly were most exposed to European colonial ideologies of all groups of Africans. In many ways the drama of colonialism is the history of the clash between the European colonizers and this emergent bourgeois class. Although native to Africa, the African bourgeois class depends on colonialism for its legitimacy. It accepts the principles implicit in colonialism but it rejects the foreign personnel that ruled Africa. It claims to be competent enough to rule, but it has no traditional legitimacy. In order to *replace* the colonizers and rule its own people it has invented a number of interest-begotten theories to justify that rule. (Ekeh 1975: 96)

In a strong way, as Peter Ekeh demonstrates, colonialism produced through its education system and ideological machinery a class of Africans that might have been black in skin colour and African by nativity but were to be the new colonisers of Africa who became managers of the modern and colonial world system in African countries. Elements of the western bourgeois that colonised Africa found themselves challenged by elements of an emerging African bourgeois class that had their own elitist interests that were removed from the will and interests of the mass of Africans:

The 'fight' for independence was thus a struggle for power between the two bourgeois classes involved in the colonization of Africa. The intellectual poverty of the independence movement in Africa flows from this fact, that what was involved was not the issue of differences of ideas regarding moral principles but rather the issue of *which* bourgeois class should rule Africans. (Ekeh 1975: 102)

The European bourgeois class of colonisers and the African bourgeois class of nationalist decolonisers were both driven by elitist, violent and domineering interests that were colonial in nature. In that way, by producing through education and ideologisation an African pretentious middle class, colonialism produced political leaders such as Mugabe who became the new colonisers of Africa that were black but used colonial sensibility and securocratic methods of ruling and misruling their countries. It is for that reason that Heidi Holland (2008: 84) argues that at the end of the day Ian Smith and Mugabe, the coloniser and the decoloniser, needed each other in order to exist. In pretending to crash terrorism and instil civilisation and development in Rhodesia Ian Smith found his political legitimation, and in pretending to fight settler colonialism, Mugabe also found his political claim to fame in the struggle against colonialism, yet both of them were despots powered by an elitist will to power.

Not only the complicity and competition between the bourgeois colonising class and the bourgeois class of the colonised infected the emerging class of African leaders like Robert Mugabe with a culture of colonial politics. Colonial political culture seems to have infected the politics of the nationalist liberation fighters and given it a violent toxicity that haunted the post-independence era. Colonialism and its violent and authoritarian politics seem to have inevitably corrupted the political mindsets of those that were fighting against it:

Colonial authoritarianism, far from deepening a commitment to democratic norms and practices on the African nationalist elite, merely consolidated an incipient authoritarian psyche in the nationalist leadership. The authoritarianism of the colonial era reproduced itself within the nationalist political movements. The war of liberation too reinforced rather than undermined this authoritarian culture. (Mair and Sithole 2002: 21)

In the bitter fight against colonialism, supposed fighters for liberation such as Mugabe learnt toxic lessons from the enemy and were to reproduce the colonial politics upon their people and countries in the post-independence era. In truth, it appears that "Robert Mugabe's political education came from the autocrat Ian Smith, who had learnt his formative lessons from imperious British colonisers" (Holland 2008: xv). What Peter Hudson (2013: 263) calls the "colonial unconscious" is the way in which at a sub-conscious level, even those that fight coloniality easily tend to learn from it and eventually reproduce it. In many ways therefore, the very struggle against colonialism became a school in political violence and authoritarianism. Unconsciously, Mugabe and his like came to reproduce and repeat colonialism.

Noted above, the same historical narrative about "discipline and punishment in ZANLA: 1964–1979," in reference to the guerrilla movement that Mugabe led and which in many ways conditioned him, Gerald Mazarire (2011) describes festivals of violence in form of shootings in cold blood, torture, assassinations and other inhuman forms of punishment in the guerrilla camps. In his own words Mugabe graphically described the way the guerrillas operated and dealt with dissent: "The ZANU-PF axe must continue to fall upon the necks of rebels when we find it no longer possible to persuade them into the harmony that binds us all" (Mair and Sithole 2002: 22); that is, where political persuasion failed violence and physical elimination became the only option for Mugabe. Coming from that political tradition of the "axe" and political culture of eliminations and assassinations, Mugabe was in actuality not formed for democracy but for tyranny and a nihilist political will to power. The unity that Mugabe talked about was unity only under his leadership, a passion for one man and one-party rule that led him to commit the Gukurahundi Genocide and eliminate ZAPU as an opposition political party, as I note in this book.

So far it appears that Mugabe was conditioned by colonialism and also shaped by the liberation struggle itself into a political thinker and actor that was not ready for democracy but was charged with a tyrannical will to power. However, it also appears that a permitting international relations political climate also existed that allowed Mugabe's tyrannical will to power to thrive and flourish into its bitter fruition. In reference to the post-independence Gukurahundi Genocide, Timothy Scarnecchia (2011), as I will elaborate later, gives details on how Mugabe was able to carry out the genocide because the world superpowers looked aside as they saw Mugabe as a pillar against Russian communism in Southern Africa, and they were keen that post-independence Zimbabwe should be a success. At the time the white and the western world was animated by the right political noises of peace and reconciliation that Mugabe was making (Saunders 2000: 17) and there was no simple indication that a genocide might be unfolding in Zimbabwe. At the time "Britain saw Zimbabwe as a foreign office trophy" (Holland 2008: xiii) "mainly because white people were not being attacked." As a white person that once supported Mugabe, Heidi Holland regrets that: "I realise that I and other well-intentioned individuals may have helped Mugabe to become the man he is today, if we reacted differently to the early signs of paranoia, could Zimbabwe have been saved" (Holland 2008: xiii). Mugabe was the darling of the western world at a time when he should have been condemned and opposed; even the queen of England knighted him soon after the genocide (Holland 2008: 214). In that way, Mugabe also became a product of international relations negligence and blunders. Mugabe's vaunted struggle against settler colonialism and western imperialism, looked at carefully, therefore, becomes what Slavoj Zizek (2016) called a "pseudo-struggle" where one imperial fundamentalism clashes with another fundamentalism in a struggle that is not of interest or of any benefit to the mass of the people. His anti-colonialism, as noted earlier, was a pseudo-struggle of a decolonising effort that was caught up in coloniality.

Mugabe does not seem to have been willing or able to overcome the limits of his faulty anti-colonialism and colonial influence. What Timothy Chappell (2005: 11) calls the "inescapable self" is a philosophical challenge based on the truth that each individual cannot escape the problem that some of his most deeply held certainties about life might be illusions and imprisoning imaginations and fantasies. As noted elsewhere in this book, Mugabe suffered a problem of the "inescapable self" and became unable to overcome his biases. What Mugabe practiced as political ideas and beliefs had become mental prisons. The ideas he used as a fortress to defend his actions quickly turned around to be mental prison walls that prevented him from sensing alternative realities. The strong personal opinions he held turned around to hold him captive.

Mugabe does not seem to have escaped what Erich Fromm (1986: 1) describes as the "chains of illusion" that bind the mind to false realities and beliefs. The Lacanian narcissist that Malcom Bowie (1991) discusses is such a person as Mugabe whose superior education and believed pre-destination of greatness removed him from the real world and located in a hyperreality of the will to power. The paranoiac that Slavoj Zizek (1996) notes as the performer that has two fathers and wears seven veils is also such a person as Mugabe whose life had to be a performance of illusions

and beliefs that he wished could be realities, after believing in his predestined rule for life he performed the life and world of that kind of political messiah. Even after being overthrown from power in a coup, he acted
as the betrayed and crucified messiah whose opponents knew not what
they were doing. In the sum of his conditioning and formation by the
many and different factors discussed above, Mugabe seems to have become
the Fanonian colonised and colonising native, for "the native is an
oppressed person whose permanent dream is to become the persecutor"
(Fanon 2001: 41). Mugabe's experience of life and colonialism did not,
unlike Nelson Mandela, condition him into a liberator and conciliator but
into a coloniser of a kind.

On the Politics of the Will to Live

Mugabe's infamous rule in Zimbabwe gives truth to the cliché that politics
is a dirty game and that political leaders can be dirty and also dangerous
people. The cliché that politics is a dirty game unfortunately seeks to give
respectability and acceptance to a current of thought which holds the false
belief that there will never be fairness and justice in politics. The cliché that
like all clichés is tired and boring but keeps finding fresh relevance in political thought and practice, the world over, maintains that politicians will
always be tricksters or violent rogues. Following the questionable wisdom
of that cliché, Mugabe, in all the will to power to which he was formed and
produced, would be understood and rationalised as but another politician
among other politicians in the world and in the game of politics.

Critical humanist and decolonial philosophers from different directions
of the world have tried to propose another politics that is not the will to
power and have described another kind of politician that are not formed
into tricksters and violent rogues. In all his limits and ignorance of any
other world besides the white European world, Immanuel Kant (1981: 1)
in his rumination on the "answer to the question: what is enlightenment?"
proposed a politics where politicians make "public use of reason" and
strive towards "perpetual peace" where even an enemy in politics can be
trusted to respect the humanity of his adversaries and not practice the politics of annihilation. In imagining a political enemy that can be trusted
Kant imagined a politician that would understand and treat his opponents
as adversaries and not ultimate enemies that are to be eliminated. Mugabe's
political example is an example that did not value either the public use of
reason or the treatment of opponents and enemies in a trustworthy and

critically humane manner. Mugabe largely did not see his political opponents as the tolerable other but as sinners and enemies whose due treatment was elimination. So much like in the will to power that Nietzsche
(1990: 54) describes, Mugabe had more need for enemies than friends, in
opposition and advance against an enemy did he find himself necessary
and fulfilled. Mugabe was at his best and inevitable self when ranting, distributing threats and pronouncing declarations and military operations.
He seemed much more comfortable and real when angry and on the war
path than in peace.

I, in this book, seek to reflect on the politics and philosophy of liberation that is opposed to the political example of Mugabe and the will to
power. For instance, Ramon Grosfoguel (2011: 1) has proposed "anti-
systemic politics" that proposes life and the human beyond "Third World
and Eurocentric fundamentalisms" where "we can overcome Eurocentric
modernity without throwing away the best of modernity as many Third
World fundamentalists do." This is a liberatory politics that does not
imagine precolonial innocence and purity, nor does it fantasise some post-
colonial authenticity that is removed from modernity, but seeks a liberated
and empowered here and now. In this politics, narcissist nihilism that goes
with the will to power does not have a place.

In being nativist, for instance, asking Tony Blair to keep to England
and insisting that he would keep his Zimbabwe, the Mugabe who once
promised that Africans will one day throw away their shoes in rejection of
western culture (Hope 2003) was practicing Third World fundamentalism
that makes the world a small and inhuman place. Mugabe's fundamentalist, nationalist and nativist territorialism had him imagine Zimbabwe as his
personal property and the people his personal subjects. He fantasised of a
pure and innocent Africa that would be removed from the world, isolated
and closed to itself. Similar to Grosfoguel, Paulo Freire (1993) proposed
a politics of liberation where the oppressed, that is the colonised peoples
of Africa and Latin America, did not only seek to liberate themselves but
also free the oppressors who were imprisoned in their being oppressors.
Such liberators aim to create a human universe:

> A good example of this is the Zapatista struggle in Mexico. The Zapatistas
> are not anti-modern fundamentalist. They do not reject democracy and
> retreat into some form of indigenous fundamentalism. On the contrary, the
> Zapatistas accept the notion of democracy, but redefine it from a local indig-
> enous practice and cosmology, conceptualizing it as "commanding while

obeying" or "we are all equals because we are all different." What seems to be a paradoxical slogan is really a critical decolonial redefinition of democracy from the practices, cosmologies and epistemologies of the subaltern. (Grosfoguel 2011: 36)

Mugabe was unable to redefine democracy from a Zimbabwean and African cosmology; instead, he duplicated and repeated the colonial imagination of nations and countries. In his fight against colonialism, imperialism and the toxicity of western modernity and coloniality, Mugabe, as I seek to show in this book, does not seem to have managed to seek to redefine coloniality; he degenerated into affirming and confirming it the way Third World fundamentalists do. He fought colonial domination but failed to overcome its seductions and trappings, and ended up participating in repetitions and reproductions of coloniality. In explaining the "miracle" of the South African transition from apartheid to democracy, a highly unexpected political eventuality, Willie Esterhuyse (2012) said the transition happened reasonably peacefully because blood enemies that were not supposed to see and talk to each other decided to make unlikely friendships and talked. Attempts of and gateways to liberation can at times be occasioned by seemingly impossible friendships and understandings between enemies and opponents in politics.

Mugabe, by the foregoing, does not seem to have been formed and produced to be able to form unlikely friendships and to climb down to talk to enemies; his will to power forbade that level of humility which Kenneth Kaunda (1966) defined as African political humanism, which I will elaborate on later on, in the conclusion, as critical decolonial humanism of the will to live (Dussel 2008) that is opposed to the politics of the will to power. Over and above a critique of Mugabe's politics of the will to power therefore, this book, at its conclusion, posits to propose a critical humanist politics of the will to live. A politics that is neither repetitive nor reproductive of the politics of domination and coloniality. The politics of the will to live departs and overcomes the repetitions, reproductions and multiplications of conquests, dominations and exploitations that define the character of the postcolony. The desire to conquer, dominate and oppress, which is a colonial desire, is what Mugabe failed to overcome, and that is how he failed to be a liberator.

References

Anderson, B. (1983). *Imagined Communities: Reflections on the Origin and Spread of Nationalism*. London & New York. Verso Books.

Arendt, H. (2006). *Eichmann in Jerusalem: A Report on the Banality of Evil*. London: Penguin Books.

Barthel, M. (1984). *The Jesuits: History and Legend of the Society of Jesus*. New York. William Morrow and Company Inc.

Bhebhe, N., & Ranger, T. (eds.). (1995). *Soldiers in Zimbabwe's Liberation War Vol 1*. Harare: University of Zimbabwe Publications.

Bowie, M. (1991). *Lacan*. London: HarperCollins Publishers.

Burbach, R. (2003). *The Pinochet Affair: State Terrorism and Global Justice*. London/New York: Zed Books.

Campbell, H. (2003). *Reclaiming Zimbabwe: The Exhaustion of the Patriarchal Model of Liberation*. Claremont: David Philip Publishers.

Chappell, T. (2005). *The Inescapable Self: An Introduction to Western Philosophy Since Descartes*. London: Orion Publishing Group.

Chesterton, G. K. (1995). *Orthodoxy*. San Francisco: Ignatius Press.

Donato. (2008). In H. Holland (Ed.), *Dinner with Mugabe: The Untold Story of a Freedom Fighter Who Became a Tyrant*. Johannesburg: Penguin Books.

Dussel, E. (2008). *Twenty Theses on Politics*. London/Durham: Duke University Press.

Ekeh, P. (1975). Colonialism and the Two Publics in Africa: A Theoretical Statement. *Comparative Studies in Society and History, 17*(1), 91–112.

Elon, A. (2006). Introduction. In H. Arendt (Ed.), *Eichmann in Jerusalem: A Report on the Banality of Evil*. London. Penguin Books.

Esterhuyse, W. (2012). *Endgame: Secret Talks and the End of Apartheid*. Cape Town: Tafelberg.

Fanon, F. (1961). *The Wretched of the Earth*. New York: Grove Press.

Fanon, F. (2001). *The Wretched of the Earth*. London: Penguin Classics.

Fanon, F. (2008). *Black Skin White Masks*. London: Pluto Press.

Foucault, M. (1977). *Discipline and Punish: The Birth of the Prison*. London: Penguin Books.

Freire, P. (1993). *Pedagogy of the Oppressed*. London. Penguin Books.

Freud, S. (1994). *Civilization and Its Discontents*. New York: Dover Publications.

Fromm, E. (1970). *The Crisis of Psychoanalysis: Essays on Freud, Marx and Social Psychology*. Middlesex: Penguin Books.

Fromm, E. (1986). *Beyond the Chains of Illusion: My Encounter with Marx and Freud*. London: Sphere Books.

Gaidzanwa, R. (2014). Grappling with Mugabe's Masculinist Politics in Zimbabwe: A Gender Perspective. In S. Ndlovu-Gatsheni (Ed.), *Mugabeism?: History, Politics and Power in Zimbabwe*. New York. Palgrave Mcmillan.

Godwin, P. (2008). *The Fear: The Last Days of Robert Mugabe*. New York: Picador.

Grosfoguel, R. (2011). Decolonizing Post-Colonial Studies and Paradigms of Political Economy: Transmodernity, Decolonial Thinking, and Global Coloniality. *Transmodernity: Journal of Peripheral Cultural Production of the Luso-Hispanic World, 1*(1), 1–34.

Gudhlanga, E. (2013). Shutting Them Out: Opportunities and Challenges of Women's Participation in Zimbabwean Politics—A Historical Perspective. *Journal of Third World Studies, 30*(1), 151–170.

Hill, G. (2003). *The Battle for Zimbabwe: The Final Countdown.* Cape Town: Zebra Press.

Hofstadter, R. (1964). The Paranoid Style in American Politics. *Harper's Magazine*, pp. 77–86.

Holland, H. (2008). *Dinner with Mugabe: The Untold Story of a Freedom Fighter Who Became a Tyrant.* Johannesburg: Penguin Books.

Hope, C. (2003). *Brothers Under the Skin: Travels in Tyranny.* London: Pan Macmillan.

Hudson, P. (2013). The State and the Colonial Unconscious. *Social Dynamics: A Journal of African Studies, 39*(2), 263–277.

Kant, I. (1981). *An Answer to the Question: "What is Enlightenment?"* London: Penguin Classics.

Kaunda, K. (1966). *A Humanist in Africa: Letters to Colin M. Morris from Kenneth Kaunda President of Zambia.* London: Longmans.

Khadiagala, G. M. (2010). Two Moments in African Thought: Ideas in Africa's International Relations. *South African Journal of International Affairs, 17*(3), 375–387.

Kirk-Greene, A. H. M. (1991). His Eternity, His Eccentricity, or His Exemplarity: A Further Contribution to the Study of His Excellency the African Head of State. *African Affairs, 90*, 163–187.

Lessing, D. (2013, March 1). The Jewel of Africa. *The New York Review of Books*, p. 1.

Little, S. (1952). In Rene Fullop-Miller (1930), *The Power and the Secret of the Jesuits.* New York. The Viking Press.

Lloyd, R. B. (2002). Zimbabwe: The Making of an Autocratic "Democracy.". *Current History, 101*(655), 219–224.

Macaphulana, D. (2014). Robert Mugabe: An African Head of State and the State of an African Head. *Bulawayo24 News.* 19 December 2014.

Macaphulana, D. M. (2016). Robert Mugabe: The Head of State and State of the Head. In *Bulawayo24 News.* Retrieved February 25, 2016, from https://bulawayo24.com.

Machiavelli, N. (2003a). *The Prince and Other Writings.* (Wayne A. Rebhorn, Trans.). New York: Barnes and Noble Classics.

Machiavelli, N. (2007). Life of Castruccio Castracani. In P. Constantine (Ed.), *The Essential Writings of Machiavelli.* New York: Random House, Inc.

Mair, S., & Sithole, M. (2002). *Blocked Democracies in Africa: Case Study of Zimbabwe Harare.* Harare: Konrad Adenauer Foundation.

Malinowski, B. (1938). Introduction. In J. Kenyatta (Ed.), *Facing Mount Kenya*. London: Heinemann.

Mandela, N. (1994). *Long Walk to Freedom: The Autobiography of Nelson Mandela*. London: Little, Brown and Company.

Mangcu, X. (2008). *To the Brink: The State of Democracy in South Africa*. Scottville: University of KwaZulu Natal Press.

Matyszak, D. (2015). Coup De Grace? Plots and Purges: Mugabe and ZANU-PF's 6th National People's Congress. *Research and Advocacy Unit*. Retrieved July 10, 2019, from www.researchand advocacyunit.

Mazarire, G. C. (2011). Discipline and Punishment in ZANLA, 1964–1979. *Journal of Southern African Studies, 37*(3), 571–591.

Mbembe, A. (1992). Provisional Notes on the Post-colony. *Africa, 62*(1), 3–37.

Mbembe, A. (2001). *On the Postcolony*. Berkeley: University of California Press.

Mbembe, A. (2002a). On the Power of the False. *Public Culture, 14*(3), 629.

Mbembe, A. (2002b). African Modes of Self-writing. *Public Culture, 14*(1), 239–273.

Memmi, A. (1974). *The Coloniser and the Colonised*. London & New York. Earthscan.

Meredith, M. (2002a). *Robert Mugabe: Power, Plunder and Tyranny in Zimbabwe*. Cape Town: Jonathan Ball Publishers.

Meredith, M. (2002b). *Our Votes, Our Guns: Robert Mugabe and the Tragedy of Zimbabwe*. New York: Public Affairs Publishers.

Mkandawire, T. (2005). *"Introduction" African Intellectuals: Rethinking Politics, Language, Gender and Development*. London & New York: Codesria Books/Zed Books.

Moorcraft, P. (2012). *Mugabe's War Machine*. Cape Town: Jonathan Ball Publishers.

Moore, D. (2008). Mamdani's Enthusiasms. *Concerned African Scholars Bulletin, 82*, 49–53.

Moore, D. B. (1991). The Ideological Formation of the Zimbabwean Ruling Class. *Journal of Southern African Studies, 17*(3), 472–495.

Mouffe, C. (2005a). *On the Political*. Abingdon: Routledge.

Mouffe, C. (2005b). *The Return of the Political*. Verso: New York/London.

Mugabe, R. (1987). Struggle for Southern Africa. *Foreign Affairs, 66*(2), 311–327.

Mugabe, R. (2002, July 2). Follow in the Footsteps of Father Zim, In *The Herald*.

Mugabe, R. (2008). Campaign Speech. In Ndlovu-Gatsheni, S. "Rethinking Chimurenga and Gukurahundi in Zimbabwe: A Critique of Partisan National History." *African Studies Review 55* (3). pp. 1–26.

Mujuru, J. (2013, January 13). Mugabe Challengers Bonkers: Mujuru. Retrieved March 10, 2018, from www.newzimbabwe.com.

Ndlovu-Gatsheni, S. (2003). Dynamics of the Zimbabwe Crisis in the 21st Century. *African Journal on Conflict Resolution, 3*(1), 99–105.

Ndlovu-Gatsheni, S. (2009). Making Sense of Mugabeism in Local and Global Politics: 'So Blair, Keep Your England and Let Me Keep My Zimbabwe. *Third World Quarterly, 30*(6), 1139–1158.

Ndlovu-Gatsheni, S. (2016). *The Decolonial Mandela: Peace, Justice and the Politics of Life.* New York: Bergham Books.

Nietzsche, F. (1969). *Thus Spoke Zarathustra.* London. Penguin Books.

Nietzsche, F. (1990). *Twilight of the Idols/ The Anti-Christ.* New York: Penguin Books.

Nkrumah, K. (1964). *Consciencism: Philosophy and Ideology for Decolonisation and Development with particular Reference to the African Revolution.* London: Heinemann.

Norman, A. (2004). *Robert Mugabe and the Betrayal of Zimbabwe.* London: McFarland & Company Publishers.

Onslow, S., & Plaut, M. (2018). *Robert Mugabe.* Johannesburg: Jacana Media.

Plato. (1993). *Republic.* Oxford: Oxford University Press.

Power, S. (2008). How to Kill a Country: Turning a Breadbasket into a Basket Case in Ten Easy Steps-the Robert Mugabe Way. *Atlantic Monthly, 292*(5), 86–101.

Ranger, T. (1980). The Changing of the Old Guard: Robert Mugabe and the Revival of ZANU-PF. *Journal of Southern African Studies, 7*(1), 71–90.

Rene Fullop-Miller. (1930). *The Power and the Secret of the Jesuits.* New York. The Viking Press.

Said, E. W. (1999). *Out of Place: A Memoir.* London: Granta Books.

Saunders, R. (2000). *Never the Same Again: Zimbabwe's Growth Towards Democracy.* Harare: Edwina Spicer Productions.

Scarnecchia, T. (2011). Rationalising Gukurahundi: Cold War and South African Foreign Relations with Zimbabwe, 1981–1983. *Kronos, 37*(1), 89–55.

Schmitt, C. (2007). *The Concept of the Political.* London & Chicago: University of Chicago Press.

Shamu, W. (2011). Mugabe is like Cremora: Shamu. *News Day.* Newsday.co.zw: Accessed 2 March 2019.

Tendi, B.-M. (2011). Robert Mugabe and Toxicity: History and Context Matter. *Representation: Journal of Representative Democracy., 47*(3), 307–318.

Walsh, G. G. (1930). The Power and the Secret of the Jesuits by Rene Fulop-Miller, F.S. Flint and D.F. Tait. *The Catholic Historical Review, 16*(3), 338–340.

Wilber, K. (2017). *Trump and a Post-Truth World.* Colorado: Shambhala.

Zizek, S. (1996). The Seven Veils of Paranoia, or, Why Does the Paranoiac Need Two Fathers? *Constellations, 3*(2), 139–156.

Zizek, S. (2013). Some Bewildered Clarifications: A Response to Noam Chomsky. *International Journal of Zizek Studies, 7*(2), 1–8.

Zizek, S. (2015). *Trouble in Paradise: From the End of History to the End of Capitalism.* London: Penguin Books.

Zizek, S. (2016). *Against the Double Blackmail: Refugees, Terror and Other Troubles with the Neighbours.* London: Allen Lane: Penguin Books.

CHAPTER 4

When the Monsters Go Marching In: Mugabe the Production and Its Spectacles

Mad bob Mugabe is concealing significant secrets and lessons of history…humanising the monster, finding the three dimensional Mugabe instead of a cartoon villain is a process of understanding and not exoneration.
—Heidi Holland (2008: xiv)

As the women's League, (to President Mugabe) we are going to support you. Some want you to be life President, but we say you are irreplaceable to the Presidency. We will appoint you President even in your grave at the National Heroes Acre because you are our unifier. You are faithful before the Lord. Before you were even born God knew you. You were set apart because God did not want you to mix and be contaminated by evil.
—Grace Mugabe (2018: 139–140)

Truly Speaking, in heaven there is God and here on earth there is an angel called Robert Gabriel Mugabe. (To President Mugabe) You are representing God here on earth.
—Kudzai Chipanga (2018: 143)

When political opponents stood up to him and challenged his power, Robert Mugabe frequently went into public rage. Enraged, Mugabe would throw political tantrums and give fiery speeches dispensing threats and curses, pronouncing doom upon his enemies. An angry Mugabe was always a spectacle to watch. Mugabe's true insanity, however, did not

171
W. J. Mpofu, *Robert Mugabe and the Will to Power in an African Postcolony*, African Histories and Modernities, https://doi.org/10.1007/978-3-030-47879-7_4

emanate from the anger that opponents drove him into. More than his opponents and political enemies that drove him into a madness of rage when they challenged him, it is in actuality Mugabe's supporters and flatterers that drove him into an insanity of delusions of grandeur. In swallowing hook, line and sinker, the flattery of sycophants that told him he was "irreplaceable" and that he was a "representative of God here on earth," Mugabe became insane as he got lost in a world of political fantasy. Political power in the hands of such a deluded leader, with a god-complex and gigantic ego, became a weapon in the hands of a dangerous lunatic. In power, controlling spies, soldiers, the police, militias and the public media, Mugabe became a true insane production whose cinematic excesses were acted out on the stage of Zimbabwean history and politics. Mugabe became a spectacular performer of power at its highest madness.

Understanding the political Mugabe, therefore, as a monster and also a pathetic personage, requires a measure of analytical courage. The courage to see and peel the many layers of what is a true political and historical onion might be what it takes to arrive at a kind of settlement on the simple and also complex performer of power that Mugabe became, a production of a kind. There is truth in the observation of Heidi Holland (2008: xiv) that behind the monster that Mugabe became are rich historical and political lessons on how even some of the simplest, the sophisticated and some refined people can be turned into despots. One of my principal observations in this book is that from childhood Mugabe was a fragile and vulnerable human being whose love for power was based more on the fear of powerlessness. The fear of weakness and powerlessness more than the sheer love for power drove Mugabe's desire for power and dominance.

In his vulnerability and its forbidding power over his personality, Mugabe took rather too seriously the prophecies about his divine anointment and anticipated greatness. Derek Matyszak (2015) notes that some around Mugabe circulated the belief that he was divine sponsored, a messenger of God, while the extremists amongst them held the alarming belief that Mugabe was divine himself. There grew a fanatic and Pentecostal political religion around Mugabe that could only madden a fragile soul.

Supporters and flatterers who really did not love him but loved what they could do with his name and power did not help the situation by creating a kind of political cult around him. With prayerful words, they constructed a messiah out of a fearful and ambitious personality that in helplessly believing their supplications became a prisoner of delusions of grandeur that insulated him from the real world.

Grace Mugabe and Kudzai Chipanga, quoted above, only exemplify the many people around Mugabe who, with their own fears, desires and dreams, created around him a world where he was a messiah. Mugabe became a true "mad Bob" in the way in which he became removed from the real world and was located in a fantastic universe of powerful messiahs, saints and deliverers. Mugabe lived, pathetically, a larger part of his time in the dreamland of power where he was unable, even if he wished, to experience the true world. That the thousands of people that gathered before him in the many rallies were mostly hungry villagers and hapless school children that were forced and also bribed to attend was lost to him. What he saw was massive crowds of supporters and believers in him and his power, and so did Bob really lose his mind. Mugabe became a production in two meaningful ways. The first way is that his power and its excesses were enabled and therefore produced by people around him, and permitted by national and international institutions that could have done something to stop his growth into a monster. The second way is how he became a performer of power and its spectacles where the Zimbabwean postcolony became an expanded stage on which he strutted the stuff of his monstrous political shows.

After believing in his political messianism, that his opportunistic supporters preached, Mugabe had to live, speak and act like the saint and the deliverer that he was imagined to be. In power politics, however, the saint and the monster can be one. The wisdom of George Orwell (1949: 1) that "saints should be judged guilty until they are proven innocent" was what was needed to protect Mugabe from the maddening fantasies and other energies of power. When Dinizulu Macaphulana (2017a, b: 1) under the influence of Jean Baudrillard described Mugabe as a "photocopy without an original," he pointed to the authentic work of art, fake but real, that Mugabe had become. Mugabe became a compelling collection of appearances and performances that in their drama and spectacle concealed the commanding actuality of a faulted human being that needed help, sobering advice, and not the worship that he received from selfish flatterers and enterprising hangers-on. The flattery and sycophancy of political entrepreneurs and other ambitious self-serving politicians and business people around Mugabe got him totally lost and mad.

The people around Mugabe, Zimbabweans at large and the world, should have treated Mugabe with what Slavoj Zizek (2017: xi) after Giorgio Agamben called the "courage of hopelessness," a proverbial pessimistic belief that what appears like some light at the end of the tunnel is actually a ghost or an approaching train coming to crash everyone and everything. Mugabe should not have been seen and treated as a messiah and a saint but a monster, and so was he and Zimbabwe going to be saved from what Geoff Nyarota (2018) has called a "graceless fall." Mugabe needed protection from the maddening energies of power not the worship that enterprising followers gave to him, and that way the world and humanity were to be protected from what became a monstrosity. Worsening the trouble is that journalists and scholars that have written on Mugabe have not appreciated how Mugabe was first formed and then produced and enabled, by people, historical conditions and circumstances, into a complex performer and monstrosity of power. Understanding how Mugabe came to be a monstrosity should have helped Zimbabweans, especially ZANU-PF supporters, and prevented them from receiving the limited and faulted Emmerson Mnangagwa, Mugabe's successor, with the same euphoria and worship that is presently driving him mad. Choirs of flatterers and singers for supper and breakfast combined surround Mugabe's successor and are feeding him fantasies and dreams of endless power. One of the songs that is being sung is that Mnangagwa should be in power well up to 2030 because of the repair job he has to do in the country after many years of Mugabe's misrule. Post-political worship of leaders inevitably forms them into monsters that turn around to eat the country. Chantal Mouffe (2005a) warned about the post-political enchantment of failing to treat politics, and therefore politicians, as antagonistic, conflictual and violent. Mugabe should have been treated with suspicion and strong institutions and systems built around him and his party, to prevent his abuse of power that grew from the personal fragility of a toddler, to a little self-confidence of an educated school teacher and then exploded into the terror of an angry prison graduate that came to power in Zimbabwe. The love for power of a weak human being that perpetually fears losing power and dreads suffering the consequences that come with the loss produces, even the most chosen political messiah, into a monster of biblical proportions.

Some Uncritical Everydayness

A kind of simplification and uncritical everydayness has accompanied some readings and writings on Mugabe. There has been a concentration on the symptoms and effects of Mugabe's rule and not his production into a monster for which Mugabe himself, some Zimbabweans and the world must share guilt. There is a need to own Mugabe and account for how some people built and enabled his monstrosity. Journalists such as Geoff

Nyarota that was one of Mugabe's propagandist supporters during the Gukurahundi Genocide of the early 1980s can now write, to opportunistically and much self-servingly, wonder how Mugabe as an entity managed to destroy the Zimbabwean economy and polity:

> Just how Mugabe managed to reduce so prosperous a nation, which was endowed with so many natural and human resources, to such levels of destitution during his presidency makes for a benchmark study in misgovernance. (Nyarota 2018: 69)

Conveniently forgotten by such journalists as Nyarota that now win awards for courage is that at some point, until they were dismissed and did not resign on their own in contempt of the corrupt system, they were part of the human resources that helped Mugabe destroy the country. Even in the present as a writer that has gained fame as a fearless opponent of Mugabe's tyranny, Nyarota (2018: 24) cannot hide the post-political enchantment he once held for Mugabe who he regarded as "the enigmatic Mugabe, the leader of the much-feared ZANU-PF." In ever naively treating Mugabe as an enigmatic political messiah and allowing ZANU-PF to be feared in the first place, such later opponents of Mugabe as Nyarota who spent a larger part of their careers as his supporters share in the production of Mugabe and guilt for his tyrannical rule. After his fall from power and before his eventual death, Mugabe became an object of condemnation even by some that supported him and were enforcers of dark rule in Zimbabwe. Even the British and American political establishments that incubated his rule in the 1980s and irrigated his tyrannical ego condemned him as a creature unknown to them. Mugabe died a sad and lonely old mad, once more vulnerable and rejected as he was as a child whose father was absent.

Part of the courage of hopelessness and critical pessimism that can lead to a future for Zimbabwe beyond tyranny is to own Mugabe as a son of his parents, product of his supporters and opponents, and also a product of the modern colonial and imperial world system. To simplify Mugabe as a singular monstrosity and one-man system that is solely guilty of the destruction of Zimbabwe is not only uncritical everydayness but also analytical cowardice and political opportunism. The courageous effort of "humanising the monster, finding the three dimensional Mugabe instead of a cartoon villain is a process of understanding and not exoneration" (Holland 2008: xiv). I attempt in this book to locate Mugabe behind the appearances, performances and illusions that are scattered by the product and the production that Mugabe became. Authoritative writers such as Nyarota use their authority, unhelpfully, to conceal rather than reveal the true Mugabe, and that is why Percy Makombe (2004: 1) noted far earlier on that more than commitment to the revelation of truths about Mugabe and the Zimbabwean tragedy, "Nyarota attempts to spin his mistakes" and wash his hands of the complicity he had in Mugabe's destruction of Zimbabwe. After the fall of Mugabe, and in the years of his decline and death, many of his enablers, enforcers and accessories that were beneficiaries of his rule conveniently re-invented themselves as warriors for democracy and champions of human rights.

To collapse the Zimbabwean problem into an item of what Mugabe did or did not do in Zimbabwe, the way Nyarota does, is to simplistically avoid analysis. This avoidance of sober analysis is not different from the post-political mistake that was made by some black and white Zimbabweans in ever thinking that Mugabe was to be a deliverer that would solve all their problems. In his account that attempts to answer the question "what went wrong in Zimbabwe?" Richard Bourne is perhaps closer to the truth in that: "What went wrong in Zimbabwe is not just a tragedy made possible by Robert Mugabe, or the British, or the international community" (Bourne 2011: 3). Mugabe at a certain level became an agent of an unfortunate history and world political system that looked aside from evil if that evil did not threaten certain important interests. Mugabe became, otherwise, a baby of many mothers and fathers that used him and were used by him for power at its madness.

In the attempt to maintain clean hands, Britain, the USA and other international powers have tried to erase and silence their complicity in the production of Mugabe as a monster and the betrayal of the people of Zimbabwe. The mistake Richard Bourne and other writers seem to make is to hold the impression that the Rhodesians handed a great country to a regime of black politicians that went on to run it down. There was nothing great about Rhodesia because it was a settler colony, whatever political and economic prosperity was there belonged to a minority of whites. Whatever economic and political boom there can be in a country, if it is racially or tribally distributed, it becomes a facility of evil. In their blame of Mugabe, some journalists and scholars have failed to reflect on what a troubled and troubling country and political system the Rhodesians handed over to the Zimbabwean post-independence government. Journalists and scholars that are supposed to be defenders of the truth and witnesses of history have participated in concealments rather than revelations. Nyarota, rather tragically, exemplifies journalism as the clever art of concealment in the way he tip-toes around how he and many others forcefully contributed to the growth of Mugabe into a political monster that in many ways ate Zimbabwe.

During Zimbabwe's darkest hour, which was the Gukurahundi Genocide, powerful world countries looked aside as Mugabe dealt death to political opponents. Timothy Scarnecchia (2011) has written of how Cold War political relations permitted the UK and the USA to overlook Mugabe's human rights abuses in Matabeleland and gave him financial and political support just to create a buffer against the encroaching spectre of communism from Eastern Europe. Quoted in Scarnecchia is Geoff Hill who narrates the reaction to Gukurahundi of the then British High Commissioner to Zimbabwe:

> Sir Martin Evans, High Commissioner in Harare at the time, admitted on camera that his instructions from London were to 'steer clear of it' when speaking to Mugabe. 'I think Matabaleland was a side issue,' he said. 'The real issues were much bigger. We were extremely interested that Zimbabwe should be a success story, and we were doing our best to help Mugabe and his people bring that about. (Hill 2003: 83)

On the altar of political and economic expediency, the rights and lives of the victims of Gukurahundi were sacrificed. Mugabe's political insanity was not only promoted by such loud but small voices of his ambitious wife Grace Mugabe and naïve flatterer Kudzai Chipanga but also super powers of the modern colonial world system came to Mugabe's political show and, in a way, permitted his growing appetite for power and excess. The UK and the USA, like Geoff Nyarota, might preach long jeremiads about tyranny and human rights abuses in Mugabe's Zimbabwe, but true history has it that they were complicit in Mugabe's rehearsals of tyranny and genocide. Mugabe's political ego, his will to power and bravado grew upon the permission and promotion that some supposedly exemplary powers in the world gave him.

On Mugabe, Steven Chan (2003: 4) is correct that "it remains a provocative thought that the man, characterised by many British newspapers as a mad dictator, may be instead some sort of ruthless romantic" that was "romantic, ruthless, well-organised in operational issues, given to rhetoric." Mugabe was not only given to rhetoric but he became a rhetoric rather than a reality himself when he actualised the role of a performance and a production acting to the winds of his own fears and desires, and the agendas of super powers that were using him and other tyrants of the Global South to design a world after their interests. I insist that Mugabe cannot be fully understood without a cold and dry appreciation of how at some point, in his early days in power, he became a knowing and willing political client and indeed puppet of the West. There was, and still is, a racist and colonial stereotype in the West that chaotic and dark Africa needs strong leaders in shape of tyrants and despots that, even if they loot economies and massacre people, can create the order that global corporations need to prosper in the continent. Mugabe became a product of Western cynicism about Africa and Africans.

More than anything in the emergence and growth of tyrannical regimes and totalitarian governments in the countries of the world, Thomas Dotcherty (2016) blames the complicity of citizens, and in a way, that of neighbouring countries and the world at large. Tyrants do not just rise and perform their tyranny, but they are given a stage upon which they act and an audience before which they perform themselves as productions. In the book, *On Tyranny: Twenty Lessons from the Twentieth Century,* Timothy Snyder (2017) explains how tyrants prosper from voluntary and "advance obedience" of opportunists before they profit from coercing the unwilling. Before tyrants enjoy the following and "support" of clobbered victims, they are relished with the promotions and permissions of opportunistic persons and forces. In reference to such domineering leaders as Donald Trump and Mugabe, Snyder recommends that societies and countries protect themselves from tyranny by "defending institutions" such as parliaments, the courts, press, trade unions and others that must have the independent ability to check the excesses of tyrants. The ability and duty to "take responsibility for the world" that Snyder teaches is the important task of societies to critically defend the truth and unmask cheap propaganda wherever it appears from flatterers, sycophants, scholars and even enterprising journalists seeking to found personal legacies on simplifications and falsifications of history around tyranny. Mugabe, just like Mnangagwa in the present, had clubs of flatterers around him.

Uncritical everydayness that is, simplifications and falsifications of history are the fertiliser that nourishes tyranny. Tyrants live and feed fat in the "alternative universe" of lies, false prophecies and fake religions built with the words of praise singers and self-serving worshippers. What Ken Wilber (2017: 11) calls "aperspectival madness" is the political insanity of scholars and politicians that get sold to contempt for all truth and reality and are bought by beliefs in illusions and fantasies of a world in their own political imagination. Mugabe, in his helm, became prisoner to a false and "alternative facts" post-political world in which he was an unquestionable messenger and ambassador of God. Wilber (2017: 43) describes the condition as "narcissist nihilism" when such a leader as Mugabe loves and believes in his own version of truth and reality to the point where the whole world can end if it does not agree with him. Mugabe was helped by flatterers and other followers to grow into a narcissist nihilist that would watch Zimbabwe die just to dig in and insist on his political position as the right position.

The lives and histories of tyrants are productions and enablements by people, circumstances and systems. For that reason, important writers such as Geoff Nyarota cannot, in justice, support Mugabe and ZANU-PF when it suits them, the way they did, and then deride him and his party opportunistically to promote their international legend and personal legacies. That slippery hide and seek game with the truth and history is itself a kind of Mugabeism. As a monstrosity and a spectacular political production, Mugabe cannot be narrowed into a simple and typical political problem from dark Africa because he is partly produced by exemplary states and captains of the world order in shape of the USA and the UK, that in the early days of his rule gave him permissions and promotions that energised his transformation into a monstrosity. It is for that reason that if the world is to succeed in "wrestling tyrants," Christopher Blakesley (2017: 176) believes a robust international justice system is needed to curb our frequent common inhumanity to each other at local and international scales. Political and historical problems such as Mugabe and other tyrants require human and international solutions, to condemn them as monsters and celebrate them as saints, depending on where one stands politically is only part of the problem.

THE SPECTACLE OF THE SAINT AND THE MONSTER

Like a true production, wherever he appeared in literature and in life, Mugabe appeared in excess and spectacle. Both those who affirmed him and those that negated him did so in extremes. For his supporters and beneficiaries of his rule, he was the irreplaceable saint that may even rule from his grave after death because there is no one like him as the appointed representative of God on earth, a political kind of messiah. After his death,

Mugabe's body lay in state for many days as the Mnangagwa government and his wife negotiated on where he was to be buried. Jokes circulated in the social media that Mugabe's wife hoped that like a true Messiah Mugabe would resurrect in true political glory to deliver his family and supporters from the military junta that topped him from power. Eventually, he was buried in a low key funeral at his home in Zvimba, not at the Heroes Acre, the shrine that Mugabe so venerated. Loss of power and death seemed to reduce Mugabe back to the ordinariness, loneliness and vulnerability of his youth.

In his helm, Mugabe became a monster to those that did not enjoy his protection and that did not support him. For his opponents and victims, Mugabe became a definition of "the fear" that Peter Godwin (2008: 1) describes as enveloping the country due to the spectacles of violence and festivals of cruelty. The festivals of cruelty were described by Catherine Buckle (2003: 1) as evil that was "beyond tears" as it was too much even for mourning. The story of Mugabe became a tale of "a freedom fighter" that tragically "became a tyrant" (Holland 2008: 1). For Zimbabwe and the world, Mugabe defined "catastrophe" (Bourne 2011: 1) and in that way betrayed Zimbabwe and humanity (Norman 2003) by failing to deliver to the promise of revolution and freedom that he so embodied earlier on.

With the many mass graves and countless victims of the wounded, bereaved and angry, Mugabe turned the Zimbabwean postcolony into a big crime scene. Contrary to the narratives of degeneration and betrayal which hold that Mugabe once carried promise but tragically turned around to deliver terror and catastrophe, Blessing-Miles Tendi (2011) notes that from the beginning, actually, Mugabe was toxic. The question that must haunt observers is how exactly did a toxic individual smuggle himself into, not only a hero, but also a kind and saintly messiah for some in Zimbabwe, and a monster for others. How did one person come to inspire so much worship from some and fear from others in what was supposed to be the same country is a political question to ask.

Mugabe became a saint and a monster at the same time, while Nelson Mandela of South Africa in one became a saint and traitor. Whether he is a saint or a monster, the hero is a traitor to some people. In his widely debated engagement with what he called "Mandela's socialist failure," Slavoj Zizek (2013: 3) lamented how the celebrated but controversial South African departed from being a socialist revolutionary to a political saint in the way he failed to fulfil the promises of delivering liberation. In the view of Zizek, political sainthood is the prize Mandela won for the political defeat he suffered and the victory enjoyed by champions and beneficiaries of apartheid who gave him political power and retained the economy at the expense of the poor majority of blacks. The political dilemma that Zizek (2013: 3) tables before us is the challenge "in short, how to move further" from the compromising example of the saintly Mandela and still avoid the "catastrophe of the totalitarian temptation" of "becoming Mugabe" the monster. Politically, the monster and the saint are failures because of their excess and extremity. Political sainthood and political monstrosity are performances and spectacles of power, two sides of the same rusty coin of political fundamentalism. In many ways, as I demonstrate later in this book, Mugabe became a true political fundamentalist.

Concerning Mahatma Gandhi, the ultimate political saint, George Orwell (1949: 1) asks a stubborn question: "To what extent was Gandhi moved by vanity- by the consciousness of himself as a humble, naked old man, sitting on a praying mat and shaking Empires by sheer spiritual power." In other words, political sainthood may be a conscious performance of humility that is fundamentally based on pride and is as violent, in its own way, as "fraud and coercion" that Orwell understands as the corruption in politics. To Christopher Hitchens (1995: xi), the worldwide reputation of the saintly Mother Teresa as "wizened, shrivelled old lady, well stricken in years, who has consecrated her entire life to the needy and the destitute" was all a choreographed performance of not only religious but also political sainthood. Behind the spectacle of humility and charity, Mother Teresa was in actuality a "self-sacrificing zealot, or chair of a missionary multinational" corporation who privately did the opposite of what she promised by forcing her religious beliefs on the poor and vulnerable, consorting with dictators, receiving money from thieves, being a propagandist for the Vatican and talking about a kingdom that is not of this world when she served kingdoms of this earth with zest. Hitchens unmasks how the saint, in Mother Teresa, lived an unaudited life of so much evil as that of a "hell's angel" but enjoyed the following of a saint. She was, not known to the world, guilty of constructing and performing poverty, pain and misery for a religious reputation. The heroism of the saints and their other side, the monsters, is all a spectacular performance of power and privilege. Mugabe, in one body, represented both the saints and the monsters, and therefore perfected tyranny. He became a living collection of spectacular performances that hid his actuality.

For becoming a saint for some and a monster for others, Mugabe suffered a double failure and came to embody two extreme and contesting political fundamentalisms. The saint brandishes bright hope and the monster a true black hole, and both are painful destinations for followers and opponents alike. There is no conceit that equals the affected modesty of the political saints as much as there is no evil that equals the "antipolitics" of political monsters (Hitchens 1995: 86). The combination of conceit and antipolitics in one person makes Mugabe a true monstrosity in whom pelf meets power. In the successful performances of political sainthood and monstrosity, the tyrant as the actor is not the only one to blame but also the gullible audiences, of followers and fanatics, who choose to believe an act and take it for history. Mugabe, in Zimbabwe and beyond, became that handmade god. With their minds those who made him with their hands imagined him a true god. With their hearts, they manufactured the faith to follow him without question. They worshiped him too far and until it was too late, and the god of their making began to demand impossible sacrifices including the burnt offering of the country itself. In some prevalent uncritical everydayness, most scholars and journalists in their post-political failure, their faith in illusions of heroism, have not overcome the spectacular performances of sainthood and monstrosity, and that way have not understood the true Mugabe.

On his part, Mugabe suffered an intense hunger for admiration that is similar to the appetite for being worshipped that Betty Glad (2002: 17) describes concerning Joseph Stalin. It is a hunger for worship that frequently conceals the deep insecurity of externally powerful but internally fragile individuals such as Mugabe and some other tyrants. Saddam Hussein is said to have enjoyed the worship of a close cousin of his who frequently repeated the statement "everything that you did in the past was good and everything that you will do in the future is good" (Miller and Mylroie 1990: 45), and this was exactly when Hussein was conducting massacres and ruining Iraq. Such followers of tyrants as Saddam Hussein's cousin, Grace Mugabe and Kudzai Chipanga invent their tyrants into saints not out of love but fear of political monstrosities. Towards the end of Mugabe's rule and eventual death, Grace Mugabe became more afraid and insecure as the death or retirement of her powerful husband would expose her to the wrath of the many enemies and victims that were awaiting their revenge on the Mugabes. Dinizulu Macaphulana (2015: 3) observed of Grace that "by appointing herself the referee of Zanu-PF politics, she aims to eliminate all the players to leave only herself as the last woman and man standing. She suddenly has to eat people or she will be on the menu herself." Imagining her fragile and aged husband as a saint that would even rule the country from the grave was not a statement of her deep faith in him but an unconscious construction of her deep fears of persecution and monstrosities when her husband lost power. It was her pathetic and unconscious hope that even the grave of her husband would protect her from the many enemies.

Grace Mugabe's fears were to be confirmed when Mugabe was deposed in a coup that exposed him and his family to the mercy of the new rulers. The fears were dramatised in how she delayed the burial of Mugabe's body as if to cling to some wish for protection from his mortal remains. Tyrants are sick to accept the worship of followers, and the followers that make a saint and a god out of a faulty mortal are sick as well. Political wellness and wisdom for leaders is to lead, and for followers and supporters is to follow, in such a fair and just way that the loss of power need not be so feared. Mugabe led and was followed as if he was never going to lose power or die one day. That is the problem of political messianism. It is removed from reality. Saints and monsters are all rather unreal people whose end is always demystifying and exposing of their ordinariness.

The "ruthless romantic" that Steven Chan (2003: 4) described in Mugabe and the "mad Bob" that is observed by Heidi Holland (2008: xiv) are all references to Mugabe as a kind of actor and performer of power. He had to perform true sainthood for his supporters and beneficiaries of his power and also dispense monstrosity to his victims and opponents. He became a man apart, torn between two dark extremes. As a result, there was "this ability" of Mugabe "to say one thing and to do another," which "has baffled his opponents ever since" (Hope 2003: 77). Betty Glad (2002: 5) correctly understands the tyrant to be a creature of "paradoxes" that is perpetually full of surprises. "What counts in a tyrant" Christopher Hope (2003: 73) notes "is not what he says or even how he comes across, it is rather to distinguish, if one is lucky, his essence" for instance "the essence of Mugabe was dissimulation, and superstitious, unforgiving malevolence." Many observers and writers have missed Mugabe's essence as at once a saint and a monster that was removed from reality to a point of insanity.

Mugabe, because of the political religion around him, suffered a faulty relationship with reality. What is called "flawed reality testing" (Glad 2002: 2) is when the tyrant effectively becomes insulated from the true world and is suspended in an unreal or super-real universe where he becomes vulnerable to injuries and even death. For instance, Mugabe ignored all the telling signs of an impending coup against him; even a graphic powerpoint presentation by the then Minister of Higher Education, Professor Jonathan Moyo, detailing how a coup was afoot, could not jolt Mugabe out of the slumber of a false sense of invincibility. Some weeks before the coup, on prime time national Television, Mugabe sounded a chilling warning to those that might have wanted to grab power from him by unconstitutional means, "I am warning you," he said. The coup had taken place already, only he was too blind and power-drunk to see.

Mugabe was effectively caught up in some "aperspectival madness" that is described by Wilber (2017) as a tendency to totally ignore all truth and hang on to a fabricated reality. The individual tyrant, such as Mugabe, becomes an actor after a script of power in the same way that Rainer Stollmann (1978: 47) describes how fascist politics becomes at the end of the day a true work of art where fictions, myths and illusions are produced for the image making and image management of fascist dictators and organisations. Most scholars, journalists and other writers on Mugabe and his politics seem to have concentrated on the person and missed the political persona and actor who was able to be intellectual and also to be soldierly, to be humble and also scathing and brutal, depending on the dictates of the will to power, and the direction of the winds of power. In that political ability to be many people and many things in one person and at once, Mugabe himself became a political product and a production in a real but compellingly cinematic way.

THE PRODUCTION OF THE POLITICAL ROBERT MUGABE

Mugabe, like many other tyrants, was perpetually hungry for reputations and legacies. The tyrant wants to be known as a legend of many glories. For instance, "Stalin also claimed expertise in a variety of fields where he actually had no training, such as economics, biology, physics and especially military science" (Conquest 1991: 193–194) and this was on top of the claim to be a "fountain of wisdom" and the "successor to Marx, Engels and Lenin as a Marxist philosopher" (Tucker 1990: 316–324). Hitler got thousands of German soldiers killed when he pretended to be a great military General and personally deployed soldiers to their deaths in poorly planned operations. Not only that, but he considered himself "an intellectual and creative giant, an expert in virtually every field of endeavour, in 1919 he planned a massive work about the history of mankind, entitled

'Monumental History of Humanity' though he had no formal training in history" (Glad 2002: 6); before his suicide, thinking of his death as a loss to all humanity, he exclaimed "what an artist dies in me" (Schramm 1965: 323). What is worrying about tyrants is not that they make all these outlandish claims about themselves to mislead populations of supporters and opponents but that they actually also believe the strange claims to be truths.

Mugabe initially produced and recommended himself in politics as a competent scholar and an articulate diplomat which were credentials that were in demand amongst black Rhodesians at the time. The fight against white settler colonialism required, not only brave guerrillas, but also intelligent and articulate black elites that could excel in public speech and private negotiations. Later, as argued below, Mugabe was forced to act out the role of a competent guerrilla and an uncompromising warrior leader to suit the demands of the times and win the support and following of guerrillas that were based in Mozambique. At the end, Mugabe became both a doubtful intellectual and a questionable guerrilla leader who appeared to be in politics for power and nothing more. As a result, what Sabelo Ndlovu-Gatsheni (2009: 1139) called Mugabeism became, in a cinematic and theatrical way, productions of certain "political controversies" that were accompanied by "political behaviours" based on "political ideas" that made him circulate "utterances" that were designed by and were for his will to power and nothing else.

The Mugabe who joined the liberation struggle as a diplomat, "eloquent, literate and intellectually rigorous," and who had "clear ideas as to what was fair and acceptable when negotiating the future of his country with Rhodesian and British politicians" (Norman 2004a: 58) was to end up a product of a violent guerrilla culture that not only believed in war and brutality but also boasted of it. Mugabe ended up a leader who "entertains a superiority complex and belittles other contenders for power- especially those without higher education- including aspiring successors from his own political party" (Compagnon 2011: 6). The tyrant fundamentally can be anything and wants to be everything for power, a philosopher, a soldier, a prophet and an artist combined, it seems. Below I treat the different and also multiple productions of Mugabe, which is the many ways he was constructed and shaped, politically. There is also an exposition of how Mugabe performed his multiple political identities.

THE PRODUCTION OF THE INTELLECTUAL ROBERT MUGABE

As noted earlier, it was at a protest rally of the National Democratic Party (NDP) in July 1961 that Mugabe formerly entered politics. As a scholar of repute and travelled gentlemen that was then based in Ghana, a liberated country, he was asked to address the rally (Meredith 2002a: 26–27), and he gave an oration that impressed the crowd and the political leadership who saw in him an able and articulate spokesperson of their ideas. In that rally, Mugabe spoke the English language better than the British and impressed black masses with his contrived accent and charged delivery that was to become his claim to fame in politics. Mugabe made full use of his education to claim political fame and leadership much the same way that Friedrich Nietzsche (1968: 227) noted that "the so-called drive for knowledge can be traced back to a drive to appropriate and conquer" and dominate others. From Hitler to Stalin, and Augusto Pinochet to Mugabe, the tyrant wants to be counted as an intellectual of sorts and one who knows and understands what the masses don't, a kind of political prophet. Mugabe frightened many ambitious colleagues and political opponents with his performance of knowledge, his pretence to be a fountain of the deepest and the latest wisdom under the sun. Most of the fright he caused with the sound and accent, and not compelling sense of his words. In speech, Mugabe was prevalently lyrical and dramatic even, and not always sensible. Sound and not exactly sense overtook his presentations and dominated his output.

The fluent and impressive use of the English language became for Mugabe a weapon and a code of political elevation. Mugabe became "the colonised" leader that Frantz Fanon (2008: 9) describes as the leader who feels that he "is elevated above his jungle status in proportion to his adoption of the mother country's cultural standards, he becomes whiter as he renounces his blackness, his jungle," and in a way impresses and scares others into subordination to his political will. Mugabe's accent and intonation of the English language, even at the end of his reign, was that which was designed and performed to create a distance between himself and others, as he invented a superior model of himself with language. And so did he enchant the massive rally of oppressed masses of black Rhodesians in 1961. In Public speech, Mugabe was a true drama prince that enchanted even his opponents.

To be recognised as a leader, in the struggle against colonialism, one had to possess some noticeable intellectual qualities. As Peter Ekeh (1975) argues, education and intellectualism gave black African politicians in the liberation movements a sense of superiority over their own black brothers and sisters and a kind of equality to the white colonisers. The education, culture and the language of the coloniser give the colonised a sense of equality with the coloniser (Fanon 2008: 14) and political superiority over other colonised peoples. Critically, Sabelo Ndlovu-Gatsheni notes that:

> One distinguishing feature of the first generation of African nationalists is that they initially fought for inclusion into the colonial power structures. They used personal acquisition of modern education as a justification for demanding inclusion. It was when colonialism proved to be too inflexible to accommodate the black elite that they engaged in politics of anti-colonialism. (Ndlovu-Gatsheni 2015: 1)

As part of this founding generation of African politicians that fought colonialism, Mugabe fully utilised his modern education as a recommendation to political superiority and entitlement to leadership. Peter Godwin (2008: 29) notes how faced with the political challenge of the lesser educated Morgan Tsvangirai in the 2000s, feeling "hyper-educated," Mugabe dismissed his opponent as an ignoramus who must not come near national leadership. In his will to power and drive for dominance, Mugabe began to see his superior education as a qualifying fetish for himself and a disqualifying curse for his opponents, no doubt he also looked down upon less educated comrades and colleagues in the liberation movement, carrying himself as an anointed spokesperson and advocate.

The image of an inspired and even chosen thinker and visionary is the relish of the tyrant. In the battle to justify his tyrannical stay in power, Saddam Hussein is said to have, at one point, circulated a suspicious poster "all over Baghdad (that) showed him as the heir of Hammurabi, the great lawmaker of 18th Century B.C Babylon" (Glad 2002: 7). Mugabe constructed such a vivid image of himself as a formidable intellectual so much so that in the scramble to succeed him, many politicians in ZANU-PF and soldiers and police officers got into a stampede for doctorates, mostly fake from briefcase universities and plagiarised copy, just to seem to fit the shoes of Mugabe, the intellectual giant.

As noted in the previous chapter, Mugabe believed he was born to rule (Holland 2008: 192) based on a "prophecy" by a leading Jesuit priest and the passionate beliefs and faith of his mother. This belief in his predestined rule combined with a good education, compared to many of his contemporaries, morphed into a stubborn will to power and an entitlement to dominance, making it worse is that his supporters also seemed to believe in his divine political anointing (Holland 2008: 192). Regarding himself as the unquestionable leader and also teacher of his inferior people, at the same rally where Mugabe launched his political career, he started his degeneration into senseless political populism. Mugabe's populism led him to ask the mass of the rallied people to take off their shoes in apparent rejection of western civilisation, and they did, "today you have removed your shoes, tomorrow you may be called upon to destroy them altogether, or to perform other acts of self-denial" (Meredith 2002a: 29). Using his new reputation as a superior thinker and knowledgeable visionary, he had begun to produce himself, and to perform his identity, and to be produced by his supporters that blindly obeyed him, into an unquestionable high priest of political wisdom, a priest and a preacher who demanded sacrifices and self-denialism from his flock. At the time his enchanted admirers did not know that one day he was to take the country out of the comity of nations of the world and reduce it to a pariah of some barefooted Zimbabweans that survived on second hand clothes, including underwear, from faraway places of the world. With a collapsed economy and impoverishment at a large scale, Mugabe reduced Zimbabweans in actuality to shoelessness.

Not everyone was fooled, however. Those that observed Mugabe closely noted that "from the beginning" there were "many worrying signs of Mugabe's thirst for power, his recklessness, and his lack of concern for the wellbeing of his fellow countrymen and women" (Compagnon 2011: 1) that he regarded as mere raw-materials for building his power and not dignified people. Mugabe's much storied education became "the creation of this ideological smokescreen," the building of "political mythology" and construction of passionately desired legendry (Compagnon 2011: 2, 5). In that way, Mugabe's education did not become the education for liberation and humanisation, or the education for critical consciousness that Paulo Freire (1993) advocated for the colonised and the oppressed. Mugabe became educated in the same arts of dehumanisation and domination that were employed and deployed by colonialists. His education created an alienating distance between him and his people, and the distance between him and the white colonisers, no matter how he tried, could not be reduced. In that way, Mugabe became a removed, isolated and lonely personage with a kind of identity crisis.

In spite of his outlandish request that his people resist and reject western culture to the extent of throwing away their shoes, Mugabe himself embraced western culture and relished the colonial and modern education that he received, to the extent that he became a thoroughgoing Anglophile

(Godwin 2008; Moorcraft 2012; Hope 2003). Mugabe put on Savile Row suits, spoke English fastidiously, enjoyed Graham Greene novels and was to be Knighted by the Queen of England in 1994 (Godwin 2008: 18). In demanding that his people reject artefacts of western civilisation, even such universal human heritages as shoes, Mugabe was not only practising cheap populism but was also objectifying his audience and supporters as tools in the game of power, people that can be forced to do what the leader himself would not do. The black Rhodesians of the 1960s like the Zimbabweans of the 1980s to the 2000s were reduced by a scheming and calculating political performer to a herd of obedient followers. Throughout his political career, Mugabe seems to have seen, understood and treated Zimbabweans as objects and simple items in his power game. He invested in Zimbabweans as unthinking raw materials in the infrastructure of his power.

In the scheme of tyranny, education can be usable for dark purposes. Used and politically instrumentalised for the will to power, even the finest education and knowledge degenerates into simplistic populism. Sabelo Ndlovu-Gatsheni (2009: 1141) argues that "Mugabeism" also manifested itself as "populist reason" which describes simplistic political ideas that may be misleading and opportunistic in nature. By nature, Ndlovu-Gatsheni continues, "populism as a phenomenon is marked by ideological simplicity, emptiness, vagueness, imprecision and multiclass character" that is directed to supposedly unthinking masses that follow demagogues without question. In addressing his audiences as such, Mugabe treated them as what Friedrich Nietzsche (1968: 132, 215, 389) described as people with a "herd consciousness" that are guided by "herd instincts" and are good candidates for domination by a powerful and intelligent master who has to think on their behalf and dictate their entire life actions to them. Even at the darkest depths of the Zimbabwean political and economic crisis, some ZANU-PF supporters followed Mugabe like a faithful herd.

Contracted to a will to power that used populist reason in all its simplicity, Mugabe for his ideology and political insights made opportunistic and simplistic selections from different political schools of thought such as Marxism, Stalinism, Maosim, Nkrumahism, Nyerereism, Garveyism, Negritude, Pan-Africanism, African neo-traditionalism and so on (Ndlovu-Gatsheni 2009: 1141). In that way, Mugabe produced himself and was produced into an accessory of a populist reason in politics. A populist reason that was "a way of constructing the political through articulation of various interests, demands and claims" but was also "an empty signifier, representing absence" (Laclau 2005: ix–xi) rather than presence of a vision of liberation. David Moore (2015: 30) correctly notes how Mugabe became an "intellectual Manqué" that in his pretences of intellection was not following any solid ideas but got blown around by the winds of power to any direction that looked politically victorious. Instead of receiving education well and becoming refined and balanced in thought and practice, Mugabe took education and corrupted it, turned it into a base and arrogant claim to power and domination, he gave good education a bad name.

Ali Mazrui wrote at length and in some depth of the connection between the Pan-Africanist liberation movements and intellectualism, and opined that "we can imagine" African "intellectualism without Pan-Africanism but we cannot envisage Pan-Africanism without intellectualization of the African condition" (Mazrui 2005: 56). In other words, Mazrui saw African intellectualism as a driver of Pan-Africanism and the liberation wars in the continent. Mazrui (2005: 56) defined the intellectual as "a person who has the capacity to be fascinated by ideas and has acquired the skill to handle many of them effectively." "The quality most apparent" in Mugabe was indeed "his intellectual rigour" and "he had this ability to listen to argument, then dissect it, take it to bits" (Meredith 2002a: 29); however, all this intellectualism was not meant for the search for truths and justice but was simply instrumentalised for the search for power. Education was not only wasted in him, but it suffered in the mind and a hand of Mugabe as it was turned into an ignorance of life and its moral demands. When education stops being a facility that enables one to pay attention to truth and justice, and becomes an excuse for a Mugabe to ignore the same, it does not only become education for the domination of others but also for the demnation of society.

In a way, Mugabe ended up being an informed person with many university degrees but still uneducated in that his information did not condition him in ethical leadership and liberatory sensibility. Heidi Holland (2008: 46, 47, 52) notes how Mugabe ended up an intellectual face of a rogue military organisation; he used educated language and mannerisms to cover up violent crimes of the guerrilla movement. Mugabe possessed an intellectual veneer that concealed an unthinking mind, unlike true intellectuals and liberators he was against and got wounded by criticism and opposition. Similar to Mugabe, Joseph Stalin in spite of his intellectual pretensions suffered critique and opposition very badly. For Stalin, friends and allies quickly became enemies as soon as they critiqued him "no matter how long and how well he had known the person concerned, he would now put him down as an enemy" (Alliluyeva 1967: 78–79). True intellectuals tend to relish argument and critique and not escape to enmity whenever they are challenged. The political ability to possess an intellectual reputation but really not be an intellectual, in justice, is a quality of the will to power that can successfully deploy illusions and fictions in pursuit of power. In the hands of the tyrants, the Mugabes and the Stalins, intellectualism is performed as an act and not actualised as a practice.

THE PRODUCTION OF THE GUERRILLA LEADER

After his production and recognition by others as a scholar and an intellectual that was equal to the leadership of a liberation movement, for the same role, Mugabe urgently needed to be seen and known as a competent guerrilla leader. The reputation of a competent soldier and gallant warrior is a coveted trophy of the typical tyrant. It is recorded that "despite a complete lack of military training, Saddam Hussein also saw himself as having military talent" so much so that "in the early phases of his war with Iran, he was directly in charge of the disposition of his troops in battle" and "as any amateur might do, he made many mistakes" (Bulloch and Morris 1991: 43) that cost the lives of many soldiers. If all human beings, as Aristotle opined, are political animals, then the tyrant is the political animal par excellence, as he wants to be recognised for excellence in all the spheres of life even those to which he is a distant stranger.

As noted earlier, Mugabe seems to have produced himself and also been produced by those that trusted his mind into the Zimbabwean liberation struggle initially as a reluctant, doubtful, scholarly and diplomatic leader, "a doubtful political factor and even temporary leader" (Tekere 2007: 16). If Mugabe became a doubtful visionary leader to start with, he later became what was initially an unwanted guerrilla leader. The typical tyrant, Betty Glad (2002) argues, is that one survivor who overcomes obstacles, may be reluctant to assume power to start with and may also face resistance and some forbidding circumstances, but once in power, his extreme fantasies and love for power go on the loose. Mugabe was not only reluctantly accepted by the guerrilla movement as a leader but was intensely resisted even by supportive presidents of neighbouring countries such as Samora Machel of Mozambique. Ibbo Mandaza states that Mugabe and Tekere had to join the guerrilla war, desperately in April 1975, as civilian onlookers (Tekere 2007: 14) since guerrillas were carrying on with the war without politicians in their leadership let alone, such questionable leaders as Mugabe, supposed intellectuals and diplomats that had no reputation for armed struggle.

Mugabe's intellectual, scholarly and diplomatic pretensions were so convincing that even David Lamb (1990: 103) who is scathing of and sceptical about Africa and African leaders to a point of being racist described him as "Robert Gabriel Mugabe, the scholarly" and "disciplined" African politician. However, Mugabe could not easily pretend the same to guerrilla war competencies and leadership as he did the scholarly and diplomatic habits. He was quickly identified as a pathetic pretender. The Zimbabwe National People's Army guerrillas (ZANLA) that were based in Mozambique, and Samora Machel himself and his Frelimo movement that was in government were reluctant to accept Mugabe as a leader of the Zimbabwean liberation movement; Joshua Nkomo and Ndabaningi Sithole were the known and acceptable leaders. There are arguments that actually Samora Machel feared that the fine-English speaking Mugabe was "an agent of Ian Smith, the Prime Minister of Rhodesia (Nyarota 2018: 9–10). As this book will show, even if Mugabe did not report to Smith, in many ways he became an agent of colonialism to his people and the country. Not only did he reproduce colonialism, but he also founded and perpetuated a kind of colonial domination over the country. The cardinal tragedy of Mugabe's legacy is that he can be described, in justice, as the black leader that became a colonial overload over Zimbabweans.

After his release from the eleven-year-long detention in a Rhodesian prison in 1974, Mugabe and Edgar Tekere in March 1975 journeyed to Mozambique to join the ZANLA guerrilla army that was advancing the war upon the Rhodesian regime (Norman 2004a: 68). Samora Machel and Frelimo put Mugabe "on protective custody" in Quelimane (Norman 2004a: 68) and prevented him from meeting with ZANLA guerrillas. Tekere (2007: 80) described the custody as a "detention" that arose from Machel and Frelimo's distrust of Mugabe. In hindsight, Zimbabwe and the world now wish Mugabe had been distrusted more in his political life. In distrust of Mugabe, Machel was to say to Tekere, "I respect Mugabe, but he does not measure up to this scale of military operation and planning, he does not belong as a soldier" (Tekere 2007: 88). As a President of Mozambique and a guerrilla leader himself, Machel observed Mugabe to be an armchair and also opportunistic leader. The ZANLA guerrilla commander, Josia Magama Tongoogara, in "anger against Mugabe" admonished Tekere for bringing a suspicious person into the guerrilla camps in Mozambique, "you are the one who brought a sell-out here!" (Tekere 2007: 89). It was with a will to power that combined perseverance, courage, skill and trickery that by 1977, Mugabe consolidated his leadership of ZANU-PF and the ZANLA guerrilla army, and this after some Zimbabwe People's Army (ZIPA) guerrillas who questioned and resisted his leadership were arrested and some of them shot dead in extra-judicial assassinations in the camps (Holland 2008: 179; Compagnon 2011: 13). Even as he seems to have stoically suffered the humiliation of being resisted and refused as a guerrilla leader until he was eventually accepted, Mugabe does not seem to have forgiven those that resisted him, as in one way or another, they were all later punished or eliminated. Deep inside himself, Mugabe saw the obstacles to his ascendancy to power as trials and tribulations of a true political messiah that must drink from the bitter cup of suffering before he ascends to political glory.

It was eventually the guerrilla leaders, Rex Nhongo (Solomon Mujuru) and Josia Ntongoogara themselves that used brute force to coerce guerrillas into accepting the leadership of Mugabe (Compagnon 2011). Gerald Mazarire (2011: 572) notes how "the release of the members of the Dare and High Command from the Zambian prisons in late 1976 and their return to the ZANLA camps after the Geneva Conference signalled the tragic end of ZIPA" that had been strong ideologically and disciplined militarily, and this end led to "the reassertion of the old ZANLA High Command, and the elevation of Robert Mugabe to the party's presidency," Mazarire notes. Mugabe's final acceptance by the guerrillas and his ascendancy to full leadership of ZANU is described by Dinizulu Macaphulana thus:

> Robert Mugabe entered politics as a fire-eating orator and some kind of an intellectual. He had a compelling and bewitching manner of putting arguments across and he electrified his audiences with his passion, and anger. The men of action, guerrillas such as Rex Nhongo and Josiah Tongoogara needed such a person in the political wing of Zanu PF. These guerrillas were men of hardihood who believed in expiring even their own comrades in arms in the name of the struggle... It was a recipe for historical disaster. The fragile Mama's Baby (Robert Mugabe) had found some hard boys from the bush to whom human life was not more than that of a chicken. The sissy had found a "war machine" and was going to use it. Rex Nhongo first and Josiah Tongoogara next were influential in replacing Ndabaningi Sithole with Robert Mugabe in 1974. Mugabe struggled to get acceptance from such

African leaders as Samora Machel, Kenneth Kaunda and even Julius Nyerere who later became his fanatical backer. (Macaphulana 2016: 3)

After growing up weak and angry as a sissy that was spoilt by his mother, Macaphulana notes, Mugabe finally found at his service strong and dangerous men that he could use to vent out, and to dispense war and violence that were bottled up in him. The typical tyrant enjoys the use and abuse of extreme cruelty that eventually becomes "his self-defeating behaviour" (Glad 2002: 14) that leads him to such monstrosities as crimes against humanity and the production of many victims and enemies that bay for his blood, all traps that Mugabe neatly fell into. The plan of the guerrillas, which they executed, was that "the party as the supreme authority" was to be "the vanguard of the revolution" and through it the revolution was to "be planned, waged and prosecuted and finally consolidated" (Mazarire 2011: 574). The guerrillas were to be the gun and Mugabe the political face. There was, from 1974 up to the present, a tussle on whether the gun or politics was to be the most prominent weapon of the struggle for liberation as imagined by ZANU-PF. No doubt the guerrillas thought they had found someone to use in Mugabe, and deep inside, he knew he had found an armed force to use. The coup of November 2017 suggests that Mugabe had always been, behind all pretences to the contrary, a tool and a captive of some figures in the guerrilla movement that became the senior army details that orchestrated the coup.

The Mugabe that entered politics as a scholar was drawn by guerrillas to the dark and grim realities of the war. As the guerrillas were powerful and influential, "the gun had thus not only triumphed over the party but a new form of punishment—execution by the gun" (Mazarire 2011: 578)—gained currency in the liberation movement under Mugabe's leadership. At the time, Mazarire (2011: 586) notes that the Secretary for Information, Eddison Zvobgo, circulated a document that described the "ZANU idea" as "the gun idea" in emphasis of violence and preparedness to shoot black and white enemies to death. Even as a pretender to diplomatic and sophisticated intellectualism, Mugabe had to act out a "gun idea" personality and deportment in order to remain the leader of the military and political movement. As Mugabe did likewise, a campaign was carried out to fortify his leadership:

This began with a campaign by Eddison Zvobgo in 1975. He wrote, 'Robert (Bob) is a very intense, single minded, inflexible, unswerving and brilliant human being ... who is the most acceptable for the job of commander-in-chief of the legions of ZANU armies'. This view flooded the pages of the Zimbabwe News before and soon after the Geneva Conference. (Mazarire 2011: 583)

Mugabe was thus being successfully produced and also sold as a deserving and legitimate guerrilla and political leader of the liberation movement even by such intellectuals as Zvobgo. In 1978, to produce and maintain himself as a true "gun idea" guerrilla leader, Mugabe was to utter that:

The justice of our gun is the justice of our cause, and the justice of our cause is the justice of our gun. Our fight is just because our cause is just. Equally because our cause is just, our fight is just. (Mugabe 1978: 6)

The man who acted the scholar in the horror movie of power was now acting the soldier. Clearly, the man who entered politics as a man of ideas had been persuaded or forced, pulled and also driven by a will to power into being an ardent gunman. Liking it or not, Mugabe had to valorise the gun and elevate the guerrilla ahead of the politician in his speeches and presentations (Mazarire 2011). More than any other person, Mugabe knew where power lay, in the hands of the guerrillas. Mazarire, in a strong way, validates what Mandaza argued that it is the politicians like Mugabe who became desperate to join the guerrillas that were carrying on with the armed struggle seemingly in no need for the leadership of politicians. The need by the guerrilla movement for a spokesperson, one who would address international audiences and give the guerrilla movement the look of a government in waiting, worked in Mugabe's favour. As far as knowledgeability and communication skills were concerned, Mugabe had become the proverbial one-eyed man in the land of the blind; the guerrillas had no choice but accept his leadership.

To fit in as a convincing guerrilla leader, Mugabe was to cultivate a reputation for such statements as that "genuine independence can only come out of the barrel of a gun" (Lamb 1990: 335). Ever the performer, in his language Mugabe became more soldierly than the true soldiers. Totally sold to the idea of the gun and war, Mugabe was opposed to the idea of a negotiated settlement in bringing about Zimbabwean independence, "Mugabe was hostile to the idea of negotiations" (Meredith 2002a: 2), as he needed the "joy of having militarily overthrown the colonial regime" (Meredith 2002a: 6). It might as well be true that it is the pretenders and performers, those who truly do not know the gun, who sing its praises and believe that it is the solution to political problems. Just as Mugabe became a dubious intellectual, he became a doubtful guerrilla leader of questionable war credentials who overestimated the uses of the gun in politics. Ironically, or rather logically, it was to be soldiers and their guns that forced Mugabe out of power.

Later in the years, in power, Mugabe "ran the government and ZANU-PF in a strictly hierarchical fashion, military style" (Tsvangirai 2011: 85). As he was promoted by military Generals into power, Mugabe was to be observed,

power, to be "captive to Generals, Chiwenga and Shiri" (Godwin 2008: 122) who later removed him from power in a military coup. Towards his ouster, when his power was threatened by the military, Mugabe turned around and cried that in Zimbabwe "politics must lead the gun"(Mugabe 2017: 3) and not the other way round. Even as this call was made in a terse speech, it was still a pathetic cry. Deep inside, behind the grandiose performances of the saint and the monster in the tyrant, there is always a fragile human being pleading for help and love.

Clearly, Mugabe's production into a questionable intellectual politician and unstable guerrilla leader became a result of a will to power in form of luck, cunning calculation and the ability to act to the script of the winds of power and the direction whence they blew. The production of Mugabe was the production of a mind and body that knew where power lay and how to act accordingly, and had the brutality of purpose for it. Josiah Tongoogara much earlier, on the 26th of December 1979, and Solomon Mujuru much later in time, in August 2011, both died under circumstances that were suspicious, and Mugabe has been blamed for assassinating them (Holland 2008: 201; Nehanda Radio 2013). A political narrative exists therefore that Mugabe could have organised the killing of the same people who made his much resisted leadership of the guerrilla movement possible, and thereby, in the true fashion of the will to power, finding and keeping power at the deadly expense of his benefactors, promoters and producers.

The above description of the intellectual and guerrilla production of Mugabe is important to this book as it helps explain how many scholars and journalists have not correctly read and understood the formation and production of Mugabe. True, Mugabe desired power, but did not singularly make his disastrous rule a reality. Mugabe was supported and enabled by people, organisations, forces and circumstances. Tyrants, as saints or monsters, have worshippers and supplicants that cement dreams of their own futures on the political fortunes of the tyrant. Tyranny creates jobs and makes careers; the tyrant is an employer and promoter that attracts singers for supper around himself. The leaders of the NDP that appointed Mugabe their spokesperson in 1961 and the guerrilla leaders that reluctantly accepted him as their leader were obviously not thinking about Mugabe but themselves and their own political fortunes at the time. Little did they know that Mugabe was thinking of nothing, of nobody but himself. The true tyrants have a "lack of commitment to their comrades in arms and the values they espouse" (Glad 2002: 22). They are not even committed to their countries. Hitler rose to political prominence on the claim "and his grandiose dream of becoming a Fuhrer of an Aryan race that would create the greatest empire known in the modern world" (Glad 2002: 29). As power and hatred consumed him, Hitler could not separate the Jews and the Germans as objects of domination and violation, "German is not worthy of me; let her perish" (Waite 1977: 392), he would say. After loss of power, Mugabe demonised ZANU-PF in anger and pathos. He entertained Zimbabwe and the world with some performances of victimhood. As I will show later in this book, Mugabe fundamentally did not care much about the Zimbabwean people and nation. Truth, justice, peace and happiness were all summarised in his personal power and interest. The tyrant does not only personalise the nation but he also nationalises his person, and threats and oppositions to himself are seen as threats to the nation. What Ken Wilber (2017) has forcefully circulated as aperspectival madness is exactly that state of mind when a politician or scholar begins to think that only his truth is the only truth and his interests the only interests. In his own Hitler-like aperspectival madness, Mugabe thought that even the nation of Zimbabwe was not worthy of him and Zimbabweans were supposed to eternally grateful for his great leadership.

The Imaginations of Robert Mugabe

For power, Mugabe constructed and styled himself into many things from a scholar and orator to a guerrilla leader. Scholars and journalists, from their many different positionalities, have also imagined and understood Mugabe in many different ways that are revealing and also misleading. As a result, the flourish of journalistic and scholarly literature on Mugabe is accompanied by a scarcity of understanding and knowledge of his essence. Journalists and scholars have not been successful in separating constructions, inventions and fictions of Mugabe from what Giorgio Agamben (1987: 18), after Plato, has called "the thing itself." Personas, characters and performances of Mugabe have severally concealed Mugabe "the thing itself" and the actuality of the political animal. Inventions and imaginations of Mugabe by scholars and journalist have not freed themselves from the trappings of seeing saints or monsters in political leaders. The binary of the saint and the monster does not in itself reveal actualities of political leaders. There are also Garden of Eden narratives by such writers as Sue Onslow and Martin Plaut (2018) that circulate the largely colonial imagination that Mugabe's crime in power was that he tragically destroyed a prosperous country that he inherited from the Rhodesian regime. Rhodesia was a colonial and racist establishment whose prosperity was reserved for a minority white population and as such Mugabe inherited a fragile, unequal and faulty country in the very first place. Most journalists and scholars have also ignored the important social and political formation of Mugabe that this book treats in the previous chapter. The way Mugabe produced himself and was produced is important in seeing, understanding and knowing his will to power.

Mugabe's formation and production became in him what Timothy Chappell (2005: 12) describes as the "inescapable self" where his certainties and beliefs about himself became both a fortress that he used to defend himself and a prison that he could also not escape. He did not only hold convictions about his predestination and power, but the convictions grew to hold him hostage and insulate him from reality. Flatterers, opportunistic sycophants and enterprising power mongers around him built a false universe of divinity and grandeur around him that enveloped and insulated him from the real world. In his eventual embodiment of a saint and a monster in one, both illusory and fake identities, Mugabe became a living and powerful accident that could only continue happening until such an event as the coup that delivered him out of power in 2017. Somehow, the coup was the event that liberated Mugabe from the fake paradise and also the prison that he lived in. The coup restored Mugabe to the vulnerability and fragility that he had always hidden behind performances of bravado and might.

The aphorism by John Dalberg-Acton that "power tends to corrupt, and absolute power corrupts absolutely" which Ronald Roberts Suresh (2007: 5) engages with is closer to the description of how the will to power as a passion and a drive consumes the tyrant and eventually leads him to the cross of crucifixion. Like a spell and a possession, it leads the tyrant to the destruction of others and finally to his own destruction. Mugabe's beliefs about himself and his divine election increasingly became messianic and missionary and therefore more tragic and misleading as he began to see sinners and lost souls in his otherwise legitimate opponents.

What made Mugabe's political messianism more compelling and consuming is that his colleagues and potential successors such as Joice Mujuru also believed and publicly spoke of his divine pre-destination to rule for life. Before a full rally and religious congregation in January 2013, Joice Mujuru (2013) accused Mugabe's political enemies and opponents of being "bonkers" and insane for "wasting their time" contesting the leadership of one who was as early as "the age of 10" aware that he was sent by God to rule Zimbabwe until the end of his life. Mugabe's political drives and passions may not be fully understood without an appreciation of the religious myth and fiction of his pre-destination to rule which morphed into a messianic will to power that made him see his political opponents as the anti-Christ that were challenging divine will and order. Holland (2008: 148) noted but did not take seriously the truth that "Mugabe believes sincerely, like his late mother, that he is some sort of saviour sent to Zimbabwe by God-and he behaves accordingly." Such long time loyalists of Mugabe as Didymus Mutasa, who also later became an enemy, forcefully circulated a political idea that Mugabe was a kind of monarch that was not supposed to be put through the indignity of leaving office but should die in power (Holland 2008: 187). Even such, now celebrated, champions of independent journalism as Geoff Nyarota (2018: 27) once did not only hold but circulated ideas and myths that Mugabe was "enigmatic, principled" and the best thing to happen to Zimbabwe. Openly some of the opportunistic loyalists circulated the view that to put Mugabe through elections was an insult to royalty and disrespect for a great leader.

Mugabe himself believed that he did not seek power but that power sought him, as he told Jonathan Moyo that "people always came to me. They wanted me without me doing anything to promote myself" (Holland 2008: 188). Many scholars, journalists and other interlocutors of the political thought and practice of Mugabe have not reckoned sufficiently with how his belief in his divine chosenness became an imprisoning psychological framework that did not permit him to experience true reality of the world and politics. Mugabe did not even see himself as a politician, but like Adolf Hitler whose psychological "core identity was that of a charismatic prophet" (Glad 2002: 15), he experienced and carried himself as a deliverer come to save Zimbabwe. Hitler's encounter with true reality in defeat led him to a suicide, and Mugabe's re-introduction to the cold and dry real political world was a coup, a symbolic crucifixion of a kind. Deluded political prophets and messiahs also end up at the cross, somehow.

As noted above, Timothy Chappell (2005: 13) describes how beliefs grow into certainties and that certainties, especially in politics and philosophy, become a fortress against other beliefs and also graduate into a prison that confines and holds captive the believer. This book holds that Mugabe's certainty about his own political messianism started as an assuring fortress and ended up a true prison beyond which he could not see or experience reality, and he began by instrumentalising his belief in his political permanence and ended up being an instrument and a victim of the same belief. In many ways, Mugabe could no longer escape himself but was bound to end up a victim of his deluded mental framework.

There is, therefore, little doubt that Mugabe in seeing enemies and opponents to his rule, in imagining and inventing them as lost sinners , he saw himself as a Christ-like figure pitted against forces of darkness that he was duty-bound by the divine reality to overcome, and believed he would eventually overcome them. This Christ-like sensibility of the will to power is the same as that which possessed Friedrich Nietzsche himself who in his experience of critics and opponents to his ideas understood himself as messianic and prevalently signed off his essays as "the crucified one" (Badiou 2009: 2) who dies on the cross in defence of his high truths and a kind of divine order of a Christian who did not really believe in Christ but himself. This is the same way in which this book notes the Jesuitised Mugabe as a Christian without Christ. The will to power, in many ways, becomes a Christ-consciousness that bends to the idolatry of self-belief and self-worship and is therefore suicidal and tragic.

Because of his own political self-belief and idolatry of self-celebration and worship, Mugabe has attracted studies and critiques that ignore structural and systemic factors that produced him and concentrate on him as a person and a subject of study. In reactions to these studies and critiques of Mugabe, Sabelo Ndlovu-Gatsheni (2012a: 316) warns that scholars should go "beyond Mugabe-centric narratives" that do not make visible the larger historical and systemic factors that produced his kind of political thought and leadership. Similar to Sabelo Ndlovu-Gatsheni's critical caution, Sandra Maclean (2002: 513) notes that Mugabe as a subject of study has "defied systematic analysis" because scholars ignore "the political economy of conflict" and international and historical factors that have structured, conditioned and produced Mugabe's political thought and leadership. Mugabe is also fundamentally a political individual that became contracted and client to cultures, systems and structures of power. To understand Mugabe, "the thing itself" beyond constructions and inventions requires a kind of critical excavation and archaeology to unravel.

Further and deeper than the individual person of Mugabe, in the systemic and cultural individual, might be where the truth hides. Richard Bourne (2011: 3) has also emphasised the need for scholars to look beyond and further than Mugabe the person in order to appreciate his political thought and political conduct in Zimbabwe, Africa and the world. In that way, Mugabe can also easily be understood as a creature of the world historical and political system. This also suggests that anyone, put in the same position, can easily become a Mugabe if institutions and systems are not put in place to check excesses and degenerations. While this understanding of the political Mugabe that is large scale, structural and world systemic is appreciated in this book, emphasis is placed on his will to power as an individual that fed from and fed into structural and systemic factors. Mugabe's will to power found systemic and structural factors and conditions that were permitting and enabling. Zimbabwe and the world conspired to give birth to Mugabe the monstrosity, in other words.

As I have noted in the previous chapter and above, Mugabe was brought up, conditioned and produced, even actively produced himself into a historical and political agent. In an interview with Heidi Holland, Jonathan Moyo, an astute observer of Mugabe and a close colleague once, an enemy and opponent later, and a trusted colleague again, noted that Mugabe as then a teacher "accepted a (political) career that was not his chosen one, he becomes a shrewd and calculating politician who must develop a philosophy and a style as he hits the ground running" (Holland 2008: 182). In other words, Mugabe had to perform to a political script that was given to him but that coincided with his will to power. In a way, not to understand Mugabe as a performer and an actor might be to miss his essence. Like Hitler who rehearsed his demagogic speeches to an imaginary audience and industrially prepared himself to sound and look like the messiah that he thought he was (Glad 2002: 17), Mugabe saw Zimbabwe and the world as a stage upon which he had to seem and look like the saviour that he imagined himself to be.

Correctly, Holland (2008: 183) notes that "a reluctant politician initially, Mugabe appears on the political stage as a puppet of other people's passions" and as "having entered politics through the persuasion of others rather than his own conviction." Ultimately, Mugabe became a puppet of power itself. What, in the view of this book, both Heidi Holland the interviewer and Jonathan Moyo the interviewee did not immediately note is that as reluctant as he was Mugabe carried a belief that he was chosen before birth to lead, those who came to persuade him to join politics were in his mind instruments of the divine, human raw materials of his divine anointed power. When Grace Mugabe and others sang to him the myths about his messianism, they were singing a song that they knew Mugabe understood and believed about himself. There is a family of scholarly ideas, as seen below, that understands or constructs Mugabe as having been a tragic figure or else a creature of tragedy. These ideas are in many ways continued inventions of Mugabe that neglect his formation and production into the monstrosity that he grew up to be.

Mugabe: The Tragic Figure

Tragic figures are usually those individuals that initially embody good for themselves and others but end up declining to some evil and disaster. Prominently, Holland (2008: 1) describes the political and historical story of Mugabe as "the untold story of a freedom fighter who became a tyrant," which description advances the suggestion that Mugabe was once a liberator and declined tragically to a tyrant. The political story of Mugabe, to Daniel Compagnon (2011), was a "predictable tragedy" that resulted in the "collapse of Zimbabwe," suggesting that there were always signs and reasons why Mugabe would end so tyrannically and badly for the country. Also holding the tragic and the unfortunate fall from grace to grass of Mugabe is Bourne (2011: 1) who bemoans the "catastrophe" in Zimbabwe and asks "what happened?" in perplexity and regret of the great degeneration of a promising leader and hopeful country. In the determination against post-political, simplistic, naïve and also innocent understandings of the political Mugabe, this book notes that it was a mistake ever to invest so much blind hope in Mugabe, as the optimism about his liberator and hero status was premature and misguided.

An exploration of the literature, be it biographies or hagiographies of Mugabe, betrays a trend in which he is seen and understood as once having carried hope for the world. Biographers prevalently observe in Mugabe an evil man who tried and failed to be good, or who started off with a promise and fell. Hagiographers prevalently observe a great man who was tragically overcome and overtaken by evil. In his essay of "the birth of tragedy," Nietzsche (1972) explains that all tragedy is made out of the great Apollonian spirit of calm, peace and good intentions and at the same time the evil and violent spirit of the force of the Dionysian. In that way, tragedy is divided between good and evil. In that respect, Mugabe would seem to be a tragic figure in that he is on the one hand extremely admired for his heroism and on the other reviled for his evil, and an Apollonian and a Dionysian conflict seems to be situated in his life, political thought and practice. This book notes that, true, Mugabe once carried promise for Zimbabwe but gradually and later delivered violence, catastrophe and tyranny, tragically. However, the book maintains that behind the initial promise Mugabe had concealed inside him a will to power and Christ-like political sensibility and consciousness that was always going to be disastrous as it was not informed by anything democratic, liberatory or humanist, but was driven by a god-like will to power that was insulated from cares of ethical politics. The true tragedy about Mugabe, perhaps, like many other tyrants that "go too far" (Glad 2002: 1), is that he found believers and supporters that were more than ready to feed his illusions of messianism and affirm him as a divinely appointed deliverer. From the start, in Zimbabwe and the larger world, Mugabe was not received with the caution and suspicion that all politicians should be treated with. The important art of "wrestling tyrants" and combating despotism in the world that Christopher Blakesley (2017: 1) describes suggests total disinvestment of trust in individual heroes, no matter how promising, but an investment in working laws and institutions that effectively check the excesses of leaders.

Mugabe: The Traitor

Related to the understanding of Mugabe as a tragic figure, who was produced by and also produced tragedy, is the understanding that he was a traitor. To Andrew Norman (2004a: 1), the life narrative of Mugabe is a tale of "the betrayal of Zimbabwe" where "Mugabe instead of leading his people to the promised land, has on the one hand amassed a fortune for himself, his family and followers" and also "presided over the deliberate murder, torture and starvation of those who opposed him." Like JudasIscariot, Mugabe is understood to have initially been a trusted insider to Zimbabwe who reneged from the confidence of his people and brought upon them what Martin Meredith (2002a: 1) describes as a tale of "power, plunder and tyranny in Zimbabwe." Much like the understanding of Mugabe as a tragic figure, the notion that he betrayed Zimbabwe holds a mistaken view that he was once a true messiah that was supposed to deliver his people some promised land, was a trusted disciple like Judas once was and then fell on the way. In politics, it seems to me, the belief in messiahs leads to the betrayal of the believers and the crucifixion of the believed. This describes in exactitude what became of Zimbabweans and Mugabe.

Such large-scale violence as the Gukurahundi Genocide of 1983 to 1987 in Zimbabwe started too early in Mugabe's career for observers to believe in an earlier Mugabe that was a liberator. More convincing is that Mugabe was a "predictable tragedy" (Compagnon 2011: 1) and that "from the beginning he was toxic" (Tendi 2011: 1). Those that saw the early Mugabe as a deliverer and were later disappointed when he not only failed to deliver but occasioned catastrophe are the same people that were misled by their own beliefs in saints and messiahs in politics.

Mugabe, it appears in the view of this book, was always burdened by what Timothy Chappell (2005: 12) calls the "nightmare" of the "egocentric predicament" where even if he wished or tried, he could not overcome the beliefs and fundamentalisms inside him that became his misleading mental universe, that an overwhelming paradise and forbidding prison. The belief in his chosenness and hence his righteousness became an energy and passion that drove his ego and forcefully defined him. Tyrants are most times romantic imaginists that come to be imprisoned in the worlds of their fantasies and get lost to the real world. Holland (2008: xiii) is correct in the much belated discovery that "I realise that I and other well-intentioned individuals may have helped Robert Mugabe to become the man he is today" and "if we had reacted differently to the early signs of his paranoia, could Zimbabwe have been saved from its current abyss." Insisting that Mugabe also became a product of white political blunders and naïve dreams, Holland (2008: xiii) is also correct to note that "if whites in the country had been more realistic and acknowledged the impossibility of shifting smoothly from a police state of their creation to the democracy of their self-serving dreams, would they have been more respectful, less provocative?" to "mad Bob." By initially supporting him as a deliverer and then later demonising him as a monster, some whites in Zimbabwe and outside gave Mugabe the excuse to be himself and pretend to some victimhood that justified, in his mind, some of his hatred and violence. Tyrants need excuses that give them an opportunity to be angry and to hate and attack certain individuals and communities. Many writers, especially white writers, understand Mugabe to have betrayed a great country that he inherited from the Rhodesians, which as I have stated earlier is a limited and compromising view. Pan-Africanist writers such as Horace Campbell (2003: 7) understand Mugabe to have betrayed a "Great Zimbabwe" of the African ancestors and pre-colonial rulers that respected the land and honoured human life. To such writers, Mugabe did not become any better than the whites who colonised the country, dominated and exploited the people. In failing to deliver liberation after the collapse of administrative colonialism but perpetuating a kind of colonialism, Mugabe became another colonist of a kind and a true traitor to his people first and next to the white colonists that expected him to be true to the forgiveness and reconciliation he offered them at the independence of Zimbabwe in 1980.

MUGABE: THE SCHOLAR AND THE DIPLOMAT

Mugabe's performances of intellectualism and pretensions to diplomacy that I describe earlier have had some believers and also sceptics in the scholarly and journalistic communities. Intellectualism and diplomacy were the first masks that Mugabe wore, the two qualities he performed to sell himself as a leader and which were slowly exposed as exactly that, performances and pretensions, however convincing.

Mugabe's game was not concealed to every observer. In the interview with Heidi Holland, Jonathan Moyo correctly notes that somehow Mugabe as a contented teacher was persuaded into politics by those that, unlike him, had always been in the struggle against colonialism when he was not. Those who invite him, at the time "they want him, not because he is committed to their cause but because he is educated, he sounds good, he speaks English well," said Moyo (Holland 2008: 181). Mugabe performed well in good argumentation and respectable modern manners and character that he could stand shoulder to shoulder with any white man at the time. Thus Mugabe was invited into the struggle for liberation from colonialism not as another political activist but as an intellectual, diplomat and spokesperson that the struggle and its nationalists and Marxists at the time could use. In a way, Mugabe entered political leadership as an elite and an opportunist rather than a willing cadre, hence Sabelo Ndlovu-Gatsheni (2015: 1, 2) opines that such leaders as Mugabe became anti-colonial but not exactly decolonial as they were also ambassadors of the same colonial system that they were supposed to overthrow. Such leaders began to fight colonialism using colonial logic hence their failure to totally vanquish colonialism. Instead of totally defeating colonialism and instituting liberation in its place they only achieved to bring into place venal native colonialism such as that which Mugabe imposed on Zimbabwe.

As I have demonstrated earlier, and still to reflect in the chapter that will follow this one, Mugabe became a pretender to both intellectualism and militarism. David Moore (2015: 33) notes correctly and argues convincingly that Mugabe became an "intellectual manqué" whose intellect was more pretended and feigned than it is real. Educatedness, in the typical post-colonial, is dramatised as intellectual weight that recommends one to leadership of the many uneducated, but in actuality, it is barren. He was not a principled thinker who firmly stood against colonialism and imperialism but was tempted and willing to share in the luxuries of the colonial world behind the back of the suffering black masses. As such, Moore observes, Mugabe was so drawn to the allure of England, Europe and the elite life that modernity offered. He was to be found pleading with the British to house his wife when he was in detention, willing to have the law broken for this (Moore 2015: 37). Mugabe pestered the British demanding the same human rights for himself that he was later to deny many Zimbabweans, a reflection of his opportunistic double standards. As a diplomat too, Mugabe has been found to be fake and wanting. Timothy Scarnecchia (2014: 78) notes how Mugabe enjoyed presenting himself as an "intransigent diplomat" when in actuality he was always more than willing to appease western powers and show himself as willing to co-operate with them and be their point man in Zimbabwe and Africa. Intellectualism and diplomacy became useful emblems that symbolised Mugabe's suitability as a leader but were not his true qualities. As this book will show in the next chapter, Mugabe in many ways became a pretender to what he was not and also pretended not to be what he exactly was in typical simulation and dissimulation of the will to power. Inside himself Mugabe had a pride and a "loftiness" that "is due of course, to the prophecy of greatness his mother supposedly received from God via Father O'Hea while he was a child" (Holland 2008: 188), and he was willing to rehearse and act to any script as long as that script seemed to validate the fiction of his chosenness by God.

There is a meaningful way in which in his will to power, Mugabe became fundamentally Cartesian and even more. It has been noted by scholars such as Andrew Norman (2004a: 47) that "Mugabe would have been inspired to hear from" his key formative mentor "father O'Hea about Ireland's struggle for independence from Britain; one which

Mugabe probably noticed was achieved not with the pen but with the sword; or in this case, the gun." The idea of a thinker who could also fight was justified in Mugabe's mind as possible and even right. In actuality, "as well as instructing Mugabe on the catechism and Cartesian logic, Father O'Hea gave him a feel for Irish legend and revolution, describing the struggle the Irish sustained to attain independence from Britain" (Meredith 2002a: 21). Mugabe was effectively sold dreams that he went on to believe and sell about the struggle and himself. Possessing an easily teachable mind, which Mugabe did, may be the same as being easily influenced and corrupted.

Enrique Chavez-Arvizo (1997: x) explains how Rene Descartes was brought up by the Jesuits who taught him the arts of mediation until he grew up to become not only a philosopher but once joined the army, combining militarism and philosophy until he produced the "I think therefore I am" aphorism that is a kind of will to power and belief in the self to conquer with thought and mind. Timothy Chappell (2005) observes that in the belief in himself as existing because he thought, Descartes settled on that the ultimate truth and reality belonged to God that is true perfection not an individual thinker. In a strong way, Descartes believed in his personal powers but still submitted to God as the ultimate authority and truth (Chavez-Arvizo 1997: xvll). Mugabe on the other hand does not seem to have tempered his cartesianism with a love or fear of God, or a respect for ethics, as this book will show.

In a way, the true tragedy and treachery of Mugabe may be that he was driven to power believing that he was sent of God, when he got into power or when the prophecy seemed to be fulfilled, he forgot about God and replaced God with himself in the true fall of Lucifer and other expelled angels. Much like the true Lucifer that reneged against the Kingdom that created him and gave him power, Mugabe was to betray the movement for the liberation of the colonised that made him the powerful man that he became. Testimony to Mugabe as a pretender and failure in intellectualism is that he has left behind no document of ideas from his own mind and pen the way many founding African liberation leaders such as Kwame Nkrumah, Julius Nyerere and Kenneth Kaunda have done. What can be called Mugabeism as a political philosophy and even ideology remains an absence rather than a reality, and it is that absence that allowed Mugabe to believe in everything and nothing at the same time, and just follow the winds of power not any clear political principles. There is no clear and followable political philosophy, as I show later, that can be called Mugabe's principled political ideology, except slogans, operations and other experiments for the preservation of his continued hold on power.

MUGABE: THE LUCIFER

A joke circulates in Zimbabwe that a true Zimbabwean found himself in Hell with a South African and a Zambian. The three persuaded the prince of Hell, Lucifer, to allow them to use his cell phone to call their friends back in Zambia, South Africa and Zimbabwe in that order. Being the true devil, Lucifer insisted on charging them an amount of money for the favour. The South African and the Zambian fainted at the sight of their bills that were in the high thousands and the Zimbabwean was pleasantly shocked at how low and affordable his was in the cool cents, "yours is a local call," the Devil explained. In short, Zimbabwe under Mugabe had become hell and the real Devil's headquarters where all the ghastly properties of Hell had become localised.

Those that have not known and experienced Mugabe as the messiah and saint that his beneficiaries and supporters have constructed him as prefer to see him as the true prince of darkness. The perception of Mugabe as a monstrous merchant of darkness is found expressed in literature that casts him as a dark figure that is opposed to the Saint and Messiah that some of his followers cherished. Life in Zimbabwe under Mugabe has been described by Judith Todd (2007) as a painful experience "through the darkness" of various forms of oppression and violations. The cruelty that Mugabe has subjected his enemies, opponents and victims to has been observed to be "beyond tears" (Buckle 2003); in the way, he has punished the people and destroyed what was once a promising country. From the Gukurahundi Genocide to the violence that accompanied land invasions and the elections of 2008, Peter Godwin (2008) summarises the Zimbabwean political condition under Mugabe as "the fear" and terror of a "smart genocide" where people get slowly killed off behind a façade of a working and stable country. Paul Moorcraft cites a US intelligence cable that described Mugabe as a devil that must be given his dues:

> To give the devil his due, he is a brilliant tactician. However, he is funda-
> mentally hampered by several factors: his ego and his belief in his own infal-
> libility; his obsessive focus on the past as justification for everything in the
> present and future; and his deep ignorance on economic issues coupled with

the belief that his 18 doctorates give him the authority to suspend the laws of economics, including supply and demand. (Moorcraft 2012: 188)

Mugabe's belief in his "infallibility" and righteousness, and his belief that he is bigger than politics and economics have driven him to commit evil that includes the Gukurahundi Genocide. His dramatisation of intellectual prowess that is treated above conceals basic ignorance and detachment from the real world of politics and economics, making him a kind of prince of darkness in the sense of ignorance and evil. The imagination that laws of politics and economics could be suspended by his will was a kind of the "aperspectival madness" that allowed him to put himself above commonsense and normalcy.

In the narrative of *Eichmann in Jerusalem: A Report on the Banality of Evil*, Hannah Arendt (2006) demonstrates how evil can be idiotic and banal but get covered up with pretences to reason and high mindedness. An idolatrous god-complex and Christ-consciousness seems to have misguided Mugabe into impunity and evil, "not once has Mugabe taken responsibility for his decisions and the actions of those around him" (Moorcraft 2012: 20). One of the foundational pillars of the philosophy of Rene Descartes, a Jesuit trainee like Mugabe, was the fear and suspicion that his beliefs might have been sponsored by an evil demon that was bent on misleading him, hence his surrender to God as the only perfect and supreme thinker (Chappell 2005: 10). Descartes checked his otherwise wild imagination with the fear of God as the only true and just truth, in his view. As an intellectual pretender and also a pretender to militarism, Mugabe in his devilish self-righteousness does not seem to have subjected his beliefs and opinions to any necessary doubt and question. Belief in his own infallibility and the evil that he occasioned led Mugabe into becoming a kind of a Lucifer that did not fear any truth. Mugabe personified the will to power as that which "drives" in order to "propel to power" and "power" that is "maintained over the self and over others with cruelty, mastery and domination" (Nietzsche 1997a, b: 1). The boast about "degrees in violence" and his "monstrous ego" (Meredith 2002a: 76, 228) that does not permit him to own up to wrong doing made Mugabe politically devilish. Like Hitler that "was not destroying to build, he was building to destroy" (Glad 2002: 32), Mugabe turned all what he touched including the country into either ruins or a true Hell where the devil himself reigns. In his negation, over years, of the true liberation and happiness of Zimbabweans, Mugabe became a real angel of darkness for a people that optimistically believed the end of colonialism to be the arrival of a paradisal era of the proverbial milk and honey.

What has sustained an image of Mugabe as a kind of messenger of darkness is not the condemnations of leaders of western countries, such as George Bush Junior, that frequently referred to Mugabe's Zimbabwe as part of the global locations of evil and darkness. Rather Mugabe as a devilish monster is defined by the political violence that he administered in Zimbabwe and the climax of which became the Gukurahundi Genocides of 1982 to 1987. The many thousands dead, millions displaced and dispossessed by political violence bespeak Mugabe's capacity for evil. Making Mugabe's dark record of evil worse is his continued denialism and refusal to account for his responsibility in the murders, massacres and the genocide. The closest he got to acknowledge the evil but distanced himself from the wrong doing is when Mugabe (2000) described the genocide as having been a "moment of madness." In saying so, Mugabe instead of being accountable distributed the blame generally, implicating even the victims and suggesting that they shared in the madness. Mugabe was devilish enough to suggest the victims of his genocide were implicated in the madness of the large-scale killings.

PRESENTATIONS AND REPRESENTATIONS OF MUGABE

In this account, I make the observation that Mugabe as a performer of power presented himself as a hero of the liberation struggle when in actuality he was something else, an opportunist power monger that was conditioned and produced into a tyrant. Both the biographies and hagiographies of Mugabe by scholars and some journalists seem to frequently misunderstand him and how he was formed, produced and unleashed into the history of Zimbabwe and the world. What Heidi Holland (2008) terms the "obscenity of understanding" is the difficulty of understanding Mugabe without apologising for evil or doing the negligent thing of not passing harsh judgement where it is due. When it comes to writing on Mugabe, scholars and journalists have battled the dilemma of fearing to condone evil and also being cautious about levelling uncritical condemnation of the man and his spectacular performances of power. Staying in power for too long, Sue Onslow and Martin Plaut (2018: 13, 15–16) believe, is what faded and cast into darkness the good that Mugabe did, dark and bloody deeds came to cloud and overshadow all other otherwise noble achievements that he made. The way the guerrillas grudgingly accepted him as leader and later how some of them as leaders of the Zimbabwe national army finally became the force that toppled him suggests that Mugabe may, throughout his term in power and in charge of ZANU-PF, have been a puppet of the soldiers as I have noted. It is possible that he became an invention, a production and also captive puppet of those that used him and his power for their own financial, social and economic benefits. In turn, as a practiced opportunist, Mugabe used the support that he was given by the securocrats and politicians in his party to fortify his personal hold on power. Not surprisingly, scholars such as Onslow and Plaut (2018: 17) make the bold conclusion that throughout his life in power, "Mugabe served the interests of the military, political and business elites who kept him in power for nearly four decades, until they finally turned on him, fearful that he would install his wife, Grace, in the presidency."

Mugabe was finally removed from power by the same people and forces that produced and maintained him in power against the will of Zimbabweans for decades. Behind all his bravado and loud rantings of a powerful tyrant, Mugabe might have been concealing a pathetic captive of rogue former guerrillas and soldiers. It is now public knowledge that Zimbabwe's military involvement in the DRC war in 1998 that was costly financially and in human lives, as many soldiers died, enriched some ministers and military generals. The same soldiers and politicians are mentioned in the story of the looting of the more than Fifteen Billion United States Dollars' worth of diamonds at Chiadzwa, looting which Mugabe publicly complained about in his last days in power. Fear not only that he would install his wife as his successor but that he might arrest them for the theft might also have fuelled the coup. As long as he allowed them to become rich, by whatever means, the former guerrillas and some politicians allowed him to stay in power by any means necessary until he began to consider punishing them for their crimes, their resort was to simply take away the power that they had given him in the very first place. In that way, Mugabe came to be consumed by the same politics of rent-seeking and patronage that was the scaffolding and fulcrum of his long stay in power.

For the reason that he was always a spectacular performer of power and strength, Mugabe's captivities to the securocrats and some politicians remained concealed, as he acted in charge. The backers and supporters that became rich and powerful using his power also publicly performed undying loyalty to him as their one and only leader and saviour. The refrain "you are the only one!" (Meredith 2007: 79) from 1987 onwards was a slogan that ZANU-PF loyalists sang to Mugabe to assure him of their unwavering support even when he became a true executive hooligan that had no respect for the law and for human life. Warlord politics of the African postcolony allows symbiotic and also parasitic relations between those that hold state power and those that benefit from it, in the true opportunism of the politics of spoils.

As much as Mugabe appears to have produced a cabal of a greedy military, political and economic elites in Zimbabwe, that cabal seems to have invented and produced him as well, in political relations of co-invention and co-production that eventually came to be his final undoing. Tyranny is that self-loving and self-eating power not only in that the tyrant is a self-worshipping narcissist but also that the very source of his invention and the production of his power is the same that comes to consume him, finally. Because Mugabe had never been alone in his Mugabeism, but had always represented a political system and a monstrosity that had individuals, organisations and forces that backed and benefited from him, understanding him frequently becomes a task that has thrown analysts off. Seeing Mugabe as a simple saint that has been betrayed and crucified or a singular monster that was particularly evil can be to simplify what is a complicated entanglement and a multiple invention. Many scholars and journalists have done just that.

Early after Zimbabwe's independence David Smith, Ian Davies and Colin Thompson (1981) wrote a flowery account of Mugabe's humble peasant beginnings, his prison life and education and his deserved ascendancy to power. Even then, the three admirers of Mugabe noted the sad reality where Mugabe regarded the two main provinces of Zimbabwe, Matabeleland and Mashonaland, as two separate countries (Ndlovu-Gatsheni 2014: 11). The regard by Mugabe of Matabeleland as another country, and Joshua Nkomo's country, not a part of the nation of Zimbabwe might explain the tribal hatred and genocide that government forces committed in the region. Mugabe's passionate Shona nationalism and patriotism did not permit him to see another tribe as Zimbabwean, which is the same way in which colonisers expelled natives from full citizenship and pushed them into native reserves and homelands. Mugabe possessed a troubling xenophobia and nativism. Writers such as David Smith, Ian Davies and Colin Thompson, in their hagiography of Mugabe, were part of that time in Zimbabwe when Mugabe was made a saint and a saviour whose glaring faults such as tribalism and xenophobia were easy to ignore. These were the intoxicating times of post-politics and blinding euphoria in Zimbabwe where a faulty and dangerous man was mistaken for national liberation itself, and behind that mistake, a monster that would eat the country grew.

Another narrative that supported the Zimbabwean liberation struggle and shed Mugabe in very good light came from David Martin and Philip Johnson (1981). The book, as Sabelo Ndlovu-Gatsheni (2014: 11) notes, was so pleasing to Mugabe that he had it distributed to all schools in the country as it portrayed him as an example for all Zimbabweans, especially the school children and youth. That self-promotion and personal political marketing on the part of Mugabe might explain his later refusal to leave office and his belief that he was irreplaceable. Tyrants tend to take the words of hagiographers and some false prophets rather too seriously. The early years of independence were the time when Mugabe received much scholarly and journalistic affirmation and praise. Fay Chung (2006) described Mugabe as an unwavering revolutionary and far sighted visionary, who perhaps did not have like-minded people around him, or has been let down and betrayed by incapable and less gifted ministers. Mugabe as a betrayed and let down political messiah is a representation that Mugabe himself was known to relish; his failures are explained as the failure of the people around him who cannot keep up with the high standards of the ruler. But as this book notes, Mugabe carried failure inside him in that he avoided engaging with reality and clung to beliefs, fantasies and illusions of power and divinity. Blind support and uncritical praise singing only helped Mugabe's blindness to himself, his faults and the world of reality around him.

The renowned historian, Terence Ranger (2003) who had earlier written favourably of Mugabe, blamed his authoritarianism on the liberation war and nationalist struggle against colonialism that demanded high handedness and authoritarianism from the fighters and their leaders. In the view of Ranger which I appreciate in this book, Mugabe was culturalised and conditioned into political violence before and during his leadership of the violent guerrilla movement, the violent struggle against colonialism infected him with its political culture of cruelty. In a way, and in his own will to power and inner vulnerability and fragility, Mugabe grew to imitate the same violence and cruelty that the Rhodesian regime had deployed against him and other black Rhodesians. Mugabe lacked the emotional and mental stamina to resist the temptation to be a coloniser in his own right.

I have noted in the previous chapter that part of Mugabe's political conditioning was in the cruelty and suffering he endured in jail and also the violence that he became part of in the liberation struggle. Mugabe cannot be fully understood and represented outside the consideration that he fought colonialism and its violence until he became, not an alternative, but a symptom of it. He fought oppression but failed to overcome the infection by the oppressive order that he went on to embody and reproduce to tragic effects. Biographers and hagiographers of Mugabe have not sufficiently understood and expressed the way Mugabe came to admire and sought to reproduce the Rhodesian colonial military and political machinery.

In his imitation and reproduction of the violent colonial political culture, Mugabe somehow became a traitor to the liberation struggle and its authentic ideals of democracy and human rights for black people that had endured venal colonialism. A veteran of the Zimbabwean liberation struggle, Wilbert Sadomba (2011), wrote of Mugabe as a cunning opportunist that usurped and appropriated the liberation struggle and personalised it in order to monopolise power. Mugabe appeared to Sadomba as an educated person who took advantage of the illiteracy of fellow comrades in the liberation struggle to centralise himself in the life of the country. Sadomba notes how the war slogan "*Pamberi neChimurenga*" (forward with the liberation war) was dropped for "*Pamberi na Robert Mugabe*" (forward with Robert Mugabe) to signal that the person of Mugabe had replaced in importance the entire national liberation struggle.

When a personal legacy of an individual leader surpasses that of the collective national struggle, that leader would have become significantly powerful and important, and Mugabe seems to have fully instrumentalised this prestige to the extent of competing with the country itself for importance. In political importance, Mugabe became the state and the nations. Mugabe was allowed and enabled to achieve such importance by not only the poets that composed slogans in his name but also opportunistic loyalists in his party and the world at large that negligently embraced him as a gallant hero. Michael Auret (2009: ix) notes how "the transformation of Robert Mugabe from a hero and international symbol for African freedom to a villain and an international outcast has been a depressing spectacle to witness." More depressing however, I note, is the political and critical carelessness of allowing an individual politician to ever personalise a collective struggle to the extent of becoming its international symbol. National liberation should, by its nature, be too weighty and grand a human ideal to be surrendered to the heroism of individuals, no matter how heroic the individuals may be.

The heroism that Mugabe was given and which he effectively used for personal advantage made him an opportunist rather than a deserving liberation leader. Similar to Wilbert Sadomba, another veteran of the Zimbabwean liberation struggle, Wilfred Mhanda (2011) portrays Mugabe as a true villain who betrayed and usurped the liberation struggle for personal power and prestige. The image of Mugabe as an opportunist who used his western education to usurp the legacy of the liberation struggle and to overtake less educated nationalists in leadership is a prevalent representation of his political practice. Most Africans that became leaders of their countries after independence from colonialism were mainly those that had achieved western education. Mugabe's education, I note in this book, did nothing to cover him in any glory, but he actually soiled the name of education in the way he conducted himself as a monster not a polished and reasoned political thinker and actor. David Blair (2002), as a result, satirises Mugabe's vaunted educational credentials and describes him as a leader who had "degrees in violence" and whose struggle had been for personal power not national liberation.

Power and violence are the true legacy of Mugabe; the rest was pretence in the view of Stephen Chan (2003) who describes Mugabe as a power monger that put up all kinds of acts and performances to cover his tyrannical motives. Understanding Mugabe as a pretender is a critical way of seeing through his performances that made him an actor who fooled his spectators. The effects of Mugabe's performative self-inventions and inventions by both admirers and detractors are summarised by Trevor Ncube (2009: x) who confesses that "Mugabe had all of us fooled for one reason or another and at different times, he made each of us believe he was one thing when infact he was something else." The capital lesson that Mugabe has taught Zimbabwe and the world is that politicians should be treated with critical suspicion and political caution as they frequently are something else other than what they promise and pretend to.

A Political Philosophy of Mugabeism

Given that Mugabe became more of a performer of power and pretender to some grand ideals, driven more by his will to power, than the ideal of liberation, it is important to question his political philosophy. The search for what Sabelo Ndlovu-Gatsheni (2014) has called "Mugabeism" in reference to Mugabe's political philosophy is a search for what is both an absence and a presence. As noted earlier, Mugabe has given no body of literature that may betray what can be called his political philosophy except for speeches and other rants, some of which were crafted by aides and hired spin-doctors. What are present are performances and pretences to radical anti-imperialism and simulations of gallant nationalism and Pan-Africanism that degenerated into racism, nativism and Afro-radicalism. Mugabe is a member of the group of first-generation African leaders who used their education and participation in liberation struggles as a justification for inclusion in the leadership of their countries and as such, they were produced by the history of colonialism and colonial education as much as they wished to produce a history of African liberation from colonialism (Ndlovu-Gatsheni 2014: 1). In a way, such leaders as Mugabe were products of the colonial intellectual and political culture, reproducing aspects of colonial, political and intellectual leadership, became easy as they understood no other world except the colonial one. Colonialism gave them a language and a template of power that landed itself easily for application in ruling and misruling their people, I note in this book.

The absence of a body of knowledge produced by Mugabe is one of the reasons why a scholar that has studied Zimbabwean history and reflected on it in impressive detail and depth, David Moore (2014: 30), describes Mugabe as "an intellectual manqué," as noted above. As such Mugabe became a political thinker that either did not achieve his potential against his wishes or a pretender to thought who has no tangible ideas except slogans and catchphrases. Moore fortifies his observations with detailed illustrations of how Mugabe has not produced or stood for any ideas in a consistent way besides being blown by the historical and political winds of power. For such a political pretender as Mugabe, committing any ideas to paper and preserving them for later evaluation may not be wise as it would betray his propensity to hold no ideas at all but to follow the winds of power. That is why Trevor Ncube (2009: x) complains that once the world thought in Mugabe it had a Marxist-Leninist in the mould of Mao Ze Dong only to realise rather too late that he was a pragmatic nationalist that soon enough proved to be a "callous megalomaniac" with genocidal tendencies.

Not only a pretender but also one given to imitation, Mugabe repeated and duplicated what he saw other leaders do, including racist colonialists such as Ian Smith. Alois Mlambo (2014: 45) observes that Mugabe was not as extra-ordinary as he was assumed to have been. He became a nationalist leader who like many others was drawn to ideas of economic nationalism, such as in the fast track land reform programme that he disastrously championed apparently for social justice but in actuality for political expediency and survival. Similar to Idi Amin who, to disastrous national consequences, expelled Indian from Uganda in 1972, Mugabe was prepared to drive the white population out from Zimbabwe in his performance of radical land reform that was not exactly an enactment of liberation, but only an opportunistic show for personal hold on power in Zimbabwe. Land retrieved from white commercial farmers was redistributed along party lines, with ZANU-PF politicians benefitting the most. National assets, otherwise, were used to buy political support and votes for a political party and its leader. Both Moore and Mlambo clearly suggest the uses of pretence and manipulation of public opinion by Mugabe to present himself as a gallant hero of his people that is guided by revolutionary principles. Gorden Moyo (2014: 61) is more specific in that Mugabe survived for so long in politics by use of simulating nationalist and Pan-Africanist ideals when in reality he was a "neo-sultanist" ruler with deep propensities to tyranny. The tyrant is the ultimate performer to an invisible script of power and that way he can fool his spectators. The very hard way did an initial admirer of Mugabe, Trevor Ncube (2009: xiv), realise that stripped of his eloquent anti-colonial rhetorical performances, Mugabe was a pathetic old man that was desperate to stay in power by all means necessary.

It appears to me that most observers and students of the political thought and practice of Mugabe notice a way in which he simulates and pretends to grand political and revolutionary ideas and ideals. For instance, Timothy Scarnecchia (2014: 78) shows in detail how Mugabe acted out as an "intransigent diplomat" in his dealing with western countries, pretending not to change his positions, when in actuality he was an "insider outsider" who did everything to impress and earn the good opinion of America and Britain. In his "friendship" with the West, Scarnecchia shows, Mugabe would deploy threats when it suited him and employ solicitations when it was right, meanwhile carefully keeping the countries close to him. Scarnecchia gives an impression of Mugabe as a leader who had no fixed truth but shifted positions in pursuit of advantage. Facing rejection by Western countries in 2003 and determined to grow his friendship with the Chinese and other Eastern countries, Mugabe famously declared that "we have turned East, where the sun rises, and given our back to the West, where the sun sets" (Onslow and Plaut 2018: 116), poetically and performatively concealing that it is the West that had turned its back on him. Philosophically, Mugabe was neither West nor East, right or left, but actually a performer to the blowing winds of power that became the music to whose sound he danced. Mugabe became a true "narcissist nihilist" that Ken Wilber (2017: 7) describes as someone that believes in "no truth" but anything and everything that sustains his intellectual and political position, no matter how wrong it is. Mugabe loved and believed in himself and his power too much to love or believe in anything besides, like a true narcissistnihilist.

Foremost of Mugabe's performances was violence that he much infamously claimed to have degrees in and which David Blair found ironic of a supposedly educated and cultured leader. One who gets degrees in any discipline is also one who has been taught and learnt well. For Mugabe, the culture of violence was partly learnt from the colonial regime and the guerrillas whose acceptance he desperately needed in Mozambique as I have illustrated above. The real owners of violence and teachers of it did not publicly boast about their violent crimes or did they make obscene threats of it.

Only as an overzealous student of violence did Mugabe find himself having to be exhibitionist about cruelty, in reference to Ian Smith and other Rhodesian whites, he once loudly claimed "we will kill those snakes among us, we will smash them completely" (Mpofu and Ndlovu-Gatsheni 2014: 130). I note in the previous chapter how in actuality Mugabe grew up a coward, a sissy and a "mama's baby" that could not even personally throw the fist of the proverbial coward. The tyrant that is a coward but wants to be known and feared for courage frequently goes too far in the exhibitionism of violence. To impress his soldiers and generals that he belonged to the world of violence and killings and was not a pretender, which he was, Saddam Hussein called out the names of those to be executed, "throughout he stopped to puff on his cigar, sometimes relighting it" as he forced some people that were present "to join him in the actual executions of the condemned" (Miller and Mylroie 1990: 44–45). Mugabe's own loud threats and boasts about guns were the performances of one who personally did not even know how to fire a revolver but could only deploy and delegate others to do it on his behalf. When the typical tyrant publicly displays and openly boasts of violence, he frequently does so to conceal his inner cowardice, mental fragility and fear.

Mugabe's exhibitionist violence was indeed violent, but it did not become a revolutionary philosophy or practice of liberation, but it became "festivals of cruelty." Such non-revolutionary violence is the typical "self-defeating behaviour" of the tyrant (Glad 2002: 14). Part of the reason

Mugabe had to cling to power until he was forced out became the fear and guilt of a man that had committed violent crimes against humanity and faced the possibility of being arraigned before an international criminal court (Auret 2009: viii), because his violence was evil and not calculated, he went too far. Mugabe went too far in not only threatening and systematically and methodically applying violence but going on to unleash wanton executions, assassinations and severe beatings that included burnings and the amputation of limbs of the victims. Once he sat on the throne of the many skulls of his victims, Mugabe could not contemplate retirement for fear of revenge and other reprisals.

It is the typical "sissy" and "Mama's Baby" that wants a reputation for being a real hard man. Mugabe went too far to perform and show off the real man of hardihood. The way Mugabe allowed, and by that encouraged, his ministers to compare him to a monarch in praise and to publicly kneel before him showed a "masculinity politics" where he treated even other grown men and colleagues from the struggle as docile women (Gaidzanwa 2014: 157). Gaidzanwa explores how even during the days of the liberation struggle, women were infantilised, treated like children, while men were feminised, treated like docile women under the leadership of Mugabe. Gaidzanwa sees in Mugabe a leader who did not only love power but wanted to see his power in the way colleagues and supporters behaved around him; he wanted to witness performances of his power and dramatisation of his authority. As what Macaphulana (2016) calls a "sissy" and "Mama's Baby" who grew up under the protective skirts of his mother, Mugabe performed excessive manliness and masculinity to hide the little girl that lived inside him. Mugabe was, in actuality, always something else and something other than what he presented himself as, and these performances of what he was actually not have misled most journalists and scholars, who have represented him in many but misleading portraits and characterisations.

THE MADNESS OF ROBERT MUGABE

Mugabe's will to power became a passionate political insanity from which he could not save himself. Once in a while, it appears that he saw into his own madness. At a memorial service in honour of Joshua Nkomo on the 2nd of July 2000, Mugabe for the first time described the Gukurahundi Genocide as having been "a moment of madness." While Mugabe referred to the madness of the Genocide in general terms, the evil and the insanity of the violence was squarely his and that of the political culture and system he personified. "Mad Bob" as Heidi Holland (2008: xiv) refers to Mugabe suffered a kind of "aperspectival madness" that Ken Wilber (2017: 11) describes and which as a concept refers to a person that is incapable of seeing any truth besides their own fantasies and illusions about reality. As an aperspectivally mad person, Mugabe rather took too seriously the statements of such people as his wife Grace Mugabe (2008: xiv) that claimed he was irreplaceable as the president of Zimbabwe and promised that, by the will of God, he would rule the country even from his grave.

Supporters such as Kudzai Chipanga (2018: 143) that told Mugabe "you are representing God on earth" were mad to indulge in such flattery of a fallible human being. Mugabe was even more insane to take such statements for gospel. Taking such words of insane flattery for gospel truth expelled Mugabe from the real world and located him in an alternative universe, an insane universe where he was an invincible deputy to God that could rule Zimbabwe and violate the people without accounting to any mortal. Mugabe should have taken seriously his opponents and not supporters. Tragically, the opponents and political enemies that questioned and challenged the view of himself as a saint, he insanely understood them as some kinds of heretics and sinners that needed to be punished. Mugabe was a political animal and monstrosity that, in hindsight, needed more opponents and enemies than he had supporters. Mugabe needed to listen to his opponents and enemies more than he did praise singers. Mugabe's supporters and flatterers helped him grow a god-complex that was to become his tragic undoing. With their words, his supporters and flatterers protected Mugabe from reality and enveloped him in fantasy and illusion. In the way, Mugabe became insulated from reality and lived in delusions of his grandeur, he became insane and power in his hands became a weapon in the disposal of a dangerous lunatic.

References

Agamben, G. (1987). The Thing Itself. *Contemporary Italian Thought*, *16*(2),53, 18–28.

Alliluyeva, S. (1967). *Twenty Letters to a Friend* (P. J. McMillan, Trans.). New York: Harper & Row.

Arendt, H. (2006). *Eichmann in Jerusalem: A Report on the Banality of Evil*. London: Penguin Books.

Auret, M. (2009). *From Liberator to Dictator: An Insider's Account of Robert Mugabe's Descent into Tyranny*. Claremont: David Philip.

Badiou, A. (2009). Who Is Nietzsche? In D. Hoens, S. Jöttkandt, & G. Buelens (Eds.), *The Catastrophic Imperative* (pp. 195–204). New York: Palgrave Macmillan.

Blair, D. (2002). *Degrees in Violence: Robert Mugabe and the Struggle for Power in Zimbabwe*. London: Continuum.

Blakesley, C. (2017). Wrestling Tyrants: Do we need an International Criminal Justice System? *Scholarly Works, 10*(24), 2–14.

Bourne, R. (2011). *Catastrophe: What Went Wrong in Zimbabwe?* London & New York: Zed Books.

Buckle, C. (2003). *Beyond Tears: Zimbabwe's Tragedy*. Cape Town: Jonathan Ball Publishers.

Bulloch, J., & Morris, H. (1991). *Saddam's War: The Origins of the Kuwait Conflict and the International Response*. London: Faber and Faber.

Campbell, H. (2003). *Reclaiming Zimbabwe: The Exhaustion of the Patriarchal Model of Liberation*. Claremont: David Philip Publishers.

Chan, S. (2003). *Robert Mugabe: A Life of Power and Violence*. Michigan: University of Michigan Press.

Chappell, T. (2005). *The Inescapable Self: An Introduction to Western Philosophy Since Descartes*. London: Orion Publishing Group.

Chavez-Arvizo, E. (1997). Introduction. In *Descartes: Key Philosophical Writings*. Hertfordshire: Wordsworth Editions.

Chipanga, K. (2018). In G. Nyarota (Ed.), *The Graceless Fall of Robert Mugabe: The End of a Dictator's Reign*. Cape Town: Penguin Random House.

Chung, F. (2006). *Re-living the Second Chimurenga: Memories from Zimbabwe's Liberation Struggle*. Uppsala: Nordic Africa Institute.

Compagnon, D. (2011). *A Predictable Tragedy: Robert Mugabe and the Collapse of Zimbabwe*. Philadelphia: University of Pennsylvania Press.

Conquest, R. (1991). *Stalin: Breaker of Nations*. New York: Viking.

Dotcherty, T. (2016). *Complicity: Criticism Between Collaboration and Commitment*. London: Rowman and Littlefield.

Ekeh, P. (1975). Colonialism and the Two Publics in Africa: A Theoretical Statement. *Comparative Studies in Society and History, 17*(1), 91–112.

Fanon, F. (2008). *Black Skin White Masks*. London: Pluto Press.

Freire, P. (1993). *Pedagogy of the Oppressed*. London: Penguin Books.

Gaidzanwa, R. (2014). Grappling with Mugabe's Masculinist Politics in Zimbabwe: A Gender Perspective. In S. Ndlovu-Gatsheni (Ed.), *Mugabeism?: History, Politics and Power in Zimbabwe*. New York: Palgrave Macmillan.

Glad, B. (2002). Why Tyrants Go Too Far: Malignant Narcissism and Absolute Power. *Political Psychology, 23*, 1–37.

Godwin, P. (2008). *The Fear: The Last Days of Robert Mugabe*. New York: Picador.

Hill, G. (2003). *The Battle for Zimbabwe: The Final Countdown*. Cape Town: Zebra Press.

Holland, H. (2008). *Dinner with Mugabe: The Untold Story of a Freedom Fighter Who Became a Tyrant*. Johannesburg: Penguin Books.

Hope, C. (2003). *Brothers Under the Skin: Travels in Tyranny*. London: Pan Macmillan.

Hitchens, C. (1995). *The Missionary Position: Mother Teresa in Theory and Practice*. London: Verso.

Laclau, E. (2005). *On Populist Reason* (pp. ix–xi). London: Verso.

Lamb, D. (1990). *The Africans: Encounters from the Sudan to the Cape*. London: Mandarin Publishers.

Macaphulana, D. M. (2015). Zimbabwe: Let Us Say Grace. In *ZimbabweSituation. com*. Retrieved October 8, 2018, from www.zimbabwesituation.com/news/ zimsit_w_analysis-zimbabwe-let-us-say-grace/.

Macaphulana, D. M. (2016). Robert Mugabe: The Head of State and State of the Head. In *Bulawyo24 News*. Retrieved February 25, 2016, from https:// bulawayo24.com.

Macaphulana, D. M. (2017a). Mnangagwa and the Theft of History. In *Bulawayo24 News*. Retrieved February 14, 2019, from https://bulawayo24. com/index-idopinion-sc-columnist-byo-122102.html.

Macaphulana, D. M. (2017b). Robert Mugabe the Physical Man Naturally Retreats. In *Bulawayo24 News*. Retrieved August 4, 2017, from bulwayo24.com.

MacLean, J. S. (2002). Mugabe at War: The Political Economy of Conflict in Zimbabwe. *Third World Quarterly, 23*(3), 513–528.

Makombe, P. (2004). Nyarota Attempts to Spin His Mistakes. In *The Standard*. Retrieved October 2, 2018, from https://www.thestandard. co.zw/2004/12/03/nyarota-attempts-to-spin-his-mistakes/.

Martin, D., & Johnson, P. (1981). *The Struggle for Zimbabwe*. London: Faber and Faber.

Matyszak, D. (2015). Coup De Grace? Plots and Purges: Mugabe and ZANU-PF's 6th National People's Congress. *Research and Advocacy Unit*. Retrieved July 10, 2019, from www.researchand advocacyunit.

Mazarire, G. C. (2011). Discipline and Punishment in ZANLA, 1964–1979. *Journal of Southern African Studies, 37*(3), 571–591.

Mazrui, A. A. (2005). Pan-Africanism and Intellectuals: Rise, Decline and Revival. In T. Mkandawire (Ed.), *African Intellectuals: Rethinking Politics, Language, Gender and Development*. New York: Zed Books.

Meredith, M. (2002a). *Robert Mugabe: Power, Plunder and Tyranny in Zimbabwe*. Cape Town: Jonathan Ball Publishers.

Meredith, M. (2007). *Mugabe: Power, Plunder, and the Struggle for Zimbabwe's Future*. New York: Public Affairs.

Mhanda, W. (2011). *Dzino: Memories of a Freedom Fighter*. Harare: Weaver Press.

Miller, J., & Mylroie, L. (1990). *Saddam Hussein and the Crisis in the Gulf*. New York: Random House.

Mlambo, A. S. (2014). Mugabe on Land, Indigenisation and Development. In S. Ndlovu-Gatsheni (Ed.), *Mugabeism? History, Politics and Power in Zimbabwe*. New York: Palgrave Macmillan.

Moorcraft, P. (2012). *Mugabe's War Machine*. Cape Town: Jonathan Ball Publishers.

Moore, D. (2015). In S. Ndlovu-Gatsheni (Ed.), *Mugabeism? History, Politics, and Power in Zimbabwe*. New York: Palgrave Macmillan.

Moore, D. B. (2014). Robert Mugabe: An Intellectual Manqué and his moments of Meaning. In S. Ndlovu-Gatsheni (Ed.), *Mugabeism? History, Politics and Power in Zimbabwe*. New York: Palgrave Macmillan.

Mouffe, C. (2005a). *On the Political*. Abingdon: Routledge.
Moyo, G. (2014). Mugabe's Neo-sultarnist Rule: Beyond the Veil of Pan-Africanism. In S. Ndlovu-Gatsheni (Ed.), *Mugabeism? History, Politics and Power in Zimbabwe*. New York: Palgrave Macmillan.
Mpofu, B., & Ndlovu-Gatsheni, S. (2014). Robert Mugabe: The Will to Power and Crisis of the Paradigm of War. In S. Ndlovu-Gatsheni (Ed.), *Mugabeism? History, Politics and Power in Zimbabwe*. New York: Palgrave Macmillan.
Mugabe, R. (1978). "Imperialist Plotting to Create a Neo-Colonialist Buffer Zone in Zimbabwe" Address to The Zimbabwe Nation in Radio Maputo's Voice of Zimbabwe on the eve of his return from the Malta Constitutional Conference on 24 February 1978, *Zimbabwe News*, 10, 1.
Mugabe, R. (2000). Mugabe Madness of Matabale Deaths. *BBC News*. news.bbc.ca.uk/2/hi/Africa. Accessed: 17 February 2021.
Mugabe, R. (2008). Campaign Speech. In Ndlovu-Gatsheni, S. "Rethinking Chimurenga and Gukurahundi in Zimbabwe: A Critique of Partisan National History." *African Studies Review 55* (3). pp. 1–26.
Mugabe, R. (2017). Politics Leads the Gun: Mugabe, *Nehanda Radio News*.
Mujuru, J. (2013, January 13). Mugabe Challengers Bonkers: Mujuru. Retrieved March 10, 2018, from www.newzimbabwe.com.
Ncube, T. (2009). Foreword. In M. Auret (Ed.), *From Liberator to Dictator: An Insider's Account of Robert Mugabe's Descent into Tyranny*. Claremont: David Philip.
Ndlovu-Gatsheni, S. (2009). Making Sense of Mugabeism in Local and Global Politics: 'So Blair, Keep Your England and Let Me Keep My Zimbabwe. *Third World Quarterly, 30*(6), 1139–1158.
Ndlovu-Gatsheni, S. (2012a). Rethinking "Chimurenga" and "Gukurahundi" in Zimbabwe: A Critique of Partisan National History. *African Studies Review, 55*(3), 1–26.
Ndlovu-Gatsheni, S. (2014). Introduction: Mugabeism and Entanglements of History, Politics, and Power in the Making of Zimbabwe. In S. Ndlovu-Gatsheni (Ed.), *Mugabeism? History, Politics, and Power in Zimbabwe*. New York: Palgrave Macmillan.
Ndlovu-Gatsheni, S. (2015). *Mugabeism? History, Politics, and Power in Zimbabwe*. New York: Palgrave Macmillan.
Nehanda Radio. (2013). Who Killed Tongoogara and Mujuru? *Nehanda Radio*. Nehandaradio.com. Accessed 10 November 2020.
Nietzsche, F. (1968). *The Will to Power*. New York: Vantage Books.
Nietzsche, F. (1972). *The Birth of Tragedy*. New York: Modern Library Press.
Nietzsche, F. (1997a). *Homer's Contest*. In J. Lungstrum & E. Sauer (Eds.), *Arenas of Creative Contest* (pp. 35–45). New York: State University of New York Press.
Nietzsche, F. (1997b). *Daybreak*. London: Cambridge University Press.
Norman, A. (2003). *Robert Mugabe and the Betrayal of Zimbabwe*. North Carolina / London: McFarland & Company Inc Publishers.

Norman, A. (2004a). *Robert Mugabe and the Betrayal of Zimbabwe*. Jefferson: McFarland and Co.

Nyarota, G. (2018). *The Graceless Fall of Robert Mugabe: The End of a Dictator's Reign*. Cape Town: Penguin Random House.

Onslow, S., & Plaut, M. (2018). *Robert Mugabe*. Johannesburg: Jacana Media.

Orwell, G. (1949). Reflections on Gandhi. *Partisan Review, 16*(1), 85–92.

Ranger, T. (2003). *The Historical Dimensions of Democracy and Human Rights in Zimbabwe. Volume 2: Nationalism, Democracy and Human Rights*. Harare: University of Zimbabwe Press.

Sadomba, W. (2011). *War Veterans and Zimbabwe's Revolution: Challenging Neo-colonialism and Settler International Capital*. Harare / Oxford: Weaver Press / James Currey.

Scarnecchia, T. (2011). Rationalising Gukurahundi: Cold War and South African Foreign Relations with Zimbabwe, 1981–1983. *Kronos, 37*(1), 89–55.

Scarnecchia, T. (2014). Intransigent Diplomat: Robert Mugabe and His Western Diplomacy, 1963–1983. In S. Ndlovu-Gatsheni (Ed.), *Mugabeism?: History, Politics and Power in Zimbabwe*. New York: Palgrave Macmillan.

Schramm, P. E. (Ed.). (1965). *Hitlers Tischegessprache im fiihrehauptquartier, 1941–1942*. Stuttgart Germany: Seewald Verlag.

Snyder, T. (2017). *On Tyranny: Twenty Lessons for the Twentieth Century*. London: Bodley Head.

Stollman. (1978). In Rene Fullop-Miller (1930), *The Power and the Secret of the Jesuits*. New York. The Viking Press.

Suresh, R. R. (2007). *Fit to Govern: The Native Intelligence of Thabo Mbeki*. Johannesburg: STE Publishers.

Tekere, E. (2007). *Edgar "2boy" Zivanai Tekere: A Life Time of Struggle*. Harare: SAPES Books.

Tendi, B.-M. (2011). Robert Mugabe and Toxicity: History and Context Matter. *Representation: Journal of Representative Democracy., 47*(3), 307–318.

Todd, G. J. (2007). *Through the Darkness: A Life in Zimbabwe*. Cape Town: Struik Publishers.

Tsvangirai, M. (2011). *At the Deep End*. London: Penguin.

Tucker, R. C. (1990). *Stalin in Power; The Revolution from Above, 1928–1941*. New York: Norton Publishers.

Waite, R. G. L. (1977). *The Psychopathic God: Adolf Hitler*. New York: Basic Books.

Walsh, G. G. (1930). The Power and the Secret of the Jesuits by Rene Fulop-Miller, F.S. Flint and D.F. Tait. *The Catholic Historical Review, 16*(3), 338–340.

Wilber, K. (2017). *Trump and a Post-Truth World*. Colorado: Shambhala.

Zizek, S. (2013). Some Bewildered Clarifications: A Response to Noam Chomsky. *International Journal of Zizek Studies, 7*(2), 1–8.

Zizek, S. (2017). *The Courage of Hopelessness: Chronicles of the Year of Living Dangerously*. London: Allen Lane: Penguin Books.

CHAPTER 5

A Career of Madness: Performances of the Will to Power

Robert Mugabe is still battling with the ghosts of colonialism; in his mind it is probably still 1975, and the 'criminal gang' of Westerners still have to be defeated. Perhaps Mr Mugabe is also suffering from some kind of Post-Traumatic Stress Disorder, or old age dementia or some kind of tropical disease affecting the brain; and the ruling clique of the African National Union-Patriotic Front is exploiting Robert Mugabe's tenuous hold on reality for their benefit; to remain in power and perpetuate dictatorship in Zimbabwe.
—Mark O' Docherty (2016: 7)

President Robert of Zimbabwe has emerged as one of the most controversial figures, eliciting both admiration and condemnation. What is termed 'mugabeism' is a summation of a constellation of political behaviour, political ideas, utterances, rhetoric and actions that have crystalised around Mugabe's life.
—Sabelo Ndlovu-Gatsheni (2009: 1139)

Mugabeism is a politics of reconstruction and 'return to the source', in which there is a clear and vicious selective reproduction of the people in a selectively reproduced and redistributed landscape. This landscape is a tight matrix which is more than a metaphor of the 'house of stone', is a mindset which is as inflexible as it is stony in its timelessness and imperviousness ... the Third Chimurenga is a revival of essentialist and nativist politics, something comparable to Adolph Hitler's ideal of the Aryan race.
—Robert Muponde (2004: 177)

© The Author(s) 2021
W. J. Mpofu, *Robert Mugabe and the Will to Power in an African Postcolony*, African Histories and Modernities,
https://doi.org/10.1007/978-3-030-47879-7_5

225

Fighting such a monstrous system as colonialism can be sickening. It can be maddening. So maddening that after the fight the fighter is bereft of the mental resources that allow one to be ready to practice liberation. Robert Mugabe did not only become bereft of liberatory resources but got possessed of the passion to conquer and dominate the Zimbabwean postcolony. What came to possess Mugabe and define his political identity is a specifically maddening will to power that combined fears of defeat by political opponents and desires for more power in Zimbabwe. The will to power as a spirited drive for power and domination that combines both desires and fears is a specifically maddening passion. Once one possesses it and is possessed by it as did Mugabe, it takes on a truly maniacal flight. That Mugabe might have been a kind of mental patient that was haunted by the ghosts of colonial history and injuries, and had not freed himself from traumas of the struggle against colonialism is a persuasive idea. More persuasive, to me, is the idea that Mugabe fought colonialism and came to absorb its politics for use and abuse in search of his own domination of the Zimbabwean postcolony. Even more appealing, in light of his dethronement by his own trusted soldiers and ministers in 2017, is the idea that O'Doherty (2016) advances that Mugabe's disturbed mental condition, that is his madness for power, might have been taken advantage of by an elite clique in ZANU-PF that used him to corruptly amass wealth and eventually to capture state power. What is also true is that Mugabe also consciously and methodically used the elite military and political clique as a "war machine" and political instrument to retain power by force and fraud in Zimbabwe.

There developed, over time, an instrumental relationship of co-creation, co-production and co-captivity between Mugabe and the securocrats that eventually became big business tycoons and looters in the Zimbabwean postcolony. They were willing to keep him in power by hook or crook as long as he looked aside as they milked the economy, ransacking diamond mines, monopolised the land, solicited big kick-backs from foreign investors and traded in the foreign currency black market. Only when Mugabe began to threaten their interests, entertaining the insane idea of appointing his wife as successor, the securocratic black marketeers dispensed with him in what became a kind of benevolent coup where his life and that of his family were spared. The coup that removed Mugabe from power was a designer coup, carried out by people that loved him and were grateful to him for their immense wealth, but had in their own will to power become too impatient to wait for his death or his never coming retirement. The fear that another leader besides Mugabe could rise, take power and hold them to account for the corruption, mass murders and evil manner in which they acquired their massive wealth filled the securocrats with fear and a burning desire to seek, find and hold power for themselves in the Zimbabwean postcolony. The militarised faction that removed Mugabe from power and presently holds power in the Zimbabwean postcolony is a group of extremely angry, guilty and fearful rich men, some of whom are understood to be richer than the country itself. Terrified tycoons and fearful black marketeers are in power in Zimbabwe and the governing and organising idea is not only the poverty of leadership but also rule by terror itself. Armed, rich and terrified men in power make the Zimbabwean postcolony a true warlord state that is still haunted by Mugabeism and its violent politics.

What Sabelo Ndlovu-Gatsheni (2009) notes as Mugabe's controversial behaviour in shape of political ideas, utterances, rhetoric and actions are the insane performances of the will to power that made Mugabe a creature of spectacular excesses. The parasitic and securocratic clique in ZANU-PF needed such an excessive and extremist performer that would create the climate of political disorder and lawlessness that allowed looting and monopolisation of mines, farms, factories and big business deals for the benefit of the favoured of the Zimbabwean postcolony, ZANU-PF politicians and some army generals. The Zimbabwean postcolony, under the tyranny of Mugabe, became a spectacular site of epical theft, murder, hoarding of public resources by powerful politicians and soldiers, and massive eating that Achille Mbembe describes of the Cameroonian postcolony.

Mugabe came to embody and dramatise a fundamentalist will to power that true to the observation of Robert Muponde (2004: 177) became comparable to that of Adolf Hitler who insanely believed himself to be a deliverer of a pure German race and saw opponents as sinners. Mugabe shared with Hitler not just that prominent moustache but insulation from reality that amounted to lunacy. In his embodiment of unreal and insane ideas about himself, his power and the world, Mugabe arrived at the mental prison of what Timothy Chappell (2005: 11) called "the problem of the inescapable self." The political passions, desires and fears that Mugabe held began as his fortress and cause but ended up being the prison of unreality and lunacy that he could not escape from. Mugabe eventually became a prisoner of a troubled and also troubling mental universe from which he could not save himself. He suffered a debilitating "egocentric predicament" that consumed him like a haunting illness. Mugabe's early socialisation, education by the Jesuits and ideologisation into Marxism and nationalism, imprisonment and colonial subjection and suffering, in the view of this book, combined to form a political universe that he was not able to see and feel beyond. Mugabe's social formation and political upbringing became a tyrannical mental and emotional framework that governed him like a stubborn demon, conditioned and programmed his political insanity.

Thus far this book has fleshed out the will to power as a passion for absolute power and domination that Mugabe possessed and which eventually possessed him, making him a mono-maniac of power. Here the book proceeds to explore Mugabe's career of political madness. Those in the Zimbabwean polity that assumed Mugabe was to deliver the nation to the promised land were mistaken. They innocently on the one hand and naively on the other entertained post-political dreams of a paradisal Zimbabwe led by a messianic deliverer that turned out to be a nightmarish monster that embodied a kind of treacherous Lucifer. For power and in power, Mugabe became mad. Tragically, he was totally blind to his insanities and excesses that decayed the Zimbabwean economy and corrupted the polity to almost beyond repair. He was so aperspectively mad that he saw those that did not vote for him and his party and those that opposed his rule as sinners that must "think again" and repent from their treachery. The voters that voted for the political opposition, in Mugabe's uneasy mind, were lost, and the opposition political parties were just sell-outs and not legitimate Zimbabweans:

> You are Zimbabweans, you belong to Zimbabwe which was brought by the blood of our heroes lying here and others scattered throughout the country. Should we give it away to sell-outs here in Harare? This is our capital city. You are sons and daughters of revolutionaries. What wrong have we done you? Harare: think again, think again, think again! (Mugabe 2005a, b, c: 1)

Mugabe uttered these words after his ZANU-PF party was defeated in the elections by the MDC that took control of Harare and Bulawayo, the two major cities. It was a painful paradox to witness Mugabe berating residents of Harare for voting the political opposition and loudly wondering what wrong him and his party had done to deserve the rejection by voters. It was neither political silliness nor naivete that Mugabe did not understand his and ZANU-PF's unpopularity with the voters, but it was a consuming kind of political insanity that was denialist of reality. At that dizzy height of his political insanity Mugabe saw himself as a humble steward of the nation and fountain of political wisdom that was an indispensable messiah for the Zimbabwean postcolony. That he was the butcher of the nation and electoral fraudster that kept power by force and fraud was totally lost to him. In his dismissal of the poets in his imagined ideal Republic, Plato (1993: 200) condemned the poets for being imaginists and performers of "unreality" that were unwanted in a world of concrete history. The world of "unreality" and insane imaginism is where Mugabe had become citizen. In that world he saw himself as an unquestionable revolutionary and liberator. In this chapter I engage with Mugabe's insane performances of the will to power where he, like a true maniac, sought to turn into commonsense what was a real nightmare. Mugabe's relationship with common truth and the real world had become troubled in that he saw nothing wrong with his excesses and believed his opponents to be misguided sinners.

The Power in Robert Mugabe, and Robert Mugabe in Power

Once in power and fully entrenched, Mugabe denied ever seeking power or campaigning for political office (Holland 2008). Mugabe wanted it known and believed that power itself sought and found him. In his interesting world, his responsibility and duty to God was to protect the power in his possession from malcontents in his party and the political opposition. It was wrong in Zimbabwe to aspire for the office of the President and Head of State. Not once but severally, Mugabe publicly laughed at the insanity of politicians in his ruling party and the opposition that wished to be presidents of Zimbabwe.

When he emerged victorious in the first independence elections of Zimbabwe whose results were announced on the 4th of March 1980, Mugabe's mother, Bona, was the first to complain and oppose his election; she cried "he is not capable of doing it. He is not the kind of person to look after other people" (Godwin 2010: 16). Bona's way of celebrating Mugabe's elevation to power, an event she much believed in and waited for, was to condemn it. She had, as I have argued, birthed Mugabe, nurtured his political ambitions and had him believe in his predestined and divine anointed rule. At the announcement of Mugabe's election, she was the one to birth the opposition and resistance to his power that followed him until the announcement of his dethronement in a military coup that came on the 14th of November 2017, many years after her death. Mugabe's will to power was in that way born together in one with the seeds of its opposition and ultimate demise. In that metaphoric and symbolic way, Mugabe's primary source of the will to power became the principal beginning of his tragic and pathetic end. Mugabe's political rise and fall were born and grew together with him.

A story is told that in 1974, the President of ZANU, Ndabaningi Sithole, had to be removed from his post following a vote of no confidence in his leadership. As the Secretary General of the party, Mugabe was to be elevated to the presidency. Dramatically Mugabe resisted the removal of Sithole and abstained from the vote in protest. This was erroneously understood as his nobility and humility. Earlier on in 1962, when Joshua Nkomo as leader was being ousted, by party cadres, and a split of ZANU-PF from ZAPU was being engineered, Mugabe showed the same reluctance to accept elevation to power. Even as the overthrow of Nkomo was to elevate him politically, Mugabe opposed the political move and was reluctant to accept the split (Holland 2008: 42). In all these reluctances to accept political elevation, Mugabe was not being polite but was performing his deeply held myth that he was not to seek power but power itself would seek and find him, it seems.

In the true nature of the will to power that is assured of itself and its right to domination, Mugabe was not being simply humble about power or was he being magnanimous in inevitable victory, he was exercising that humility of the will to power that is the same as pride which Friedrich Nietzsche (1968: 99) describes. As one who believed he was born with power and believed that power was already in him, he would not celebrate power as seemingly given to him by other people, his was from God. Any one that pretended to promote Mugabe politically was being rude to assume that power which belonged to God. Mugabe was too insane to suffer gratitude to any mortal for political elevation; political promotion for him, in his world of "unreality," was the job of destiny. In his insane certainty about his power and its divinity, Mugabe saw all the signs that the coup that would topple him was unfolding but he ignored all the warnings, including a graphic powerpoint presentation by the then Minister of Higher Education, Jonathan Moyo. Moyo was to disclose that Mugabe trusted Emmerson Mnangagwa and Constantine Chiwenga, the coupsters, totally to believe that they could topple him one day. In truth, Mugabe trusted himself and his power too much to believe that he could be overthrown. He had an insane and religious kind of faith in his entitlement to power in Zimbabwe. Mugabe was too insane to accept promotion or demotion from other mortals. He was above common souls.

Further, as one who believed himself with power from God, the idea of any other leader, such as Nkomo and Sithole, being deposed from power was unacceptable as it seemed to foretell his own possible removal one day to come. In that way, Mugabe's reluctance to accept opportunities for power was not out of humility or polite reluctance but out of pride of the will to power, a disinterest that is indicative of a much deeper and higher interest. Mugabe in his will to power did not want to go down in history and destiny as one that was once empowered or brought to power by other mortals, and he did not want around him comrades and colleagues that believed that they can make and unmake leaders, for he was a natural leader for life, in his mind. The contempt Mugabe had for voters, especially those that voted for the opposition, arose from his contempt of the idea of being elected when he believed that he was divinely appointed. For Mugabe elections were an insane political lottery of common souls that he despised as he carried himself, politically, like a kind of medieval monarch that ruled with divine commission.

In the real world, however, the electoral victory that delivered Mugabe to power in 1980 had been forced using violence and terrorisation of the electorate to the extent that General Peter Walls wrote to the British Prime Minister asking that the elections be nullified as they were neither free nor fair (Meredith 2002a: 12). As noted earlier, much corruptly, such powerful African leaders as Julius Nyerere had threatened chaos if Mugabe did not prevail in the historical election. Mugabe's victory was exactly that, an engineered and manipulated victory which he chose to understand and believe as God's work. Powerful African statesmen such as Julius Nyerere contributed to the growth of Mugabe into a monster that insanely frowned upon democratic elections and believed in stole victories.

Supporters of ZAPU, the rival political party, were "terrorised" and "brutalised," while Joshua Nkomo's protestations were ignored. Ignoring ZAPU and its leader's protestations, (Bourne 2011: 98) was the beginning of Mugabe's impunity that was to be a hallmark of his leadership. To Mugabe the elections were a formality to satisfy international expectations and provide a semblance of legitimacy, otherwise he already had the power in himself. Mugabe's dismissive attitude to elections was betrayed in the run up to the 2008 presidential elections when he faced stiff challenge from the MDC and its popular leader, Morgan Tsvangirai. Mugabe expressed what I have quoted before in this book and that I repeat because it summarises his insane attitude to life and to power. Mugabe called the coming vote not only a formality but a waste of time:

> You can vote for them [MDC], but that would be a wasted vote. I am telling you. You would just be cheating yourself. There is no way we can allow them to rule this country. Never, ever. We have a job to do, to protect our heritage. The MDC will not rule this country. It will never, ever happen. We will never allow it. (Mugabe 2008: 2)

In a modern country that aspires to be counted as democratic and that boasts of a legacy of liberation, here was the President flying in the face of the freedom of political choice, free and fair elections. To vote the opposition was, in Mugabe's world, to waste votes. Zimbabweans were cheating themselves in supporting the opposition and rejecting the natural leader and his party; that is how insane and lost Mugabe was to the world of the real. He exuded such arrogant impunity and negligence towards democratic processes that he considered unnecessary and a waste of time, and that showed his insane irrelevance to the world of reality. As noted earlier, for Mugabe and his charged will to power, only violence represented by and symbolised in the gun was the insurance and assurance to power, and so Mugabe, as quoted before, said:

> Our votes must go together with our guns. After all, any vote we shall have, shall have been the product of a gun. The guns which produces the vote should remain its security officer- its guarantor. The peoples' votes and people's guns are always inseparable twins. (Meredith 2002a: 1)

Mugabe's conflation of democratic choice of the ballot and the violence of the gun is another telling window into his insane understanding of politics and the ethics of free choice. The ballot as a democratic substitute for the bullet was not in Mugabe's consideration or care. Hidden behind his boast about the gun, and revealed in his fear of democratic elections, is that the man was a coward that feared punch ups and dreaded the idea of being defeated. This book takes an interest in how Mugabe's will to power ballooned to that level of impunity, arrogance and bellicosity. The coward had found in the gun a hiding place and potent weapon to frighten those that he feared. Meanwhile the real gun-bearers, the securocrats in ZANU-PF that were using the climate of tyranny and disorder to make big money, had found a useful tool in Mugabe. Mugabe's cowardice and the greed of the securocrats became the fears and desires that tied ZANU-PF together as a criminal organisation that relished in corruption and political violence, for survival. I illustrated in the previous chapter how the gun idea became the ZANU idea and how Mugabe had to perform the role of a true gunman to win and keep the trust of the guerrillas in Mozambique.

Under the leadership of Mugabe ZANU-PF became a kind of strange mafia family of sorts. The idea of the family became a true organising idea as Mugabe turned the political party and government into a family to which he was the patriarch and godfather. Mugabe's family background, as I noted in the previous chapter, stamped a bold signature on his psychological makeup and drove his political insanity to the dizzy heights. In his study of "human passions," Malcolm Bowie (1991) explores the work of Sigmund Freud and Jacque Lacan who both emphasise the importance of family life and conditions in the social and political formation of individuals and in giving them the philias and phobias that drive their thoughts and actions. The family becomes a psychological "force field" that is the battery that energises and drives an individual (Bowie 1991: 5). Frantz Fanon (2008: 109) also notes that the political and social behaviour of adults, in the view of psychoanalysis, can be traced to their infantile and formative conditioning in the family and lower schooling. In that way, the Jesuit prophecy about his predestined greatness and leadership which his mother insisted to Mugabe and family in his years as toddler (Holland 2008) came to not only be an attitude of his but a total identity and an inescapable self of his, a fortress and a prison to the self.

Mugabe's family life became a trigger to his political insanity. Freud noted how the family provided the forming child with oedipal influences that got him to overcome and symbolically "kill his father" as he gains his own manhood and identity (Bowie 1991: 33). Lacan noted that the child goes through a "mirror stage" in the family where he receives an image and an imagination of himself and can say "I am that" while he goes on to perform that identity (Bowie 1991: 21) to its fulfilment. Both Freud and Lacan saw "narcissism" as self-love and self-worship that can develop into a delusion and paranoia that drives a grown human being into a kind of insanity and lunacy of his own image and power (Bowie 1991: 33). The dismissal of elections and belief in "guns" and power by any means necessary became a true insanity of Mugabe who now believed in "government through military operations" (Rupiya 2005: 116). The gun, as a symbol of violence and an instrument of power, had become a possession that also possesses one as in a fetish and a talisman. Mugabe saw himself as an anointed father of the nation that had a mission to use the gun to defend his position against aspirants and upstarts. To keep power by any means necessary became "a job to do" and a kind of fatherly duty to God and the national family. It was itself an insanity to turn a diverse nation of many identities, classes and ideological groups into his family. Mugabe's idea of the nation and the family was an insane idea.

In the Freudian and Lacanian senses, it is a self-loving, self-worshipping and therefore paranoid and insane Robert Mugabe who did not only dismiss democratic elections but ignored court judgements and rulings in Zimbabwe. Regarding the illegal and chaotic seizure of white owned commercial farms that the courts ruled against, Mugabe exclaimed:

> The courts can do whatever they want. But no judicial decision will stand on our way… my own position is that we should not even be defending our decision before the courts. This country is our country and this land is our land … They think because they are white they have a divine right to our resources. Not here. The white man is not indigenous to Africa. Africa is for Africans, Zimbabwe is for Zimbabweans. (Meredith 2002a: 203)

Mugabe could, with a stony belief in his own reason and truth, charge that the British and white commercial farmers did not have "divine right" because he believed that he had divine right to Zimbabwe, Zimbabweans and the land. In that way, Mugabe could stand on the international and national stage of public opinion and judgement and utter the insanity that "no judicial decision will stand on our way" (Meredith 2002a: 18). Divine right that he denied the white commercial farming community is the same right that he generously gave to himself. Mugabe was too insane to notice the paradox that he had become a settler himself who reigned over Zimbabwe and Zimbabweans with nativist impunity.

If power and political legitimacy did not need democratic elections and court rulings then it was power and legitimacy that was in Mugabe himself as a divine appointee, which is ordinarily an insane and removed understanding of the world in the present. The guns and violence that Mugabe understood as the twin and assurance of his power were perhaps, in his view, instruments of what Walter Benjamin called "divine violence" that needs no justification as it is from God himself and human beings have to suffer it with not only stoicism but gratitude.

In a psychological and political way, Mugabe was driven by the lunacy of the will to power and had become a lunatic in power that made real his own description of the Gukurahundi Genocide that he said he committed at a "moment of madness." In the understanding of power and the will to power in its maddening effects, Heidi Holland (2008: xiv) is perhaps correct that "Mad bob Mugabe is conceasecrets and lessons of history," one lesson being exactly how a human being can be driven to lunacy by appetites for absolute power. Like Friedrich Nietzsche who in his own will to power in philosophy had come to "construct his own category of truth" (Badiou 2009: 2), Mugabe constructed a political universe of his own where he enjoyed god-like powers and privileges, where democratic elections and judicial decisions did not matter. It was, in actuality, an insane universe, which was tragically removed from the real world.

MUGABE IN PERFORMANCE, SIMULATION AND DISSIMULATION

Insanity, and in particular political insanity in the case of Mugabe, becomes a kind of constructive imagination that builds a world after the image of the tyrant and the appetites of his passions. Political insanity re-evaluates all values and challenges commonsense. Correctly, Friedrich Nietzsche (1968: 3) described the will to power as a desire and a passion whose drive was spirited and aimed "at a revaluation of all values" and a construction of a nihilist intellectual and political universe. In that way, Muponde (2004: 177) is correct that "mugabeism is a politics of reconstruction" that is accompanied by a "vicious selective reproduction" of political values to suit Mugabe's own will to power. To achieve the revaluation and reconstitution of the political, Mugabe had to produce and perform what Sabelo Ndlovu-Gatsheni (2009: 1139) has correctly noted as "political behaviours" and political "utterances" that sought to bring to reality his own political world that affirmed his illusions and delusions of political grandeur that were rooted in believed divine anointing and inspiration. Mugabe's stated historical and political goal became the reconstitution of Zimbabwe into a one-party state (Meredith 2002a: 60; Norman 2004a, b: 93; Smith 1997: 370; Bourne 2011: 265) under himself as the executive president for life that ruled with pretences of democracy but effectively and ultimately like a monarch with divine powers and rights. In spite of his exaggerated modernist pretensions and choreographed sophistry, deep inside Mugabe was a big pre-colonial monarch with a gigantic and shiny ego.

In many ways, to bring his mythical monarchy into reality, Mugabe had to believe and perform the monarchy to get Zimbabweans and all others to believe and affirm it in actuality. After ensuring that he was Head of State, Chancellor of all universities, Head of Government and Commander in Chief of the Defence Forces, he allowed some ministers to call him "ruler for life" and the "second son of God" (Meredith 2002a: 79). A Twenty-First February Movement was created to commemorate his birthday, his dwellings were overly fortified and a huge motorcade accompanied his official limousine. Frequently on public holidays, before a stadium full of a crowd, Mugabe would be seen bowing down and saluting his own portrait, not in so many words, inviting Zimbabweans to do the same, worship the leader. With the importance of democratic elections minimised and the rulings of the courts severally ignored, Mugabe instituted a regime of executive hooliganism and disorder in Zimbabwe where his pretences to omnipotent and omniscient power became a kind of populist reason. In the observation of Ernesto Laclau that is noted earlier, populist reason works through radical disorder:

> [I]n a situation of radical disorder, 'order' is present as that which is absent; it becomes an empty signifier, as the signifier of this absence. In this sense, various political forces can compete in their efforts to represent their particular objectives as those which carry out the filling of that lack. To homogenise something is exactly to carry out this filling function. (Laclau 1996: 44)

In a way, in the absence of order, Mugabe instituted an order of his own, a disorder as the order of the day in the Zimbabwean postcolony. He did not only create an absence of democratic order but also invented and inserted an order after his own sign and image as a real but actually "empty signifier" of imagined divine commission. As a personalised sign and signifier himself, Mugabe had to perform, simulate and dissimulate politics to actualise his wished for and imagined power. Much like in Stalinist performances and memorialisations, and performances of North Korean politics and leadership (Meredith 2002a: 77), Mugabe had to mobilise activities, ceremonies, signs and rituals that represented and sought to naturalise and normalise his power. Mugabe's performances of power are the same as what is described by Judith Butler (1988: 519) as "performative acts" that produce and maintain meaning and seek to construct reality as a kind of self-fulfilling prophecies of power. Judith Butler (2010: 147) further described what she called the "performative agency" of individuals and communities in the production and maintenance of political meanings, "performative politics refers to acts of self-constitution" that consist of "speech acts," what is said and "illocutionary" or "perlocutionary" messages that name reality or seek to construct reality and manufacture the truth.

The politician such as Mugabe becomes in one a performer and spokesperson that seeks to produce and maintain some realities. Some performances erase and silence reality while others make real and existent actually absent realities. Jean Baudrillard (1994: 3) distinguished between performance of simulation and dissimulation; "to dissimulate is to pretend not to have what one has" and to "simulate is to feign to have what one doesn't have." In his performances of the will to power and drive to manufacture the reality of his power, Mugabe combined both simulation and dissimulation. Effectively, Mugabe became a performer of power. In his description of Mugabe in a rally in rural Lupane, Christopher Hope noted performance and manufacture of the reality of power thus:

> Robert Mugabe, on the public platform, had the role taped; he embodied its absurdity, its menace, its suffocating fragrance, its location midway between Hollywood and Hell, its supernatural pretensions, its angry self-importance. He fulfilled that strange requirement of a tyrant, expansion. Each time you looked there seemed to be more of him. More of them. Despots flowed, one into another, consorting, and merging like mercury. (Hope 2003: 19)

In a way, Mugabe was witnessed to enact and produce a larger than life image of himself that is expanded and multiple and conceals his humanity while projecting a wished for divinity, that is therefore fake. Mugabe typified some of the most venal dictators of the world in his dramatisation of power. Notably "if you look at the portraits of Stalin you see the phenomenon: it is as if someone (is) not content with the face of the man as it was" (Hope 2003: 57) and seeks to exaggerate it into that of a deity. In total, Christopher Hope (2003: 73) witnessed that "the essence of Robert Mugabe was dissimulation" which was fundamentally to effectively conceal the real man that he was and to produce an image of a metaphysical personality and a kind of one-man majority with a commanding presence. The moustache of Hitler that Mugabe wore (Holland 2008: 158) may not just have been a simple symbol to irritate prison warders, as he explained it, but an internalised admiration of Adolph Hitler that Mugabe carried and which possessed him. The imitation of the Hitler look might have been part of his unconscious political universe that was framed by an aspiration to be feared and to be a menace for the world. To trouble the world and be troubled by it is the stuff of the political Jesuit that Mugabe had become.

A collection of performances, simulations and dissimulations, can morph into a representation and a sign on its own that may at once be revealing and concealing of reality. Simulation, notes Jean Baudrillard, does more than representation and misrepresentation as it produces hyper-reality, becomes a simulacrum that may have four different significations: "It is the reflection of a profound reality; it masks and denatures a profound reality; it masks the absence of profound reality; it has no relation to reality whatsoever; it is its own pure simulacrum" (Baudrillard 1994: 6).

Baudrillard states that as a reflection of profound reality the sign is an honest appearance that reveals what is hidden. As it masks profound reality the sign is "evil appearance" that misleads by hiding reality. As it pretends to be appearance it is in the "order of sorcery," in its deception. And as it becomes its own simulacrum it becomes pure simulation that misleads and seeks to reconstruct reality (Baudrillard 1994: 6). The sign is pure evil when it seeks to replace reality with its own manufactured reality. Here and further in this book I observe that Mugabe relished in several representations that became not only an order of sorcery but were pure simulacrum. He circulated signs, symbols and myths of himself that were misleading and productive of a convincing but fake reality. Mugabe became not only a pretender but a performer that brought the unreal about himself to life. To separate Mugabe the "thing itself" from the many personas and characters he performed is what has eluded many authors.

Like any other performer Mugabe loved audiences and ceremonies. Mugabe did not only have a "penchant for ceremony and Tradition" (Tendi 2013: 965) but even as his popularity and political following were compromised, he made sure that people were coerced and persuaded, taken by trains and buses from remote areas to create for him "colossal gatherings" of political rallies that "strike fear in the competition" (Tendi

2013: 966) and project him as popular. He relished in showing the human electricity of multitudes behind him, even if they did not in reality exist. Rented crowds and school children that were forced to abandon classes (Hope 2003: 16) to boost the attendance of his rallies became part of Mugabe's performances and constructions of otherwise absent popularity. In November 2017, an equally rented and constructed crowd was used to force Mugabe to resign. The paradox of Mugabe the owner of colossal crowds being removed from power by the show of a colossal crowd by coup-makers brought to life Achille Mbembe's description of the political contradictions of the postcolony where:

> Dictators can go to sleep at night lulled by roars of adulation and support, only to wake up in the morning to find their golden calves smashed and their tablets of law overturned. The applauding crowds of yesterday have become today a cursing, abusive mob. That is to say, people whose identities have been partly confiscated have been able, precisely because there was this pretence, to glue together the bits and pieces of their fragmented identities. By taking over the signs and language of officialdom, people have been able to remythologise their own conceptual universe while in the process turning the commandment into a sort of Zombie. (Mbembe 1992: 10)

The same crowds that Mugabe constructed to perform and display his power turned around to pull down his mask, to demystify his power and re-introduce reality where unreality had been naturalised. His own fictions, myths and performances were paid back to him, in his own currency. In other words, power that ignores legitimacy and credibility of elections and judicial decisions can one day be exposed for what it is, a performance and not a reality. The people that have been zombified have a way of claiming back their humanity and giving the tyrant his true status and condition as the first zombie that is imprisoned by its inevitable and inescapable self, otherwise. It may take a manufactured crowd to liberate the tyrant from his inevitable and inescapable self. The will to power involves the leader turning the led into zombies. It is only when the led zombify the leader does a political rupture take place. Under a tyrannical leader positive change takes place when the victims of the tyrant find their agency and use it to topple the potentate. In that way, the overthrow of Mugabe was his liberation from the imprisoning mythical universe he created around himself and which choirs of flatterers and sycophants impressed upon him.

Mugabe and the Simulation of Reconciliation and Peace

After such a conflicted history as the history of the colonisation of what became Zimbabwe, healing, reconciliation, peace and unity become exalted ideals. As I seek to demonstrate in this book, Mugabe who seems to have always believed in total war and revenge of the will to power, had in the same will to power, to simulate grand ideals and practices of reconciliation, peace and unity through spectacular performances. In the argument of Friedrich Nietzsche (1968: 50), such grand human ideals as revolution, equal rights, love, peace, justice and philanthropy are always, in the scheme of the will to power, simulated and pretended as "flags" and other impressions to beguile the masses and fool them into believing that the otherwise monstrous leaders are deliverers. In the political universe of the will to power monsters can perform messiahs. Similar to Nietzsche, Niccolo Machiavelli (2003: 71) stated that the foxy and cunning prince should always build a reputation for being good but in practice should neither keep his word nor abandon the ways of the beast and preparedness to harm his opponents. It would seem to me that Mugabe handled his relationship with whites and former Rhodesians after independence with much Nietzschean and Machiavellian will to power. Following his performances in "a series of conciliatory speeches, both to whites and African opponents" (Bourne 2011: 98) after Zimbabwe's independence, Mugabe enjoyed the good reputation of a magnanimous statesman. Mugabe effectively used that reputation to attain national support and international affirmation but it later emerged that he had retained his vengeful agenda as "more recent events" went on to prove that "these speeches were a sham, a façade for a long-term Marxist manipulator" (Bourne 2011: 99). The mask was always going to fall, and it was a post-political blunder in the very first place for Zimbabweans to take a political mask for a face. In spectacularly simulating unity, peace, reconciliation and national healing, Mugabe once again fooled the unsuspecting world.

An Original Intention to Revenge

Behind the conciliator, peaceful unifier and statesman that Mugabe performed with cinematic efficiency, there was a vengeful manipulator impatiently waiting to pounce on the white community. Not everyone was fooled, such scholars as Daniel Compagnon (2011: 1) have always maintained that "from the beginning" Mugabe concealed his vengeful intentions but there were "many worrying signs" that one day the monster in him will emerge from behind his performances of peace and reconciliation to cause immense chaos. Martin Meredith (2002a: 7) notes that "while in exile," Mugabe "had repeatedly insisted on the need for a one party Marxist state" in Zimbabwe after independence, and that "Ian Smith and his criminal gang" of whites "will be tried and killed" while "white exploiters would not be allowed to keep an acre of land" in the new Zimbabwe. That bleeding grudge and intention to extract his pound of flesh from the white community was artfully concealed by Mugabe behind lyrical rhetoric of reconciliation. Nihilist revenge was carefully embellished behind soothing promises. National unity and reconciliation as grand ideals were worn as a mask to conceal the frown on the face of a political monster.

Zimbabwean independence from Rhodesian colonialism as it is known was delivered through a negotiated settlement of Lancaster House in 1979, in the UK. Attentive historians, journalists and scholars have noted for instance that "but Mugabe was hostile to the idea of negotiations" he was so "hardened by prison" and "he did not need a compromise (Meredith 2002a: 2) with Rhodesians but an armed takeover of the state by guerrillas under his leadership. In his own words, Mugabe regretted the negotiations, "we wanted an armed takeover of the state" in "the field" of war; it made him an "unhappy man" to talk peace (Meredith 2002a: 7, 8). Lord Carrington who was instrumental in the talks and the preparations that preceded them noted that "there is no doubt Mugabe would not have signed the Lancaster House Agreement if Presidents Julius Nyerere of Tanzania and Samora Machel of Mozambique hadn't prompted him" (Holland 2008: 61).

Mugabe's view of the Frontline Heads of States that, as this book shows, persuaded and pressured him to the talks was that "we thought the heads of state were selling us out (Meredith 2002a: 3) by insisting on talks with the Rhodesian regime." The British-appointed care taker Governor of Rhodesia at the time was Lord Soames whose view of Mugabe then was that of a monster that was driven to bloodletting, "I had the same picture that everybody had, that he was something of a Marxists ogre, and that he'd soon slit your throat as look at you, and that he was a bad man" (Meredith 2002a: 11). Similar to Augusto Pinochet who declined to talk to the Salvador Allende regime that he toppled in the 1973 coup in Chile, insisting that "we want unconditional surrender, we don't want to talk" (Burbach 2003: 18), Mugabe wanted the satisfaction of the surrender and pleas for mercy of the Rhodesians, he felt that talks let them go without the pain that they deserved from his hands. True to the ways of the will to power that carries itself as "peace and innocence" to conceal its violence and "insurrectionary" tendencies, which must "conquer through extreme mildness, sweetness, softness" (Nietzsche 1968: 109), Mugabe concealed his intention to revenge and to harm behind simulations and performances of conciliatory politics. In that way, Mugabe became a true green snake in the grass that sang peace while hiding a lump in the throat.

Revenge was foremost in Mugabe's post-independence political agenda. Researches by a number of scholars and journalists have revealed that massive persuasion and pressure from the Frontline States compelled Mugabe to reconcile and make peace with white Rhodesians that he originally intended to punish in the true vengeance of the will to power. Mugabe is noted to have arrived at Lancaster House in 1979 to denounce the proposed talks and declare continuation with the armed struggle. Samora Machel who hosted the ZANLA guerrillas in Mozambique and much begrudgingly accepted Mugabe as their leader sent a trusted messenger to deliver the promise and the warning to Mugabe that "If he did not sign the agreement, he would be welcome back in Mozambique and given a beach house where he could write his memoirs, but Mozambique will make no further sacrifices for a cause that could be won on the conference table" (Meredith 2002a: 8). In other words, Samora Machel used a threat to pressure Mugabe to talk peace and to sign a political settlement testament. Otherwise it was never in Mugabe's intentions to even contemplate forgiveness of and reconciliation with the white population.

Even after the agreement had been signed Samora Machel personally warned Mugabe not to antagonise the white population in Zimbabwe lest he caused further trouble for the country, its polity and economy, "don't play make believe Marxist games when you get home" he said "you will face ruin if you force the whites there into precipitate flight" (Meredith 2002a: 9). When Mugabe continued to argue on the merits of armed takeover of the state, the collective of the Frontline States, headed by Samora Machel, Kenneth Kaunda and Julius Nyerere, insisted that "we hear what you are saying, but we know you will hear us when we say the war must end" (Norman 2004a, b: 76). Clearly, and true to Lord Carrington's observation, if the Frontline Heads of States had not used their influence and authority to persuade and pressurise Mugabe to a negotiated settlement, he would have preferred a continuation of the armed struggle in hope to overthrow and punish the Rhodesian regime and the white population. By its nature as a drive that is also a desire for conquest and domination of one by the other, the will to power, Friedrich Nietzsche (1968: 347) states, derives much "pleasure" and relish in "revenge" as its "pleasure includes pain" of others, "pleasure as feeling of power" and celebration of conquest. The warning that came to Mugabe from the Frontline States was a sober wisdom from their experience of decolonisation, Samora Machel, for instance, had learnt from the angry exodus and withdrawal of whites from Mozambique between 1974 and 1975, which led to a depression in the economy of the country (Bourne 2011: 99). Mugabe was to dramatically turn that pragmatism from bitter historical experience into a fiction and an empty signifier of a kind of populist reason that was articulated and performed but really not meant. The reconciliation that Mugabe became a hero for was borrowed wisdom and stolen political pragmatism that he was to abandon and return to the agenda of revenge that he demonstrated in crashing ZAPU and punishing white Zimbabweans.

As the will to power believes in "falsification" of events and the truth (Nietzsche 1968: 277), Mugabe did not disclose that the political wisdom of reconciliation that he was performing was a gift pressed upon him by wiser and much more experienced leaders. He presented and performed it as his own, with apparent disdain and a spirit of plagiarism towards those who truly owned the idea. To disclose the source of his newly found wisdom would have, in his mind, minimised his power, "perhaps he feared that someone would find out that he was not really God's chosen one, but an ordinary little boy with defects as well as attributes" (Holland 2008: 210). The fear to be seen to be human, ordinary, fallible and correctable seems to have perpetually haunted Mugabe that deep down remained up to his death a terrified little boy. True it is that "Mugabe gives the appearance of disdain because he wants to be acknowledged as superior, perhaps to get as far away as possible from the opposite, inferiority which he dreads" (Holland 2008: 62). Borrowed and even stolen wisdoms and truths were used by Mugabe to opportunistically and timeously cultivate a political reputation of a statesman that he was actually not.

The postcolony, such as Zimbabwe was and still is, becomes what Achille Mbembe (1992: 3) says is "a rather dramatic stage on which are played out" a multiplicity of mirages and facades of power, where power seeks to stage its "magnificence and prodigality" (Mbembe 1992: 7) to circulate its myths and fictions as the solution to the problems of society. In its performance of the stolen wisdom of reconciliation, Mugabe's speech, as captured by Peter Stiff, was messianic and prophetic in form, tone and content:

> Our nation requires every one of us to be a new man. If yesterday I fought you as an enemy, today you will become a friend and ally…it could never be a correct justification that because the whites oppressed us yesterday, when they had power, that the blacks should oppress them today because they have power. An evil remains an evil. Our majority rule could easily turn to inhuman rule if we oppressed, persecuted or harassed those who do not think like the majority of us… we will ensure there is a place for everyone in this country. I want a broadly based government to include whites and Nkomo. (Stiff 2000: 27)

That Mugabe so clearly understood the ethics of liberation and the wisdom of forgiveness and reconciliation makes all the worse that in practice he went on to do the very opposite. That he knew "evil" and the problematic of the "inhuman" and "oppression" but knowingly went on to visit the same on the people that he claimed to be his new friends and allies makes him a knowing and therefore a much guiltier offender. On the night of Zimbabwe's political independence Mugabe was heard on radio and appeared on national television screens performing the fiction of reconciliation. Being the voice and the face of reconciliation made Mugabe a true performer of cinematic extents, a Lucifer that recites the scriptures:

> In the evening Comrade Robert Mugabe strolled into white living rooms countrywide. Promising reconciliation rather than revenge, he told television viewers that he would honour the British-brokered Lancaster House Agreement, thus guaranteeing white pensions and property rights… the monster of the morning had begun to morph into a responsible leader by the third beer that night. (Holland 2008: xiii)

Even those that had long suspected and believed that Mugabe was a monstrosity changed their minds about him that evening and night. Even the Rhodesian leader, himself a monster, Ian Smith who had always regarded Mugabe as the "Apostle of Satan" that night confessed to have experienced him anew as "reasonable" (Meredith 2002a: 15). Adding more poetry to his performance, Mugabe waxed that "let us deepen our sense of belonging and engender a common interest that knows no race, colour or creed" (Meredith 2002a: 13). Mugabe performed reconciliation in the same way that the biblical Lucifer as a personification of evil recites the scriptures more eloquently than the preachers and the chosen ones. The "new man" that Mugabe asked of every Zimbabwean was as represented in himself, a fake man, and a mere persona that concealed the true will to power that drove him and that he drove in pursuit of power and domination. The very old man that Mugabe died as remained, in essence, a fragile and vengeful little boy.

Mugabe's performance of statesmanship and political wisdom simulated an era of hope not only in Zimbabwe but regionally and internationally. The effects of Mugabe's performance and simulation created what Achille Mbembe (1992: 4) called "the mutual zombification" of the performer himself who acts out a ridiculous falsehood and the wide audience that is taken up and fooled by the lie. Such influential states in the world as "Britain saw Zimbabwe as a Foreign affairs trophy" (Holland 2008: xiii) and were proud to support Mugabe's regime in Harare:

> Virtually everyone who should have cried foul looked the other way; whites because they were grateful to be out of the range of fire; the British government because it had to stand by its man up North while trying to bring majority rule to apartheid South Africa; and the international media because it had backed Mugabe to the hilt and could not contemplate its flawed judgement. (Holland 2008: xiii)

Engrossment with the prospects of Zimbabwe was so palpable that as large a figure as "Her Majesty, the Queen of England, in a personal message to Mugabe, wrote that it is a moment for people of all races and all political persuasions to forget the bitterness of the past" (Norman 2004a, b: 90) and build a better country. Under the cover of national, regional and international excitement and indeed post-political euphoria that his performance of wisdom and simulation of reconciliation created, Mugabe committed the Gukurahundi Genocide where more than 20,000 people were killed and hundreds of thousands dispossessed and displaced from the Matabeleland and the Midlands areas of Zimbabwe. The genocide unfolded as "on the international stage Zimbabwe was accorded star status" and "one country after another lined up to help the new government." "We are the darling of the world," Mugabe told a meeting of white farmers, "and since we are on honeymoon and honeymoons don't always last too long. We ought to take advantage of it" (Meredith 2002a: 46) which indicates that he knew that soon enough his mask will fall away and his performances of virtue make way for the real monstrosity that he truly was.

In their numbers, white people, especially commercial farmers, were to be killed (Norman 2004a, b: 146). Mugabe was to "whip up hysteria against Britain in particular" (Norman 2004a, b: 67). Not only did he ban the international media in Zimbabwe, but he also exercised authoritarian control of the political arena in the country, used violence as the cornerstone of his rule, plundered the economy, subjugated the opposition political parties and created an international crisis in the region (Compagnon 2011: 8–254). The country that was once famously called by Julius Nyerere of Tanzania "the Jewel of Africa" was turned into what George Bush called an "axis of evil."

Mugabe's monstrosity was not only ignored but also purposely incubated by world super powers such as Britain and the USA that wanted Zimbabwe to stabilise and be usable as a pillar in the struggle against communism in Southern Africa (Scarnecchia 2011). As well as Britain refused to abrogate and nullify the elections that brought Mugabe to power even as they were unfree and unfair, and Governor Lord Soames agreed to let the elections go ahead in the interests of stability in Zimbabwe (Meredith 2002a: 12), there are signs that Mugabe's victory was corruptly assisted by Britain and some of the Frontline States. Lord Carrington states that "Julius Nyerere had earlier told me in London during Lancaster House that his man Robert Mugabe had better win because if he didn't, the frontline states were not going to accept it" which was an undemocratic and corrupt threat. "Nyerere's foreign minister had been sent to me," said Carrington, after Mugabe's electoral victory to say "Julius wants you to know he is pleased Mugabe won, but why did you let him win by so much?" (Holland 2008: 69). After all, it appears Mugabe did not really win, but was made to win; his victory was constructed and manufactured by super powers that mistakenly saw in him a client and an ally in their own imperial agendas. Besides the electoral fraud that Britain is suspected of having used to enable a Mugabe victory, looking aside from his violence and terror allowed him to force victory. In other words Mugabe became the spoilt little brat of the international community.

THE REVOCATION OF RECONCILIATION

In his interesting world, Mugabe saw the reconciliation he extended to the Zimbabwean white community as a benevolent personal gift that he could at will take back. Reconciliation was not a grave nation building strategy to be preserved but a gracious gift from the tyrant for which the whites were supposed to be perpetually grateful. Concealment of the real behind the fictitious seems to have been Mugabe's stock in the trade of power, even the way he made sure that he always was "the man dressed in elegant suits" (Holland 2008: 159) seems to be a symbolic way in which he concealed the monster in him behind civil and refined looks. In actuality, Mugabe believed that his supporters should "strike fear in the hearts of the white man, our real enemy" (Meredith 2002a: 17). After the white population, some parts of it in fact, continued to back Ian Smith in the 1985 election, and later to support the opposition MDC, Robert Mugabe was willing in prime-time television to describe them as crooks and unworthy people:

> These crooks we inherited as part of our population. We cannot expect them to have straightened up, to be honest people and an honest community. Yes, some are good people, but they remain cheats. They remain dishonest. They remain uncommitted even to the national cause. We would actually be happier if some country were to accept them, and since Britain said it wanted them to come to Britain, we can open our doors to them, but we will not force them out. There are some who are good, but I think the bulk of the people we would rather do without. (Meredith 2002a: 210)

It was time for Mugabe to abandon Samora Machel's sober counsel. By continuing to vote Ian Smith the white populations were "telling the new President that their old leader Ian Smith" was their choice, "white Zimbabweans as a group would not hold Mugabe's hand, they conveyed to him the decision to stick to their own kind" (Holland 2008: 114) which drove Mugabe mad. Their rejection of his leadership gave him the excuse he needed to pounce. The continued political support for Smith was possibly racism but their right to vote whomever they wanted was protected in the national constitution, and Mugabe refused to respect that right. Mugabe angrily ranted that, "the voting has shown that they have not repented in any way," the whites "still cling to the past and support the very man who created a series of horrors against the people of Zimbabwe"

(Meredith 2002a: 56). Refusing to vote Mugabe showed that the whites "they remain dishonest, they remain uncommitted even to national cause" as Mugabe said. In his world, those who rejected him were actually rejecting the nation and were being treasonous. Mugabe also failed to make the distinction between white individuals and a white system. Earlier in 1974, Mugabe had shown sophistication of understanding on the matter. Michael Nicholson, of the Independent Television News, asked him whether he had been embittered against whites by his lengthy imprisonment, "no" he replied "we are fighting a system that is wrong. We don't hate the whites; we will have no racial discrimination in an independent Zimbabwe" (Bourne 2011: 99). Yet his contempt for the whites and their free vote showed the opposite that his acceptance of them was conditional to voting him. The performances of reconciliation that Mugabe put up had created euphoria regionally and internationally and various countries made generous financial and other donations to Zimbabwe, the post-political optimism had taken a sure grip and Mugabe's will to power found fertile ground to grow. Now he was, for power, prepared to squander all the goodwill.

Nigeria, for instance donated a large sum of money that Mugabe used to buy media houses in order to monopolise and control the flow of information in the country. "Mugabe had already used the money donated by Nigeria to buy the South African company that controlled the majority of Zimbabwe's newspapers," pursuantly, "he had sacked the white editors and replaced them with government appointees," the newspapers began to spin "propaganda" for the new government (Norman 2004a, b: 91). Mugabe's government that was displaying signs of its own racism in its discrimination of whites had also begun the discrimination and marginalisation of other black people along the lines of ethnicity and clans. Reconciliation was a personal gift and a political weapon that Mugabe could give and take, and use to punish the whites. In a terse speech before the election of 2000 where the white population was accused by Mugabe of supporting the opposition, he said "the national reconciliation policy we adopted in 1980 is threatened, gravely threatened, by the acts of the white settlers in this country and we shall revoke that national reconciliation, we shall revoke it!" (Mugabe 2000: 1). In his will to power, Mugabe became a monstrosity that turned back to consume the very people, communities and powers that incubated and brought it up. Like any angry jealousy god that withdraws his grace when offended, Mugabe declared reconciliation revoked and all white people became candidates for violation and death.

ROBERT MUGABE AND THE WHITE MAN

Robert Mugabe's hatred and fundamentalist reduction of all white people to racist and settler imperialist colonisers was a strange but true kind of love. His storied contempt for people and things white was another performance that concealed his aspiration to whiteness. Mugabe's relationship with the white man and whiteness at large, I observe, was a power relationship that Albert Memmi (1974) nuanced as the dialogue and also the clash between "the coloniser and the colonised." The relationship between the coloniser and the colonised can be characterised by troubling philias and phobias. The contempt between the two, oppressor and oppressed, may strangely but truly involve some attractions. A white man is what Mugabe unknowingly but truly wished to be. Frantz Fanon (2008: 3) described how in the colonial encounters, at a psychopathological level, "the white man is sealed in his whiteness the black man in his blackness" while the colonised "black man wants to be white" and the colonising "white man slaves to reach human level." In that traumatic way, the relationship between the coloniser and the colonised is a mutually dehumanising relationship. Mugabe that was formatively educated and mentored by white Jesuit priests had his colonial love and hate relationship with white people and whiteness as a system, and this book will note that Mugabe, in his typical will to power, tried to manipulate this relationship for political power and privilege.

Instead of Mugabe's relations with the white man and whiteness leading to his liberation from being a colonial subject they seem to have led to further trauma that projected itself from his person and sensibility as hate and exaggerated nativism. In many ways, as I argue, Mugabe became the Fanonian "black man" who "wants to be like the white man" because "for the black man there is only one destiny. And it is white. Long ago the black man admitted the unarguable superiority of the white man, and all his efforts are aimed at achieving white existence" (Fanon 2008: 178). Mugabe struggled to prove himself rather too much before the white person and whiteness.

Mugabe's traumatising and dehumanising relationship with the white man and whiteness is perhaps most vividly captured in an anecdotal incident where, in his will to power and drive to dramatise reconciliation with Rhodesian whites after the independence of Zimbabwe, he wanted to show how far he had forgiven Ian Smith. Smith visited State House and he met a friendly and forgiving Mugabe who pulled him close and said "come and seat next to me" on the sofa (Holland 2008: 86) and performed the friendliest gesture of hugging and "holding hands" with Smith. This was a most vivid dramatisation of reconciliation on the part of Mugabe who had been jailed by Smith for eleven years and during the jail term was denied the compassionate leave to attend the funeral of his only child. Perhaps dramatising his own status as a coloniser par excellence Ian Smith spurned Mugabe's powerful gesture, Smith said to Heidi Holland "well I don't like people holding my hand. So I got my hand out of his and moved to the other end of the sofa" (Holland 2008: 87). In its symbolism, this incident demonstrates how Mugabe tried to reach out to whites and to whiteness and was rejected, in the process traumatised and embittered. In a "decolonial critique of Robert Mugabe," Morgan Ndlovu (2014: 237–238) uses a "structure and agency" analysis to demonstrate how supposedly "post-colonial" African leaders such as Mugabe effectively remained colonial subjects that had limited ability to restructure and reconstitute colonial power relations. With all his power, real and imagined, Mugabe failed to alter his bitter relations with former colonisers. Mugabe learnt of his enduring colonial subjection the very hard way when Ian Smith dramatically and symbolically reduced him to his political size, an insignificant person that aspired to be accepted by a contemptuous white system. Frantz Fanon (2008: 86) illustrates the trauma of a black colonial subject that overreaches to the white coloniser and gets spurned, his cry is "what? while I was forgetting, forgiving and wanting only to love, my message was flung back in my face like a slap" most painfully "I was told to stay within my bounds, to go back where I belonged" (Fanon 2008: 86). Smith physically and symbolically pushed Mugabe to where he belonged, in the peripheries of being. In his insane admiration of white power, Mugabe went too far in the attempt to please and polish the white ego and was rejected, making him bitter. How Mugabe came to be maddened against all white people is a truism that is yet to be understood.

It is perhaps in the blindness and even naiveté of the will to power that Mugabe thought his elevated education and his status as a political leader could suddenly erase his colonial subjection. Mugabe fell into the existential trap of "the colonised" who imagines that he "is elevated above his jungle status in proportion to his adoption of the mother country's cultural standards, he becomes whiter as he renounces his blackness, his jungle" (Fanon 2008: 9). Much simplistically this colonised person believes that "the language of the coloniser gives" him as "the colonised a sense of equality with the coloniser" (Fanon 2008: 14). The Robert Mugabe that Ian Smith dramatically and symbolically rejected is a man who espoused Englishness and white sensibility to some dramatic levels:

> As Mugabe emerged from the carapace of Rhodesian propaganda, there was much to surprise us: his obvious Anglophilia, his Savile Raw suits, his fastidious English, his penchant for Graham Greene novels, his admiration of the Queen, especially after she had knighted him in 1994, for services to Anglo-Zimbabwe relations, his love for tea and cricket, a game, he said, that civilises people and creates good gentlemen. I want everyone to play cricket in Zimbabwe. I want ours to be a nation of gentlemen. (Godwin 2010: 18)

Mugabe did not only espouse borrowed English sensibility and finesse, but he somehow sought to weaponise his colonial acculturation to elevate himself above other black people, like the colonial white man, as their civiliser and saviour. Correctly, Andrew Norman (2004a, b: 154) notes that when Mugabe was saying "I want ours to be a nation of gentlemen, it was at that time that the notorious 5th Brigade" under Mugabe's chief command "were ethnically cleansing, that is murdering tens of thousands of Ndebele in Matabeleland," a genocide that this book treats below. Mugabe had tragically become a colonising colonial subject that was unfortunately, for himself, being rejected by the same coloniser he tried to emulate and reach out to as an equal. Because of his grand education and British mannerisms that were accompanied by articulate speech, in the liberation movement, "Mugabe was trusted to stand shoulder to shoulder with whites, Rhodesian and British politicians in debate" (Norman 2004a, b: 58). That, however, did not make Mugabe equal to whites in the racist and colonial scheme of things, he could only wish. Albert Memmi (1974: 59) notes how the coloniser initially admires and encourages the colonised that aspire to his status and that mimic his culture but eventually the coloniser does not permit the colonised to reach his station, he puts them back in their zone of inferiority and failure that marks the permanence of colonial relations. Even as he powerfully wished, Mugabe's will to power could not elevate him to the station of a true coloniser; he remained only a colonising colonial subject that was to stay in his place. Yet Mugabe never stopped trying, Heidi Holland (2008) notes how Mugabe came close to tears when he spoke about the British Royal Family and reminisced about the good old days when he was the darling of the world. The ranting and public yelling that Mugabe regularly made concerning the evil of the UK and the West at large concealed an embittered love and feeling of rejection at being sanctioned and banned from travelling to Europe and North America.

The Allure of White Power and Privilege

All forms of power and privilege are the true temptation of the will to power, being on top and powerful is the true ambition of the power monger. The power and prestige of the white coloniser seems to be what Mugabe most desired. He fully understood white power and privilege within the colonial system, and in his understanding of it did not get repulsed by its cruelty and inhumanity, but in his will to power, he came to admire and aspire for the same for himself. Mugabe came to envy the immense power of the white coloniser and to wish to possess it for himself. As a subject of white colonial power in Rhodesia, Mugabe noted that "we were brought up in a society which actually worshipped the white man as a kind of god" (Meredith 2002a: 22). Not only that but the white man had become a world that loomed large, and Mugabe noted thus:

> He was infallible. He was the rule to be obeyed. Whoever was white therefore not only had the power but also the privilege of demanding respect from every black. And so we feared the white man. After the defeat of the blacks in 1897, our parents and grandparents accepted rule by the white man as something unavoidable. There was no way we could get rid of the white man. He was power. He had guns. He had subdued everybody through the security forces. And therefore all we could do was to seek from him the removal of our grievances. If we could get some form of justice within the system, that was that people sought to be achieved. And we accepted this as youngsters. (Meredith 2002a: 22)

It appears to me that Mugabe might have subconsciously internalised the fear and also admiration of the white man's power and also the power machinery of the colonial system at large. Mugabe became that Fanonian black subject who wanted to share in the superiority of the white man. Fanon observed that in the colonial climate "white men consider themselves superior to black men" and "black men want to prove to white men at all costs, the richness of their thought, the equal value of their intellect" (Fanon 2008: 3). Mugabe's storied education and his performance of Englishness in speech and manners symptomatised his deep desire for the prestige of colonial whiteness. He deeply desired equality and fraternity with whites.

Mugabe tried too hard to demonstrate his own "richness" of thought through elevated education and also the political habit of befriending and working with white men. Ian Smith seems to have seen this in Mugabe's performances of friendship and warmth. Mugabe was not befriending white men as a human gesture of common humanity but as an attempt to fortify his own power and elevate himself above other blacks and colonial subjects. Smith noted thus about Mugabe:

> He was a very clever bloke and he worked with me for as long as he thought it was going to help him. Once again, it was just to keep himself in power. I give that answer to all questions about Mugabe because that is all there is to it. Everything he has ever done is about keeping himself in power. Dictators and fascists all over the world think like that. (Holland 2008: 88)

The convincing suggestion that Smith makes is that Mugabe, in feigning friendship with him and other whites, intended to mobilise white people like him and their power to build his own power and fortify his own hold and dominion over the Zimbabwean postcolony. Smith was perhaps the right person to make this observation and advance the suggestion as he of note was another technician of power and tyrant that once publicly expressed the desire to perpetuate white colonial power for more than a million years in Rhodesia. It is possible that in spurning Mugabe, pulling out his hand and leaving to sit on the other side of the sofa to symbolise rejection, Smith meant to deny Mugabe the political capital and political resource of white power and privilege that Mugabe desired and which Smith represented. As a colonial politician of some hardihood himself and powered by his own storied will to power, Ian Smith was not going to donate the capital and symbolic resource of his power to Mugabe, but Mugabe was not going to give up that easily as he was determined to be accepted as the unquestionable leader, a black strongman who was above other blacks in education, civility and gentility, Mugabe was struggling to be white.

Not every time did Ian Smith see through and resist Mugabe's will to power and performance of reconciliation and love. After another meeting with Mugabe, in his own words, Ian Smith was totally bewitched and mesmerised by the performance. Smith reported that "I was welcomed most courteously" by a Mugabe who "said he appreciated the vital need to retain the confidence of the white people so that they would continue to play their part in building the future of the country" and ensuring progress:

> His appreciation seemed genuine, and as he escorted me to my car he expressed the wish that we would keep in contact... when I got back home, I said to Janet, that I hoped it was not a hallucination, he behaved like a balanced, civilised westerner, the antithesis of the communist gangster I had expected, if this was a true picture, then there could be hope instead of despair. (Meredith 2002a: 41–42)

Ian Smith's celebrations of Mugabe's political gestures were also for the wrong reasons that Mugabe acted in the courtesy that he associated not with human beings in general but "civilised westerners." Smith was racist to fixate good manners only to westerners. Mugabe was also racist to think that befriending Smith and proving his westernised deportments meant that he was superior. In a way Smith and Mugabe appear to be one person in different bodies and skins. Mugabe and Smith needed each other for the fulfilment of their bigotries and fundamentalisms (Holland 2008: 84). The two were caught up in an unhygienic, racist and colonial relationship where the white man was impressed that a black man could behave like a white westerner and the black man was working overtime to win the approval of the white man.

For some time, Smith and the white population in Zimbabwe celebrated Mugabe as "Good old Bob!" (Meredith 2002a: 45). In turn, "Mugabe made few changes that directly affected the white community" (Meredith 2002a: 48) in a performance of fake generosity. Mugabe protected the white population from changes that must normally come with decolonisation and liberation after colonialism. Not only that, to appease the apartheid regime in neighbouring South Africa, Mugabe made sure that there were to be no African National Congress camps on Zimbabwean soil (Meredith 2002a: 47) in a performance that negated his vaunted anti-colonialism. Publicly, Mugabe rationalised this political performance and move, "we are against apartheid" he said and we "have a duty to assist our brothers and sisters," in South Africa but "no nationalist guerrilla bases would be established on Zimbabwean territory" (Norman 2004a, b: 92). This performance that was clearly for the pleasure and comfort of apartheid South Africa was in spite of the fact that Tanzania, Zambia and Mozambique had taken the risk to host guerrilla bases of other countries including Zimbabwe. The generosity that other countries showed, at great risk, to Zimbabwe during the liberation struggle, Mugabe was not willing to extend to the liberation movements in South Africa. In that way, Mugabe gave political support to the racist apartheid regime of South Africa.

While Mugabe became good at publicly acting out the figure of a radical opponent of imperialism and empire, he privately, as David Moore (2015: 37) correctly notes, was willing to seek favours and personal accommodation with Empire. Knowing that Lord Soames, the care-taker governor of Rhodesia, was the eyes and the ears of the British Empire at the time, Mugabe was willing to humble himself before the governor and confess his limitations. After his contested electoral victory in the independence elections Mugabe made appeals to Lord Soames: "Lord Soames's private secretary recalls a daunted Mugabe," pleading with Lord Soames "he said I have no experience of running a country and neither has any of my people. None of us has run anything and so we need your help" (Meredith 2002a: 14). Mugabe was to make the very strange request that Lord Soames should remain in Zimbabwe for a number of years after independence, a request that Soames laughingly rejected. It amused Soames that a black African radical that spent more than a decade in prison and led a bitter bush war fighting for the dignity and freedom of blacks was suggesting that he and his people were not ready to govern. That Mugabe once, cap in hand and the proverbial tail between the legs, pleaded with a white politician to remain in power in Zimbabwe is unthinkable to those in Africa that took his black radicalism seriously.

Mugabe was acting the clever native who knows his limits and the limits of his people and appealed to the white man for "recolonisation," even if the request was couched as a request for capacity building in an immature postindependence African polity. Suddenly, to Mugabe, the face, eyes and ears of the British, Lord Soames, "was so good a friend" (Meredith 2002a:

14). In performance, Mugabe did not only trust Soames the British envoy but grew to love him: "I must admit that I was one of those who originally never trusted him, and yet I ended up not only implicitly trusting him but also fondly loving him as well" (Meredith 2002a: 14), Mugabe remarked. Knowingly or unknowingly, in expressing unpreparedness to rule without white help Mugabe was feeding the colonial stereotype about the "colonised" black people as naturally incompetent, lazy and unable (Memmi 1974: 123). Mugabe's behaviour gave the unfortunate suggestion that the black person was also naturally burdened with what has been called a "dependency complex" which means "colonisability" (Memmi 1974: 132).

It is noteworthy that Mugabe who grew up without a father figure had suddenly found in the powerful white man a father that he could trust, love and appeal to. Through his education by the Jesuits, imprisonment by the white Rhodesian security machinery and final recognition as a worthy leader, Mugabe had become a good product of whiteness in the Fanonian sense that "white civilisation and European culture have forced an existential deviation on the Negro" to the extent that "what is often called a black soul is a white man's artefact" (Fanon 2008: 6). Mugabe was, from his experience from prison to school, a white man's artefact.

It was as a product of whiteness and white power that Mugabe could say to Mary Soames, wife of Lord Soames, over a cup of tea that "well we had the good fortune to have been colonised by the British" (Holland 2008: 71). Mary Soames was to meditate over this statement "did he mean it, I wonder, or was it said just to pull me along? Did he fool Christopher (that is Lord Soames) who was quiet a canny bird and who came to like Mugabe very much indeed..." (Holland 2008: 71). In his performance of his own will to power, Mugabe had become too desperate for white affirmation and support. The British and former Rhodesians were also too pleased to receive his gestures affirming them as friends and mentors, much in the manner in which "the presence of the Negro besides the whites is in a way an insurance policy on humanness, when the whites feel that they have become too mechanised, they turn to the men of colour and ask them a little human sustenance" (Fanon 2008: 98). Around a fawning and grovelling Mugabe, the former colonisers felt some good validation.

Not all British representatives were delighted, comforted and fooled by Mugabe's performances. Lord Carrington, for instance, observed of Mugabe that "even when he was being polite there was a sort of reptilian quality about him...Mugabe wasn't human at all...he was an awfully slippery sort of person-reptilian as I say" (Holland 2008: 63). The monster was not concealed to everyone, even as it seemed that for feel-good post-political delusion, everyone was willing to pretend that the monster was an angel, and that what was to be hell was a paradise in Zimbabwe.

Most scholars agree that somehow Mugabe "did everything to appease white fear of black rule" (Holland 2008: 114). What most of them do not observe is that Mugabe had another agenda beside the pragmatic politics of retaining some whites in his government to keep the confidence of the former coloniser and the good will of the international community at large. In his will to power, Mugabe also meant to inherit the colonial white securocratic machinery for his own use and abuse in Zimbabwe. In inviting the former Rhodesian intelligence chief, the dreaded Ken Flower, to work for him, Mugabe was willing to play down their enmity and the fact that Flower previously and severally attempted to kill him. Even as Flower was prepared to apologise for the attempts at his life, Mugabe shrugged and laughed off the remorse "we were trying to kill each other that is what the war was about" (Meredith 2002a: 42). What Mugabe as new coloniser wanted was not a repentant Ken but the same dangerous Flower at his service this time. If Ken Flower had apologised and repented of his killing ways, Mugabe would have lost a dangerous tool that he needed to use against his political opponents. Flower just needed to shift his killing services from Smith to Mugabe as the new colonial overlord. In that way, Mugabe reproduced colonialism and its violence in Zimbabwe. Ken Flower was to be Mugabe's key advisor in the planning and execution of the Gukurahundi Genocide.

The hard man, Mac McGuiness, the prison warder that was in charge of Mugabe and other political prisoners was also retained, and "far from trusting McGuiness as a friend, Mugabe probably wanted the former policeman to head his own intelligence network because he knew McGuiness as a ruthless person" (Holland 2008: 35) who would deal with Mugabe's own political challengers with cruelty. That is how Mugabe became a post-colonial leader who admired colonial power and the power of the coloniser and did all he can to inherit the oppressive machinery of the colonial system to use it in the fortification of his own hold on power. To have white men in his service gave Mugabe some fulfilment and sense of arrival at a certain destination of power.

For white Rhodesian securocrats Mugabe abandoned the storied guerrilla leaders that, against some odds, had eventually accepted him as leader of the movement and enabled his political career. After the independence of Zimbabwe, Mugabe preferred to appoint General Peter Walls, the former leader of the Rhodesian colonial armed forces that the guerrillas were fighting, as leader of the National Army. Walls was the General who had written a letter to the British government asking them not to recognise the election results of 1980 as the vote was not free and fair because of political violence. General Walls was shocked that Mugabe appointed him, "I said to him, but how can I as an avowed anti-Marxist work for a person like you? He gave me a lecture on how the principles of Karl Marx were the same as Jesus Christ" (Meredith 2002a: 12). Mugabe was prepared to mix and rationalise Marxism and Christianity just to be accepted by a colonial army General as his new boss, to step into the boots of Ian Smith and be the new strong man is what also occupied Mugabe's ego, beside the need to assure the white population of a peaceful future in Zimbabwe. An ambition to be white and to be of whites seems to have consumed Mugabe who was, behind all pretences and performances, a colonial subject. While Mugabe later earned a reputation for rebuking Nelson Mandela for bending over too far in accommodating whites after the end of apartheid, Mugabe himself seems to have bended over too deep and in much embarrassing ways. For a man that was supposed to be an example of black excellence and African pride, Mugabe went far too far to seek white approval and to demonstrate black incapacities.

Keen observers have noted that Mugabe's first cabinet after independence was "a cabinet full of anglophiles" (Holland 2008: 110), and that he did not accept his parliamentarians as Africans, he wanted them westernised, even "his own dress and manners tended to mirror English rather than African norms." Perhaps for the pleasure and approval of the British and white sensibility, Mugabe demanded that his ministers if they "want to be in cabinet" must dress in suits in the way it is done in the British parliament (Holland 2008: 110). Besides the white former Rhodesian securocrats who headed the army, the police and the intelligence after Zimbabwe's independence, Mugabe appointed whites to head the ministries of Agriculture, Commerce and Industry and two other ministries (Holland 2008: 114). Besides reflecting Mugabe's lack of confidence in himself and his war time colleagues, this showed his ambition to please the same white supremacy and fortify the same colonialism that he professed to revile and to fight. Mugabe's cabinet appointments reflected a sad maintenance and reproduction of the colonial order of things.

Further, Mugabe maintained such colonial legislations as the Law and Order Maintenance Act and the Presidential Powers (Temporary Measures)

Act under which Smith had jailed him and his colleagues in the struggle. Mugabe's maintenance of colonial securocrats and colonial legislations after independence betrayed a troubling reality that for him colonialism was bad only when it was perpetuated by others and not him, otherwise he did not mind being a coloniser in a black skin that used the technologies of the same colonialism he fought to oppress other black people.

Behind his spectacular performance of black heroism and anti-colonialism, Mugabe might have suffered the pathology of what E.W.B Dubois called a double consciousness which "is a peculiar sensation, this double consciousness, this sense of always looking at one's self through the eyes of others, of measuring one's soul by the tape of a world that looks on in amused contempt and pity… warring ideals in one dark body" (Dubois 1969: 45). White standards and colonial sensibility might have been the measure and method with which Mugabe looked at and judged himself, hence the desperate need to please the former coloniser and win his approval. After all, no matter how well they conceal it behind radical-ism, "those that experience themselves as inferior often overcompensate" (Fanon 2008: 167) in trying to prove their equality to the oppressor.

Mugabe struggled too hard to prove his equality to whites and superi-ority to other black people, a personal struggle that was racist and colonial in its essence. Frantz Fanon was condemning that kind of drive for superi-ority of the will to power when he asked the black person who competed with the white person for superiority: "superiority? Inferiority? Why not quite simply attempt to touch the other, to feel the other, to explain the other to myself? Was my freedom not given to me then in order to build the world of the you?" (Fanon (2008: 181). Mugabe did not try to relate with other blacks and whites as fellow human beings. He got engrossed in the search for superiority. Mugabe should have sought that Fanonian kind of relations and engagement with whites and the British and not to seek to be seen as superior or equal to them. He should have sought human rela-tions, not relations that maintained the structure of colonial relations where educated blacks elevated themselves above other blacks and tried and failed to achieve equality with whites. Mugabe failed to practice the liberating politics of mutual rehumanisation that liberates the former oppressed and former oppressors from colonial relations.

Much like the attempt with Ian Smith in the sofa incident that is described above, the way in which Mugabe went out of his way to please whites and demonstrate lack of confidence in himself and his colleagues was always going to end in rejection and bitterness for him. His spirited attempt to please the white population did not earn him their vote, they continued to vote Smith and later the opposition Movement for Democratic Change (MDC) that he contemptuously accused of being white puppets. In their numbers white people did support the MDC and Mugabe who relished the support of whites before could not sleep or wake well knowing that Morgan Tsvangirai now enjoyed the admiration and support that was once his.

Much bitterly, Mugabe dismissed from work a white Minister after the white community voted for Ian Smith en masse in the elections of 1985. In dismissing Denis Norman, a white man who was the Minister of Agriculture in 1985, Mugabe expressed, not in so many words, bitterness: "you be white and we will be black," he said and "you go your own white way and we will go ours" (Holland 2008: 115). Denis Norman had to take individual punishment for all the whites that voted Smith and not Mugabe. To start with, Mugabe was wrong to appoint and please whites in order to buy their vote. That was the opportunism of his will to power. Secondly he was wrong to maintain a strict binary between whites and blacks in Zimbabwe, some whites voted for him and others did not and some black people did vote for Ian Smith, Mugabe was most likely just invoking racism for his own political ends. Importantly, in Mugabe's tone and diction "you be white and we will be black," one can read the bitterness of a rejected lover, someone who so loved the idea of Britain and of whiteness and got embittered when rejected, which is the true sour grapes of the will to power. Mugabe's love for whites and the British could not be concealed even by his performances of the will to power and pride. Under western sanctions that were passed in 2001 and forbidden from travelling to Europe, frequently "Mugabe seemed on the brink of tears as he remembered the Royal family" (Holland 2008: 235), he really missed their love and friendship of the days when he was the darling of the British. Peter Godwin, cited in Paul Moorcraft, notes that:

> I've noticed that when he speaks of Britain, he subconsciously lapses in to a magniloquent sub-Churchilian cadence- betraying his agonizing Anglophilia. "We are not an extension of Britain," he thunders now. "I will never stand for it, dead or alive, even my ghost will not stand for it. (Moorcraft 2012: 21)

Behind this vivid performance of hatred of whites and Britain by Mugabe, observers cannot miss the bitter cry of a baby pleading to be accepted back by parents that have abandoned him. Such enhanced hatred of whites as expressed in such words as "we will kill those snakes among us, we will smash them completely" (Meredith 2002a: 57) are expressions that hide love. Mugabe's was deep anger and hate that can only come from one who loved so much but was rejected. "We were supposed," Mugabe said, "to put the whites before a firing squad" (Meredith 2002a: 52) instead of reconciling with them after independence. This kind of anger and bitterness that Mugabe exuded is "fervor" which "is the weapon of choice of the impotent" (Fanon 2008: 2). Before white people, when they supported him and when they condemned him, Mugabe became impotent; he could only react with fervour at their rejection of himself and what he stood for.

I observe elsewhere in this book and here that Mugabe's will to power was more out of fear of weakness rather than simple love for power. The weakness of being disliked and rejected, like he was by his father as a toddler, Mugabe re-lived it with much anger and bitterness in being spurned by Britain and some whites. In his will to power, Mugabe loved to be loved and the idea of being hated and rejected was traumatising to him, it invoked the injury of his rejection by his father in childhood.

As Frantz Fanon (2002: 180) argues, "the tragedy of the Man is that he was once a child." The tragedy of Mugabe was the stubborn child that refused to grow inside him. He seems to have been dogged by his childhood traumas, a wounded and infuriated baby boy continued crying and throwing tantrums in his heart and mind. He failed to overcome the angry and troubled child inside himself. Frequently the angry and bitter boy inside him jumped out to throw rants and perform other spectacles of anger and hate. As an elder, anger and hate became Mugabe's identity. Behind the fury and fervour of Mugabe was a demand to be loved that was at once pathetic and determined. Early childhood abandonment by his father drove him to seek the world to father and love him while at the same time his drive for power was an attempt to be everyone's father. In whites and in the idea of Britain, Mugabe had found a symbolic father, punitive and oppressive and at times loving and powerful, and like his biological father, the symbolic father rejected him and he lost his sanity in anger and bitterness. Mugabe did not suffer well rejection and abandonment of any kind. His delusions about being a son of God and a kind of messiah and everyone's chosen deliverer made Mugabe into an insanely lovesick old man that expected to be worshipped by Zimbabweans.

MUGABE AND THE LANGUAGING OF HATE

A lot about Mugabe was concealed and also revealed in the language that he deployed. Mugabe's words and the gestures that accompanied them hid and revealed a lot about the political nature of the man. His languaging of issues, description and naming of opponents and enemies is one avenue of entering and understanding his political performances and will to power. As a proponent and also celebrant of the will to power, boasting about the nobility of his birth and imagined purity of blood, Friedrich Nietzsche (2004a, b: 6), for instance, described his father as a man who "the angels must look like" but his mother and sister as the "lower rung" of humanity, with "pettiness of instincts" and such a "canaille" type of people that were "a blasphemy against" his "divinity" of birth and being. Nietzsche's celebration of himself and his father, and his denunciation of his mother and sister used language that invented superiority of the self and constructed inferiority of the other. The will to power can be dehumanising not only in its insatiable appetite for violence but also its toxic language and demeaning expression. Mugabe's political language housed the war that was always brewing in him.

The typical tyrant names and calls the world around him in bitter and angry language of hate and war. In his study of Augusto Pinochet's personality, language and performance of power, Roger Burbach (2003) describes how Pinochet employed and deployed dehumanising language in naming and describing President Salvador Allende that he and others deposed in the violent coup of Chile in 1973. Pinochet described Allende and his supporters as "cocks," the "son of a bitch" whose people were "fuck heads" that were also "fools" and "bastards" if they were not "snakes" (Burbach 2003: 26) that should be destroyed. Describing enemies and opponents in animalistic and dehumanising terms cushions the political extremist and fundamentalist from the guilt of violating other human beings and gives him or her the psychological comfort that he or she is only violating animals and things, in the same way that the proverbial dog is given a bad name so that he could be hanged with a clear conscience. Once a political opponent has been called a sell-out, an element, a dog or a pig, as Mugabe frequently labelled his hated ones, that opponent effectively becomes a candidate for hate and elimination.

The language of the political fundamentalist and extremist is an important site from which his otherwise concealed and hidden desires and fears can be deciphered. Malcolm Bowie (1991: 48) states that to Jacques

Lacan the unconscious is always betrayed in the language of the communicator that almost always carries clues to his deeper drives and passions. To Sigmund Freud too, Malcom Bowie (1991: 49) notes, language is understood to provide a clearer passage to the world of the unconscious as a universe of desires and fears, "human speech and conduct are continuously intelligible" and related. In other words, words in speech as sounds in the air and in print as signs on space are important signifiers that carry clues to the desires, phobias and philias of the communicator. The tyrant's language, his choice of words and the names he gives his opponent cannot be ignored if his mental universe and political intentions are to be understood.

The hatred and humiliation that Mugabe endured under colonialism he was more than prepared to reproduce it and pass it on to others, in language and practice. There is a humiliating incident when Mugabe and Eddison Zvogbo, doing their form 4, were invited to a vicar's house for tea and some talk. When they left their seats, they noticed the vicar's wife using an unknown substance to disinfect the seat on which they were seated (Onslow and Plaut 2018: 39). The white racist could not sit on the same seat on which hated blacks were sitting without sterilising the seat. Mugabe and Zvogbo personally witnessed the performance of extreme hatred. Mugabe does not only seem to have suffered the humiliation but also learnt from it and was going to inflict it on other blacks, even some comrades in the struggle for liberation.

Anecdotally, Paul Moorcraft records an incident in London when Julius Nyerere as an African elder statesman called Mugabe and Joshua Nkomo to an office seeking to mediate in their conflict and bring peace and unity between the two and their political organisations that were competing and feuding for power in Rhodesia, and that were being encouraged to contest the important independence elections as a united Patriotic Front. Joshua Nkomo was the first to have a discussion with Julius Nyerere and left the office to allow Mugabe to also converse in private with Nyerere. Coming after Nkomo, Mugabe refused to sit on the same chair that Nkomo had sat on, and said to Nyerere "If you think I am going to sit where that fat bastard just sat, you will have to think again" (Moorcraft 2012: 20). Possibly, Mugabe would have loved the chair to be disinfected before he could sit on it, that is how far deep and colonial his hatred for Nkomo had become. Nyerere was depressed not just by the pettiness of Mugabe's hatred but also the vulgarity and contempt of his angry determination, he was "utterly shocked" by the uncouthness of Mugabe's talk. What Nyerere did not immediately see was just how far Mugabe had perfected imitating the coloniser in hatred and contempt for the other.

The Mugabe, who was to seek to symbolise his forgiveness and reconciliation with Ian Smith by inviting him to sit next to him on the sofa and hold hands with him, a gesture that was humiliatingly rejected, found sitting on the same chair that a fellow black fighter for Zimbabwean liberation was sitting on unacceptable and offensive. To Mugabe's will to power and imagination of intense enmity and his hate, Joshua Nkomo had become a pollutant and a kind of germ to be avoided and all proximity to his body and presence shunned, which is a kind of extremist hate and political imagination that drives ethnic cleansing and genocides, where opponents are seen as toxins and pollutants in the land. In the description of the racist hatred of apartheid white racists against the black people of South Africa, J.M. Coetzee (1991: 24) notes how the hated blacks were understood and treated as people that were infected with disease, demon possessed and dirty, and therefore contact with them and their clothes and bodies being a thing to be avoided like "contagion" and malady. Mugabe had degenerated, in his hatred of Nkomo, to that apartheidic and extremist hatred. Mugabe probably did not understand how much of the white racist in a black body he had become. Deep inside Mugabe the black radical anti-colonialist sat on a contemptuous white racist bigot that was willing to treat other black people, including heroes of the liberation war, with racist contempt.

In the pick of the Fast Track Land Reform Programme where Britain severally expressed disappointments and appeared to side with the political opposition to Mugabe and ZANU-PF, Mugabe made many fiery and also hateful speeches. In one of them, he argued "we say to Britain here and now: Hands off, hands off, don't keep interfering, hands off" (Buckle 2003: 78). Mugabe and his supporters derived pleasure in comparing British Prime Minister Tony Blair to a "Blair toilet" (Buckle 2003: 140), a type of lavatory used in Zimbabwe for rural and semi-urban sanitation and hygiene. The association of the political enemy and opponent with a toilet and the dirt that it is associated with bespeaks extreme contempt and a subconscious desire and wish to consign the adversary to the waste.

In some interesting and also alarming poetry of anger and hate, on national television and in prime time, Mugabe could appear and describe the British Broadcasting Corporation (BBC) that were disseminating messages that were opposed to him and his regime as the "British Bum

Cleaners" (Godwin 2010: 316), another metaphor that associated his political opponents with toilet activities and faecal matter itself. Seeing and describing his political opponents as those people if not those things that belonged to the toilet signified a deep and hateful political disposition. The fundamental desire for the ultimate elimination and erasure of the enemy and opponent is not concealed where the toilets and waste matter are used to imagine and describe them. What regularly, made Mugabe's hateful speeches and imagery more forceful and effective in their suggestion and effect is that "his speeches reverberated long distances from the campaign venue, courtesy of a brand new crisp public address system" (Tendi 2013: 970). Mugabe made sure that his speeches were magnified, amplified and spread throughout the country. In that way, his hateful messages were amplified and magnified through technology and other media effects. Hatred that constructs and imagines the hated in terms of toilets and toilet matter is intense hatred that builds psychological borders and fences between one and the other, borders that are impossible to mend in as much as wasted matter that has been excreted and disposed of is not to be recovered or retrieved for any human uses or benefits. That kind and level of hate is fundamentalist and extremist in its elimination of future opportunities for human reconciliation. Mugabe's language of political conflict was never near that of heroes and statesmen but belonged to the vulgar world of bullies and hateful extremists.

Interestingly but also expected of him, in his language of hate, Mugabe was frequently and severally prepared to invoke nature, God and morality as a reason for his hatred. Much the same way in which racist practitioners of apartheid regarded mixing blood and sharing space with blacks immoral, unnatural and ungodly (Coetzee 1991), Mugabe hid his hate and contempt behind self-righteous morality, naturalism and even religiosity. Mugabe described the gay, homosexual and lesbian population in Zimbabwe as people that were "immoral" and unwanted "sodomists" that were "sexual perverts" and practiced "sub-human behaviour" for which his government was "to root out the evil" because they were "worse than pigs and dogs" extremely, he believed and said "we don't believe they have any rights at all" (Meredith 2002a: 130–131). In the biblical narrative, sodomites specifically were people and are people to be destroyed by fire. Perverts, pigs and dogs are all descriptions of those people and animals that are considered dirty and must be despised. Not only to animalise and dehumanise, but also to totally erase the human rights of a population is extremist and fundamentalist to the point of being genocidal. Mugabe wished that the people he hated did not exist. If Mugabe's performance of hatred was a strange but true kind of love, his obsessive hatred for homosexuals, gays and lesbians became a vigorous attraction. He would spend hours berating them in rallies and funerals where their relevance was difficult to see. Christopher Hope (2003: 16) correctly observed the "pseudo-religiosity" with which Mugabe advanced his political opinions and personal beliefs. To claim to think and even to hate and be angry in the name of the godly and the natural makes one, such as Mugabe, feel insulated from human and earthly cares, and empowered by metaphysical power and the divine to do as he wishes with the other. And that is the stuff of political and religious crusaders who ultimately become genocidal.

Following the treatment by Carl Schmitt of the concept of the political, Chantal Mouffe (2005a, b) describes how the political par excellence allows that room for the political enemy to be legitimised, engaged with and even preserved even within intense political rivalry and competition. In that scheme of the political proper, the enemy becomes an adversary who is to be opposed but not eliminated or destroyed. Mugabe's hateful political imagination did not seek to preserve but to eliminate and erase the opponent as an enemy in totality. It is in that way that Mugabe became a political fundamentalist. The gay and lesbian community of Zimbabwe did not have to be Mugabe's political enemy, but he elevated them to that and used them as a favoured object to dramatise his anger and hatred. He loved to perform his hatred of the community. It remains a subject of curiosity exactly why Mugabe became so personally and intensely offended by gays and lesbians.

Of the existence and political prospects of the political opposition in Zimbabwe, Mugabe wished for total absence and erasure "there will never come a day when the MDC will rule this country" and "never, ever" (Meredith 2002a: 210) he vowed. Elsewhere, he said "I am firmly asserting to you that there will never come a day when the MDC will rule this country- never ever" (Buckle 2003: 67). To speak in vows and oaths and in curses, in the language of casting of spells and damnation became Mugabe's stock in political trade. In the study of "extremism left and right," Clayton Waddell (1972: 28) and C.W. Scudder (1972: 76) both but separately dismiss that "strong differences of opinion" and "strong convictions" on their own constitute extremism, but they insist that pretences to strong views and convictions are used by extremists to conceal their raw fundamentalism and hatred that have nothing to do with the protection of some deeply held values or beliefs. As this book has noted above, Mugabe severally and frequently performed and simulated behaviours and even ideas that he truly did not believe in, just for the will to power and to be in the right side of power, Mugabe effectively became a performer of simulations and dissimulations. In the political belief that only he and his political party had the right to exist and to have a political future in Zimbabwe, Mugabe had become an extremist and a fundamentalist for whom violence and the elimination of the other had become not only sensible but natural.

The Languaging of Violence

Political and religious fundamentalists deludedly hold onto their beliefs and interests as true and just dogma. Severally and frequently, Mugabe described his political opponents and enemies as wrong and totally wrong, while he and his party were totally right in their position and beliefs. This fundamentalism turned politics for Mugabe into a kind of rigid religion that is blind to all political alternatives and wide awake to its own imagined and believed godly righteousness. In the way, he went far too far in punishing his opponents for what he thought were their wrong ideas, Mugabe became a true political extremist that had lost a sense of moderation and measurement. The Gukurahundi Genocide that is treated below is an example of political extremism that came to be Mugabe's political identity.

Instead of awakening to his own political hate and violence as sin, Mugabe understood his political opponents as sinners that must repent. Speaking like a true political high priest and judgement day prophet, Mugabe on the Heroes Day celebrations of 2003 asked his opponents and those of his party ZANU-PF in the opposition MDC to repent of their sins:

> Those who would go together with our enemies abroad cannot at the same time want to march alongside us as our partners in the nation-building efforts that are underway. We say no to them; they must first repent. There is room for them to repent, there is room for them to say we were wrong yesterday, we shall not be wrong tomorrow. (Mugabe 2003: 1)

The language of repentance invokes the religious and the judgmental. Those that are judged to be wrong must either repent or be condemned to destruction and demnation. Seeing political opponents as sinners whose only chance is in repentance or demnation and destruction bespeaks the threat of violence and elimination of one by the other. The sinners and the condemned are those that must be burnt in hell and removed from amongst those that are holy and chosen. To add the religious, behind his otherwise human and partisan beliefs and interests, is not only threatening to opponents, but it also gives the fundamentalist and the extremist some comfort that his violence has the backing of the right and the divine, which makes him even more dangerous and unreasoning. Mugabe possessed a dangerous sense of political self-righteousness that made him unaccountable to himself and to others.

Mugabe's vicious reaction to revolts and uprisings against his rule began during the guerrilla war in Mozambique. When a revolt of the Zimbabwe People's Army (ZIPA) and the Vashandi arose in Mozambique in the 1970s amongst the guerrillas, demanding Mugabe's ouster as leader amongst other things, violence was threatened and carried out with alarming viciousness. After the revolters were killed and others disciplined in different ways Mugabe said: "We warned any person with the tendency to revolt that the ZANU axe would fall on their necks: *Tino tema nedemo* ['we will axe you']" (Masunungure 2004: 147–192). The axing and the beheading of opponents and challengers that Mugabe describes bespeak the crucifixion and violent elimination of religious and political opponents. When Joshua Nkomo and his ZAPU party were the enemy, Mugabe stated that "ZAPU and its leader Dr Joshua Nkomo are like a cobra in a house. The only way to deal effectively with a snake is to strike and destroy its head" (Nkomo 1984: 2). In the biblical religious narrative, the snake or the serpent by another name are the ultimate enemy that caused the fall of man in the garden of Eden, and all believers are required to not only avoid but also dutifully crash the head of the snake when it is seen.

The true political fundamentalist and extremist that he was, Mugabe did not see moderate but only final and total enemies that were necessarily supposed to be crashed like serpents. Heidi Holland (2008: 150) notes that Mugabe, caught up in violence all his life, developed an "eye for an eye mindset" of violent revenge against opponents and enemies. Describing his political fighting against opponents, Mugabe said he would when cornered "fight like a wounded lion" (Tendi 2013: 963), viciously and ruthlessly. Elections and political competition were frequently described by Mugabe as a "boxing" match and a pugilistic game of inflicting injuries and avoiding punches. Not in so many ways and words, Mugabe took politics not only as a dirty game but also practiced it as such, and as not war by other means but war itself. In many ways, psychologically and politically, Mugabe was a deeply wounded monster that post-political thinkers amongst scholars and journalists, and populations in the world had mistaken for a hero. Mugabe was a wounded soul that practiced politics as the art and science of inflicting wounds and getting even with real and imagined enemies.

The Gukurahundi Genocide: A Spectacle of Evil

The Gukurahundi Genocide of 1982 to 1987, in Matabeleland and the Midlands provinces of Zimbabwe, that was conducted by a special force, the Fifth Brigade, trained by North Korean specialists on torture and mass murder has been widely written about. What has not been widely discussed is how the genocide was a performance of evil in the pursuit of absolute power by the Robert Mugabe regime. Mugabe did not only wish for an armed takeover of the country from the Rhodesian regime so that he could have total control of the country but he also deeply desired a "one party state along North Korean lines" (Hope 2003: 96) in Zimbabwe so that he could be a president for life, uninterrupted by any political opposition. Joshua Nkomo and his ZAPU party were a serious obstacle to the burning desire of a life presidency and one-party state that consumed Mugabe, hence the deep animosity between himself and Nkomo and their respective liberation war armies, ZANLA and ZIPRA. The "liberation war rivalry and the contested independence election set a possibility for civil war in Zimbabwe" (Meredith 2002a: 59) and history has proven that it led to a genocide. Besides fighting the Rhodesian regime and its military, ZANLA and ZAPU fought against each other whenever an opportunity arose or when they encountered each other in the bush. After Zimbabwe's independence Mugabe held on to the grudges from the bush war and was burning to settle some political and military scores.

Mugabe's desire for a life presidency and one-party state (Meredith 2002a: 60) made Nkomo and ZIPRA a target of elimination, Martin Meredith believes that the fact that ZIPRA was mainly composed of Ndebele soldiers and ZANLA of the Shona only added tribal fuel to the fire of animosities. And Mugabe relished enmity. Much the same way in which Mugabe wished to militarily conquer the Rhodesians and achieve total power, he had to find a way of eliminating ZAPU, Nkomo and ZIPRA if not subdue and neutralise them forever in order to monopolise power in the Zimbabwean postcolony. In the true performance of the will to power, the genocide had to be staged, excuses and pretexts had to be created, searched for and found to permit a military onslaught on ZAPU, Nkomo and ZIPRA:

> The real aim was to break the will of the Ndebele people to resist-and it worked. His soldiers killed, and went on killing, until Joshua Nkomo capitulated. In 1987, Nkomo signed something called a Unity Pact, he was appointed vice-president and thereafter ceased to matter in Zimbabwean politics. His physical death was a formality. (Hope 2003: 26)

In the Gukurahundi Genocide and its cruelty, Mugabe did not only seek to feed liberation war grudges and animosities between his party and that of Nkomo, and between the Ndebele and the Shona people. He also intended to achieve one-party and personal rule for life in Zimbabwe. If the reasons for a genocide did not exist, he was prepared to invent them, and if the reasons existed but were not enough, he was ready to enhance them. In that way the Gukurahundi Genocide became a political performance as much as it became a spectacle of evil. In the way it was planned, the cruelty of its execution and later the rationalisation and denialism that followed the genocide, Gukurahundi carried what Hannah Arendt (2006) in reference to the Holocaust in German called "the banality of evil" that is performed with idiocy and cunning combined.

When it broke out, the Gukurahundi Genocide appeared like an accidental and random break out of violence. Initially, Mugabe himself denied knowledge of what the soldiers were doing in Matabeleland and the Midlands. What can no longer be denied is that the massacres and the genocide were programmatically planned, Mugabe's minister of police, Enos Nkala, at the time said:

> As from today ZAPU has become the enemy of ZANU-PF. The time has come for ZANU to flex its muscles. Our supporters must now form vigilante committees for those who want to challenge us. There must be a general mobilisation of our supporters. Organise yourselves into small groups in readiness to challenge ZAPU on its home ground. If it means a few blows we shall deliver them. (Meredith 2002a: 61)

Enos Nkala specifically incited and organised ZANU-PF supporters for violent attacks against ZAPU and its supporters. The aim was to eliminate all political opposition to ZANU-PF as a party and to Mugabe as a person once and for all. The "few blows" that Nkala referred to were to be large-scale violence and a true banality of evil that was later at worst denied and best rationalised by the perpetrators and their sympathisers. From Enos Nkala's influential position in ZANU-PF and in the government then, especially his resolution that "from now on," can be deduced the fact that the armed onslaught on ZAPU, Nkomo and ZIPRA was carefully deliberated and planned. The genocide was a political and military project.

Similar to Augusto Pinochet's attack on the Chileans that supported Salvador Allende (Burbach 2003: 43) and Joseph Stalin's Great Terror of the Thirties (Hope 2003: 112), the Gukurahundi Genocide was carefully reflected upon and planned. In spite of later denials and revisionist reconstructions of it by Mugabe himself as having been minor violence that was exaggerated by enemies of the state (Hope 2003: 118) or a "moment of madness" (2003: 127) where violence was conducted without much sober thought, the genocide and its cover ups, concealments and excuses were calculated, contemplated upon and executed with decided ruthlessness. Mugabe did not only state that "we have to deal with the problem" of Nkomo, ZAPU and ZIPRA "quiet ruthlessly" (Meredith 2002a: 68), but he also noted that an extra-legal operation of revenge has to be carried out: "Some of the measures we shall take are measures that will be extra-legal…an eye for an eye and an ear for an ear may not be adequate in our circumstances, we might very well demand two ears for one ear and two eyes for one eye" (Meredith 2002a: 65). That Gukurahundi was to be a crime against humanity and violence beyond the scale of biblical violence was something that was clear to Mugabe from the very start.

Genocidal thinking had always accompanied Mugabe and the political ethic of his ZANU-PF party. Irritated by opposition voters that continued to vote the MDC in the 2000 and 2002 elections, a key member of ZANU-PF and government minister wished that all Zimbabweans would be erased and silenced until the party was left with only its members in the country. Zimbabwe, Didymus Mutasa said, "would be better off with only six million people, with their own people who support the liberation struggle" (Compagnon 2011: 51) not the rest of the population in the country. Such thinking and sentiment is fundamentally genocidal, and made by a powerful politician may incite violence and murder at a large scale. Led by Mugabe, ZANU-PF aspired for a Zimbabwe where political opponents were all dead and only supporters were around to affirm the party and its leader for life.

Manufacturing the Gukurahundi Genocide

Well before the genocide, Mugabe had not only stated his wishes for a one-party state in Zimbabwe but also his deep personal hatred for Joshua Nkomo, so much of it that he would not sit on a chair where Nkomo had been sitting. As mentioned above Mugabe had already publicly mused on extra-legal and large-scale violent revenge on ZAPU, Nkomo and ZIPRA. For Gukurahundi to be carried out with some rationality and cover of legality, there had to be sound excuses and pretexts to simulate threats to state security and national interests in Zimbabwe by ZAPU and Nkomo's ZIPRA dissidents, which were dissidents that were largely a construction. Before committing genocide, genocidists construct excuses and rationalisations of their crime against humanity. Emmanuel Eze (2005) observes that perpetrators of genocide create "epistemic conditions" for their crimes by constructing an entire "ideology" that explains their actions as rights and correct even when, like Mugabe and his regime were, "dedicated thieves and murderers." A former Central Intelligence Organisation senior officer and therefore state security insider in Rhodesia and Zimbabwe, Kevin Woods, importantly disclosed that the Fifth Brigade had a habit of disguising themselves as ZIPRA dissidents, committing atrocities and then blaming them on Nkomo and ZAPU, in the process killing innocent civilians in large numbers:

> Fifth Brigade were not shy when it came to dressing up like dissidents, visiting a rural homestead for food, and then returning the following day to check if any strangers had been around. And of course the locals, being terrified of reprisals from the dissidents would deny any such thing, and be killed on the spot for supporting them. (Woods 2007: 70)

From Woods's disclosure, it is clear that where genuine dissidents and terrorists were not found, the state security agents were used to act as dissidents and terrorise people so that the same state agents would be unleashed on the same civilians. In that way, amongst other ways, the Gukurahundi Genocide became a true performance of cruelty and evil of the will to power, of inventing enemies and attacks, so that revenge would be justified in the eyes of the world. Eze (2005) notes that part of the ideology and epistemic conditions that are constructed by perpetrators of genocide before they commit their crimes against humanity is the "ideological warrants" that give them room to later deny that the genocide ever took place or that they were the perpetrators and the criminals against humanity. The perpetrators of the Gukurahundi Genocide performed the massacres in such a way that they could deny responsibility and blame other invisible forces for the crimes.

The Kidnapping of International Tourists

Six white and international tourists were kidnapped on Victoria Falls road and later killed and buried in shallow graves in the area. The kidnappers circulated a ransom note in which they suggested they were ZAPU and ZIPRA fighters. Joshua Nkomo (1984: 233–234) denied knowledge and involvement and strongly argued that state security agents staged the kidnapping to build propaganda against ZAPU and ZIPRA as dangerous terrorist organisations, especially that the tourists were western persons from different countries, ZAPU, Nkomo and ZIPRA would lose all international standing and support. There clearly was, on part of Mugabe and ZANU-PF, political intention to mobilise world opinion against Nkomo, ZAPU and ZIPRA. The act of kidnapping and killing citizens from overseas for purposes of creating bad press for a political rival in an African postcolony that Zimbabwe is appears like grave political evil that should have worried the whole world.

Proof that the kidnapping was designed to infuriate the international community is that some Zimbabwean women that were in the same car with the tourists were released by the kidnappers and were driven back to Bulawayo by the police. Joshua Nkomo (1984: 234) observed the anomaly that "one of the cars seen by the released women passengers to have been involved in the ambush was later used by the police to transport the driver of the damaged vehicle back to town" and Nkomo correctly noted that "I really don't believe in dissidents who drive about in private cars that are later used by the police." The kidnapping was by all appearances an internal security stratagem that was choreographed to besmirch the name of Joshua Nkomo and ZAPU. Given the disclosure by Kevin Woods that state security agents used to simulate terrorist and dissident acts, Nkomo's argument holds much water. Christopher Hope notes that "doubt still persists on who the real culprits were," who kidnapped the tourists "but it hardly matters- for the kidnap of the tourists became the pretext for launching in Matabeleland one of the most sustained programmes of torture, terror, kidnapping and murder that the country had ever seen" (Hope 2003: 99). After the dethronement of Mugabe in 2017, a ZANU-PF former minister Patrick Zhuwawo (2018: 1) and a nephew of Mugabe disclosed that to his knowledge then Minister of Security Emmerson Mnangagwa and then Commander of the National Army, Constantine Chiwenga, organised the kidnapping of the tourists and their subsequent murder to soil the name of ZAPU, discredit ZIPRA and get Joshua Nkomo isolated internationally. Emmerson Mnangagwa and Constantine Chiwenga became instrumental in the eventual dethronement of Mugabe from power with Mnangagwa becoming President, replacing Mugabe and Chiwenga the Vice-President. It is in that way in which the removal of Mugabe from power only served to elevate his enforcers and handlers that were only going to enhance than undo Mugabeism in the Zimbabwean postcolony.

THE ARMS CACHES

The other pretext and excuse for the Gukurahundi Genocide became the discovery, on the 7th of February 1982, of an Arms Cache at ZAPU-owned farms, Nest Egg Farm and Ascot Farm near Bulawayo. After the discovery of the arms Mugabe publicly claimed that ZAPU, Nkomo and his ZIPRA army were planning a coup d'état, "these people were planning to overthrow and take over the government" (Meredith 2002a: 63) and in true performance of grief his "heart was torn to pieces" by the discovery. However, the known truth is that Arms Cache belonging to both ZANLA and ZIPRA were a well-known fact since independence (Meredith 2002a: 63), and both armies hid arms in fear that the Rhodesians might renege from the Lancaster House agreement and go back to war. Joshua Nkomo admitted that "there were weapons in those places, the numbers found were swollen by the ferrying in of arms from elsewhere by the investigators" (Nkomo 1984: 225) to simulate that ZAPU and ZIPRA were planning an armed insurgency. International journalists and other observers were ferried to the site and the weapons were displayed to the whole world to portray ZAPU and ZIPRA as armed terrorists that deserve punishment. Mugabe publicly declared that "ZAPU and its leader Dr Joshua Nkomo are like a cobra in a house. The only way to deal effectively with a snake is to strike and destroy its head." (Nkomo 1984: 2). In the process of collecting the arms, historical records of ZAPU and ZIPRA were also collected by state security agents. These records were later used by the Fifth Brigade to trace the homes and families of ZIPRA cadres that were to be targeted during the genocide (Woods 2007: 78), and these records were also hidden and as a consequence ZIPRA war veterans do not appear in the national roll of honour. Gukurahundi became at once a genocide and an epistemicide and a theft of history and erasure of the truth. The theft of the ZAPU historical record (Nkomo 1984: 228) became part of the way in which history and information were to be managed and manipulated against ZAPU, Nkomo and ZIPRA (Meredith 2002a: 67) to rationalise and even justify the Gukurahundi Genocide, which was a true performance in its simulations and dissimulations. Just like the dissidents that were largely invented, the Arms Cache became an opportunity for Mugabe to construct a crime scene and frame Nkomo, his party and supporters for treason, and rationalise the genocide.

THE INVENTION OF THE DISSIDENTS

I have already noted above, using the confessions of Kevin Woods, that the Fifth Brigade staged dissidents. They would send soldiers that would move around villages dressed like and pretending to be some ZAPU bandits. Pretending to be pursuing these bandits the Fifth Brigade would terrorise and murder unarmed civilians. The kidnapping of foreign tourists, discussed above, the discovery of arms caches and dissident menace all became excuses and pretexts that the state either simulated or enhanced in order to create political grounds for the genocide. Mugabe was consumed by hate, fear and vengeance (Woods 2007: 50) and could not tolerate the existence of ZAPU, Nkomo and ZIPRA in Zimbabwe. Besides Richard Gwesela who remains to this day unaccounted for, one of the most infamous dissidents was Gayigusu who became known for robberies, murders and rapes in Matabeleland. Importantly, Kevin Woods discloses that Gayigusu was a recruit and an implant of the state security system, "Gayigusu, he had been recruited, equipped, and was being deployed and moved around the province in CIO and Fifth Brigade vehicles to do the bidding of his political masters" (Woods 2007: 97) in ZANU-PF and its securocrats. In that way, some prominent and most notorious dissidents were staged actors of the state and performers of its designed evil.

Further, Kevin Woods discloses that apartheid South Africa trained, armed and deployed dissidents to destabilise Zimbabwe and fan what they wanted to be civil war (Woods 2007: 91). The Gukurahundi Genocide was not on its own a proceed of a civil war but an attack on unarmed civilians by a crack unit designed for the purpose by the state. Furthermore, Martin Meredith states that the same white securocrats that Mugabe in his performance of reconciliation inherited and retained from the Rhodesian regime became the "white CIO officers working clandestinely for South Africans" that "had already managed to fan the flames of suspicion (Meredith 2002a: 64) between ZAPU and ZANU, fuelling the Gukurahundi genocide. Mugabe's political connivance with the apartheid regime is a subject that is yet to be fully probed and understood. Even if it is possible that there were some ZAPU and ZIPRA dissidents at large, "the dissident problem was far smaller than the government contended. At the time the number of dissidents in Matabeleland North was no more than about 200" and at their most they "never exceeded 400" (Meredith 2002a: 66) and therefore did not justify the genocidal reaction from the Robert Mugabe regime. The government knew this but Mugabe needed a good excuse to destroy Nkomo, his party and ZIPRA cadres, to eliminate them from the Zimbabwean political landscape and create a one-party state under his life presidency. The Gukurahundi Genocide was, therefore, a carefully planned large-scale accident that was designed for the benefit of achieving a one-party state under the life presidency of Mugabe in Zimbabwe. That Mugabe could not only contemplate but also carry out a genocide for purposes of achieving a life presidency in a one-party state in the Zimbabwean postcolony only shows how deep and evil his will to power had ballooned from political ambition to a consuming appetite for domination.

Gukurahundi Genocide as the Banality of Evil

The evil intentions behind the operations of the Fifth Brigade were not so cleverly concealed. Even the planning and execution of the genocide were accompanied by common idiocy expressed in public statements that remain in the public domain. For the evil intentions behind the formation of the Fifth Brigade and its cruelty to be understood, it is important to focus on the force itself and how it was designed and structured. In the Fifth Brigade Mugabe created an army that was separate from the national army, and the national army was an outfit that was otherwise not trained for genocide. Martin Meredith records that this was done after a "secret agreement with North Korea in October 1980" following which "in August 1981 Mugabe disclosed that a team of 106 North Korean instructors had arrived in Zimbabwe to train Fifth Brigade" about which "Nkomo" complained that Mugabe was creating "a special partisan army divorced from the national army for the possible imposition of a one-party-state" (Meredith 2002a: 62). In a strong way, the Fifth Brigade was a kind of partisan and even personal militia and army that belonged to Mugabe. On record is also that "the bond between Mugabe and the god-king Kim Chong II, 'Beloved Leader' of North Korea was strong" (Hope 2003: 101). Mugabe openly admired the grip on power of the North Korean leader and wished the same for himself in Zimbabwe. Personally, Mugabe admired the power and cruelty of some of the most venal tyrants of the world including Adolf Hitler whose moustache Mugabe religiously copied for his own shave style.

The Fifth Brigade was not trained for peace-keeping but for purposes of being what Paul Moorcraft (2012) correctly called "Mugabe's war machine" that would deal with his political enemies ruthlessly and with cruelty. Mugabe himself said about the Brigade, "the 5th Brigade were trained by North Koreans because we wanted one arm of the army to have a political orientation which stems from our philosophy as ZANU-PF" (Meredith 2002a: 66). It was a personal and partisan army whose training Kevin Woods described as basic and consisting more of indoctrination:

> Their instruction consisted of basic military tactics taught by the North Koreans and considerable brain numbing-ideology drummed in by Mugabe's political indoctrination staff. Upon completion of their five month training they emerged as brain washed zombies, armed to the teeth, and with blood lust in their eyes. All they needed was a convenient target and avenue to be set loose upon. (Woods 2007: 50)

This was the army on whose basis Mugabe could openly threaten ZAPU, Joshua Nkomo and ZIPRA: "we will show evil ZAPU our teeth, we can bite and we will certainly bite-ZAPU is destined for destruction" (Woods 2007: 70). Colonel Perence Shiri, the former Air force commander that is now a Minister of Agriculture, also instructed the force at its pass out parade, "from today on you will start dealing with dissidents. Wherever you meet them, deal with them, and I don't expect a report back" (Woods 2007: 51). Not expecting a report back, in military speak, meant that the Brigade was not to be accountable in the manner in which all regular armies are. The Brigade was a crack unit created knowingly for crimes against humanity. Their political purpose was "to nullify Joshua Nkomo" (Woods 2007: 58) and to successfully see to the "elimination once and for all of Joshua Nkomo" (Woods 2007: 59) from Zimbabwean politics. From the beginning of his career, in power, Mugabe did not want any political opposition. After the training of the Brigade, Mugabe used symbolic language to describe their work "the knowledge you have gained here will make you work with the people, plough and reconstruct. These are the aims you should retain" (Woods 2007: 50). The genocidal work of ethnic cleansing and rebuilding of the nation, after eliminating political opponents, were not so concealed in the language. ZAPU people had become the weeds to be weeded out in the project that sought to produce a Zimbabwe without political opposition to ZANU-PF. In that way, with his insane will to power, Mugabe killed his way to absolute dominion of the Zimbabwean postcolony, and did so in a banality of evil that Hannah Arendt so ably described of Hitler and the Holocaust in Germany.

TRIBALISM AND THE WILL TO POWER IN THE GUKURAHUNDI GENOCIDE

The most denied truths about the Gukurahundi Genocide in the present are that it was planned, was a tribalist project and that it is a continuing crime that victims are still suffering from. Much like racism, tribalism is usable as a political passion that constructs and justifies hatred and elimination of opponents. Besides denying tribalism, there is a durable attempt by fearful and guilty politicians and securocrats in ZANU-PF to reduce the Genocide to a "closed chapter" of history. It seems to me that Mugabe did not create the Fifth Brigade and conduct the Gukurahundi Genocide with any national interests in mind but with regionalist and much tribalist agendas. It should be remembered that much earlier on Mugabe had suggested to Lord Soames that Mashonaland and Matabeleland were separate countries where he owned Mashonaland and Nkomo-controlled Matabeleland. This was after Nkomo had complained that Mugabe's militias were disrupting his campaign rallies in Mashonaland. Mugabe memorably said:

> Look Lord Soames, I am not new to this game, you know. That's my part of the country, Manicaland, that's mine. The fact that Nkomo can't campaign there is down to the fact that I control it; I've had a cell there for five years. Is it surprising that people don't turn out there for Nkomo? Would I go to Nkomo country (Matabeleland) and expect to raise a crowd there? Of course I wouldn't. (Smith and Simpson 1981: 181)

There is not much surprise then why the Fifth Brigade was recruited from only "Shona speaking x-ZANLA forces loyal to Mugabe" and structured to be "answering directly to Mugabe" (Meredith 2002a: 65). It is noted that "the strategy of the force was pursued by the establishment of a Shona, ZANU-loyal military formation which was additional to the unified army being trained by the British" (Bourne 2011: 104). In the operations of the force, only the "ethnic Ndebele who supported Nkomo were killed" and much cruelly "villagers were forced at gunpoint to dance on the freshly dug graves of their relatives and chant pro-Mugabe slogans" (Holland 2008: 199). In Mugabe's racist, regionalist and tribalist mind, "some Zimbabweans are more indigenous than others" (Hope 2003: 98), and such people as the Ndebele became dispensable and also disposable by genocidal means. Much the same way in which colonialists used racism to rationalise the oppression and killing of black people in Rhodesia, Mugabe deployed tribalism as an ideology of identity politics that made the genocide commonsensical.

The hateful, violent and impassioned ethnic, racist, tribal and regionalist politics such as that of Mugabe seems to be a central component of the politics of the will to power. Friedrich Nietzsche (2004a, b: 4) in his will to power even regretted the ethnic, racial and regional origins of his own mother. Mugabe's own tribal bigotry, as noted by Christopher Hope, compared to that of the apartheid theorist and practitioner, Hendrik Verwoerd, who possessed "a political creed that declared not just that all countries were tribes at heart, sons and daughters of the soil, but that some tribes were more valuable because more indigenous, and thus purer by blood and breeding than those who fell outside" (Hope 2003: 36). Black people under apartheid and the Ndebele under Mugabe had fell outside the protection of power. It is for that reason that "Fifth Brigade members told the women and girls they raped that they would bear Shona babies that should populate Matabeleland" (Compagnon 2011: 50) to replace the Ndebele nation. What the Jews were to Hitler's Germany the Ndebele people had become in Mugabe's Zimbabwe.

The name Gukurahundi itself meant that "the rains that blow away the chaff" in reference to Ndebele people as disposable pollutants of the land that could be dispensed with as part of national and political sanitation and hygiene. Being a force that had "fanatical ideological loyalty to Mugabe" (Moorcraft 2012: 105) in person and also being a "North Korean-Trained and Shona-recruited Fifth-Brigade (Compagnon 2011: 49), the force was as tribalist and partisan as it was cruel and deadly. Their job which they did is that "they beat, killed, raped, tortured and burnt homes; they sought to make Ndebele speakers talk in Shona" (Bourne 2011: 107). Simplistically, some interlocutors have sought to portray the Gukurahundi Genocide as an attack by Shona people on the Ndebele population of Zimbabwe. Truth is that tribalism and ethnic rage, and populism, were mobilised by Mugabe, his party and its securocrats to achieve some political goals. Ancient Shona versus Ndebele animosities became ready political resources for a tyrant with a burning will to power and evil securocrats on his side. It was for power that Mugabe was willing to sink to tribalism and nativism as populist methodologies of genocidal hatred of political opponents.

Genocidal tribalism is part of the politics of the African postcolony that Frantz Fanon condemned. Fanon described and critiqued such tribalist and regionalist politics as that of Mugabe when he treated the subject of "pitfalls of national consciousness" in post-colonial Africa. "National consciousness, instead of being all embracing," Fanon (2001: 119) argued, became a "travesty of what it might have been," the venerated "nation is passed over for the race, and the tribe is preferred to the state" and this politics is owed to, Fanon says, "the intellectual laziness" of leaders. Frantz Fanon might as well have been writing of ZANU-PF and Mugabe when he stated that:

> As far as national unity is concerned the party will also make many mistakes, as for example when the so-called national party behaves as a party based on ethnical differences. It becomes in fact the tribe which makes itself into a party which of its own will proclaims that it is a national party, and which claims to speak in the name of the totality of the people, secretly sometimes even openly organises an authentic ethnical dictatorship. (Fanon 2001: 147)

In the Gukurahundi Genocide and his understanding of Zimbabwe as an essentially divided country on regional and ethnic grounds, and racial grounds when it came to punishing and excluding whites, Mugabe failed in the important political project of nation building. His became the art and science of dividing the nation for personal and partisan power. Because his Shona tribe had majority numbers in the country, Mugabe saw political advantage and employed and deployed tribalism. Kevin Woods saw it thus:

> President Robert Mugabe, perhaps with foresight, but almost certainly consumed by paranoia and with evil in his heart, ordered that a new full Zimbabwe National Army Brigade be formed consisting only of his staunch

supporters-erstwhile ZANLA guerillas from the liberation struggle... and very strictly screened young men of the *same tribe as himself*, who were still to be trained. (Woods 2007: 50)

The cruelty and evil described below describes the extent to which Mugabe would go in punishing Nkomo, ZAPU and ZIPRA. Nkomo had to say in reaction, "I have never done anything wrong and Mugabe knows it, I tell you this is for personal power" (Hope 2003: 99). Nkomo did not have to do anything, Mugabe was prepared to invent and construct allegations, simulate crimes and apply terror in order to perpetrate a genocide in pursuit of absolute power. Notably, "What Verwoerd pioneered was the way of making tribalism respectable across Africa" and "no other leader in African today more closely resembles Dr Verwoerd than Robert Mugabe" (Hope 2003: 37). When leaders choose tribe, race and other narrow identities ahead of the nation and humanity, the way Mugabe and others have done, Frantz Fanon (2001: 148) argued, "these heads of government are the true traitors in Africa, for they sell their country to the most terrifying of all its enemies: stupidity" because the political power that is rooted in such fragile foundations as tribalism, regionalism and nativism is perishable and also violent and evil. Andrew Norman summarised the cruelty, evil and excess of Gukurahundi thus: "Mugabe unleashed barbaric massacres against the entire Ndebele people of the region: once again he had responded to what appeared to be a small, local problem in an entirely disproportionate manner, rapes, beatings, torture, burnings and deliberate starvation were the order of the day" (Norman 2004a, b: 95). The Gukurahundi Genocide became a work of cruelty and evil that could only be driven by an insane appetite for political victory and power.

Systematic Cruelty and Organised Evil

For Mugabe and ZANU-PF cruelty became systematised as a tool to inspire fear and secure power. Evil itself became part of the identity of the person of Mugabe and the party, ZANU-PF. Institutionalised violence is the term that Lloyd Sachikonye (2011) used to describe the culture and tradition of political violence in Zimbabwe for the past sixty years. Similarly, David Coltart (2007) compared political violence in Zimbabwe to a disease. As institutionalised violence and also a political malady, political violence in Zimbabwe found its worst and most tragic expression in the Gukurahundi Genocide that exceeded in its cruelty and evil. In describing

Gukurahundi as having been a "moment of madness," Mugabe unintentionally explained his own paranoia that drove him to excessive violence. As understood by Jacques Lacan paranoia is a kind of madness in that it is "delusional fear" (Bowie 1991: 37) that can lead to excessive violence and evil. In many ways including in the Gukurahundi Genocide, Mugabe became what Wallace Stevens referred to as a "lunatic of one idea" (Bowie 1991: 43) and in this case an idea of power by all means necessary. The spirited drive for power led Mugabe into insanity and poor imagination. Insanity and evil constitute the banality of evil that Hannah Arendt (2006) condemned of the extremes of both Nazism and Zionism as political passions.

Besides the Security Minister, Emmerson Mnangagwa, Perence Shiri, Constantine Dominic Chiwenga and others, Colonel Lionel Dyke, a securocrat that Mugabe inherited from the Rhodesian regime, was a key genocide enforcer that supervised curfews (Woods 2007: 52). The genocide became a neatly supervised and enforced operation of killings. Christopher Hope summarised the cruelty and evil of the Gukurahundi Genocide thus:

> Five Brigade burned victims alive, tortured them with electrodes, drowned them, locked them in camps where they succumbed to starvation and disease, and then threw their bodies into mass graves or dump them down old deserted mine-shafts. There were times when Five Brigade exceeded its own record of cruelty. In order that families of their victims should suffer as extensively as possible-for the Ndebele find it intolerable that the dead should not be properly buried and decently mourned-Five Brigade insisted that the bodies of the executed be abandoned in the bush to be disposed of by vultures and jackals and other scavengers. (Hope 2003: 101)

Alongside these festivals of cruelty and evil, a scotched earth policy was implemented. All forms of transportation were banned, shops were closed and farming and schooling activities were stopped, and the people starved to death in large numbers (Woods 2007: 53). There were also incidents of biological warfare where chemicals and poisons were used to poison and kill people in large numbers (Woods 2007: 98). Both the leaders of ZAPU, ZIPRA and ordinary operatives were targeted, and the populations of civilians too, indistinguishably. At the beginning of the genocide, Enos Nkala said of the leadership, "we want to wipe out the ZAPU leadership. You have only seen the warning lights. We are not yet full speed. ZAPU is a murderous organisation and its murderous leadership must be hit so hard" (Woods 2007: 71). Unarmed civilians were not spared. Concerning civilians, Mugabe himself announced: "Don't cry if your relatives get killed in the process...where men and women provide food for the dissidents, when we get there we eradicate them, we do not differentiate who we fight because we can't tell who is a dissident and who is not" (Meredith 2002a: 68). On the same subject of innocent civilian casualties, Defence Minister, Sydney Sekeramayi, reasoned thus: "That innocent people could well be suffering and that this was acceptable, can Nkomo identify a dissident, a dissident supporter or an innocent civilian" (Woods 2007: 63). In that way the killing of civilians was licensed. It is also in that way that civilians were slaughtered in large numbers in Southern Zimbabwe. The state feigned inability to distinguish who was from who was not a dissident. All the people of the region became candidates for death. Intentional ignorance is what tyrannical and genocidal regimes feign in order to perpetuate evil with impunity.

The Gukurahundi Genocide was an evil operation that was led by evil men. As an insider and also observer at the time, Kevin Woods noted that "one thing I did realise, very early in my CIO days was that Mugabe is manifestly evil and that his security Minister, Emmerson Mnangagwa, was running a close second in that dubious distinction" (Woods 2007: 123). On how the civilian population was to be systematically starved and killed off, an armed to the teeth Gukurahundi operative is recorded to have said: "First you will eat your chickens, then your goats, then your cattle, then your donkeys. Then you will eat your children and finally you will eat the dissidents" (Meredith 2002a: 70–71). Martin Meredith concludes that all the ministers and soldiers said these outlandish and cruel statements of evil because at the top, Mugabe gave license and permission, "the author of this terror was Mugabe. His own speeches licensed it" (Meredith 2002a: 75).

Interesting but also rather typical of most genocides and other forms of large-scale violence is how the godly and the religious was mobilised and deployed in the Gukurahundi Genocide. "Five Brigade," Christopher Hope notes, "were fond of Biblical allusions, and several of its commanders appropriated the name of Jesus, the 'black Jesuses' had power over life and death and they liked their terrified victims to be aware of their supernatural status" (Hope 2003: 102).

Some victims tried to reach out to Mugabe to appeal for his mercy. One captive of the Fifth Brigade, a man that was to be killed, pleaded with the

Security Minister, Emmerson Mnangagwa, for audience with Mugabe. The answer that he received was that Mugabe was God, and said Mnangagwa, "if you want to speak to God," meaning Mugabe, "go through his son" (Woods 2007: 71) in reference to himself. Where Mugabe had become the God, his ministers and soldiers became disciplines and sons. Addressing an audience in Victoria Falls which is an area where the genocide was also at its most intense, Mnangagwa said: "Blessed are they who will follow the path of the government's laws but woe unto those who choose the path of collaborating with dissidents, for we will surely shorten your days" (Woods 2007: 71), in clear adaptation and imitation for evil purposes of the beatitudes of Jesus Christ in his Sermon on the Mount teachings. Further, Mnangagwa preached: "Blessed are they who hunger and thirst after justice for they shall find peace" (Hope 2003: 103). Mugabe had taken the place of God, and his followers and enforcers of violence had become the Christs and other disciples. God had been suspended, replaced by a man, in a setting where evil had become a religion that was to be faithfully implemented. Mugabe was no longer the imaginary "son of God" and was now a God himself in whose name masses of people were massacred. Survivors of the Gukurahundi Genocide cringed in 2017 when Mnangagwa replaced Mugabe in power in 2017 and made his slogan the statement, "the voice of the people is the voice of God!" Mnangagwa had been known and experienced by the victims and survivors of Gukurahundi as a personification of evil and enemy of God. Mnangagwa is the man who in that same rally in Victoria Falls called Ndebele people cockroaches that must be fumigated out of existence in the country.

Mugabe did not take kindly to cries about the Genocide and the evil of the Security Minister. At the height of the Genocide some concerned religious ministers approached Mugabe to complain about the killings in Matabeleland. It was in March 1983. In true performance, "the Prime Minister listened with sympathy" and "seemed to be genuinely shocked and saddened," looking at Security Minister, Mnangagwa, he asked "why didn't you tell me?" that people are dying. In the whole of it, "it was an extra-ordinary performance: a dissembling modesty mixed with cunning" (Hope 2003: 104–105). Mugabe promised to urgently attend to the matter. Dramatically Mugabe appeared on national television that evening lambasting the religious ministers as "a band of Jeremiahs" that was up to mischief in the country. Through cunning and pretences mixed with pure denialism, Mugabe and his Security Minister went on with the genocide.

The God of the moment of madness was Mugabe himself, anyone speaking or pretending to speak for God as the Catholic priests did was an enemy. Mugabe did not only sanction and license the killings but he immediately pardoned and freed any security officials that were brought before the courts for the violence and crimes (Woods 2007: 73). In punishing some and pardoning others, Mugabe came to act godlike. Unlike Rene Descartes, the Jesuit mentee who questioned all knowledge except the existence and superiority of God (Chavez-Arvizo 1997: xvii), Mugabe became the Jesuit trainee that developed a god-complex and came to hold contempt for the Christian church and its messengers. Mugabe, in the words below, was prepared to accuse the Catholic Church, that brought him up, of colonialism but not to address his own blatant violations of human rights:

> The most insidious side of the resurgence (of colonialism) of white power came by way of the pulpit and in the human form of church figures who do not hesitate "to render unto God" things that belonged to Caesar. Especially in Suburban parishes and in rural Matabaleland, prayers became full blooded politics and congregations became anti-ZANU-PF political communities united around hackneyed grievances to do with the tensions we had before the Unity Accord. (Meredith 2002a: 193)

The church was supposed to be silent on human rights in respect of the Unity Accord that Mugabe signed with Nkomo after the Genocide. Political contracts between politicians, in the imagination of the will to power that possessed Mugabe, became more important than social justice and biblical calls for human rights. The silencing and erasure of other voices became a preoccupation of a Mugabe that had become totally hostage to a consuming will to power. In his god-complex of the will to power, Mugabe could threaten the church ministers. In reference to the critical and outspoken Archbishop Pius Ncube who openly challenged him on human rights violations, Mugabe said "we will respect him if he remains within the confines of the church but, once he shows off his political tentacles, and if those tentacles are harmful, we will cut them off" (Hope 2003: 23). That human rights and social justice were within the confines of the church and a central part of the Christian religion was deliberately and conveniently forgotten by Mugabe who had become a law unto himself, an executive hooligan.

During and after the genocide, information on and about the mass killings was carefully concealed from the international media (Meredith 2002a: 67). A commission of inquiry led by Justice Simplicius Chihambakwe released a report which Emmerson Mnangagwa vowed "will never be made public" (Woods 2007: 83). Just as ZAPU historical records were hidden (Woods 2007: 78), all information on the genocide became secret which makes Gukurahundi both a genocide and an epistemicide where information and the truth had to be destroyed for purposes of securing the power and privilege of the perpetrators. A key result of the genocide was that Joshua Nkomo and ZAPU capitulated and signed a Unity Accord with Mugabe and ZANU-PF (Meredith 2002a: 73), resulting in a de facto one-party state in Zimbabwe. The genocide achieved the political purpose for which it was designed. The fear that the genocide caused amongst the people is still a useful political resource in Zimbabwe as the people of Matabeleland and the Midlands remain cowed and intimidated. The sheer memory of the genocide and its spectacles of cruelty keep the people of Matabeleland and the Midlands fearful and politically cowed, the smallest threat of violence scares them to silence.

The complicity of the international community in the Gukurahundi Genocide is a least discussed subject. Condemning international complicity in the genocide and troublesome British double-standards, Paul Moorcraft notes that "even after Mugabe's North Korean trained Fifth Brigade had slaughtered tens of thousands of Ndebeles in the early 1980s, Queen Elizabeth awarded him an honorary knighthood" and "only much later in 2003 after the killing of a small number of white farmers" in Zimbabwe "the British Prime Minister was asked in Parliament" if Mugabe should not be de-knighted, only "in June 2008 the Queen annulled the honour"(Moorcraft 2012: 21). If Gukurahundi as Mugabe argued was indeed a moment of madness, it was his madness that had the will to power itself as a drive, a passion and a desire. In many ways, the Gukurahundi Genocide became non-revolutionary violence which Mahmood Mamdani describes as futile and tragic violence:

> What do I mean by non-revolutionary violence? I mean by it a kind of violence in which different groups of more or less equally impoverished and disempowered people are pitted against each other. Fanon called such people the wretched of the earth. When the wretched of the earth divide into

contending groups that take it out on one another, that violence is non-revolutionary. When the battle-lines are not defined by wealth or poverty, but by a difference that is not economic, such as religion or ethnicity or race, the violence it gives rise to is non-revolutionary. (Mamdani 2001: 1)

The Ndebele ethnic people, ZAPU as a political party, Joshua Nkomo as a politician and ZIPRA as an army were like ZANLA, Mugabe and ZANU-PF, oppressed entities that were supposed to emerge from a history of colonial and racist domination. The genocide became non-revolutionary violence in reproducing and repeating a kind of colonial violence of one against another in such a very large scale. That reproduction and repetition of the colonial and the racist in a post-colonial setting is an example of the tragedy and also evil of the will to power. What makes the evil of the Gukurahundi Genocide worse is that, on record, more Zimbabweans died in the genocide than in the war against settler colonialism. Worse still, the genocide divided the country almost beyond repair. The Gukurahundi Genocide complicated the Zimbabwean national question. It produced not only dead bodies and many mass graves but angry widows, widowers and orphans, bitter survivors and exiles. It produced secessionist movements that have reason to believe that the country should be split into two or more countries. Mugabe's genocidist nationalism did not graduate Zimbabweans into nationhood.

PERFORMING THE NATION

After so dividing the country through a genocide, when it suited his political ends, Mugabe was willing and able to play the nation builder and unifier of the country. Through the Gukurahundi Genocide as evil and also non-revolutionary violence, Mugabe participated in poor imagination of the nation of Zimbabwe and failed in the project of nation building. With the Gukurahundi Genocide, Mugabe brought to life what Frantz Fanon (2001: 128) condemned as the resurrection of ancient tribal rivalries after independence from colonialism in Africa. This resurrection of ancient rivalries is as a result, Fanon noted, of the political and intellectual laziness of elite political leaders of the class that inherited power from the colonialists. These elite but lazy leaders easily became new colonisers of Africa. Ndabaningi Sithole, one of the founders of the Zimbabwean liberation movement and architects of ZANU-PF, bemoaned Mugabe's opportunistic tribalism and divisions of the nation of Zimbabwe:

> When we formed ZANU in 1963, it was called the Zimbabwe African National Union, but by 1974 and the beginning of 1975, it had become in practice 'Zimbabwe African Tribal Union' masquerading under the respectable garbs of the ZANU of 1963. The tribalised or regional Dare had therefore ceased to represent ZANU as we know it. It had come to represent in effect ZATU (Zimbabwe African Tribal Union) or ZARU (Zimbabwe African Regional Union). (Sithole 1979: 310)

In this lamentation of the division and death of the nation, Ndabaningi Sithole also reflects on how Mugabe and others performed the nation as in simulating nation building rather than enacting it in earnest. For political power, national unity and peace were sacrificed on the altar of opportunism and the will to power; power was sought, found and kept at the dear expense of national unity and justice in Zimbabwe. What was supposed to be a liberation movement led by Joshua Nkomo and Mugabe was reduced to a school of violence and hatred where party cadres, soldiers and party functionaries were, in the argument of Ngwabi Bhebhe, taught to hate each other and given reasons to attack each other:

> The reason was very simple. These young men and women were trained to hate each other by their leaders, who wanted to justify the separate existence of their parties. Each party had its own Commissariat Department, whose task was to teach recruits the history of the party, how the party was different from the other, who the leaders were and how they were different from the less revolutionary or sell-out leaders of the rival party. Thus, the cadres were brought up to hate. (Bhebhe 2004: 256)

After Mugabe's dethronement and death Zimbabwe remains a country whose nationhood cries for re-imagination. Hate, which in many ways is the true oxygen of violence and evil, was privileged and elevated to the status of political education and allowed to infect the liberation movement that was reduced to a movement of new domination and oppression. Where the coloniser had become absent, in true non-revolutionary history, the former colonised turned and colonised each other and violated the nation that they meant to liberate and re-build. After this violation of the nation, Mugabe was willing to perform and simulate nation building, for nothing else but power. In his performative words, Mugabe could say: "Zimbabwe is one entity and shall never be separated into different entities. It's impossible. I am saying this because there are some people who are saying let's do what Lesotho did. There is no Lesotho here. There is one Zimbabwe and one Zimbabwe only" (Mugabe 2005a, b, c: 1). Indeed, Mugabe had torn the country asunder but for power he wanted a reputation as a unifying leader and nation builder. He wanted to be reputed for what he was not. Denialism and convenient amnesia became some of the telling symptoms of Mugabe's madness.

In his madness, Mugabe wanted to minimise the genocide to a closed chapter of Zimbabwe's history. Whenever he was reminded of the Gukurahundi Genocide that divided the nation and killed many nationals, Mugabe demanded that it be forgotten and left to freeze as the dead past: "If we go by the past, would Ian Smith be alive today? What cause will there be to impel us to keep him alive? Perhaps I will be the man to go and cut his throat and open up his belly," as supposedly a good leader he thought "but no we shall never do that. We have sworn not to go by the past except as a record or register. The record or register will remind us of what never to do. If that was wrong, if that went against the sacred tenets of humanity, we must never repeat, we must never oppress man" (Mugabe 1997: 1), he said. That Mugabe knew that "we must never oppress man" is truism that his many victims would be bewildered by. The same leader that was guilty of genocide was now demanding that the victims and the world forget the atrocities. The leader who had oppressed and killed man was paradoxically seeking to build a reputation for liberation and national unity. The will to power works in cruel paradoxes and crude ironies. Conveniently and also opportunistically, Mugabe dwelt on the wrongs of Ian Smith and colonialism and erased his genocidal crimes against humanity, which is another ironic and paradoxical performance of the political holiness of the will to power that neither sees nor hears its own evil. Mugabe was then living in a paradisal but truly insane world where he could forgive and forget his own crimes against Zimbabweans and humanity, and then compel Zimbabweans to do the same.

In the important argument that nations are imagined communities, Benedict Anderson (1983) meant that nations as populations within such countries as Zimbabwe could be imagined, constructed and united into working and just settings. Mugabe's imagination of the nation became poor and was infected with the will to power, personal, partisan and narrow power for that matter. Where he could not build the nation, he simply performed and simulated it. K.M. Askew (2002: 14), in the case of Tanzania, describes how the nation can be performed for the better or the worse, using music and the cultural politics of art and symbolism. In the case of Zimbabwe, Mugabe performed the nation by use of what Sabelo

Ndlovu-Gatsheni and Wendy Willems called "cultural nationalism" that can be abused in simulating rather than actualising genuine nation building. In Zimbabwe:

> Performing the nation involved the conflation of state, nation, ruling party and the person of Robert Mugabe into one symbol of national sovereignty that needed to be jealously guarded. It ranged from singing a national anthem to the wearing (by the ZANU-PF Women's League) of identical dresses with Mugabe's portrait emblazoned on the fabric. (Ndlovu-Gatsheni and Willems 2009: 952)

Instead of imagining the nation and enacting its building, Mugabe imagined power and himself as the fulfilment of the nation. Mugabe became the powerful but also pathetic nationalist that Frantz Fanon described as "the leader, who once used to call for African unity" but went on to be the one who "thought of his own little family" (Fanon 2001: 148) instead of thinking of all the tribes and races of the nation beyond his own. One of the reasons suggested for removing Mugabe from power by the military junta was not that he wanted to establish a tribal oligarchy in Zimbabwe but a family dynasty where he allegedly wanted his own wife to succeed him.

Mugabe was fond of pretending that "national unity was his top priority" (Nkomo 1984: 203), but frequently went on to participate in racism, tribalism, regionalism and factionalism. Surprisingly therefore, "Robert Mugabe, whose intelligence should have set him above this faction-fighting, had become its servant" (Nkomo 1984: 217). Once asked by Joshua Nkomo what the supreme body was in the Zimbabwean nation, he said: "the supreme body in Zimbabwe is the central committee of ZANU-PF, my party" (Nkomo 1984: 3). This was an understanding of the nation that was partisan, narrow and of poor imagination. This poor imagination degenerated to a point where he thought himself and his family were the nation. As Nkomo correctly noted, Mugabe's storied education and vaunted intelligence could not protect him from trappings of evil and the will to power that normalised poor imagination of the nation. The reputation of a gallant Pan-Africanist that Mugabe built was based on rhetoric and not logic; the man, as he frequently called himself, could not be a prophet of African continental unity because he could not even unite a country.

Mugabe's idea of Zimbabwe in its poverty of imagination became an idea of personal power. He used ceremonies, symbols and rituals as simulations and pretences to national unity and nation building that he was supposed to actualise and not just perform. Mugabe performed and dramatised nation building instead of enacting it. Over time Mugabe grew a "penchant for ceremony and tradition" (Tendi 2013: 965) where crowds of people rallied around him and made him feel like the messiah that he was not. Sabelo Ndlovu-Gatsheni noted how Mugabe performed the nation without enacting nation building in veracity:

The idea of "Zimbabwe for Zimbabweans" popularized by Mugabe, for example, included the "Occidentalizing' of white citizens. In 2001 a number of "galas" and "biras" were organized to celebrate the lives of Joshua Nkomo and Simon Muzenda, who had been co-vice presidents of Zimbabwe. Ironically, in the 1980s Nkomo, who was forced into exile in 1983, had been represented as the "father of dissidents"; in 2001 his status as "father of the nation" was granted posthumously. The commemoration of Nkomo, known as "Umdala Wethu Gala" ("Our dear old man gala")," emphasizes Nkomo as a symbol of national unity because he signed the Unity Accord of December 22, 1987, which enabled ZANU-PF to swallow PF-ZAPU and for Mugabe to pursue his objective of a one-party state. Muzenda, for his part, is represented as the "soul of the nation" and celebrated in what has become known as "Mzee Bira." (Ndlovu-Gatsheni 2012: 13)

Mobilising the heroism and symbolism of the dead that he could honour while they were alive became another of his strategies for manufacturing popularity. Mugabe's imagination and performance of the Zimbabwean nation was violent in its racism, tribalism and opportunism. He cultivated a political tendency of celebrating other heroes only when they were dead. In the nationalism of Mugabe in Zimbabwe, we can observe the degeneration where "from nationalism we have passed to ultra-nationalism, to chauvinism, and finally to racism" (Fanon 2001: 125). Mugabe practiced nationalism as nativism. What was supposed to be unity amongst people and political parties became an opportunity to "swallow" opposition political parties such as ZAPU and create a one-party state under Mugabe as supreme leader. What was supposed to be celebration of heroes was the abuse of their names and legacies for Mugabe's popularity and personal political image. This was a symbolic but still violent kind of cannibalism where Mugabe politically fed on other politicians whose good names he used to build his political image.

The remembrance of heroes that had passed on, such as Joshua Nkomo and Simon Muzenda, was turned into a political religion used to mobilise the nation into supporting Mugabe and ZANU-PF. Those who opposed Mugabe were imagined as sinners that must urgently repent and join the idolatry of worship and support for him and his party. During the Heroes Day commemoration of 2003 at the National Heroes Acre, for instance, Mugabe spoke religiously to the political opposition, specifically the MDC, and preached unto them the gospel of repentance: "There is room for them to repent, there is room for them to say we were wrong yesterday, we shall not be wrong tomorrow" (Mugabe 2003: 1). This is another capital statement from Mugabe that I repeat in this book as it is a telling clue to his personalised and partisan understanding of the nation, an insane understanding. Now that the British and American powers were against him, he expected every person and party in Zimbabwe not to relate with them. To oppose Mugabe and not to support him and his party was irreligious and sinful, in his imagination, the opposition needed to "repent" and return to the idol and the religion of the person and the party. Mugabe was possessed of an exclusionary nationalism and personalism that expelled his opponents from the nation and that isolated them as the usual sinners that had departed from his idolatrous religion. The heavy weight of the names and symbols of dead statesmen that were not in their lives allowed to lead Zimbabwe were carefully manipulated to blackmail Zimbabweans into supporting the leadership of Mugabe.

The Heroes Acre, like the Gukurahundi Genocide that was assisted and enabled by North Korea, was constructed with the assistance of the North Koreans and "the North Koreans, the ideological godfathers of the Mugabe revolution, built the Heroes Acre in their own image" (Hope 2003: 232). The Acre became, in Mugabe's own words, a shrine:

This National Shrine [Heroes' Acre], as indeed are the district and provincial and other shrines where our fallen heroes lie, is a place of renewal and re-dedication that strengthens our resolve and pledge that Zimbabwe shall never be a colony again. For, as we look at the pantheon of heroes and heroines who make our roll call today, what greater challenge, what greater patriotism is there, than to faithfully and resolutely guard that which cost us tens of thousands of lives to achieve? Where would our honour be if we were intimidated by imperialism's tired trickery into letting go of our sacred land? (Mugabe 2004: 1)

The shrine is described in the religious language of the "sacred" and diction of a "pantheon" of gods of which Mugabe himself imagined himself as the god of gods that lives after the others have died. It became a paradox that after weeks of negotiations, Mugabe's family, led by his wife Grace Mugabe, refused to bury his remains at the Heroes Acre, the shrine that he so treasured. In a way Mugabe's family denied Emmerson Mnangagwa's government the opportunity to preside over Mugabe's burial and use his body and image for their own propaganda. Mnangagwa, no doubt, would have loved to pontificate over the Mugabe's dead body and perform the dutiful successor, a deserving heir to the fallen tyrant.

Mugabe was good at pontificating over the dead bodies of other politicians and using them to portray an image of himself as a great leader and patriot. Patriotism as a violent passion out of which men and women are prepared to die and kill for the nation (Anderson 1983) was invoked not for nation building but for building the party and personal political support for Mugabe. In a strong but symbolic way, by using the names and the dead lives of heroes to build his own political image, Mugabe participated in cannibalism where he ate other heroes for his own political nutrition and nourishment of personal power. The will to power is no vegetarian, but it is truly cannibalistic. In the way in which Jean-Bedel Bokassa physically killed his opponents and political competitors and as a "keen cannibal" put their parts in the fridge and "ate" them (Hope 2003: 39), Mugabe symbolically fed on their bodies and names for his own name and will to power, and he profited politically from the souls of the dead in a kind of political cannibalism of the will to power. After Mugabe was buried in Zvimba and not at the Heroes Acre, the social media were full of narratives about how he personally instructed his family not to surrender his body to Mnangagwa and his political faction that he feared would harvest his body parts for purposes of witchcraft. Mugabe's will to power would not allow him to permit his remains to be used as a campaign object by the man and the ZANU-PF faction that toppled him from power, in life and in death, Mugabe carefully kept grudges and relished in revenge. Those that finally toppled him from power, even if they were his brothers in crime, were now constructed as wizards that would easily eat his body, the body of a political messiah that he imagined himself as.

Mugabe himself, in a symbolic but real way, practiced the political sorcery of forcing the ghosts of dead politicians to use their living names to campaign for him, the Heroes Acre as a cemetery became for him a kind of political rally of ghosts that he annually invited to join his political campaigns. Names of dead and some living heroes were called as from a register to endorse the image of Mugabe. Amongst the names of the departed and some living African icons and heroes that Mugabe named for special honour and remembrance at the Heroes Acre in 2005, in particular, in the celebration of Zimbabwe's twenty-five years of independence were: Julius Nyerere, Kenneth Kaunda, Samora Machel, Seretse Khama, Agostinho Neto, Leopold Takawira, Samuel Parirenyatwa, Joshua Nkomo, Simon Muzenda and Bernard Chidzero (Ndlovu-Gatsheni and Willems 2009: 956). It might look like true political politeness or just good political marketing but the act of mobilising the popularity of living and dead African heroes to use it as a perfume to scent the soiled name of Mugabe and ZANU-PF was a kind of political sorcery and cannibalism. Political profits accrued from past and departed heroes amount to dirty gains akin to those from the violation of graves in the cemetery and the commandeering of ghosts to do political campaigns for the benefit of the party and the person of Mugabe. In particular, Joshua Nkomo's name and symbol were fed upon by Mugabe for his political nutrition and will to power.

THE CANNIBALISATION OF JOSHUA NKOMO

In a strange but true way, Mugabe found political capital and made political raw materials of the dead. Politically Mugabe was much alive in the presence and company of dead heroes. In observance of Mugabe's way of using the Heroes Acre as a site of political campaigns and of his poor imagination of the nation, Kizito Muchemwa (2010: 504) called it "Necropolitan imagination" of the nation, which had as its part a strange adoration and use of the dead and their names. The dead and their names, even if they were hated and persecuted in life, like true hunted animals that are later eaten at the table, are from their graves suddenly relished and consumed as political resources and capital itself.

Joshua Nkomo in particular was much persecuted in his life by Mugabe. By Mugabe, Nkomo was called a snake and a therefore a candidate for death, "ZAPU and its leader Dr Joshua Nkomo are like a cobra in a house. The only way to deal effectively with a snake is to strike and destroy its head" (Nkomo 1984: 2). For the Gukurahundi Genocide and the way Nkomo was hunted so that he could be murdered, he cried "but nothing in my life had prepared me for persecution at the hands of a government led by black Africans" (Nkomo 1984: 1). Mugabe was determined to animalise, hunt and kill Joshua Nkomo and ZAPU, "the dissident party and its dissident father are both destined not only for rejection but for utter destruction as well" (Norman 2004a, b: 95), Mugabe threatened. Rememberably, Nkomo had once been so hated by Mugabe that he would not even sit on a chair that Nkomo had sat on, as if Nkomo had leprosy or some other contagion. Once dead and buried at the shrine, Nkomo became political relish for Mugabe.

Opportunistically profiting from the names of the dead became Mugabe's second identity. When Joshua Nkomo, for instance, was safely dead and peaceful at Heroes Acre, Mugabe was ready to resurrect and relish him for political profit. In a way. the ghost of Nkomo was again troubled and persecuted, risen and sent to campaign and fatten the image of a party and politician that persecuted him in his life. The persecution of the man and eating his political ghost was couched as remembrance and memorialisations. For example, in the national event to remember Nkomo in July 2002, Mugabe said:

> We remember him as the Father of Zimbabwe, as the one who pioneered the struggle and one who was committed to the very end to liberate his people and after liberation wanted the people to get their land. We also remember him as father of the family and politically, as father of all of us. But what's important now is that we should follow his steps on those things that he showed us as virtues and that he wanted done. And the things he emphasized most were, firstly, the unity of all Zimbabweans. That unity is important as the basis on which we can put our minds together, our energies together, and work as one and for the good of us all, the good of our children. The second issue is land and this issue must be resolved in the interests of the people of Zimbabwe. Therefore, imperialism must never be allowed to thrive and prosper in Zimbabwe. (Mugabe 2002: 1)

The Nkomo that was called the "Father of Dissidents" in his life was now in his death used as a national father figure, a rightful title he was denied in life. Now that Nkomo was no longer a political competitor his name could be celebrated before the Zimbabwean multitudes and used a campaign symbol. For Mugabe, the problem in Zimbabwe had nothing to do with his venal tyranny and corruption but everything to do with imperialism. This aperspectival madness and narcissist nihilism insulated him from reality and blinded him to what a problem he exactly was. The name of the departed Nkomo who could not speak for himself or answer any questions was mobilised and deployed to give respectability and acceptance to an infamous and chaotic land grab that was partisan political project. There is no doubt that in his life, Nkomo would not have lent his support to violence and such disorder that was partisan and frequently racist.

In pursuit of the legacy of Joshua Nkomo and its usability for political gains, Mugabe also visited the local school in Nkomo's village at Matobo. The school was named Joshua Mqabuko Nkomo in honour of the late ZAPU leader. The villagers around the school had overwhelmingly voted the opposition MDC and its leader Morgan Tsvangirai in the previous election. A few kilometres from the school is Bhalagwe where one of the biggest Gukurahundi Genocide mass graves is found. The people of Matobo have not recovered from the horror of the genocide. At the school, Mugabe made a speech that was a true symbolic eating of Joshua Nkomo. He berated the villagers:

> You gave your school the name Joshua Mqabuko Nkomo on your own voli-
> tion. On the other hand, you say you want the MDC and Tsvangirai. What
> contradiction is that? Do you still have Nkomo in mind? Do you have him
> in your heart? I heard the schoolchildren here singing a tune that says
> Nkomo is still alive. That is as it should be. However, we should show that
> he is still alive in our hearts, in our minds, in our whole lives [...]. He taught
> us to be united. He also taught us to be the owners of our land and to suffer
> for our land; to defend our land so it is not sold to the enemy.
> (Mugabe 2004: 1)

Cleverly and also ridiculously, Mugabe gave himself the freedom to accuse the angry victims of Gukurahundi of betraying Joshua Nkomo. Joshua Nkomo was brought to life and politically consumed, and also used a stick to beat and also a meal to bribe victims of Gukurahundi to vote for the person and party that had killed some of them in big numbers. In true cannibalistic fashion and in the political sorcery of the will to power, the population that was starved (Norman 2004a, b: 95) during Gukurahundi and whose pregnant women were ripped open with knives, "let's kill these dissidents before they are born" (Holland 2008: 186), said the Fifth Brigade, were being asked to, in the name of Joshua Nkomo, love Mugabe and ZANU-PF. Mugabe lived in such a fact-free universe where any guilt for the Gukurahundi Genocide on his part was not sup-posed to arise and the victims had to accept that as commonsense. In another sense Mugabe had the political denialism and also naivete of a child that could believe that a people could easily forget their victimhood after a major genocide. It was also pure insanity to expect the people of Matobo to forgive and forget a party and a man that had ordered mass murders in their community.

In the name of Joshua Nkomo, the victims of the Gukurahundi Genocide were being asked in a religious accent and tone to make peace with their suffering and death, to forget their pain and remember to support ZANU-PF and Mugabe. The use of the name and symbol of dead Joshua Nkomo for the political profits of Mugabe and ZANU-PF was in a way a real eating of a dead political rival. What Jean Baudrillard (1994: 6) refers to as "sorcery" in signification is such uses of symbols, signs and gestures for purposes of inventing reality and manipulating the truth. Mugabe never respected or honoured Joshua Nkomo in his life, but after his death, political "sorcery" permitted Mugabe to feign and perform honour for Nkomo for political reasons. Not only that, after decades of dividing the nation, Mugabe wished to be known and understood as a nation builder and unifier of the people. He did not only perform the nation as treated above but also simulated national unity that did not exist.

THE SIMULATION OF NATIONAL UNITY

In the discussion of "the trouble with Nigeria" as far as the polity and economy of the country was concerned, Chinua Achebe (1983) argued that unity at national and social levels was only as good as the intentions behind it as even criminals could unite for the purposes of committing crimes. In his will to power, Mugabe used and abused the ideal of national unity for personal, partisan and absolute power. After the Government of National Unity of 2008 where the opposition MDC was brought into government after a violent and disputed election, Morgan Tsvangirai noted that "by admitting me and MDC to government he opened himself to opportunities that might help him salvage a tattered human rights record and reclaim his long lost image" (Tsvangirai 2011: 520). The political unity that was forged with the opposition ZAPU political party in 1987 was also a ploy to inaugurate a one-party state (Hope 2003: 26) in Zimbabwe by "swallowing" a formidable opposition political party and co-opting Joshua Nkomo into the ZANU party and government. Ian Smith also noted that Mugabe was being "a very clever bloke" that "worked with me for as long as he thought it was going to help him" (Holland 2008: 88). For Mugabe, political unity at party and national levels was always instrumentalised and even weaponised for his own power, control and domination, it seems. Mugabe almost always sang and performed the ideal of national unity, but the quality and purpose of the unity he envisioned and insisted upon was for his will to power and quest for political dominance. The nation of Zimbabwe could only be a nation and unite under Mugabe as the one and only father.

Mugabe's political pleas and demands for national unity in Zimbabwe were couched and intoned in the tone of national political blackmail and a kind of political extortion where the people were not allowed room to choose their political options freely. To unite was always going be to unite under ZANU-PF and Mugabe not any other party or leader. In March 2005 at the Umzingwane District in Matabeleland South before the parliamentary elections, Mugabe said before a rally:

> We are a people-oriented Government, a people-oriented party in the first place. It is the interests of the people we look at as we formulate our programmes. But we would want the people to be with us. Give us the necessary support. It is that oneness that we require and it must be demonstrated once every five years. And now I ask: Are you going to demonstrate that unity by voting for Zanu-PF in the parliamentary elections? (Mugabe 2005a, b, c: 1)

That his party was a people-oriented party was another manufactured reality that came from an aperspectivally insane imagination. Evidence was all enveloping that his party was oriented towards himself and his power, but Mugabe's relationship with reality had always been a troubled one. While national unity and peace are a grand human ideal, but that Zimbabweans, especially the victims of the Gukurahundi Genocide, should only pursue that ideal by supporting Mugabe and ZANU-PF was problematic. To reduce national unity to a property of ZANU-PF was misleading especially in the background that Mugabe and the same party had divided the nation on racial, regional and tribal grounds when it suited their opportunistic political goals. It is Mugabe that "has defined certain group of Zimbabweans as not Zimbabwean enough" (Mlambo 2014: 57), and divided the nation accordingly. In spite of having caused and profited politically from national disunity before, Mugabe was prepared to falsify history and manipulate the truth to bully Zimbabweans into unity behind him and his party:

We were oppressed, but we fought that as a united people and we should fight as a united people, as our present shows that we are not united. We fought the war as a united front as ZIPRA and ZANLA and we were united against the enemy. This unity we must keep'... 'ZANU-PF and PF-ZAPU are the liberation parties of this country. We are the custodians of the independence of Zimbabwe and we will forever jealously guard that hard-won freedom.' (Mugabe 2004: 1)

That ZANLA and ZIPRA or ZAPU and ZANU had been a united front in the liberation struggle against colonialism was a falsification of history and a revisionist invention. The disunity and violence between the two parties culminated in a genocide and the persecution of Joshua Nkomo and ZAPU. Conveniently, Mugabe always asked Zimbabweans to remember the cruelty and atrocities of the colonial regime but never those atrocities that were conducted by him, his army and political party. Mugabe was a true artist when it came to rewriting history, editing facts and adding fables. Selective amnesia, intentional forgetfulness and deliberate ignorance seem to be one of the qualities of the will to power where the politician is deliberately blind to his crimes and much awake to those of his opponents. This is the same aperspectival madness and narcissist nihilism that defined Mugabe and held him blind to his prominent blemishes.

Without a sense of irony Mugabe confidently claimed historical custody of national unity and peace. Zimbabwean national unity and peace that Mugabe and his party were always ready to sacrifice and jeopardise for political power, in the attack on ZAPU and Ndebele people and the isolation of white Zimbabweans for political punishment during the Fast Track Land Reform Programme, became Mugabe's claim to political fame. Conveniently, the disunity and political violence in the country is blamed on western countries and the political opposition:

[T]he unity among Zimbabweans has been constantly attacked by the country's detractors and those who want to manipulate its people. Western nations, particularly Britain, are now employing some devious means of dividing Zimbabweans by creating and funding opposition political parties. The funded opposition parties such as the MDC are often dangerous and are bent on dividing the people along tribal lines. The British sponsored violence in the country by funding the MDC to embark on mass protests soon after the presidential election last year. They even tried to evoke tribal sentiments by manufacturing a document alleging that the Government had hatched a scheme to exterminate the Ndebeles. (Mugabe 2003: 1)

The extermination of the Ndebeles which was carefully planned, a special Brigade trained and deployed for the purpose and deployed was then being claimed by Mugabe to be an invented allegation by the country's enemies. Such hide and seek with history should have proven to Zimbabweans and the world that Mugabe had become insane in his insulation from reality. Apportioning blame to others, denialism and deliberate distortions of history became Mugabe's stock in trade as he sought to perform and simulate the role of unifier of the nation and nation builder. Mugabe was insane in his propensity to deny the obvious.

Even in the attempt to encourage and forge national unity in Zimbabwe, Mugabe remained stuck in understandings and imaginations of the nation and politics that are exclusionary and divisive. Those that do not support ZANU-PF or that oppose him are named as traitors, stooges and sell-outs that do not really belong in Zimbabwe:

> We have always said we don't want stooges and puppets working day and night to effect regime change with our former colonial masters. So that's the difference between us and the MDC. Zanu-PF is a revolutionary party while the MDC are counter-revolutionaries and reactionaries. For us in Zanu-PF, the power of the Government, the President and his ministers comes from the people of Zimbabwe. For the MDC, they derive their power from Mr. Blair. So there you are. You have a choice. Where do you stand? On the side of the people, or the British? If you stand with the British, you are not one of us you are a sellout, a stooge. (Mugabe 2005a, b, c: 1)

Mugabe was expert in not only manufacturing reality but peddling what is now commonly understood as alternative facts. The quality of national unity that Robert Mugabe imagined was partisan and narrow. ZANU-PF and himself were being conflated with the nation and to be a true Zimbabwean and patriot was reduced to supporting ZANU-PF and Mugabe. In failing or else resisting the important work of distinguishing the party from the nation and his person from the country, Robert Mugabe was escaping the accountability and responsibility to the people of Zimbabwe who had the ethical and democratic right to unite and rally behind a political party of their choice and leader of their own evaluation and election. In a nutshell, even as grand an ideal as national unity and nation building were, it seems, not only pretended to and simulated by Mugabe but were also appropriated, usurped and even weaponised for partisan and personal political power.

What I note here as Mugabe's insanity and also political sorcery was his ability to deny reality and perform his desires and fears as indisputable truths. Total blindness to and intentional ignorance of his blemishes made Mugabe a truly insane performer that in a fundamentalist and extremist way was sure of his divine appointment and commission. Without exonerating him from the evil he visited upon Zimbabwe and the world, it is critically important to understand Mugabe as having been a victim of his own will to power and the political opportunism of those that supported him. Mugabe's choir of supporters, fanatics, flatterers and sycophants did not build around him a world that could have recovered him from insanity. Instead they circulated myths, performances and events around him that enhanced his madness. What surrounded Mugabe was a political cult that did not help but insulated him from the real world and by that fortified his insanity. Mugabe became very mad.

References

Achebe, C. (1983). *The Trouble with Nigeria*. London: Heinemann Educational Books.

Anderson, B. (1983). *Imagined Communities: Reflections on the Origin and Spread of Nationalism*. London & New York. Verso Books.

Arendt, H. (2006). *Eichmann in Jerusalem: A Report on the Banality of Evil*. London: Penguin Books.

Askew, K. M. (2002). *Performing the Nation: Swahili Music and Cultural Politics in Tanzania*. Chicago: University of Chicago Press.

Badiou, A. (2009). Who Is Nietzsche? In D. Hoens, S. Jöttkandt, & G. Buelens (Eds.), *The Catastrophic Imperative* (pp. 195–204). New York: Palgrave Macmillan.

Baudrillard, J. (1994). *Simulacra and Simulation*. Ann Arbor: University of Michigan Press.

Bhebhe, N. (2004). *Simon Vengayi Muzenda and the Struggle for the Liberation of Zimbabwe*. Gweru: Mambo Press.

Bourne, R. (2011). *Catastrophe: What Went Wrong in Zimbabwe?* London & New York: Zed Books.

Bowie, M. (1991). *Lacan*. London: HarperCollins Publishers.

Buckle, C. (2003). *Beyond Tears: Zimbabwe's Tragedy*. Cape Town: Jonathan Ball Publishers.

Burbach, R. (2003). *The Pinochet Affair: State Terrorism and Global Justice*. London/New York: Zed Books.

Butler, J. (1988). Performing Acts and Gender Constitution. In S. Case (Ed.), *Performing Feminism* (pp. 270–282). Baltimore, MD: John Hopkins University Press, 1991.

Butler, J. (2010). Performative Agency. *Journal of Cultural Economy, 3*(2), 147–161.

Chappell, T. (2005). *The Inescapable Self: An Introduction to Western Philosophy Since Descartes*. London: Orion Publishing Group.

Chavez-Arvizo, E. (1997). Introduction. In *Descartes: Key Philosophical Writings*. Hertfordshire: Wordsworth Editions.

Coetzee, J. M. (1991). The Mind of Apartheid: Geoffrey Cronje (1907–). *Social Dynamics 17*, 1–35.

Coltart, D. (2007). Why I Cannot Join Tsvangirai's Faction. *New African: Zimbabwe*, Special Issue, 48–54.

Compagnon, D. (2011). *A Predictable Tragedy: Robert Mugabe and the Collapse of Zimbabwe. Philadelphia*: University of Pennsylvania Press.

Dubois, E. W. B. (1969). *The Souls of Black Folk*. New York: Nal Penguin Inc.

Eze, E. C. (2005). Epistemic Conditions for Genocide. In J. K. Roth (Ed.), *Genocide and Human Rights*. London: Palgrave Macmillan.

Fanon, F. (2001). *The Wretched of the Earth*. London: Penguin Classics.

Fanon, F. (2002). *Black Skin White Masks*. New York: Grove Press.

Fanon, F. (2008). *Black Skin White Masks*. London: Pluto Press.

Godwin, P. (2010). *The Fear: The Last Days of Robert Mugabe*. New York: Picador.

Holland, H. (2008). *Dinner with Mugabe: The Untold Story of a Freedom Fighter Who Became a Tyrant*. Johannesburg: Penguin Books.

Hope, C. (2003). *Brothers Under the Skin: Travels in Tyranny*. London: Pan Macmillan.

Laclau, E. (1996). *Emancipation(s)*. London: Verso.

Mamdani, M. (2001). Making Sense of Non-Revolutionary Violence: Some Lessons from Rwandan Genocide (Text of the Frantz Fanon Lecture, University of Durban, Westville, 8 August 2001), p. 1.

Masunungure, E. (2004). Travails of Opposition Politics in Zimbabwe Since Independence. In D. Harold-Barry (Ed.), *Zimbabwe: The Past is the Future* (pp. 147–92). Harare: Weaver Press.

Mbembe, A. (1992). Provisional Notes on the Post-colony. *Africa, 62*(1), 3–37.

Memmi, A. (1974). *The Coloniser and the Colonised*. London & New York. Earthscan.

Meredith, M. (2002a). *Robert Mugabe: Power, Plunder and Tyranny in Zimbabwe*. Cape Town: Jonathan Ball Publishers.

Mlambo, A. S. (2014). Mugabe on Land, Indigenisation and Development. In S. Ndlovu-Gatsheni (Ed.), *Mugabeism? History, Politics and Power in Zimbabwe*. New York: Palgrave Macmillan.

Moorcraft, P. (2012). *Mugabe's War Machine*. Cape Town: Jonathan Ball Publishers.

Moore, D. (2015). In S. Ndlovu-Gatsheni (Ed.), *Mugabeism? History, Politics, and Power in Zimbabwe*. New York: Palgrave Macmillan.

Mouffe, C. (2005a). *On the Political*. Abingdon: Routledge.

Mouffe, C. (2005b). *The Return of the Political*. Verso: New York/London.

Muchemwa, K. Z. (2010). Galas, Biras, State Funerals and the Necropolitan Imagination in Re-Construction of the Zimbabwean Nation, 1980–2008. *Social Dynamics, 36*(3), 504–514.

Mugabe, R. (2000, October 25). Speech at ZANU-PF Headquarters.

Mugabe, R. (2002, July 2). Follow in the Footsteps of Father Zim, In *The Herald*.

Mugabe, R. (2005a, July 15). In Madonko, I. Remain United – President, In *The Herald*.

Mugabe, R. (2005b, February 8). Keep Unity Alive, Says President. In *The Herald*.

Mugabe, R. (2005c, November 20). Zimbabwe Is One Nation. In *The Sunday Mail*.

Mugabe, R. (2008). Campaign Speech. In Ndlovu-Gatsheni, S. "Rethinking Chimurenga and Gukurahundi in Zimbabwe: A Critique of Partisan National History." *African Studies Review 55* (3). pp. 1–26.

Muponde, R. (2004). The Worm and the Hoe: Cultural Politics and Reconciliation after the Third Chimurenga. In B. Raftopoulos & T. Savage (Eds.), *Zimbabwe: Injustice and Political Reconciliation* (pp. 168–88). Cape Town: Institute for Justice and Reconciliation.

Ndlovu, M. (2014). African Leadership in the Age of Euro-North American-centric Modernity: A Decolonial Critique of Robert Mugabe. In S. Ndlovu-Gatsheni (Ed.), *Mugabeism? History, Politics and Power in Zimbabwe*. New York: Palgrave Macmillan.

Ndlovu-Gatsheni, S. (2009). Making Sense of Mugabeism in Local and Global Politics: 'So Blair, Keep Your England and Let Me Keep My Zimbabwe. *Third World Quarterly, 30*(6), 1139–1158.

Ndlovu-Gatsheni, S., & Willems, W. (2009). Making Sense of Cultural Nationalism and the Politics of Commemoration Under the Third Chimurenga in Zimbabwe. *Journal of Southern African Studies, 35*(4), 945–965.

Nietzsche, F. (1968). *The Will to Power*. New York: Vantage Books.

Nietzsche, F. (2004a). *Why am I so Clever?* London: Penguin Classics.

Nietzsche, F. (2004b). *Human, All Too Human* (M. Faber and S. Lehmann, Trans.). London: Penguin.

Nkomo, J. (1984). *The Story of My Life*. London: Methuen.

Norman, A. (2004a). *Robert Mugabe and the Betrayal of Zimbabwe*. Jefferson: McFarland and Co.

Norman, A. (2004b). *Robert Mugabe and the Betrayal of Zimbabwe*. London: McFarland & Company Publishers.

O' Docherty, M. (2016). *The Legacy of Robert Mugabe and the Zimbabwean African National Union-Patriotic-Front: A One Party State facilitating Dictatorship and Disregard for Human Rights*. Crystal Grove Books: North Carolina, Lulu Press Inc.

Onslow, S., & Plaut, M. (2018). *Robert Mugabe*. Johannesburg: Jacana Media.

Plato. (1993). *Republic*. Oxford: Oxford University Press.

Rupiya, M. (2005). Zimbabwe: Governance Through Military Operations. *African Security Studies, 14*(3), 116–118.

Sachikonye, L. (2011). *When a State Turns on Its Citizens: 60 Years of Violence in Zimbabwe*. Johannesburg: Jacana Media.

Scarnecchia, T. (2011). Rationalising Gukurahundi: Cold War and South African Foreign Relations with Zimbabwe, 1981–1983. *Kronos, 37*(1), 89–55.

Scudder, C. W. (1972). Psychological Dimensions of Extremism. In E. West (Ed.), *Extremism Left and Right*. Michigan: Eerdmans Publishing Company.

Sithole, S. (1979). On the Assassination of Herbert Chitepo and ZANU, 10 May 1976. In C. Nyangoni & G. Nyandoro (Eds.), *Zimbabwe Independence Movements: Select Documents*. London: Rex Collings.

Smith, D., & Simpson C. (1981). *Mugabe Illustrated*. Salisbury: Pioneer Head.

Smith, I. (1997). *The Great Betrayal: The Memoirs of Africa's Most Controversial Leader*. London: Blake Publishing.

Stiff, P. (2000). *Cry Zimbabwe*. Alberton: Galago Publishing.

Tendi, B.-M. (2013). Robert Mugabe's 2013 Presidential Election Campaign. *Journal of Southern African Studies, 39*(4), 963–970.

Tsvangirai, M. (2011). *At the Deep End*. London: Penguin.

Waddell, H. C. (1972). Common Features of Extremism. In E. West (Ed.), *Extremism Left and Right*. Michigan: Eerdmans Publishing Company.

Woods, K. (2007). *The Kevin Woods Story. In the Shadow of Mugabe's Gallows*. Johannesburg: 30 Degrees South Publishers.

Zhuwawo, P. (2018). Patrick Zhuwawo Makes Shocking Revelations about Gukurahundi. *New Zimbabwe Vision*. Newzimbababwevision.com. Accessed 10 April 2019.

CHAPTER 6

The Return of the Symptom
in the Postcolony

The situation in our country has moved to another level. Firstly, we wish to assure our nation, His Excellency, the President of the Republic of Zimbabwe and Commander in Chief of the Zimbabwe Defence Forces, Cde R. G. Mugabe and his family are safe and sound and their security is guaranteed. We are only targeting criminals around him who are committing crimes that are causing social and economic suffering in the country in order to bring them to justice.
—Major General Sibusiso Moyo (2017a: 1)

I never expected that President Mugabe would ever fire me, because in my view I had full loyalty towards him. I was committed to my party, committed to my government, committed and loyal to my leader to the end. I also believe he knew that I was loyal to him and I would never ever do anything against him.
—Emmerson Mnangagwa (2018: 1)

I don't hate Mnangagwa and I want to work with him. But he must be proper to be where he is. He is illegal. We must undo this disgrace we have imposed on ourselves. We don't deserve it. Zimbabwe does not deserve it. We want to be a constitutional country. We must obey the law.
—Robert Mugabe (2018: 118)

It is telling that the soldiers that led the removal of Mugabe from power could not find any other vocabulary of naming their action besides the

© The Author(s) 2021
W. J. Mpofu, *Robert Mugabe and the Will to Power in an African Postcolony*, African Histories and Modernities,
https://doi.org/10.1007/978-3-030-47879-7_6

paradoxical claim that they were restoring some legacy. If their move was a revolution, it was at least going to pretend to inaugurate a new order of things, politically. The telling claim became that Mugabe and Zimbabwe, in combination, were being rescued from some criminals. In that way the coup d'état of 14 November 2017 that finally dethroned Mugabe became his removal from political office that was also his strange but true return to power in Zimbabwe. It was his return to power in the way Mugabeism, the violence and deceit associated with Mugabe's rule, was to become more vulgar and even more visible after his fall. The coup was meaningfully code-named "Operation Restore Legacy." The historical and political legacy of ZANU-PF that was being restored was a bloody heritage of politics as a "gun idea" that was dominated by the name and person of Mugabe and was executed by old securocrats from the guerrilla movement. Led by former guerrillas the coup was a kind of return to the source and a resurrection of political cultures and practices that had come to be concealed and suppressed. The political cultures and practices of vulgar violence had come to be disguised and concealed as Mugabe and ZANU-PF entertained some reformists and political strategists such as Jonathan Moyo who effectively weaponised political communication and the marketing of some ideas as manufacture of political consent and persuasion. Moyo, at his helm as a leading ZANU-PF communicator, had crafted compelling manifestoes and composed lyrical jingles to refashion the old party as a new and modern political movement that had ideas as its claim to political fame. Behind the image of a party of ideas that Moyo and others were constructing remained a beastly grouping of trigger happy war types that were resisting change and were still stuck in the bush. The dethronement of Mugabe and his eventual death became a rejuvenation of native colonialism in Zimbabwe.

Over a period of time Jonathan Moyo achieved a grip of Mugabe's attention and political interest. Absent in Moyo's political language were the threats and celebrations of political violence that were the stock in trade of ZANU-PF politicians of the "gun idea." Moyo advanced a ZANU-PF of ideas and which ZANU-F Mugabe wished to be remembered for after a career of political madness and large-scale violence. It is another paradox that Mugabe expected his career of madness to be forgotten when mass graves punctuated parts of the country and the victims were still hurting at his impunity. In so enchanting Mugabe, the mighty ruler, Moyo and his allies infuriated ambitious securocrats. Departing from the "gun idea," Moyo gave ZANU-PF the political vocabulary to name political moments in Zimbabwe and in that way he earned Mugabe's admiration. Political phrases such as *Third Chimurenga*, Land is the

Economy and the Economy is Land, Zimbabwe will never be a colony again and *Hondo Yeminda* jingles were artefacts from Moyo's desk (Tendi 2008: 386), and his boast was that "Jonathan Moyo never beat anyone up." The proximity to Mugabe and advancing an idea of a ZANU-PF of ideas became criminality to the impatient securocrats that saw Moyo and his close allies exiled as the coup overtook Zimbabwe and eventually retired Mugabe from political office. A legacy of the "gun idea" was restored through armoured tanks and helicopter gunships that surrounded Harare. But that was not the end of Mugabeism.

The coup became the resurrection of the "gun idea" as an approach to politics that ZANU-PF adopted and turned into political commonsense in the guerrilla camps of Mozambique in the 1970s. The securocrats that overthrew Mugabe were former guerrillas that he produced and who also produced him and kept him in power by all means necessary against the will of Zimbabweans. As such, it was not going to be just another coup; it had to be novel and beautiful. Contrary to what Geoff Nyarota (2018) describes as a "graceless fall," Mugabe's removal from office was graceful in two ways. Firstly, and on a lighter note, Grace Mugabe dominated the political events before and during the coup, she became part of the reason or else the excuse for the securocrats to remove Mugabe in apparent concern that he was about to elevate his wife to the presidency of the party and the country. For months before the coup, Grace Mugabe had issued spectacular verbal attacks on former guerrillas and other politicians that, with their gun idea, believed liberation war credentials were an entitlement to leadership of the party and the country. In her political articulation she leaned towards a ZANU-PF of ideas and carried Mugabe along in clear support of the political marketing of the Generation 40 alliance, as Moyo and allies Patrick Zhuwawo and Saviour Kasukuwere were called.

Secondly, the coup was graceful in that, towards the person and family of Mugabe, it was carried out with elegance and generosity, with their lives secured and their safety guaranteed by the army generals. Only those politicians that did not belong to the Lacoste Faction of Emmerson Mnangagwa, the Generation 40 political outfit that were described as criminals, became targeted for elimination. These were mainly politicians that were not there in Mozambique in the 1970s and were not formed and developed in the "gun idea" as a political culture that was being restored through a coup. It is in that way that the coup was also a return to the past, a resurrection of some ways of the bush war. In the imagination of the upholders of the "gun idea" that carried out the coup political ideas such as the arts of persuasion that were held by the G40 political outfit and supported by Mugabe and his wife amounted to some political criminality. In his last days in political office, Mugabe had become a true musician of the idea that "politics must lead the gun and not the gun lead politics," an idea that infuriated the former guerrillas and their civilian fronts in ZANU-PF.

The removal of Mugabe from office was also, in that way, his separation from so-called "criminals" and a purge. Mugabe was being purified of those people that were considered pollutants because they were not of the gun idea. Those who held other ideas besides the gun idea were effectively criminalised. Concealed behind the grace and beauty of this particular coup were massacres of G40 loyalists and some securocrats that were opposed to the ouster of Mugabe. For the reason that those amongst the security forces that were killed for their loyalty to Mugabe were killed in the dark, away from the cameras, the coup became a beautiful operation to the naked eye when in its actuality it was murderous. Observant and keen researchers such as Blessing-Miles Tendi (2019: 1) have noted that the removal of Mugabe from office, in spite of denials and other embellishments of the action as "a non-coup-coup" or a "very Zimbabwean or special" political move, was a coup like any other.

The beauty of the coup was carefully choreographed to mislead the world. With heinous atrocities concealed from Zimbabweans and the world, what were witnessed were smiling army generals in new and neat combat fatigues. Armed soldiers were seen posing for selfie photographs with jubilant members of the public. One after another, on prime-time television, the coup makers marched past a seated Mugabe saluting him. Africa and the world were assured that what was happening in Zimbabwe was not a coup but a graceful "military intervention." Jubilant crowds of Zimbabweans were allowed to celebrate in the streets and climb atop of military tanks and hug soldiers. When Mugabe's resignation was announced in Parliament on the 21st of November 2017, eternal opponents, politicians from ZANU-PF and those from the MDC-Alliance were seen singing and dancing together in rare but spectacular conviviality. Elderly and some usually sombre and grave personalities were seen gyrating and swinging as if they had liquid hips. The physical person of Mugabe was successfully removed from political office but the political system and culture that he personified was in return, recharged and fortified. Zimbabweans of all walks including leaders and activists of opposition political parties were successfully mobilised to support the coup. In the social media, the coup was called "cute," and Zimbabwean soldiers and their tanks were glorified. The glorious and jubilant political climate that enveloped Zimbabwe with the news of Mugabe's fall effectively concealed that a political monstrosity was unfolding.

The man that was to replace Mugabe as President of the party and the state was his infamous hand and enforcer, Emmerson Mnangagwa. Meaningfully nicknamed the Crocodile, Mnangagwa was Mugabe's loyal hand who called Mugabe a God and appointed himself the "son of God." The rise of Mnangagwa to power was soon to prove to be an enhancement of what Willard Reno (1998) called warlord politics. The return of shootings of unarmed civilians by soldiers and uses and public threats of violence by soldiers and the police but confirmed the condition of Zimbabwe as what Achille Mbembe (2001) called a postcolony, a setting where symptoms of colonial politics and violence refuse to disappear. Political violence, violation of the constitution and general executive hooliganism became a legacy restored in Zimbabwe.

Events that invoked memories of the Gukurahundi Genocide came to be witnessed. Except during the Gukurahundi Genocide where dissidents were staged, even in the height of Mugabe's rule by terror and deceit, it was unthinkable that soldiers would shoot civilians by the day and the following morning address a press conference announcing that they are looking for the criminals that stole their guns and uniforms and shot and killed civilians the previous day. A full high table of army and police commanders announced this with straight military faces and ended the announcement with the polite request that members of the public should help the police with information if they happen to meet the uniformed and armed criminals. The claim by soldiers and the police that there were unknown and armed people that were shooting at civilians in the country reminded Zimbabweans of the invention of dissidents during the Gukurahundi Genocide. Part of the genocide was the performance of soldiers that by night dressed in rags, dangled their guns and moved around villages harassing villagers and claiming to be dissidents. By day, the same soldiers, now dressed in their neat fatigues, would patrol the villages pretending to be looking for the dissidents but actually murdering villagers and raping women.

On the 1st of August in 2018 soldiers shot dead six unarmed civilians that were part of the crowd that was protesting against suspicious delays in the announcement of election results. The elections mainly pitted Emmerson Mnangagwa against Nelson Chamisa of the MDC-Alliance.

On international television and the social media videos of soldiers using automatic rifles to gun down fleeing protesters circulated. It became part of the ludicrousness of the postcolony when the commander of Zimbabwe Defence Forces, Philip Valerio Sibanda, in a televised presentation to a Commission of Inquiry, denied that it was the army that shot and killed the protesters. Much like Mugabe's disputed electoral victories, Mnangagwa's electoral victory was disputed by the political opposition that took its grievances to the courts.

While the important court judgement was eagerly awaited by anxious Zimbabweans, the leadership of the War Veterans held a press conference a day before the court judgement on the disputed election results was to be delivered. The War Vets declared that they will accept no other outcome except the victory of Emmerson Mnangagwa. The political legacy that was restored at the ouster of Mugabe was a legacy of the hooliganism of power where the courts as an arm of government could be ignored and their decisions dismissed. Not in so many words, in that charged press conference, the leadership of the war veterans threatened the judiciary in Zimbabwe and could have influenced the court judgement in favour of Mnangagwa. The press conference was conducted by sweaty and angry men that literary walked on the constitution of the country in the name of what they called a "revolution" and its "ideology." The press conference performance of the war veterans had the air of Idi Amin and the feel of a fascist harangue that was insulated from any constitutional and democratic cares. The Zimbabwean postcolony had hit its Idi Amin moments where street wisdom and rusty fascist ideas were elevated into political importance. In that way the fall of Mugabe became a rise of Mugabeism and an invigoration of the political culture of impunity and hooliganism that Mugabe represented in Zimbabwe.

If the shooting of unarmed civilians that were protesting against the suspicious delay of election results in 2018 was tragic, the killing of dozens and injuring of hundreds of civilians that were protesting against fuel price increases and general economic decay were diabolic. On the 15th of January 2019, a nationwide protest called by trade unions commenced and provoked the ire of the government. The army was deployed apparently to stop the burning and looting that erupted in the urban areas as desperate and angry Zimbabweans blocked roads, burnt tyres and threw stones. Many women were reported to have been raped by military personnel. Hundreds of activists were arrested and detained. Internet was shut down to prevent Zimbabweans from capturing and sending photos and videos that would alert the world to the atrocities that the soldiers were committing. Zimbabweans came face to face with the cold and dry truism that the ZANU-PF idea was still the same old gun idea that was imagined and practiced during the bush war against colonialism. Mnangagwa's catch-phrase that "Zimbabwe is open for business" was proven for what it was an empty slogan as the country was totally closed for normal business and open to state terror. The political barbarism of angry and sweaty former guerrillas from the bush war that still had the bush in their minds and war in their hearts came to life in the Zimbabwean postcolony. Beaten by the G40 in the battles of ideas, they resorted to tanks, guns and the tool of abductions and assassinations.

Mugabe, as I observe earlier in this book, joined the Zimbabwean liberation movement in the 1960s as a civilian and scholarly face of the guerrilla movement. His intellectual performances and grandiose orations, even as they were pretensions, were used to cover up otherwise a rogue guerrilla movement that believed in torture, rape and murder as political methodology. Mugabe's removal from office seemed to have let loose the rogues that came out to torture and murder civilians in the streets. The rape of women as actualisation and celebration of conquest came to the fore. For their own scholarly performances and uses of ideas as weapons in politics, the G40 outfit of Jonathan Moyo, Patrick Zhuwawo, Saviour Kasukuwere and others were not only criminalised but also targeted for murder. Only quick and daring escape to exile saved them. The only "criminals" that remained behind at the mercy of the winners were the ordinary men and women of Zimbabwe that had to learn the very hard way that a militarised junta was now in power.

The gun idea of the Lacoste Faction and the Book of the G40 had from some time been jostling for Mugabe's attention with each seeking to define a certain future of ZANU-PF and Zimbabwe. Perhaps to dramatise their weaponisation of ideas as opposed to guns in politics, in 2015 the G40 group leaders enrolled to read law at the University of Zimbabwe. Mugabe and his wife Grace were drawn to this group that seemed to remind Mugabe of his younger days when his claim to fame in politics was knowledge, refined oratory and performance of learned politicking. In Jonathan Moyo in particular, an articulate and witty political communicator, Mugabe saw his younger and ideal self. The G40 outfit, as noted earlier, gave Mugabe a sense of comfort and atonement after years of presiding on and supervising diabolic political violence. Perhaps, after all, Mugabe wished to be remembered one day as having been a great man of

ideas and not the genocidist leader that he became. Mugabe's enchantment with the G40 was not as hidden as it was part of his attempt to
return to the political world of ideas and thinking as opposed to the uses
of guns. Lost in the landscape of ideas the securocrats of the Lacoste group
ran to the armoury and brought to life the gun idea in Zimbabwe. The
gun tragically came to lead politics in Zimbabwe and atrocities such as
torture, rape and murder were turned into national commonsense. The
Zimbabwe National Defence Forces under the command of former guerrilla elements had degenerated into the Zimbabwe National Attack Forces,
it seemed. If Zimbabweans, Africa and the world thought Mnangagwa was
going to be not even a revolutionary but a reformer, they were to learn
that he was more Mugabeist than Mugabe. Mugabe and Mnangagwa had
always been birds of the same feather who shared the same gun idea as a
political school of thought. And when it came to the gun idea, violence
and the impunity that goes with it in the postcolony, Mnangagwa was
Mugabe's leader and also enforcer. Evil became the organising idea that
defined the relationship between Mnangagwa and Mugabe (Woods 2007).

Birds of a Feather

As held in two epigraphs that open this chapter, Mnangagwa and Mugabe
had mutual respect, loyalty and love for each. Beyond mutual respect,
loyalty and love, the two became each other's political handler and keeper.
They enjoyed a specifically special political and personal relationship. A
national daily newspaper was forced to apologise after it referred to
President Emmerson Mnangagwa as Mr Robert Mnangagwa in one of its
lead stories just after the coup. Joke or mistake, or just political poetry, the
reference to Mnangagwa has projected his imbrication in the person and
political legacy of Mugabe. After all, Mnangagwa himself publicly boasted
of being the son of the God that Mugabe became in Zimbabwean history
and politics. That the Zimbabwean soldiery had overthrown Mugabe and
helped install Mnangagwa as his successor should not have been mistaken
for a revolution as the two were true birds of a feather that enjoyed a special personal, historical and political relationship. The two were fellow
travellers in the ideological path of the "gun idea." They shared the same
political sensibility that valorised violence as a political language. That
Mugabe could fire Mnangagwa and that Mnangagwa could overthrow
Mugabe and replace him in power is a paradox in terms and in practice as
the two were one and the same in the history and idea of ZANU-PF and

the legacy of tyranny that came to define the Zimbabwean political land-scape. The political history of post-independence Zimbabwe was, in many ways, poisoned by the violent personalities of Robert Mugabe and Emmerson Mnangagwa as especially related politicians. It was as known as a proverb in Zimbabwe that Mugabe threatened political violence and Emmerson Mnangagwa implemented it. To Mugabe, Mnangagwa became what Otto Adolf Eichmann was to Adolf Hitler in Nazi Germany.

When on the 6th of November 2017, Mugabe, standing with the G40 political outfit of ZANU-PF, fired Emmerson Mnangagwa from govern-ment and sent him into self-imposed exile, Alex Magaisa (2017: 1) noted the event to be the possible end of a "special relationship" between Mugabe and Mnangagwa. A lot of what was done by Mugabe in Zimbabwean politics was blamed on Mnangagwa as his trusted hand and Mnangagwa's own crimes were attached to Mugabe as his powerful boss. There was no Mugabe without Mnangagwa and no Mnangagwa without Mugabe. Magaisa notes that somehow, Mnangagwa became a "loyal water carrier" for Mugabe. I want to extend the observation to that the two car-ried each other's water and were each other's keeper. Largely, Mugabe was the brains and Mnangagwa the muscle in one body of ZANU-PF politics of the "gun idea." Even as political tensions had grown to the bitter heights between mentor and his mentee, from his short exile in South Africa, Mnangagwa wrote to express his enduring loyalty to Mugabe as a person and ZANU-PF as a political party:

> I never expected that President Mugabe would ever fire me, because in my view I had full loyalty towards him. I was committed to my party, commit-ted to my government, committed and loyal to my leader to the end. I also believe he knew that I was loyal to him and I would never ever do anything against him. (Mnangagwa, in Ndlovu (2018: 1)

It became common knowledge in Zimbabwe that Mnangagwa had always been a facilitator and implementer of Mugabeism. The special rela-tionship between the two began in the bush war against colonialism. The two played significant roles in the lives of each other and they shared the guilt for the degeneration of Zimbabwe into the hellish postcolony that it became.

Mugabe and Mnangagwa can very easily be understood as true broth-ers in crime. In a way, each became a product of the other as trusted allies and also accomplices. It was not for nothing that Mnangagwa called

Mugabe God and himself the Son of God during the Gukurahundi Genocide. Mnangagwa not in so many words boasted of and clarified the role he played in Mugabe's political life and the nature of the relationship between the two of them:

> This role was confirmed at the Chimoio Congress in 1977. I have been very close to the president ever since. We have avoided life-threatening situations together. I have doubled up as his personal body guard. In return the President has passed on to me life skills which have put me in the good stead throughout my long period in government. Our relationship has over the years blossomed beyond that of master and servant but to father and son. (Mnangagwa, in Ndlovu 2018: 22)

They did not only avoid life-threatening situations together, but they also together threatened and took the lives of many Zimbabweans in the Gukurahundi Genocide and other episodes of large-scale political violence in the country. Mnangagwa was, as noted earlier, Mugabe's dreaded Security Minister during the Gukurahundi Genocide. Reputed to be the brains and the hands behind Mugabe's storied electoral fraud and political violence Mnangagwa did not just become a political mentee of Mugabe but also a trusted accessory and facilitator of Mugabeism. In firing Mnangagwa, Mugabe was as well firing himself, and in dethroning Mugabe, Mnangagwa was as well not only replacing him but also reproducing him. It is in that way that the coup in Zimbabwe did not become a revolution but change without difference. Mnangagwa, not surprisingly, quickly reproduced and magnified Mugabeism very early in his tenure as President of Zimbabwe. Mnangagwa's rise to power became a strange but true return of Mugabe in the Zimbabwean postcolony. The two are creators and also creatures of the same political culture of politics as war and politicking as the "gun idea" of punishing and eliminating enemies. Grace Mugabe and the Generation 40 political outfit of ZANU-PF were up against a Himalayan mountain in trying to replace the "gun idea" with another idea as an approach to politics. The violent legacy that produced Mugabe and Mnangagwa and which they both participated in shaping is too deep-rooted to be persuaded or negotiated into the background; it requires a more monstrous approach and one with more hardihood than mere argumentation.

From the political culture and history that produced Mugabe and Mnangagwa, there was always going to be a part of Mnangagwa in Mugabe and a part of Mugabe in Mnangagwa. They were, in that way, not just birds of the same political feather but also feathers of the same will to power whose flight has utilised cruelty and violence as a political tool. Even after dismissing Mnangagwa and eventually being overthrown in a coup that elevated Mnangagwa to power, Mugabe also, not in so many words, professed his love for Mnangagwa: "I don't hate Mnangagwa and I want to work with him. But he must be proper to be where he is. He is illegal. We must undo this disgrace we have imposed on ourselves. We don't deserve it. Zimbabwe does not deserve it. We want to be a constitutional country. We must obey the law" (Mugabe 2018: 118). The law that Mnangagwa did not obey in overthrowing Mugabe was not necessarily the Zimbabwean constitution but the special political relationship of co-creation and co-production between himself and Mugabe who never believed that his trusted hand, water carrier and personal bodyguard would topple him from power. Mugabe was embittered by the personal betrayal not the violations of the country's constitution. The tradition and law that Mnangagwa violated was, to Mugabe, the invisible but real political constitution of political thought and practice as the gun idea where Mugabe was leader and Mnangagwa a dutiful follower and industrious implementer of atrocities.

The increased visibility and effect of soldiers in post-Mugabe Zimbabwe showed that a bodyguard and bouncer of a kind had come to power and would reproduce Mugabeism to spectacular heights and alarming depths of infamy. Few if any, in Zimbabwe and outside, believed that after Mugabe was overthrown and the country was purportedly open for business, women would be raped as political punishment, and that Zimbabweans would be tortured and shot dead for protesting injustices. The will to power that Friedrich Nietzsche (1968) described and valorised privileged the permanence and eternal return of power as domination of one by the other. In succeeding Mugabe in power, it seems, Emmerson Mnangagwa enabled the permanence and return of Mugabe.

As former president of Zimbabwe and invested in violence and war, Mugabe is a true absence that is emphatically present as the country remains an outpost of tyranny and a truly hellish postcolony. In many ways, both Mugabe and Mnangagwa successfully and much unfortunately reproduced the same colonial politics and colonial modes of domination that they spent years in the bush war fighting against. Their joint tragedy was to fight colonialism and then to fail to avoid being infected by its political sensibilities and practices. Instead of replacing Rhodesian colonialism with liberation in Zimbabwe, they became, in person and in practice, effective symptoms of colonialism that represented the endurance of colonial modes of domination that still persist in Zimbabwe. What Mugabe and Mnangagwa reproduced and represent in Zimbabwe after Rhodesian settler colonialism is true Zimbabwean native colonialism. It is in that symptomatic and political way in which Mugabe and Mnangagwa fought the war of Zimbabwe's liberation but failed to be liberators, and quickly became colonisers and oppressors of a venal kind. The historical and political lesson from the legacy of Mugabe and Mnangagwa in Zimbabwe is chiefly that a people may fight oppression and end up being possessed by it, becoming only ready and willing to reproduce and multiply it, even upon the people they were supposed to liberate. The example of Mugabe and Mnangagwa became that of post-colonial political culture that failed to liberate itself from colonialism.

Lions and Crocodiles of the Mafiadom in the Postcolony

After the dethronement of Mugabe, Mnangagwa was more than willing when it served his ends to pretend to victimhood. As narrated by some writers, his escape from the country to exile in South Africa was the stuff of action movies, dare-devil moves, endurance and heroism. Douglas Rogers (2019) and Ray Ndlovu (2018) describe a tough Mnangagwa accompanied by clever, courageous and loyal sons and friends walking long hours through dangerous wildernesses to escape a murderous Mugabe regime. In veracity Mnangagwa could not escape the Mugabe regime because he embodied and personified it. Later, General Chiwenga publicly let slip the truth that Mnangagwa was escorted to Mozambique by officers of the Zimbabwe Military Intelligence. The rest was myth-making and fiction. Myth-making and fiction are hallmarks of the typical postcolony in Africa. Tyranical regimes and their tyrants relish in constructing themselves as brave heroes and deliverers of the nation with the right hand while with the left hand they punish the population and pillage the country.

The postcolony is a site both of witchcraft and political gangsterism. Those like Mugabe and Mnangagwa that hold power use it, like in the true arts of sorcery, as a spell upon the conquered and dominated population. In its political character, the postcolony is a true Mafiadom where the rule of Godfathers is not only primary but also very real. In many ways Mugabe operated and carried himself like a Godfather of ZANU-PF as a mafia family and also a kind of witchcraft organisation that operated with an enclosed but real logic of its own that only privileged insiders knew and understood. Mnangagwa was from the beginning such a privileged insider, he knew, understood and lived the logic of the Mafiadom of the postcolony. In the Mafiadom of the postcolony promises and threats are presented in a specific grammar and vocabulary that is closed but seriously open to insiders. Dinizulu Macaphulana (2015) who characterised Mnangagwa as a thief, not only of power, but of history itself, gave an illustration of how even as a loyal water carrier for Mugabe, Mnangagwa always from the very beginning had his eye on the throne. Talking to the journalist, Baffour Ankomah, for instance, and well before the coup, Mnangagwa told the story about how he jokingly but politely invited Mugabe to walk with his lions at the Lion Park in Gweru and Mugabe answered him with another polite request that he should come and try swimming with his crocodiles in Kutama. The story betrays how the two captains of the Mafia family used jokes to threaten each other:

> After independence, I once joked with President Mugabe. He came to Gweru, the capital of my home area. So I said to him, 'Mr President, you know I am a Shumba, a lion, and there is Lion Park in Gweru where you can walk with lions in the morning until 11am when it becomes unsafe because the lions become a bit hungry.'…So I told the President: 'it is now 9am, I want us to go and walk with the lions but don't be afraid because I am a Shumba, a lion.' Was the President amused? He waited until he came to the podium to give his speech and then told the people: 'Mr Mnangagwa has asked me, because he is a lion himself, to go with him and walk with the lions here. Since I am the President, I am inviting him to come and swim with my crocodiles at Kutama. If he comes out alive, then, I will walk with his lions. (Mnangagwa 2015: 1)

By his totem, Mugabe was a Gushungo, a crocodile. While in his own lineage, Mnangagwa answers to the name of, Shumba, the Lion. Macaphulana read the joke and the story about it to have been a threat and a counter-threat between two political gangsters and practitioners of the political witchcraft of the Zimbabwean postcolony. In walking alongside Mnangagwa all the years, Mugabe walked with the lion that was, when it became a bit hungry in the high noon, going to bite him. In the eleventh month of 2017, using the military, Mnangagwa did bite the crocodile from Kutama. Mnangagwa had always hungered to succeed Mugabe while Mugabe's forbidding will to power could not allow him to even imagine being succeeded by anyone.

As a true crocodile and technician of power in 2017, Mugabe was found out of his dam and domain, so was he eaten. Like a patient lion that is not always a bit hungry, Mnangagwa walked happily with Mugabe in many long years of the struggle and after, he admired Mugabe so much that he called himself after the Crocodile when he was a lion in actuality, but he was always going to bite. Mnangagwa slowly stole the name, the shadow and the power from Mugabe. He carefully captured state institutions, including the soldiery, and the entire security and insecurity sector, waiting for the right time to strike. The special relationship between Mugabe and Mnangagwa was a union and partnership of love, jealousy, suspicion, fear and danger. In the Zimbabwean postcolony as a setting of political witchcraft, an art and a science that punishes victims and pays the faithful followers and supporters, Mugabe and Mnangagwa became two powerful complementing and also competing sorcerers. In their domain of such sorcerers of the postcolony, which is a very dangerous place, assassinations, poisonings, staged car accidents, abductions and disappearances become the political language that is used to dispense with opponents. Zimbabwe under Mugabe and Mnangagwa became such a dangerous place where life was fragile and that was defined by an atmosphere of what Joost Fontein (2018) called "political accidents in Zimbabwe" where lives of political opponents became disposable.

In the Zimbabwean postcolony and amongst insiders of the Mafiadom, threats and promises were daily dressed in jokes and circulated as banter, but they were always real. After positioning himself, over many years as a servant, son and mentee of Mugabe's, Mnangagwa was always going to steal power. Mugabe seems to have known this but, in the true ignorance and stubbornness of the will to power, decided not believe any of the telling signs of the coming bite of the lion. As a tyrant, every Julius Caesar ignores all warnings about the Ides of March. A large part of the confident tyrant's life in the postcolony is spent in political somnambulism, sleepwalking in a false sense of power and security, until it is truly too late. Outwardly, all good tyrants carry themselves with candour and some daredevil bravado when in actuality they are fragile and vulnerable personages. At the dizzy height of his iron will to power and strength, Mugabe was in actuality vulnerable; he owed his power to keepers that could anytime dispense with him. Mnangagwa the lion walked with Mugabe so long and so closely such that in replacing him in power he could only usurp his position, reproduce and amplify his tyranny, and not deliver change. The coup that overthrew Mugabe and enthroned Mnangagwa had been rehearsed several times before it was carried out in veracity. Like the true messiah of the postcolony of Zimbabwe, Mugabe was always going to receive the treacherous kiss of Judas, the bite of a trusted insider of the Mafiadom.

In one of her hurricane rallies across the country in late 2017, Grace Mugabe told a gathering of the Apostolic Faith Christian church that as early as 1980, the year of Zimbabwe's independence, Mnangagwa tried to stage a coup. In that early plot, Grace Mugabe narrated that Mnangagwa warned Mugabe, Morris Nyagumbo and Enos Nkala, all senior ZANU-PF leaders at the time, to flee the country to Mozambique because some Rhodesian assassins were out to eliminate them. Mugabe is said to have ignored the warning. If he and his colleagues had fled to their exile in Mozambique Mnangagwa would have remained the leader of the party and the country.

In what was another attempt at power, in 2007, retired soldiers Albert Mapoto, Colonel Ben Ncube, Major General Engelbert Rugeje and Air vice Marshal Elson Moyo were together with 400 hundred soldiers arrested for plotting and attempting a coup d'état that was to remove Mugabe and elevate then Minister of Rural Housing, Emmerson Mnangagwa, to power. After some years the case against the soldiers and their leaders was dropped by the courts. Earlier in 2004 a plot now known in Zimbabwe as the Dinyane Declaration was hatched to elevate Mnangagwa to the Vice-Presidency of ZANU-PF and position him to succeed Mugabe. Under the guise of a Parents Day event at Dinyane Secondary School in Tsholotsho a meeting was held to put flesh onto the bones of the political plan. The plan fell flat when some of the conspirators alerted Mugabe of the conspiracy and a number of the plotters were suspended from the party and some expelled. But Mnangagwa was still retained, and only the "criminal" elements around him were purged. In their special relationship, Mugabe and Mnangagwa needed each other to the end. Mugabe was a true crocodile to survive all these and other plots. It is his blind confidence and belief in his invincibility that kept him walking with a lion he knew and one that was when it got a bit too hungry, going to bite him. It is the paradox of the special political relationship that Mnangagwa the lion acted like a true crocodile, waiting for the right time to strike while Mugabe became a true lion that was sure of its power and confident of its rule of the postcolony until it was too late. Mugabe invested too much faith in the special relationship, unbending faith that always leads to the cross of the crucifixion in religion and in politics alike. Also possible is that Mugabe might not have trusted Mnangagwa but had invested too much faith in himself; the will to power is not only a maddening but also a blinding passion. Mugabe had an insanely exaggerated sense of his hold on power that made him laugh off all warnings and threats to his position.

The valorisation of animal metaphors in terms of totems about Crocodiles and Lions that Mugabe and Mnangagwa got involved in was not simple self-celebration or artefact of identity politics. The two specially and deeply related politicians were enmeshed together and one with each other in the political animalism of what Machiavelli called "the way of the beast." The Zimbabwean postcolony, under the leadership of Mugabe and his bodyguards became a beastly setting characterised by festivals of cruelty and evil that mirror the haunt of deadly crocodiles in rivers and marauding lions of the jungle. For that reason, Mnangagwa's success in replacing Mugabe in political office could not have been a revolution. It became exactly what it was called, a restoration of the legacy of tyranny and the Olympics of power and violence that accompanies it. Mistake or joke, the reference by one newspaper to Emmerson Mnangagwa as Robert Mnangagwa that is mentioned above became a semantic accident that beautifully and also powerfully projected the new president's political genealogy and actuality, a mixture of Mugabeism and his own spirited and consuming will to power. In the typical postcolony, such as Zimbabwe became, powerful and dangerous politicians do not only call themselves by names of predatory beasts but they in actuality and veracity reproduce and amplify animal behaviours and prey on individuals, communities and nations. Privileged politicians as sorcerers and gangsters of the postcolony call themselves with names of beasts because in truth the postcolony such as what Mnangagwa and Mugabe's Zimbabwe became is a real jungle where the powerless daily need lots of luck to survive.

In 2014, as a Minister of Justice in Mugabe's government, Emmerson Mnangagwa was accused by outspoken "motor-mouth" politician Temba Mliswa (2014: 1) of being "mafia." Mliswa elaborated on that in 1998 Mnangagwa teamed up with such foreign business moguls as Billy Rautenbauch and John Bredenkamp to use Zimbabwean soldiers as a personal militia that secured their mining interests in the Democratic Republic of Congo where many of the soldiers died and those that survived lived to know what working for nothing was. In veracity, Mliswa accused Mnangagwa of conspiring with foreign individuals and forces to use the Zimbabwean national army and other national and state resources to participate in looting, plundering, black marketeering and other forms of cozenage and corruption. During and after the coup that toppled Mugabe, the uses of the national army for partisan, factional and personal political interests became a tragic but true culture in the Zimbabwean postcolony. It is street wisdom in Zimbabwe that many soldiers, police officers and intelligence operatives become rich and even wealthy working as runners and errand boys for the chefs, kingpins and champions of the postcolony in shape of powerful politicians and army generals. The decay of the polity and the economy mathematically results in the obscene wealth of a few securocrats and privileged politicians.

During and after Mugabe's rule, Zimbabwe became a true beastly and exploitative Mafiadom where the interests of the nation and its institutions came secondary to the desires for money and power of privileged politicians. As noted earlier in this book, in the dying days of his rule, Mugabe openly complained that Fifteen Billion United States Dollars' worth of diamonds mined in Chiadzwa were missing. The Zimbabwean military and some Chinese business entities were responsible for exploiting the diamond fields and it became everybody's guess that some privileged securocrats and well-positioned politicians had once again teamed with the foreign business underworld to pillage and siphon Zimbabwe's resources and thereby rob the mass of the poor. As nuanced by Achille Mbembe (2001), the postcolony at its fruition becomes a site of massive eating and also immense defecation of the powerful and the privileged who eat on behalf of the majority, turning the country into a big kind of toilet in its messiness.

History has pressed itself upon Zimbabwe as a sequence of repetitions and reproductions of oppressive regimes of power. In an edited volume, David Harold-Barry (2004) captured well the paradox of Zimbabwean politics in the observation that in "Zimbabwe the past is the future." While Mugabe spectacularly reproduced and repeated the evils of Rhodesian colonial politics on the people he is supposed to have participated in liberating, Emmerson Mnangagwa did not only restore the dark and bitter legacy of Mugabe but naturalised and normalised a beastly Mafiadom that made Zimbabwe a truly dangerous place. Genocidal political violence, corruption in form of the systematic siphoning and plundering of national resources by politicians for personal, factional and partisan gain was to walk on two legs and wear a hat in Zimbabwe. The ascendancy of Mnangagwa to power made visible in Zimbabwe previously obscure but clearly dubious individuals and personalities that came to occupy powerful political positions, common idiots and random hoodlums became ministers and parliamentarians, some of them advisors to the new head of state. A cult of mediocrity, that Chinua Achebe theorised of in Nigeria, arrived in Zimbabwe. If Mugabe covered the vulgarity of his venal tyranny with pretences to thoughtfulness and elegance, Mnangagwa allowed common idiocy to unfold. For instance, after an episode of xenophobic violence in South Africa where many Zimbabweans were reported at risk, Deputy Minister of Information, one Energy Mutodi, a PhD, came out to reason with South Africans. In his argument, Zimbabwe was looking after the Ndebele population that were refugees from South Africa, for that reason South Africans should spare Zimbabweans in South Africa the violence. In one speech an entire nation within Zimbabwe was reduced to foreigners by a senior government official. The true scandal is that Mutodi's modes of political thinking seem truly and honestly representative of the Mnangagwa regime. Daily the Zimbabwean postcolony wakes up to strange stories about the present government and its officials. In November 2019, much arrogantly and insensitively, the Mnangagwa regime dismissed junior medical doctors that went on industrial action demanding better salaries and liveable working conditions. This resulted in a kind of genocide where many people died of curable diseases in Zimbabwe's hospitals, and this as government officials looked aside.

The coup in which Mnangagwa used the national army to topple Mugabe was in actuality not the real coup but a symptom of the long and deep coup that he, under the leadership of Mugabe, conducted against the nation and country of Zimbabwe over decades. Witchcraft of the political and otherwise is fulfilled when national armies and other institutions and resources are deployed for the benefit and gluttonous consumption of individuals, political factions and parties, at the dear expense of national populations whose protests are met with shootings, rapes and heavy bludgeonings. In a matter of weeks after the removal of Mugabe from office, Mnangagwa subjected Zimbabweans to some true kind of colonial domination and rule where violence and coercion became, once again, naturalised and normalised.

Not from a political platform such as that of Mliswa but from a researched scholarly perspective, Sandra MacLean (2002) described "the political economy of conflict" in Zimbabwe under Mugabe where "war" became the identity of the country. Once again Mnangagwa is noted as one of those powerful individuals that together with international companies in alliance with foreign states and global super powers benefitted handsomely from the rich pickings of diamond mining in the Democratic

Republic of the Congo. In concert with some key securocrats in Zimbabwe Mnangagwa is noted to have personally gained from the spoils of a war where a national army was deployed under the persuasive guise of Pan-African solidarity and African continentalism.

That Mnangagwa became the figure that the army elected to restore the same legacy of corruption and tyranny that he himself and Mugabe so forcefully embodied represents history, true to Karl Marx, repeating itself first as a tragedy and then next as a true spectacular farce. By telling political and historical evidence, Mnangagwa, from the Gukurahundi Genocide to the DRC war and repeated political violence during and after Mugabe's rule, came to represent and embody what was bloody, dark and tragic about the Zimbabwean postcolony under the rule of a venal Mafiadom. Jonathan Moyo, a vigorous critic of Emmerson Mnangagwa in the dying days of Mugabe's rule, repeated chilling stories of Mnangagwa's cruelty. One of the stories was that Mnangagwa found a rival suitor at one of his girlfriends' apartments in Harare. At gun point, allegedly, he asked the rival suitor to sit on a red hot stove or jump out of the window. Godfrey Majonga chose to jump from the fourth floor of the building and broke his spine upon landing, and until his death in 2019 was wheelchair bound. The torture of Majonga and his fall in fear of the gun has become just a metaphor of all Zimbabweans that presently live in fear of guns in the postcolony. And that sit on the hot stove of a collapsing economy. The gun idea is deployed not only in fights over girlfriends in the intimate economy but also in disciplining and coercing the population. Mnangagwa's reign has brought into fruition and perfection the realisation of the gun idea in Zimbabwe. The postcolony is a hot stove for the poor and unarmed civilians that have no power to enforce their will.

The history of the African postcolony at large is pregnant with alarming stories of mafia presidents and warlords that became richer than their countries and that are known for their capacity for cruelty and evil. Under Mugabe, politicians and soldiers used state power to much corruptly amass wealth and accumulate assets in and outside the country. Relying on evidence from Wikileaks cables, Gosebo Mathope (2017: 1) noted that Mnangagwa was "reputedly Zimbabwe's richest man" that grew rich from "illicit mine deals in the DRC Congo" and through under the table business deals when he was the Secretary for Finance of ZANU-PF. "Regarded as the wealthiest individual in Zimbabwe, Mnangagwa has close business links with Colonel Lionel Dyck, a white officer from the old Rhodesian army who founded Mine Tech, a landmine clearance company that secured lucrative contracts from the Zimbabwean government to clear landmines in Zimbabwe border areas after the war"(Mathope 2017: 1). Mathope fleshed out evidence from United Nations Reports that listed Mnangagwa as a personal beneficiary of trade in blood diamonds of the Congo. After becoming a living metaphor of looting and corruption Mnangagwa could not be the face of the struggle against corruption in Zimbabwe; he could only normalise and naturalise it.

For informed observers, when Mnangagwa advanced the mantra of Operation Restore Legacy and the "Zimbabwe is Open for Business" slogan, the irony and the paradox of it all was not the least concealed. A true Mafiadom was afoot in Zimbabwe after the fall of Mugabe. Folktales, myths and legends of Africa's rich despots and warlords morphed into a rude reality in the Zimbabwean postcolony. Those that had collapsed the polity and the economy and closed the country for normal business over years were now claiming to be the champions of change. Ambitious security guards and bouncers, bodyguards, came to capture state power; broken bones, blood and dead bodies punctuated the Zimbabwean postcolony once again.

What Achille Mbembe (2001: 116) called "the domain of drunkards" in the African postcolony is exactly that the insanity of believing in cheap miracles and making the strange and the bizarre appear normal. Normalising the abnormal became the commonsense of the Zimbabwean postcolony during the reign and after that fall of Mugabe. The domain of the drunkards in the postcolony turns history around into a realm of the silly, strange and the insane. In the last years of Mugabe in power, for instance, those that aspired to succeed him scrambled for university degrees especially doctorates from briefcase universities. Everyone that wanted to be counted had to dramatise some intellectualism. Zimbabwe itself, a country that was storied for its education system, became over-populated by fake doctors of this and that subject, and phony professors that bought and sold degrees in the black market. Ghost writers were engaged to write dissertations for former guerrillas and senior police and army details. Zimbabwe came to be enveloped in the fake and the phony, not only in the knowledge economy, but in every sector of its life.

Mugabe's storied education got those that wanted to fill his shoes to do everything to be counted as learned, even if by embarrassing shortcuts. Mugabe's wife, Grace, scandalised the normal world when in 2014 the University of Zimbabwe awarded her a Doctoral Degree three months after she registered for it. Suddenly everyone that wanted to be a candidate for political office had to possess, by hook or crook, a university degree, especially the coveted doctoral qualification that had become a kind of fetish of power. As a postcolony and a true domain of the drunkards, Zimbabwe fell under the spell of phony professors and prophets. Predictions of doom and that of the death of powerful politicians flourished. Pictures of powerful politicians kneeling down and consulting with prophets and sangomas impregnated the social media.

Not only Mugabe's storied education was aspired for, imitated and reproduced, even his denialism was to be rehearsed by powerful politicians. Mugabe's denialism and insane contradiction of nature and reality were to be rehearsed by his successors and repeated in some tragi-comic episodes. General Chiwenga, the towering giant that commandeered the coup that toppled Mugabe, together with his wife, became visibly unwell and were frequently noted in public with swollen bodies and colouring skin. In one weekend of February 2019 the General who also had acquired a Doctorate was under emergency circumstances lifted to a hospital in South Africa for treatment. His condition was reported critical. Three days later, the General was back, much reduced in body size, his towering frame famished and the skin wrinkled; "I am alive and well," he said in a televised interview. A visibly very sick man, forcing laughter on his face and claiming to be alive and well, reminded Zimbabweans of the tragedy of an old and ailing Mugabe claiming to be young and strong. Post-Mugabe Zimbabwe became not only a vivid Mafiadom but also a true domain of the drunkards where in a silly and insane way, politicians denied reality and pretended that all was well with their sick bodies and the decaying polity and economy of the postcolony. So effectively, Mugabe as the deluded tyrant that was intoxicated with the love for power and fear of weakness became reincarnated in those that were jostling to succeed him. Mugabeism so possessed Mugabe's successors that as self-styled crocodiles and retired generals consciously or unconsciously mimicked Mugabe's ways. Mugabe and his Mugabeism haunt Zimbabwe even after his death. In his life and time, Mugabe so dominated every part and spirit of Zimbabwe so much so that even those that claim to champion change and oppose the legacy of Mugabe actually go on to mimic and reproduce the fallen tyrant and his ways. Zimbabweans and all those in the world that believed the coup and the fall of Mugabe, and his eventual death, would deliver change are living to witness not only the durability of tyranny but also the true return of Mugabeism and colonialism by any other name.

It is stated earlier in this book that Mugabe grew up on a myth of being a God commissioned figure that was destined to rule Zimbabwe for life. To some dramatic and also comic extents, Mnangagwa and General Chiwenga invented and circulated their own foundational myths of power and glory. Through the spokesperson that he inherited from Mugabe, one George Charamba, Mnangagwa circulated a fascinating myth of his heroic birth and destiny that linked him to the great King Mzilikazi. In a story captured by the journalist, Mandla Ndlovu (2019) Charamba announced to Zimbabweans in the social media that Mnangagwa:

> grew up under the influence of this Warrior-Grandfather who raised him on the staple of heroic tales, and toughening tasks.By way of historical background to benefit those not in the know, when Mzilikazi settled in the southern part of Zimbabwe in late 1830s, his Kingdom entered a pact with Chief Chivi never to fight each other. This pact was solemnized by way of Chief Chivi giving one of his sons—the President's grandfather—to the Ndebele Kingdom for inculturation. (Ndlovu 2019: 1)

As if that was not enough historical construction and confabulation, Charamba added that Mnangagwa had a Ndebele name "Ihlupheko" which was a poor attempt at the common name "Mhlupheki" : "I am further told that at the birth of IHLUPEKO, this grandfather fired his old hunting gun—mugigwa—three times, to welcome the newly born-baby"(Ndlovu 2019: 1). The gun salute at Mnangagwa's birth is supposed to signify a destiny of power that was known prior to his birth. A kind of messianic birth. The intention of that construction, perhaps, was to get Zimbabweans to accept Mnangagwa as a destined warrior leader. General Chiwenga, who is understood to be desperately trying to topple Mnangagwa, would not be left behind. Tendi, after a probing research, noted that:

> Chiwenga's political ambitions were also rooted in a 1965 prophecy given to him by his dying grandfather who, in his youth, was an heir to a chieftainship he eventually did not manage to attain in his lifetime. As described by Chiwenga, his deceasing grandfather prophesied to him: 'what I wanted to achieve [governing] I could not achieve, but you are going to do it. You are Nyikadzino. You are Nyikadzino … you are going to fulfil this destiny'. Chiwenga made this disclosure in August 2016, soon after he changed his legal name fromConstantineChiwengatoConstantinoGuvheyaDominic-Nyikadzino Chiwenga. (Tendi 2019: 23)

Claiming old prophecies and constructing new mythical identities of themselves became the stock in political trade of Mugabe's successors. They desperately sought to fill his terrible but still big shoes through mythology and fiction. All this comic but real myth-making and fiction only goes to demonstrate how the postcoup and the post-Mugabe political era in Zimbabwe tragically became a repetition and reproduction of Mugabeism, a true restoration of a bloody genocidal legacy. It became a real return of the symptom of colonialism in the Zimbabwean postcolony.

The Return of the Post-political

Zimbabwe has failed, so far, to shake-off the legacy of Mugabe and its violence. Mugabe's ambitious successors have only achieved to repeat and reproduce Mugabeism with all the coloniality that comes and goes with it. And the post-political temptations of the postcolony that produced Mugabe are still at large. In the collection of essays on "the return of the political," Chantal Mouffe (2005a) seeks to press home the point that premature optimism about revolution and change is the tragedy of politics at a world scale. Easy revolutions and cheap heroes are the tragedy of post-political excitements. In other words, post-political temptations and inclinations with their naïve or innocent premature jubilations of political change are the very demise of real revolutions. The true understanding of politics and the political as the stuff of caution and pessimism that Mouffe advances was needed when Mugabe became the leader of Zimbabwe in 1980 and equally when he was toppled from power in the coup of 2017. It is with post-political blindness that Mugabe's elevation to power and his dethronement were equally celebrated by Zimbabweans and the wide world. The celebration of easy victories and telling of lies that Amilcar Cabral condemned is part and parcel of the post-political tendencies of the postcolony where individuals and populations urgently want to celebrate anything that might look like change and anyone that pretends to be a hero, even if they are a well-known and infamous crocodile of the postcolony. In the post-political postcolony, such as Zimbabwe, the arrival of a new tyrant is celebrated at once with the departure of the old one. There seems to be no break that is taken to soberly ask questions and apply caution before embracing and celebrating any simulation of change. The Zimbabwean postcolony in its history and nature seems to be as Andrew Meldrum (2004) states, a place where in spite of all the trials and tribulations, people find every excuse to "have hope." Hope and euphoria about change, the history of the Zimbabwean postcolony confirms, amount to tragic postpolitics that allows tyranny to keep returning and recycling itself under many different guises. In many ways, the fall of Mugabe and the rise of Mnangagwa became a true return of Mugabeism in the Zimbabwean postcolony, one can insist.

The resilient and long suffering people of Zimbabwe that carried the burden of settler colonialism for many decades and have endured tyranny for more decades had expectedly but unfortunately become too impatient for change and revolution. Even the smallest imitation of political change and performance of heroism by pretenders sparks euphoria and jubilation that are both tragically post-political. The political proper and politics at large as a game of many dangers, treacheries and tragedies are ignored whenever individuals and populations get intoxicated with euphoria and jubilation. Describing the euphoria and jubilation that enveloped Zimbabwe and captured Zimbabweans during and after the coup, Dinizulu Macaphulana (2019), who was one of the few Zimbabwean voices that counselled caution, noted that "usually vigilant lawyers abandoned their jurisprudence, astute editors forgot journalism and seasoned political activists and opposition political leaders cast away their wisdom, and the persecuted Zimbabwean populace forgot the mass graves, the wounds and memories of blood and pain" to celebrate a coup that was to be the enhancement rather than the overthrow of tyranny in the Zimbabwean postcolony.

More tragic was that opposition political leaders and supporters, some human rights lawyers and prominent journalists that had for decades suffered the tyranny of Mugabe with Emmerson Mnangagwa as his trusted hand and fixer, came out to give dignity to the elevation of Mnangagwa from being Mugabe's bouncer and bodyguard to the captain of the Zimbabwean postcolony par excellence. It was by all accounts a tragic post-political mistake that the elevation of Mnangagwa to the presidency of Zimbabwe was ever celebrated, especially by the victims of tyranny in the Zimbabwean postcolony that were supposed to be cautious and measured. The public celebrations of the coup in Zimbabwe became a true return of the post-political in the postcolony. It all became the proverbial ironic way in which chickens celebrated Christmas day, that day when they are slaughtered in big numbers, cooked and eaten with sharp objects, forks and knifes. The Zimbabwean political experiment, thus far, has taught us that post-political excitements make fertile grounds for tyranny.

The first post-political blunder was for Zimbabweans to accept without question that the removal of Mugabe from power that was conducted by the military and that saw armoured tanks roll down the streets of Harare was not a coup. Zimbabweans celebrated the fall of the dictator and failed to notice the rise of a venal military junta. The coup was called by the architects a "military assisted transition." That it was the use of the Zimbabwean National Army in partisan and even factional politics was ignored. Just like the uses of the National Army in the Congo, 1998, to secure diamond interests of certain powerful individuals, the use of the Zimbabwean soldiery to remove one tyrant to install another was tragic. Once politicised armies tend to remain political and never really return to the barracks. They might return physically but still remain in the streets politically. Zimbabwe does now and will continue to exist under the cloud of another coup that might be sprung up anytime, making the country an uncertain and very unsafe place for life and business, a risk society of a kind.

The same soldiers that were kissed and hugged as heroes in the streets of Harare were the same that were to gun down unarmed civilians after the disputed elections of 2018 and during the protests against price increases early in 2019. That in the postcolony history can truly repeat itself first as a tragedy and next as a farce became true in Zimbabwe. Trevor Ncube, the man who publicly and in print regretted how he naively celebrated and supported the rise of Mugabe to power in 1980, was to be found prominently and loudly celebrating the coup and the militarised promotion of Emmerson Mnangagwa to power. Ncube (2018) was quoted as having said "the military intervention in November was not a military coup, but a helping hand from the ZDF for ZANU-PF to resolve its succession puzzle and that through it, Zimbabweans had managed to reclaim their country." Why a sound public intellectual, business person and opinion leader such as Trevor Ncube would rationalise and celebrate the involvement of the national army in partisan and factional politics is on its own a post-political tragedy. Ncube's became a true example of how the euphoria of the post-political can intoxicate and blind even trusted thinkers, much tragically. The intentional ignorance and political opportunism of the elite is also another troubling tendency in the postcolony.

Discerning Zimbabweans, the political opposition and civil society were supposed to hold the coup makers to account, demand recognition and respect for the constitution, and ensure that the courts, parliament and other democratic institutions remained independent. Away from post-political enchantments with political change and the arrival of new heroes, the coup itself and Mnangagwa as a leader should have been received with not only caution but due suspicion and care. That the Zimbabwean national army has been reduced to a militia for certain powerful persons, factions and parties anticipates a chaotic, violent and unstable future for Zimbabwe. The Zimbabwean security sectors, especially the soldiery, will need to be reformed and rehabilitated or else Zimbabwe and Zimbabweans should make peace with more coups and military governments in the future. There is no doubt also that the Zimbabwean coup and its post-political moment will have a demonstration effect on other Southern African countries where the coup will be imitated and reproduced. Zimbabwe itself remains entrapped in a coup moment where political pro-testers and other dissenters are severely punished. Distrust punctuates relations between and amongst politicians and securocrats that live in per-manent fear of each other. The political opposition is rendered irrelevant as Zimbabweans consciously and unconsciously wait for another coup.

ZIMBABWE IN THE JAWS OF THE CROCODILE

Emmerson Mnangagwa's history as Mugabe's right hand man has always been in the public domain. His infamy as the security minister that super-vised the Gukurahundi Genocide has been equally public. The imbrication of his name in the looting of blood diamonds in the Democratic Republic of the Congo has also been a well-understood actuality of history. Scholars such as Timothy Scarnecchia (2011) have, using declassified intelligence documents of the South African Department of Foreign Affairs, disclosed Emmerson Mnangagwa's treacherous collusion and conspiracy with the racist South African apartheid regime. He, with Mugabe's knowledge and consent, in 1983, as Minister of Security, struck secret deals with the then South African Defence Forces that would prevent the South African lib-eration movement from operating from Zimbabwe, effectively betraying the African liberation struggle against colonialism and apartheid (Scarnecchia 2011: 94). Not only that but Mugabe also participated in the machinations with the South African apartheid regime to train and deploy bandits that would pose as ZIPRA dissidents in Zimbabwe, machinations that became the excuse for the Gukurahundi Genocide. In that treacher-ous way, Mugabe and Mnangagwa conspired with apartheid against Africa and manufactured political reasons for committing genocide in Zimbabwe. In such treacherous shenanigans against Zimbabweans and Africans,

Mugabe, Mnangagwa and the regime they represented actually reinforced and reproduced colonial politics and its modes of domination.

For the reasons of his dodgy and treacherous history, Mnangagwa's elevation to power was supposed to be questioned or received with vigilance but it was not. The coup itself, in all its bloodiness, was sanitised and perfumed to look and sound like a long-awaited revolution. The excitement of Zimbabweans at the news of the fall of Mugabe could be understood and also forgiven. The post-political enchantment of journalists and some lawyers, however, can neither be understood nor forgiven. Journalists in particular were supposed to ask questions and probe actualities and veracities of the coup as an event and of Emmerson Mnangagwa as a politician with a specific and known background. Machiavelli, I think, was engaged with the political, and the political proper, when he opined that men are either good or bad, but for the purposes of politics, they should be handled always as bad. Mnangagwa, much postpolitically, was not treated as bad. He was not handled with due suspicion, but he was given the status of a political celebrity and had the red carpet rolled below his feet. There was a kind of excited collective amnesia on who he was and what he had done to Zimbabweans.

The political proper, as the understanding of politics as conflictual, antagonistic and dangerous, demands sober memory and courageous confrontation with history and politicians as agents of history. Zimbabwean journalists and scholars have largely failed in this task. Mnangagwa was not subjected to due examination and probity. The tiredness with Mugabe and his rule blinded Zimbabweans to the monstrosity that his fall occasioned. After the coup, Zimbabweans could have demanded a transitional government, a caretaker council or a government of national unity that would prepare the country for democratic, free and fair elections. Allowing Mnangagwa to simply walk into Mugabe's shoes and be the one under whose incumbency the elections of 2018 were organised made it easy for him to simply become another Mugabe and entrench himself in power, and be in a position to suffocate the political opposition, and in that way colonise Zimbabwe again. Working democratic institutions were not availed to check and limit the excesses of power.

Fittingly, the rise of Emmerson Mnangagwa to power attracted journalistic attention, and articles and some books were speedily written. By Ray Ndlovu (2018), the book, *In the Jaws of the Crocodile: Emmerson Mnangagwa's Rise to Power in Zimbabwe,* carried a lot of promise, a promise that it went on to tragically break. There was expectation of critical engagement and probing narrative that would at the least ask important questions about the coup and the person of Emmerson Mnangagwa. There was even fair expectation that Ray Ndlovu would express how the rise of Emmerson Mnangagwa to power put Zimbabwe and Zimbabweans "in the jaws of the crocodile" given his reputation for cruelty and imbrications in large-scale corruption and genocide. Squandering a rich journalistic opportunity to question power and expose historical dangers, Ray Ndlovu became mesmerised by the person of Mnangagwa as a political survivor and the storied crocodile that swallowed Mugabe. Mnangagwa's escape and the intervention of his friends in South Africa, the heroism of his sons become the gist of the book. And this is while stubborn questions about Mnangagwa, the coup and Zimbabwe's future are effectively ignored. In that way, the book collapsed into a celebration of Mnangagwa and abandoned the promise of a journalistic investigation and critical historical report. The book failed to overcome the euphoria and post-political enchantments with change and heroism of the post-Mugabe Zimbabwe. That Raymond Ndlovu is a good writer with lucid prose makes it more unfortunate that excellence of form was not met with the relevance of content.

The interviews that Ray Ndlovu was granted by Emmerson Mnangagwa himself, his family and some individuals that are close to him gave him an opportunity that he squandered. Ndlovu was in a position to unmask for Zimbabwe and the world the monstrosity that was unfolding in Zimbabwe. The sense of loss and that of an opportunity squandered is made more palpable by that Ray Ndlovu actually understood well his role as a journalist but somehow allowed himself to be enchanted by Mnangagwa. As a journalist he was supposed to remove himself from the euphoria of the moment and insulate himself from the enchantments with victorious heroes and report reflectively on the historical developments in Zimbabwe, and Ray Ndlovu did not only know this but also actually expressed it:

> I did not have the chance to be part of the celebrations of what was a historic moment in Zimbabwe's history: The fall of Robert Mugabe. Even if I had wanted to, my profession as a journalist prevented me from sharing in the euphoria that swept across the country at the time. And so I emerged from those twenty-one days in November almost untouched by the dramatic events that had unfolded. I did not hug anyone on the streets and I did not kiss any stranger in those moments of celebration. I did not pose for a photo with soldiers, who at the time were celebrated as heroes for their part in

toppling Mugabe. I did not even have picture taken of myself next to one of the army tanks that were stationed for three weeks outside the seat of power, the Munhumutapa Building, once Mugabe's stronghold. (Ndlovu 2018: 163)

Ray Ndlovu knowingly let down the vocation of critical journalism. Concentration and emphasis on Mugabe's fall and the collapse of his strong hold on power prevented Ndlovu from giving a candid examination of Mnangagwa and his rise to power in Zimbabwe. Ndlovu might not have hugged and kissed strangers in the streets in excitement or taken photographs with army tanks and soldiers, but his book went on to give the coup, Mnangagwa and his rise to power the kiss treatment of a hagiography. Epistemically, Ray Ndlovu tragically joined the Lacoste political faction of Mnangagwa and other coup makers. The coup was not just about the fall of Mugabe but also the rise of Emmerson Mnangagwa a long time accessory and facilitator of Mugabe's rule. This alone should have urged an astute journalist that Ray Ndlovu is to conduct a critical examination of the rise of Emmerson Mnangagwa to power in the light of, and even darkness of, his person and history. Away from post-political enchantments, the question should have been asked how the rise to power of Emmerson Mnangagwa was possibly the return of Mugabe by another name. How Mnangagwa might have represented change without difference is a question that should not have escaped scholars and journalists even in the thickness of excitement about the fall of an infamous dictator and seeming political change in Zimbabwe. How it escaped journalists that Mnangagwa had been Mugabe's hand and fixer for many years and not his victim is a post-political puzzle.

Post-political temptations and puzzles can be overcoming even to the tried and the tested of minds, for instance, Mzilikazi wa Africa, a celebrated South African investigative journalist who sat through the conversation between Ray Ndlovu and Emmerson Mnangagwa, was also taken up by Mnangagwa's performance of victimhood. "During the interview" Mzilikazi wa Afrika (2018: ix) notes "Mnangagwa opened up about the serious challenges the country faced and the mess that the predecessor had bequeathed him. I was left with the impression that Mnangagwa does have a plan, a vision that will fix Zimbabwe." Presently Mnangagwa's vision and plan has been exposed to be a reproduction of Mugabe and a repetition of Mugabeism. That Mugabe and Mnangagwa were together in messing up the country was totally silenced. In successfully erasing and silencing his complicity in Mugabe's ruinous rule Mnangagwa was closing up and not opening up on the condition of the country and its prospects. For Mnangagwa to successfully wash his hands of all traces of his involvement in the Mugabe legacy, before two compelling journalists, was a dramatic performance by a man who prided himself of being Mugabe's son and loyalist. One who could not, in theory and practice, oppose Mugabe's legacy but only restore and enhance it.

Such obvious untruths as that Emmerson Mnangagwa was popular in Bulawayo that Ray Ndlovu (2018: 8) constructs can only show a kind of journalism that had failed to detach itself from power. Well-known and understood history is that Mnangagwa, dating back from the Gukurahundi Genocide, is a man that is not only unpopular but totally unwanted in Bulawayo and Matabeleland at large. Part of the special relationship between Mugabe and Mnangagwa was the sure way in which he was always appointed to the cabinet ministers even as he lost almost all elections that he participated in. Popular politicians win elections and not special appointments. Such celebration of a person as that Mnangagwa was a calculating strategist "whose nickname, the Crocodile, conjures images of immense patience and a canny ability to know when to seize the moment" that Ray Ndlovu (2018: 5) gives to Mnangagwa shows a journalism that is captured in postpolitics and declines into vigorous public relations that border on true praise-singing, and this was when there were stubborn historical questions to be asked about the coup and Mnangagwa himself. Ray Ndlovu neglected the responsibility to journalise and participated in the homework of public relations for Emmerson Mnangagwa. Post-political inclinations can impede even excellent journalists from executing their vocation.

Narrating his ordeal after being fired by Mugabe and telling the tell of his escape to South Africa, Emmerson Mnangagwa, as a security and also insecurity insider in Mugabe's regime, gave many clues that Ray Ndlovu could have picked up to unmask the evil of the system that Mugabe and Mnangagwa built. Mnangagwa explained that he had to flee to exile to avoid being arrested because he was going to be poisoned and killed in police and state custody. "What they want to do is to catch me," said Mnangagwa, and "once they have caught me, they are going to put me in jail and then they are going to inject me. In the morning everyone will be told that I hung myself" (Ndlovu 2018: 30). In this statement, Mnangagwa disclosed the workings of a security and insecurity system that he participated in building and leading over years. During the Gukurahundi

Genocide and after, many prisoners were reported in different mornings of Zimbabwe's history to have committed suicide in prison. This and many other unintended but telling disclosures by Mugabe's long time right hand man were ignored as Ray Ndlovu concentrated on details such as how Mnangagwa's daughter Tariro was a "deeply spiritual woman" (Ndlovu 2018: 72) that shared verses from the scriptures with his father and family (Ndlovu 2018: 75). Mnangagwa becomes a hero of the book, a God-fearing family man that courageously prevails over his evil enemies. That he is, with good reasons, considered evil by other people in Zimbabwe is ignored by Ray Ndlovu who post-politically and publicly baths Mnangagwa clean of all his monumental sins that are in the public domain in Zimbabwe and beyond. In concentrating on petty details about Mnangagwa's family Ndlovu majored on minor issues and eventually minored on major issues such as the true meaning of a Mnangagwa presidency in Zimbabwe.

Typical of experienced performers of power, when he encountered Ray Ndlovu, the journalist, Mnangagwa performed the lighter side of things; he drove the interview safely away from the hard and contentious issues. And Raymond Ndlovu was taken up and star-struck by the performer, "when I finally meet President Emmerson Mnangagwa, he gives off a hearty laugh" (Ndlovu 2018: 175) and "I sense genuineness in Mnangagwa's laughter" (Ndlovu 2018: 176). A life of prayers and laughter is what Mnangagwa performed successfully, and the shine of it blinded Ray Ndlovu to the reality that the man who had answers to questions about Zimbabwe's dark history of political violence and public insecurity was sitting before him.

Such a grave historical matter as the coup of November 2017 was in a post-political moment reduced by a politician and the journalist interviewing him to some kind of victory. "The triumph of November 2017" Ndlovu states, "symbolised a victory for the military. The military had once again confirmed its status as the ultimate kingmakers in Zimbabwe's politics" (Ndlovu 2018: 199). The tragic development that a national army had involved or been involved in party and factional politics was post-politically compressed into a victory of the military when it was a clear loss to democracy, law and order in Zimbabwe. A loss whose physical and bloody consequences was to be seen when soldiers gunned down unarmed civilians in the streets of Harare. As journalists, lawyers and scholars got enchanted by the long-awaited fall of Mugabe, the heroism and survivalism of the coup makers, the rise of Mnangagwa meant that in reality Zimbabwe and Zimbabweans were getting into the jaws of the crocodile. The coup was not to be a simple fall and loss of Mugabe, but it was also a strange but true way in which he returned, and therefore it was also a fall and loss for Zimbabwe and Zimbabweans. Mugabeism was enhanced and not abated by the coup, and clearly the coup did not liberate but further subjected Zimbabweans into colonialism and domination of a kind. The anti-colonialism that Mugabe represented and which was unable to overcome coloniality and became a kind of colonial fundamentalism and domination of Zimbabweans remained intact after Mugabe's removal from office. This is just as Mugabe himself reproduced and repeated the coloniality of the Rhodesian regime after the political independence of the Zimbabwean postcolony.

THE COLONIALITY OF THE WILL TO POWER

Under Mugabe's rule, postindependence Zimbabwe became a true postcolony that Achille Mbembe has portrayed as a site of political obscenities, exaggerations, spectacles and insanities. All these would have been entertaining if Zimbabweans were not being killed in huge numbers, the economy decayed and infrastructure collapsed as powerful politicians and military generals looted the public coffers. Zimbabwe came to be defined by what very early after independence Andre Astrow (1983) called a "revolution that lost its way" through poor political strategies, accommodation with imperialism and negations of democracy and good governance. At the end of it all, Mugabe and his ZANU-PF party became those anti-colonialists that fought against colonialism but did not actually fight for liberation from colonialism in the way they became colonisers themselves. After settler colonialism, native colonialism became a reality in Zimbabwe.

Mugabe did not need to follow the examples and obey the prescriptions of western governments to serve Zimbabweans and keep fidelity to the revolution. Such African leaders as Kenneth Kaunda (1966: 33) preached and practiced humanist servant leadership that made the killing of one's people for power unthinkable. Kaunda did not perform any miracles in Zambia. He became a benevolent dictator that gracefully stepped down from power when Zambians voted him out. In that way Kaunda did not only perform and pretend to gallant African statesmanship but enacted and lived in fidelity to the ideal. Mugabe promised a miraculous and paradisal Zimbabwe of reconciled, peaceful and happy blacks and whites after colonialism. But what he brought to reality was a hellish postcolony that became host to a major genocide. Kaunda's commitment to liberation, just across the Zambezi from Zimbabwe, was most witnessed in the sacrifice Zambia made in hosting guerrilla movements of other African countries for many years at great expense and risk. Kaunda enacted, not just a fight against colonialism in Africa, but also a fight for liberation in Southern Africa. The lesson Mugabe left behind is that negating colonialism alone does not entail affirming liberation.

In his helm, Mugabe performed anti-colonialism and anti-imperialism. In regional and international fora, Mugabe became a living metaphor of anti-colonialism for chanting such slogans as "Zimbabwe will never be a colony again" and circulating such catch-phrases as "our sovereignty is not negotiable." He projected himself as a gallant warrior against things colonial in Africa and at a world scale. And many in Africa and the entire Global South were taken up by the performance and believed Mugabe to be a brave decolonial liberator. However, as the present book has demonstrated, Mugabe's anti-colonialism did not graduate into decoloniality, it remained a mask that he wore and an alibi that concealed his own coloniality and will to power. Under Mugabe the Zimbabwean postcolony was a colony of a kind where Zimbabweans hungered for liberation from those that were supposed to have liberated them. In veracity, the political legacy of Mugabe in Zimbabwe has been a legacy of colonialism. How Mugabe participated in the struggle against colonialism and also internalised and reproduced colonial domination in Zimbabwe is a historical paradox that haunts the present book. Mugabe's struggle against colonialism and his own practice of colonial modes of power and politics against the people of Zimbabwe confirms the assertion of Jean Paul Sartre (2001: 31) who noted that after all, "colonialism is a system." As a system, colonialism was in Zimbabwe and elsewhere composed of methods and styles of conquest and domination that utilise both force and fraud. As a system, colonialism also entails the production and uses of political cultures, traditions and approaches that privilege racism, tribalism, xenophobia and contempt for the conquered.

Perhaps, it is exactly because colonialism is a system that political independence in Africa only turned former colonies into postcolonies as sites of the durability and endurance of colonial conditions and experiences, and not liberated settings. Save for the black colour of his skin and his nativity to Zimbabwe and Africa, Mugabe's political thought and practice in Zimbabwe became colonial and also predatory. In his will to power, that is his spirited drive to seek, find and keep power by force and fraud, and by all other means necessary and unnecessary, Mugabe did not only become a kind of conqueror and coloniser but also created an example, precedence and therefore a political culture and system that was imitable and followable by those that have succeeded him. In his life and times, Mugabe became an enchanting political wrong model in Zimbabwe that his supporters and even opponents have to different extents failed to escape. It is in that systemic way that what has been called Mugabeism as political thought and practice of domination and control has almost become part of Zimbabwe's identity, a colonial historical identity. That is how infectious and systemic Mugabe as a person and an idea became. To remove him from power, the coup makers could not even invent the language or articulate the practice of doing so, except the paradoxical claim that they were not dethroning him but restoring his legacy and protecting him from some criminals. It is in that way that the removal of Mugabe became a kind of restoration of Mugabeism.

What Mugabe did in Zimbabwe, from the Gukurahundi Genocide, fraudulent electoral outcomes that gave him political victory over all opponents and the uses of political violence to silence protesters mirrored practices of colonial regimes and imperial civilisations, the world over. The Rhodesian colonial regime of Ian Smith that Mugabe fought and which punished him, and which was a colonial regime and part of the colonial and imperial civilisation at a world scale seems to have found strange but true imitation and reproduction in Mugabe. In his terse indictment and description of the western civilisation as a colonial civilisation at a world scale, Aime Cesaire noted thus:

> A civilization that proves incapable of solving the problems it creates is a decadent civilization. A civilization that chooses to close its eyes to its most crucial problems is a stricken civilization. A civilization that uses its principles for trickery and deceit is a dying civilization...that Europe is unable to justify itself either before the bar of "reason" or before the bar of "conscience"; and that, increasingly, it takes refuge in a hypocrisy which is all the more odious because it is less and less likely to deceive. (Cesaire 1955: 1)

In Zimbabwe, Mugabe dramatised all the civilisational challenges that accompany colonial regimes and systems. There is still no sign that Mugabe and those that are reproducing his political legacy are capable of solving the political and economic problems that they have brought to life in Zimbabwe. The denialism and impunity of the leaders, the pretence that all is well in Zimbabwe amounts to a political regime that decadently closes its eyes to the problems it has created and also to the fact that the regime itself is a problem by its very existence. The employment of trickery, deployment of deceit and reliance on fake news as communication, points to the "dying civilisation" that Cesaire decried. The political system that Mugabe naturalised and normalised in Zimbabwe has survived by taking refuge in hypocrisy and pretences. That Mugabe fought colonialism and suffered colonial violence but over decades used colonial modes and methods of power to punish the people he is supposed to have helped liberate was as hypocritical as it was tragic. The idea and practice of fighting monstrosities until one becomes a monstrosity that Friedrich Nietzsche described is an idea and practice that Mugabe actualised in repeating the colonial oppression he suffered and fought against, and levying it upon his own people. The denialism of the present native colonialist regime in Zimbabwe amounts to what can be called intentional ignorance. Video footages of abductions and torture of political opponents that circulate in the social media are publicly denied as fake news by government ministers. 'There is no crisis in Zimbabwe' is a phrase that is dutifully recited by leaders while the polity and the economy of the country daily go to the proverbial dogs.

For the sheer love for power and fear of powerlessness, Mugabe drove himself into being a monster to his own people. The appetite for power and more power became for him a will to power and desire to dominate even if senselessly and with cruelty that amounted to evil and that could not be justified before the bar of reason or that of any conscience for that matter. The reproduction and repetition of the colonial and coloniality by those that fought colonialism in Africa approaches nihilism and reduces African struggles for decolonisation to pseudo-struggles and gives liberation a bad name. Indeed, the very words "decolonisation" and "independence" have become dirty words to such people as Zimbabweans that have witnessed how decolonisers quickly degenerate into colonisers of a kind. That is how deep the Zimbabwean postcolony is a paradox and a historical mistake.

In veracity, Mugabe's anti-colonialism became a struggle against colonialism that, as Sabelo Ndlovu-Gatsheni noted, did not become decoloniality or liberation, but remained entrapped in coloniality. For a struggle against colonialism to graduate into decoloniality and the practice of liberation, those that are leading the struggle must mature from just being fighters for freedom to being humanists and liberators. They must escape the binary of the struggle of the colonised versus the coloniser and become architects of a new universe of new people that have survived coloniality. Paulo Freire described well the elevated vocation of true humanists and liberators and their great task that includes not only liberating themselves but also liberating their oppressors:

> This, then, is the great humanistic and historical task of the oppressed: to liberate themselves and their oppressors as well. The oppressors who oppress, exploit and rape by virtue of their power, cannot find in this power the strength to liberate either the oppressed or themselves. Only power that springs from the weakness of the oppressed will be sufficiently strong to free both. (Freire 1996: 26)

During and after the struggle for political independence in Zimbabwe, Mugabe, in spite of his lyrical rhetoric of reconciliation, carried with him and inside himself too much of the baggage of colonialism, its lessons, grudges and propensities to force and fraud. Mugabe through his given and then taken reconciliation policy towards Ian Smith and the Rhodesian regime failed to liberate the colonisers from their own racism and colonialism. By retracting reconciliation and reverting back to the animosities of the colonial that defined relations between blacks and white in Rhodesia, Mugabe preserved colonialism in Zimbabwe. When he unleashed colonial forms of domination and punishment upon black Zimbabweans that opposed his rule, Mugabe did not only imitate the colonisers but became one of them except for his black skin and nativity to Zimbabwe.

Mugabe failed the humanistic homework of liberating the oppressors and liberating himself and his people. He succeeded in maintaining colonialism and colonial modes of power and control after the Rhodesians and their colonial administration had been dethroned. In hugging onto colonial grudges and racist animosities, Mugabe failed to use the power that springs from the weakness of the oppressed and elected to deploy the will to power of himself and his regime as another oppressor. One cannot, Mugabe's legacy teaches us, vanquish a colonial regime like the Rhodesian one by imitating it, copying its rules and using its tricks; one only succeeds in repeating colonialism by so doing. Mugabe's historical crime in Zimbabwe is repeating colonialism, failing to teach Rhodesian colonialists humanism and liberation but tragically learning from them and reproducing their political ways. Liberators are not simple anti-colonialists and regular decolonisers but actors from some higher political and historical ground who bring to life the wisdom that: "Liberation is thus a childbirth, and a painful one. The man or woman who emerges is a new person, viable only as the oppressor oppressed contradiction is superseded by the humanisation of all people" (Freire 1996: 31). Mugabe refused, or was unable, to demolish the contradiction between him and his political opponents that he always escalated into enemies that must be annihilated. Education, Christian religion, prison and his long tenure in power all failed to produce a new man out of Mugabe. Inside himself Mugabe remained a perpetually angry colonial child, and colonising colonial subject that was unable to be a liberator or a humanist. The freedom fighter in him remained exactly that, the man who fought freedom, and not fought for freedom. Mugabe became frozen and fossilised in coloniality and failed to be transformed so that he could be a transformer himself. The liberator, as Freire notes, is the one who first liberates himself, deals with the oppressor that is internalised inside himself, the oppressor within, before he can further the cause of liberation. Mugabe failed to defeat the coloniser and the oppressor within himself, he only succeeded in irrigating his will to power that eventually morphed into a true monstrosity.

What the philosopher of liberation, Enrique Dussel (2008: 30), has called "the fetishisation of power" is the political "idolatry" of turning political leaders into some kinds of gods. Once a political leader such as Mugabe is idolised and his name and words are fetishised he can no longer be a liberator for the reason that idols and icons dominate their followers and are, like the gods, followed without question and with blind faith. Once idolised, as Mugabe was, the political leader is imprisoned in the images, symbols and metaphors of the idol and cannot allow himself and be allowed by his followers to admit imperfection and fallibility. Admitting imperfections, allowing oneself to be questioned and corrected is one capital quality of political reformers, revolutionaries and liberators that Mugabe became bereft of. ZANU-PF as a party idolised Mugabe and fetishised his name to the extent that he became, not a correctable human leader, but a kind of god. He was idolised beyond possible repair. Mugabe himself believed in his infallibility and saw his opponents as sinners against destiny, and so did he become insane. He began to see his domination of Zimbabwe and Zimbabweans as normal, natural and a design of God. Even his storied education could not equip Mugabe with enough critical consciousness to critique and correct himself, to recover himself from the imprisoning aperspectival madness that made him feel and act like a deputy to God in Zimbabwean politics.

In believing that his domination of Zimbabwe and Zimbabweans was natural, normal and a design of God, Mugabe became captive to what Ken Wilber (2017) described as "aperspectival madness" which is the insane inability to see wrong in oneself and ones' beliefs and actions. Mugabe could not as a result of his aperspectival madness question or correct his fetishisation of power. Dussel (2008: 33) elaborates that "the fetishisation of power, as we have seen, consists of a 'Will to Power' as domination of the people, of the majority, of the weakest, of the poor." The majority of Zimbabweans lived under Mugabe's colonising will to power and by fraudulent and forceful means they were dominated, dispossessed, impoverished, displaced and violated.

In all of this, Mugabe was insanely insulated from the fetishism of his power and domination of Zimbabwe and Zimbabweans. Fawning ministers, sycophants and flatterers crowded into a political cult around him and made real the political idolatry that kept Zimbabweans in a hell on earth. Combined with his family and social upbringing that injected him with delusions of divine anointment and commission, the political idolisation of Mugabe made his aperspectival madness even more imprisoning and corrupting. With a will power that was driven by such aperspectival madness Mugabe was not equipped to be a liberator but was constructed and charged into a coloniser and oppressor. The coloniality of Mugabe's will to power, like colonialism proper, has become a legacy and a system that keeps being restored and reproduced in Zimbabwe. The struggle against coloniality and fetishism of power in Zimbabwe is therefore a struggle for liberation that will involve political atheism, heresy and rebellion against political idols, colonial legacies and systems. Under Mugabe, and under the present militarised political establishment that is reproducing, multiplying and amplifying Mugabeism, Zimbabwe remains a troubling and also troubled postcolony.

REFERENCES

Astrow, A. (1983). *Zimbabwe: A Revolution That Lost Its Way?* London: Zed Press.

Cesaire, A. (1955). *Discourse on Colonialism.* New York/London: Monthly Review Press.

Dussel, E. (2008). *Twenty Theses on Politics.* London/Durham: Duke University Press.

Fontein, J. (2018). Political Accidents in Zimbabwe. *Kronos, 44*(1), 33–58.

Freire, F. (1996). *Pedagogy of the Oppressed*. London: Penguin Books.

Harold-Barry, D. (2004). *Zimbabwe: The Past Is the Future*. Harare: Weaver Press.

Kaunda, K. (1966). *A Humanist in Africa: Letters to Colin M. Morris from Kenneth Kaunda President of Zambia*. London: Longmans.

Macaphulana, D. M. (2015). Zimbabwe: Let Us Say Grace. In *ZimbabweSituation. com*. Retrieved October 8, 2018, from www.zimbabwesituation.com/news/ zimsit_w_analysis-zimbabwe-let-us-say-grace/.

MacLean, J. S. (2002). Mugabe at War: The Political Economy of Conflict in Zimbabwe. *Third World Quarterly, 23*(3), 513–528.

Magaisa, A. (2017). Mugabe-Mnangagwa: End of 'special relationship'? In *News Day*. Retrieved February 14, 2019, from http://www.newsday.co. zw/2017/11/mugabemnangagwa-end-specialrelationship/.

Mathophe, G. (2017). Mnangagwa, 'Zimbabwe's Richest Man' and His 'Illicit' Mining Exploitations. In *The Citizen*. Retrieved February 14, 2019, from https://citizen.co.za/news/news-africa/1734187/mnangwagwa-zimbabwes-richest-man-and-his-illicit-mining-exploitations/.

Mbembe, A. (2001). *On the Postcolony*. Berkeley: University of California Press.

Meldrum, A. (2004). *Where We Have Hope: A Memoir of Zimbabwe*. London: John Murray.

Mliswa, T. (2014). Mliswa accuses Mnangagwa of being Mafia. In Mugove Tafirenyika & Lloyd Mbiba (Eds.), *Zimbabwe Situation*. Retrieved June 10, 2019, from Zimbabwesituation.com.

Mnangagwa, E. D. (2015). Mnangagwa: We Shall Miss Mugabe Dearly. Interview with Baffour Ankomah. *News DzeZimbabwe*. Retrieved February 14, 2019, from http://www.newsdzezimbabwe.co.uk/2015/08/mnangagwa-we-shall-miss-mgabe-dearly.html.

Mnangagwa, E. D. (2018). Exclusive Interview with Ray Ndlovu and Mzilikazi wa Africa. In R. Ndlovu (Ed.), *In the Jaws of the Crocodile: Emmerson Mnangagwa's Rise to Power*. Cape Town: Penguin Books.

Mouffe, C. (2005a). *On the Political*. Abingdon: Routledge.

Moyo, S. B. (2017a). In Barnes, J. Zimbabwe Coup: Military Chief's Full State Media Address after Robert Mugabe Takeover. Retrieved August 19, 2019, from https://www.express.co.uk/news/world/879796/Zimbabwe-coup-Robert-Mugabe-latest-news-full-speech-Major-General-SB-Moyo-ZBC.

Mugabe, G. (2018). In G. Nyarota (Ed.), *The Graceless Fall of Robert Mugabe: The End of a Dictator's Reign*. Cape Town: Penguin Random House.

Ncube, T. (2018). Trevor Ncube Backs Mnangagwa: Claims It Was Not a Coup. In *Bulawayo24 News*. Retrieved February 14, 2019, from https://bulawayo24. com/index-id-news-sc-national-byo-133066.html.

Ndlovu, M. (2019). Mnangagwa's Ndebele Name Revealed. In *Bulawayo 24 News*. Retrieved January 10, 2020, from https://bulawayo24.com/index-id-news-sc-national-byo-176358.html.

Ndlovu, R. (2018). *In the Jaws of the Crocodile: Emmerson Mnangagwa's Rise to Power*. Cape Town: Penguin Books.

Nietzsche, F. (1968). *The Will to Power*. New York: Vantage Books.

Nyarota, G. (2018). *The Graceless Fall of Robert Mugabe: The End of a Dictator's Reign*. Cape Town: Penguin Random House.

Reno, W. (1998). *Warlord Politics and African States*. Boulder and London. Lynne Rienner Publishers.

Rogers, D. (2019). *Two Weeks in November: The Astonishing Untold Story of the Operation that Toppled Mugabe*. Jeppestown: Jonathan Ball Publishers.

Sartre, J. (2001). *Colonialism and Neocolonialism*. London/New York: Routledge.

Scarnecchia, T. (2011). Rationalising Gukurahundi: Cold War and South African Foreign Relations with Zimbabwe, 1981–1983. *Kronos, 37*(1), 89–55.

Tendi, B-M. (2008). Patriotic History and Public Intellectuals Critical of Power. *Journal of Southern African Studies, 34*(2), 379–396.

Tendi, B-M. (2019). The Motivations and Dynamics of Zimbabwe's 2017 Military Coup. *African Affairs*, 1–29.

Wa Africa, M. (2018). In R. Ndlovu (Ed.), *In the Jaws of the Crocodile: Emmerson Mnangagwa's Rise to Power*. Cape Town: Penguin Books.

Wilber, K. (2017). *Trump and a Post-Truth World*. Colorado: Shambhala.

Woods, K. (2007). *The Kevin Woods Story. In the Shadow of Mugabe's Gallows*. Johannesburg: 30 Degrees South Publishers.

References

Achebe, C. (1983). *The Trouble with Nigeria*. London: Heinemann Educational Books.

Agamben, G. (1987). The Thing Itself. *Contemporary Italian Thought, 16*(2), 53, 18–28.

Agamben, G. (2005). *State of Exception. Chicago & London*. University of Chicago Press.

Alliluyeva, S. (1967). *Twenty Letters to a Friend* (P. J. McMillan, Trans.). New York: Harper & Row.

Althusser, L. (2010). *Machiavelli and Us* (G. Elliot, Trans.). London: Verso.

Anderson, B. (1983). *Imagined Communities: Reflections on the Origin and Spread of Nationalism*. London & New York. Verso Books.

Anderson, B. (2006). *Imagined Communities: Reflections on the Origin and Spread of Nationalism*. London & New York: Verso Books.

Arendt, H. (1955). *The Origins of Totalitarianism*. Boston: Harcourt, Houghton Mifflin.

Arendt, H. (2006). *Eichmann in Jerusalem: A Report on the Banality of Evil*. London: Penguin Books.

Aristotle. (1948). *The Politics of Aristotle* (E. Barker, Trans.). Oxford: Clarendon.

Armah, A. K. (1988). *The Beautyful Ones are not yet Born*. Oxford: Heinemann.

Askew, K. M. (2002). *Performing the Nation: Swahili Music and Cultural Politics in Tanzania*. Chicago: University of Chicago Press.

Astrow, A. (1983). *Zimbabwe: A Revolution That Lost Its Way?* London: Zed Press.

Asuelime, L., & Simurai, B. (2013). Robert Mugabe Against all Odds: A Historical Discourse of a Successful Life President? *African Renaissance, 10*(2), 51–56.

© The Author(s) 2021
W. J. Mpofu, *Robert Mugabe and the Will to Power in an African Postcolony*, African Histories and Modernities,
https://doi.org/10.1007/978-3-030-47879-7

Auret, M. (2009). *From Liberator to Dictator: An Insider's Account of Robert Mugabe's Descent into Tyranny.* Claremont: David Philip.

Badiou, A. (2009). Who Is Nietzsche? In D. Hoens, S. Jöttkandt, & G. Buelens (Eds.), *The Catastrophic Imperative* (pp. 195–204). New York: Palgrave Macmillan.

Barnette, H. H. (1972). The Anatomy of Extremism: Right and Left. In E. West (Ed.), *Extremism Left and Right.* Michigan: William Eerdmans Publishing Company.

Barthel, M. (1984). *The Jesuits: History and Legend of the Society of Jesus.* New York: William Morrow and Company Inc.

Baudrillard, J. (1994). *Simulacra and Simulation.* Ann Arbor: University of Michigan Press.

Belfield, R. (2005). *Assassination: The Killers and Their Paymaster Revealed.* London: Magpie Books.

Bhebhe, N. (2004). *Simon Vengayi Muzenda and the Struggle for the Liberation of Zimbabwe.* Gweru: Mambo Press.

Bhebhe, N., & Ranger, T. (Eds.). (1995). *Soldiers in Zimbabwe's Liberation War Vol 1.* Harare: University of Zimbabwe Publications.

Blair, D. (2002). *Degrees in Violence: Robert Mugabe and the Struggle for Power in Zimbabwe.* London: Continuum.

Blakesley, C. (2017). Wrestling Tyrants: Do we need an International Criminal Justice System? *Scholarly Works, 10*(24), 2–14.

Bourne, R. (2011). *Catastrophe: What Went Wrong in Zimbabwe?* London & New York: Zed Books.

Bowie, M. (1991). *Lacan.* London: HarperCollins Publishers.

Buckle, C. (2003). *Beyond Tears: Zimbabwe's Tragedy.* Cape Town: Jonathan Ball Publishers.

Bulloch, J., & Morris, H. (1991). *Saddam's War: The Origins of the Kuwait Conflict and the International Response.* London: Faber and Faber.

Bullock, A. (1992). *Hitler and Stalin: Parallel Lives.* New York: Random House.

Burbach, R. (2003). *The Pinochet Affair: State Terrorism and Global Justice.* London/New York: Zed Books.

Butler, J. (1988). Performing Acts and Gender Constitution. In S. Case (Ed.), *Performing Feminism* (pp. 270–282). Baltimore, MD: John Hopkins University Press, 1991.

Butler, J. (1990). Performative Acts and Gender Constitution: An Essay in Phenomenology and Feminist Theory. In S. Case (Ed.), *Performing Feminisms: Feminist Critical Theory and Theater.* Baltimore: Johns Hopkins University Press.

Butler, J. (2010). Performative Agency. *Journal of Cultural Economy, 3*(2), 147–161.

Campbell, H. (2003). *Reclaiming Zimbabwe: The Exhaustion of the Patriarchal Model of Liberation.* Claremont: David Philip Publishers.

Camus, A. (1953). *The Fastidious Assassins*. London: Penguin Books.

Cesaire, A. (1955). *Discourse on Colonialism*. New York/London: Monthly Review Press.

Chabal, P., & Daloz, J.-P. (1999). *Africa Works: Disorder as Political Instrument*. Bloomington: Indiana University Press.

Chan, S. (2003). *Robert Mugabe: A Life of Power and Violence*. Michigan: University of Michigan Press.

Chan, S. (2007). Nietzsche in Harare. *Prospect*, May, p. 134.

Chappell, T. (2005). *The Inescapable Self: An Introduction to Western Philosophy Since Descartes*. London: Orion Publishing Group.

Chavez-Arvizo, E. (1997). Introduction. In *Descartes: Key Philosophical Writings*. Hertfordshire: Wordsworth Editions.

Chesterton, G. K. (1995). *Orthodoxy*. San Francisco: Ignatius Press.

Chipanga, K. (2018). In G. Nyarota (Ed.), *The Graceless Fall of Robert Mugabe: The End of a Dictator's Reign*. Cape Town: Penguin Random House.

Chung, F. (2006). *Re-living the Second Chimurenga: Memories from Zimbabwe's Liberation Struggle*. Uppsala: Nordic Africa Institute.

Clausewitz, C. V. (1985). *On war*. Harmondsworth: Penguin.

Coetzee, J. M. (1991). The Mind of Apartheid: Geoffrey Cronje (1907–). *Social Dynamics 17*, 1–35.

Coltart, D. (2007). Why I Cannot Join Tsvangirai's Faction. *New African: Zimbabwe*, Special Issue, 48–54.

Compagnon, D. (2011). *A Predictable Tragedy: Robert Mugabe and the Collapse of Zimbabwe. Philadelphia*: University of Pennsylvania Press.

Conquest, R. (1991). *Stalin: Breaker of Nations*. New York: Viking.

Cranenburgh, O. V. (2008). Big Men Rule: The Presidential Power, Regime Type and Democracy in 30 African Countries. *Democratisation, 15*(5), 925–973.

Daloz, J.-P. (2003). Big Men in Sub-Saharan African Africa: How Elites Accumulate Positions and Resources. *Comparative Sociology, 2*(1), 271–285.

Donato. (2008). In H. Holland (Ed.), *Dinner with Mugabe: The Untold Story of a Freedom Fighter Who Became a Tyrant*. Johannesburg: Penguin Books.

Dongo, M. (2016, August 9). In Bulawayo24 News, *Mugabe War Credentials Questioned, War Prisoner not War Vet*.

Dotcherty, T. (2016). *Complicity: Criticism Between Collaboration and Commitment*. London: Rowman and Littlefield.

Dubois, E. W. B. (1969). *The Souls of Black Folk*. New York: Nal Penguin Inc.

Dussel, E. (1985). *Philosophy of Liberation*. New York: Wipf and Stock Publishers.

Dussel, E. (2008). *Twenty Theses on Politics*. London/Durham: Duke University Press.

Ekeh, P. (1975). Colonialism and the Two Publics in Africa: A Theoretical Statement. *Comparative Studies in Society and History, 17*(1), 91–112.

Ekeh, P. P. (1983). Colonialism and Social Structure in Africa. In *An Inaugural Lecture*. Ibadan: Ibadan University Press.

Elon, A. (2006). Introduction. In H. Arendt (Ed.), *Eichmann in Jerusalem: A Report on the Banality of Evil*. London. Penguin Books.

Esterhuyse, W. (2012). *Endgame: Secret Talks and the End of Apartheid*. Cape Town: Tafelberg.

Eze, E. C. (2005). Epistemic Conditions for Genocide. In J. K. Roth (Ed.), *Genocide and Human Rights*. London: Palgrave Macmillan.

Fanon, F. (1967). *The Wretched of the Earth*. New York: Grove Press.

Fanon, F. (2001). *The Wretched of the Earth*. London: Penguin Classics.

Fanon, F. (2002). *Black Skin White Masks*. New York: Grove Press.

Fanon, F. (2008). *Black Skin White Masks*. London: Pluto Press.

Fontein, J. (2018). Political Accidents in Zimbabwe. *Kronos, 44*(1), 33–58.

Foucault, M. (1977). *Discipline and Punish: The Birth of the Prison*. London: Penguin Books.

Freire, F. (1996). *Pedagogy of the Oppressed*. London: Penguin Books.

Freire, P. (1993). *Pedagogy of the Oppressed*. London: Penguin Books.

Freud, S. (1994). *Civilization and Its Discontents*. New York: Dover Publications.

Friedman, S. (2010). Seeing Ourselves as Others See Us: Race, Technique and the Mbeki Administration. In D. Glaser (Ed.), *Mbeki and After: Reflections on the Legacy of Thabo Mbeki*. Johannesburg: Wits University Press.

Fromm, E. (1970). *The Crisis of Psychoanalysis: Essays on Freud, Marx and Social Psychology*. Middlesex: Penguin Books.

Fromm, E. (1986). *Beyond the Chains of Illusion: My Encounter with Marx and Freud*. London: Sphere Books.

Fukuyama, F. (1992). *The End of History and the Last Man*. New York: Free Press.

Gaddafi, M. (2009). Libya's Gaddafi Hurls Insults as Saudi King. Address to the Arab Summit. Retrieved September 10, 2018, from https://www.smh.com.au/world/libyas-gaddafi-hurls-insults-at-saudi-king-20141031-9h9r.html.

Gaidzanwa, R. (2014). Grappling with Mugabe's Masculinist Politics in Zimbabwe: A Gender Perspective. In S. Ndlovu-Gatsheni (Ed.), *Mugabeism?: History, Politics and Power in Zimbabwe*. New York: Palgrave Macmillan.

Gappah, P. (2017). How Zimbabwe Freed Itself from Robert Mugabe. In *The New Yorker*. Retrieved October 5, 2018, from https://www.newyorker.com/sections/.../how-zimbabwe-freed-itself-of-robert-mugabe.

Gat, A. (2008). *War in Human Civilization*. Oxford: Oxford University Press.

Germani, G. (1978). *Authoritarianism, Fascism and National Populism*. Brunswick, NJ: Transaction Books.

Glad, B. (2002). Why Tyrants Go Too Far: Malignant Narcissism and Absolute Power. *Political Psychology, 23*, 1–37.

Godwin, P. (2008). *The Fear: The Last Days of Robert Mugabe*. New York: Picador.

Godwin, P. (2010). *The Fear: The Last Days of Robert Mugabe*. New York: Picador.

Gramsci, A. (1971). *Selections from the Prison Notebooks*. New York: International Publishers Company.

Grosfoguel, R. (2011). Decolonizing Post-Colonial Studies and Paradigms of Political Economy: Transmodernity, Decolonial Thinking, and Global Coloniality. *Transmodernity: Journal of Peripheral Cultural Production of the Luso-Hispanic World, 1*(1), 1–34.

Gudhlanga, E. (2013). Shutting Them Out: Opportunities and Challenges of Women's Participation in Zimbabwean Politics—A Historical Perspective. *Journal of Third World Studies, 30*(1), 151–170.

Harold-Barry, D. (2004). *Zimbabwe: The Past Is the Future*. Harare: Weaver Press.

Heidegger, M. (1967). Who is Nietszche's Zarathustra? *Review of Metaphysics, 20*(3), 411–431.

Hill, G. (2003). *The Battle for Zimbabwe: The Final Countdown*. Cape Town: Zebra Press.

Hitchens, C. (1995). *The Missionary Position: Mother Teresa in Theory and Practice*. London: Verso.

Hitchens, C. (2008). Mandela Envy: Is Robert Mugabe's Lawless Misrule Founded on Jealousy? *Fighting Words: SLATE*. Slate.comnews: Accessed 12 April 2019.

Hofstadter, R. (1964). The Paranoid Style in American Politics. *Harper's Magazine*, pp. 77–86.

Holland, H. (2008). *Dinner with Mugabe: The Untold Story of a Freedom Fighter Who Became a Tyrant*. Johannesburg: Penguin Books.

Holland, H. (2012). *Dinner with Mugabe: The Untold Story of a Freedom Fighter Who Became a Tyrant*. London: Penguin.

Hope, C. (2003). *Brothers Under the Skin: Travels in Tyranny*. London: Pan Macmillan.

Hudson, P. (2013). The State and the Colonial Unconscious. *Social Dynamics: A Journal of African Studies, 39*(2), 263–277.

Jackson, H. R., & Roseberg, C. G. (1984). Personal Rule: Theory and Practice in Africa. *Comparative Politics, 16*(4), 421–442.

Jenkins, M. (2013). Aristocratic Radicalism or Anarchy? An Examination of Nietzsche's Doctrine of Will to Power. *Pathways of Philosophy*. Retrieved July 20, 2018, from www.philosophypathways.com/fellows/jenkins.pdf.

Johnson, S. (1775). In J. Boswell (Ed.), *Life of Samuel Johnson, LL.D.* (Vol. 1, p. 478). London: Wordsworth.

Kant, I. (1981). *An Answer to the Question: "What is Enlightenment?"* London: Penguin Classics.

Kaplan, D. R. (1996). *The Ends of the Earth: From Togo to Turkmenistan, From Iran to Cambodia: A Journey to the Frontiers of Anarchy*. New York: Vintage Books.

Kaplan, R. (2002). *Warrior Politics: Why Leadership Needs a Pagan Ethos*. New York: Vintage Books.

Karsh, E., & Rautsi, I. (1991). *Saddam Hussein: A Political Biography*. New York: Macmillan.

Kaunda, K. (1966). *A Humanist in Africa: Letters to Colin M. Morris from Kenneth Kaunda President of Zambia*. London: Longmans.

Kells. (2013, April 13). Politics Leads the Gun: Mugabe. Retrieved March 10, 2018, from https//ZimetroNews.com.

Khadiagala, G. M. (2010). Two Moments in African Thought: Ideas in Africa's International Relations. *South African Journal of International Affairs, 17*(3), 375–387.

Kirk-Greene, A. H. M. (1991). His Eternity, His Eccentricity, or His Exemplarity: A Further Contribution to the Study of His Excellency the African Head of State. *African Affairs, 90*, 163–187.

Kriger, N. (2003). Robert Mugabe: Another Too-Long Serving African Ruler: A Review Essay. *Political Science Quarterly, 118*(2), 307–313.

Laclau, E. (1966). *Emancipation(s)*. London: Verso.

Laclau, E. (2005). *On Populist Reason* (pp. ix–xi). London: Verso.

Lamb, D. (1990). *The Africans: Encounters from the Sudan to the Cape*. London: Mandarin Publishers.

Lessing, D. (2013, March 1). The Jewel of Africa. *The New York Review of Books*, p. 1.

Little, S. (1952). In Rene Fullop-Miller (1930), *The Power and the Secret of the Jesuits*. New York. The Viking Press.

Lloyd, R. B. (2002). Zimbabwe: The Making of an Autocratic "Democracy.". *Current History, 101*(655), 219–224.

Lukacs, J. (1997). *The Hitler of History*. New York: Knopf.

Macaphulana, D. (2014). Robert Mugabe: An African Head of State and the State of an African Head. *Bulawayo24 News*. 19 December 2014.

Macaphulana, D. M. (2015). Zimbabwe: Let Us Say Grace. In *Zimbabwe Situation. com*. Retrieved October 8, 2018, from www.zimbabwesituation.com/news/zimsit_w_analysis-zimbabwe-let-us-say-grace/.

Macaphulana, D. M. (2016). Robert Mugabe: The Head of State and State of the Head. In *Bulawyo24 News*. Retrieved February 25, 2016, from https://bulawayo24.com.

Macaphulana, D. M. (2017a). Mnangagwa and the Theft of History. In *Bulawayo24 News*. Retrieved February 14, 2019, from https://bulawayo24.com/index-id-opinion-sc-columnist-byo-122102.html.

Macaphulana, D. M. (2017b). Robert Mugabe the Physical Man Naturally Retreats. In *Bulawayo24 News*. Retrieved August 4, 2017, from bulwayo24.com.

Machel, S. (1996). In Mamdani, M. Citizen and Subject: Contemporary Africa and the Legacy of Late Colonialism. *Perspectives on Political Science, 26.* 120–120.

Machiavelli, N. (2003a). *The Prince and Other Writings*. (Wayne A. Rebhorn, Trans.). New York: Barnes and Noble Classics.

Machiavelli, N. (2003b). *The Prince*. New York: Barnes and Noble Classics.

Machiavelli, N. (2007). Life of Castruccio Castracani. In P. Constantine (Ed.), *The Essential Writings of Machiavelli*. New York: Random House, Inc.

MacLean, J. S. (2002). Mugabe at War: The Political Economy of Conflict in Zimbabwe. *Third World Quarterly, 23*(3), 513–528.

Madonko, I. (2001). Remain United – President, In *The Herald*, 15 July 2005 Unity Gala, December.

Magaisa, A. (2017). Mugabe-Mnangagwa: End of 'special relationship'? In *News Day*. Retrieved February 14, 2019, from http://www.newsday.co.zw/2017/11/mugabemnangagwa-end-specialrelationship/.

Magaisa, T. A. (2016, February 26). The God Father Has Spoken- But Was It Much Ado About Nothing? In *Zimbabwe Independent*.

Magaisa, T. A. (2019). The Regime and its Enablers. *Big Saturday Read*. Retrieved February 5, 2020, from www.bigsr.co.uk.

Mair, S., & Sithole, M. (2002). *Blocked Democracies in Africa: Case Study of Zimbabwe Harare*. Harare: Konrad Adenauer Foundation.

Makombe, P. (2004). Nyarota Attempts to Spin His Mistakes. In *The Standard*. Retrieved October 2, 2018, from https://www.thestandard.co.zw/2004/12/03/nyarota-attempts-to-spin-his-mistakes/.

Maldonado-Torres, N. (2008). *Against War: Views from the Underside of Modernity*. London / Durham: Duke University Press.

Malinowski, B. (1938). Introduction. In J. Kenyatta (Ed.), *Facing Mount Kenya*. London: Heinemann.

Mamdani, M. (2001). Making Sense of Non-Revolutionary Violence: Some Lessons from Rwandan Genocide (Text of the Frantz Fanon Lecture, University of Durban, Westville, 8 August 2001), p. 1.

Mamdani, M. (2004). *Good Muslim, Bad Muslim: America, the Cold War and the Roots of Terror*. New York: Pantheon Books.

Mamdani, M. (2009). Lessons of Zimbabwe: Mugabe in Context. *Concerned African Scholars Bulletin, 82*, 1–13.

Mandela, N. (1994). *Long Walk to Freedom: The Autobiography of Nelson Mandela*. London: Little, Brown and Company.

Mangcu, X. (2008). *To the Brink: The State of Democracy in South Africa*. Scottville: University of KwaZulu Natal Press.

Martin, D., & Johnson, P. (1981). *The Struggle for Zimbabwe*. London: Faber and Faber.

Martin, D., Phyllis, J., & Mugabe, R. (1981). *The Struggle for Zimbabwe: The Chimurenga War*. London: Faber & Faber.

Masunungure, E. (2004). Travails of Opposition Politics in Zimbabwe Since Independence. In D. Harold-Barry (Ed.), *Zimbabwe: The Past is the Future* (pp. 147–92). Harare: Weaver Press.

Mathophe, G. (2017). Mnangagwa, 'Zimbabwe's Richest Man' and His 'Illicit' Mining Exploitations. In *The Citizen*. Retrieved February 14, 2019, from https://citizen.co.za/news/news-africa/1734187/mnangwagwa-zimbabwes-richest-man-and-his-illicit-mining-exploitations/.

Matyszak, D. (2015). Coup De Grace? Plots and Purges: Mugabe and ZANU-PF's 6th National People's Congress. *Research and Advocacy Unit*. Retrieved July 10, 2019, from www.researchand advocacyunit.

Mazarire, G. C. (2011). Discipline and Punishment in ZANLA, 1964–1979. *Journal of Southern African Studies, 37*(3), 571–591.

Mazrui, A. (1990). On Poet Presidents and Philosopher Kings. *Research in African Literature, 21*(2), 13–19.

Mazrui, A. (1995). The Blood of Experience: The Failed State and Political Collapse in Africa. *World Policy Journal, 12*(1), 28–34.

Mazrui, A. (1997). Nkrumah: The Leninist Czar. *Transition, 75,* 106–126.

Mazrui, A. A. (1974). Africa, My Conscience and I. *Transition, 46,* 67–71.

Mazrui, A. A. (Ed.). (1977). *The Warrior Tradition in Modern Africa* (Vol. 23). South Holland: Brill Publishers.

Mazrui, A. A. (1982). Africa Between Nationalism and Nationhood: A Political Survey. *Journal of Black Studies, 13*(1), 23–44.

Mazrui, A. A. (2005). Pan-Africanism and Intellectuals: Rise, Decline and Revival. In T. Mkandawire (Ed.), *African Intellectuals: Rethinking Politics, Language, Gender and Development*. New York: Zed Books.

Mbembe, A. (1992). Provisional Notes on the Post-colony. *Africa, 62*(1), 3–37.

Mbembe, A. (2001). *On the Postcolony*. Berkeley: University of California Press.

Mbembe, A. (2002a). On the Power of the False. *Public Culture, 14*(3), 629.

Mbembe, A. (2002b). African Modes of Self-writing. *Public Culture, 14*(1), 239–273.

Mbembe, A. (2004). An Essay on Politics as a Form of Expenditure. *Cahiers Etudes Africaines, 1,* 173–174.

Meldrum, A. (2004). *Where We Have Hope: A Memoir of Zimbabwe*. London: John Murray.

Memmi, A. (1974). *The Coloniser and the Colonised*. London & New York. Earthscan.

Meredith, M. (2002a). *Robert Mugabe: Power, Plunder and Tyranny in Zimbabwe*. Cape Town: Jonathan Ball Publishers.

Meredith, M. (2002b). *Our Votes, Our Guns: Robert Mugabe and the Tragedy of Zimbabwe*. New York: Public Affairs Publishers.

Meredith, M. (2007). *Mugabe: Power, Plunder, and the Struggle for Zimbabwe's Future*. New York: Public Affairs.

Mhanda, W. (2011). *Dzino: Memories of a Freedom Fighter*. Harare: Weaver Press.

Miller, J., & Mylroie, L. (1990). *Saddam Hussein and the Crisis in the Gulf*. New York: Random House.

Mkandawire, T. (2005). *"Introduction" African Intellectuals: Rethinking Politics, Language, Gender and Development*. London & New York: Codesria Books/Zed Books.

Mlambo, A. S. (2014). Mugabe on Land, Indigenisation and Development. In S. Ndlovu-Gatsheni (Ed.), *Mugabeism? History, Politics and Power in Zimbabwe*. New York: Palgrave Macmillan.

Mliswa, T. (2014). Mliswa accuses Mnangagwa of being Mafia. In Mugove Tafirenyika & Lloyd Mbiba (Eds.), *Zimbabwe Situation*. Retrieved June 10, 2019, from Zimbabwesituation.com.

Mnangagwa, E. D. (2015). Mnangagwa: We Shall Miss Mugabe Dearly. Interview with Baffour Ankomah. *News DzeZimbabwe*. Retrieved February 14, 2019, from http://www.newsdzezimbabwe.co.uk/2015/08/mnangagwa-we-shall-miss-mgabe-dearly.html.

Mnangagwa, E. D. (2018). Exclusive Interview with Ray Ndlovu and Mzilikazi wa Africa. In R. Ndlovu (Ed.), *In the Jaws of the Crocodile: Emmerson Mnangagwa's Rise to Power*. Cape Town: Penguin Books.

Moorcraft, P. (2012). *Mugabe's War Machine*. Cape Town: Jonathan Ball Publishers.

Moore, D. (2007). "Intellectuals" Interpreting Zimbabwe's Primitive Accumulation: Progress to Market Civilisation? *Safundi, 8*(2), 199–222.

Moore, D. (2009). Mamdani's Enthusiasms. *Concerned African Scholars Bulletin, 82*, 49–53.

Moore, D. (2015). In S. Ndlovu-Gatsheni (Ed.), *Mugabeism? History, Politics, and Power in Zimbabwe*. New York: Palgrave Macmillan.

Moore, D. B. (1991). The Ideological Formation of the Zimbabwean Ruling Class. *Journal of Southern African Studies, 17*(3), 472–495.

Moore, D. B. (2014). Robert Mugabe: An Intellectual Manqué and his moments of Meaning. In S. Ndlovu-Gatsheni (Ed.), *Mugabeism? History, Politics and Power in Zimbabwe*. New York: Palgrave Macmillan.

Mouffe, C. (2005a). *On the Political*. Abingdon: Routledge.

Mouffe, C. (2005b). *The Return of the Political*. Verso: New York/London.

Moyo, G. (2014). Mugabe's Neo-sultarnist Rule: Beyond the Veil of Pan-Africanism. In S. Ndlovu-Gatsheni (Ed.), *Mugabeism? History, Politics and Power in Zimbabwe*. New York: Palgrave Macmillan.

Moyo, J. (2008). In Tendi, B-M, Patriotic History and Public Intellectuals' Critical Power. *Journal of Southern African Studies, 34* (2) p. 386.

Moyo, S. B. (2017a). In Barnes, J. Zimbabwe Coup: Military Chief's Full State Media Address after Robert Mugabe Takeover. Retrieved August 19, 2019, from https://www.express.co.uk/news/world/879796/Zimbabwe-coup-Robert-Mugabe-latest-news-full-speech-Major-General-SB-Moyo-ZBC.

Moyo, S. B. (2017b). Full Statement from Zimbabwe Military on Situation in Zimbabwe. *ENCA*. Retrieved February 14, 2019, from https://www.enca.com/africa/full-statement-by-zim-army-on-state-broadcaster.

Mpofu, B., & Ndlovu-Gatsheni, S. (2014). Robert Mugabe: The Will to Power and Crisis of the Paradigm of War. In S. Ndlovu-Gatsheni (Ed.), *Mugabeism? History, Politics and Power in Zimbabwe*. New York: Palgrave Macmillan.

Muchemwa, K. Z. (2010). Galas, Biras, State Funerals and the Necropolitan Imagination in Re-Construction of the Zimbabwean Nation, 1980–2008. *Social Dynamics, 36*(3), 504–514.

Mugabe, G. (2018). In G. Nyarota (Ed.), *The Graceless Fall of Robert Mugabe: The End of a Dictator's Reign*. Cape Town: Penguin Random House.

Mugabe, R. (1976). In Meredith, M. (2002). *Our Votes, Our Guns: Robert Mugabe and the Tragedy of Zimbabwe*. New York. Public Affairs Publishers.

Mugabe, R. (1978). "Imperialist Plotting to Create a Neo-Colonialist Buffer Zone in Zimbabwe" Address to The Zimbabwe Nation in Radio Maputo's Voice of Zimbabwe on the eve of his return from the Malta Constitutional Conference on 24 February 1978, *Zimbabwe News*, 10, 1.

Mugabe, R. (1989a). Struggle for Southern Africa. *Foreign Affairs, 66*(2), 311–327.

Mugabe, R. (1989b). The Unity Accord: Its Promise for the Future. In Banana, C.S (ed.) *Turmoil and Tenacity: Zimbabwe 1890–1990*. Harare: College Press.

Mugabe, R. (1997a, May 11). Lets forget the Past. In *The Sunday Mail*.

Mugabe, R. (1997b, December 6). Speech on the Fast Track Land Reform Programme. In *The Herald*.

Mugabe, R. (2000). Mugabe Madness of Matabale Deaths. *BBC News*. news.bbc. ca.uk/2/hi/Africa. Accessed 17 February 2021.

Mugabe, R. (2000, October 25). Speech at ZANU-PF Headquarters.

Mugabe, R. (2002, July 2). Follow in the Footsteps of Father Zim, In *The Herald*.

Mugabe, R. (2003, March). Speech at the state funeral of a Cabinet minister, March 2003. Quoted in Thornycroft, Peta (26 March 2003). "'Hitler' Mugabe launches revenge terror attacks". In *Daily Telegraph* (London). Retrieved August 5, 2013.

Mugabe, R. (2003, December 22). In Chikova, L. & Mataire, L. 16 Years on Zim Remains United, in *The Herald*.

Mugabe, R. (2003, August 16). President Implores MDC to Repent, *The Herald*.

Mugabe, R. (2004, November 30). Remain United: President, In *The Herald*.

Mugabe, R. (2004, August 10). Time to Remember Gallant Liberators, In *The Herald*.

Mugabe, R. (2004). In E. V. Masunungure, "Travails of Opposition Politics in Zimbabwe Since Independence", in D. Harold-Barry (ed.), *Zimbabwe: The Past is the Future,* Harare. Weaver Press. pp. 147–192.

Mugabe, R. (2005a, July 15). In Madonko, I. Remain United – President, In *The Herald*.

Mugabe, R. (2005b, February 8). Keep Unity Alive, Says President. In *The Herald*.

Mugabe, R. (2005c, November 20). Zimbabwe Is One Nation. In *The Sunday Mail*.

Mugabe, R. (2008). Campaign Speech. In Ndlovu-Gatsheni, S. "Rethinking Chimurenga and Gukurahundi in Zimbabwe: A Critique of Partisan National History." *African Studies Review 55* (3). pp. 1–26.

Mugabe, R. (2017). Politics Leads the Gun: Mugabe, *Nehanda Radio News*.

Mugabe, R. (2018a). Statement in a Press Conference. *Eye Witness News*. Retrieved October 25, 2018, from https://ewn.co.za/2018/07/29/mugabe-i-will-not-vote-for-those-who-tormented-me.

Mugabe, R. (2018b). In R. Ndlovu (Ed.), *In the Jaws of the Crocodile: Emmerson Mnangagwa's Rise to Power*. Cape Town: Penguin Books.

Mujuru, J. (2013, January 13). Mugabe Challengers Bonkers: Mujuru. Retrieved March 10, 2018, from www.newzimbabwe.com.

Muponde, R. (2004). The Worm and the Hoe: Cultural Politics and Reconciliation after the Third Chimurenga. In B. Raftopoulos & T. Savage (Eds.), *Zimbabwe: Injustice and Political Reconciliation* (pp. 168–88). Cape Town: Institute for Justice and Reconciliation.

Mutambara, A. (2017). Zimbabwe: Mutambara-Mugabe Very Shallow, Intellectually Inadequate and Personally Insecure. Retrieved April 18, 2018, from www.allafrica.com.

Ncube, T. (2009). Foreword. In M. Auret (Ed.), *From Liberator to Dictator: An Insider's Account of Robert Mugabe's Descent into Tyranny*. Claremont: David Philip.

Ncube, T. (2018). Trevor Ncube Backs Mnangagwa: Claims It Was Not a Coup. In *Bulawayo24 News*. Retrieved February 14, 2019, from https://bulawayo24.com/index-id-news-sc-national-byo-133066.html.

Ndlovu, M. (2014). African Leadership in the Age of Euro-North American-centric Modernity: A Decolonial Critique of Robert Mugabe. In S. Ndlovu-Gatsheni (Ed.), *Mugabeism? History, Politics and Power in Zimbabwe*. New York: Palgrave Macmillan.

Ndlovu, M. (2019). Mnangagwa's Ndebele Name Revealed. In *Bulawayo 24 News*. Retrieved January 10, 2020, from https://bulawayo24.com/index-id-news-sc-national-byo-176358.html.

Ndlovu, R. (2018). *In the Jaws of the Crocodile: Emmerson Mnangagwa's Rise to Power*. Cape Town: Penguin Books.

Ndlovu-Gatsheni, S. (2003). Dynamics of the Zimbabwe Crisis in the 21st Century. *African Journal on Conflict Resolution, 3*(1), 99–105.

Ndlovu-Gatsheni, S. (2009). Making Sense of Mugabeism in Local and Global Politics: 'So Blair, Keep Your England and Let Me Keep My Zimbabwe. *Third World Quarterly, 30*(6), 1139–1158.

Ndlovu-Gatsheni, S. (2012a). Rethinking "Chimurenga" and "Gukurahundi" in Zimbabwe: A Critique of Partisan National History. *African Studies Review, 55*(3), 1–26.

Ndlovu-Gatsheni, S. (2012b). Beyond Mugabe-Centric Narratives of the Zimbabwean Crisis: Review Article. *African Affairs, 111*(443), 315–323.

Ndlovu-Gatsheni, S. (2014). Introduction: Mugabeism and Entanglements of History, Politics, and Power in the Making of Zimbabwe. In S. Ndlovu-Gatsheni (Ed.), *Mugabeism? History, Politics, and Power in Zimbabwe.* New York: Palgrave Macmillan.

Ndlovu-Gatsheni, S. (2015). *Mugabeism? History, Politics, and Power in Zimbabwe.* New York: Palgrave Macmillan.

Ndlovu-Gatsheni, S. (2016). *The Decolonial Mandela: Peace, Justice and the Politics of Life.* New York: Bergham Books.

Ndlovu-Gatsheni, S., & Willems, W. (2009). Making Sense of Cultural Nationalism and the Politics of Commemoration Under the Third Chimurenga in Zimbabwe. *Journal of Southern African Studies, 35*(4), 945–965.

Nehanda Radio. (2013). Who Killed Tongoogara and Mujuru? *Nehanda Radio.* Nehandaradio.com. Accessed 10 November 2020.

Nietszche, F. (1972). *The Birth of Tragedy.* New York: Modern Library Press.

Nietzsche, F. (1886/1966). *Beyond Good and Evil* (W. Kaufmann, Trans.). New York. Vintage.

Nietzsche, F. (1968). *The Will to Power.* New York: Vantage Books.

Nietzsche, F. (1969). *Thus Spoke Zarathustra.* London: Penguin Books.

Nietzsche, F. (1979). *"Why I Am so Clever," in Ecce Homo.* London: Penguin Classics.

Nietzsche, F. (1990). *Twilight of the Idols/ The Anti-Christ.* New York: Penguin Books.

Nietzsche, F. (1997a). *Homer's Contest.* In J. Lungstrum & E. Sauer (Eds.), *Arenas of Creative Contest* (pp. 35–45). New York: State University of New York Press.

Nietzsche, F. (1997b). *Daybreak.* London: Cambridge University Press.

Nietzsche, F. (2003). *Thus Spoke Zarathustra.* London: Penguin Books.

Nietzsche, F. (2004a). *Why am I so Clever?* London: Penguin Classics.

Nietzsche, F. (2004b). *Human, All Too Human* (M. Faber and S. Lehmann, Trans.). London: Penguin.

Nietzsche, F. (2009). *The Gay Science.* Cambridge: Cambridge University Press.

Nietzsche, F. (2016). *Why I Am so Clever.* London: Penguin Classics.

Nkomo, J. (1984). *The Story of My Life.* London: Methuen.

Nkomo, J. (2002). *The New Zimbabwe.* Harare: SAPES.

Nkrumah, K. (1964). *Consciencism: Philosophy and Ideology for Decolonisation and Development with particular Reference to the African Revolution.* London: Heinemann.

Norman, A. (2003). *Robert Mugabe and the Betrayal of Zimbabwe.* North Carolina / London: McFarland & Company Inc Publishers.

Norman, A. (2004a). *Robert Mugabe and the Betrayal of Zimbabwe.* Jefferson: McFarland and Co.

Norman, A. (2004b). *Robert Mugabe and the Betrayal of Zimbabwe.* London: McFarland & Company Publishers.

Norman, A. (2008). *Mugabe: Teacher, Revolutionary, Tyrant.* Gloucestershire: History Press.

Nussbaum, M. (1998). Political Animals: Luck, Love and Dignity. *Metaphilosophy, 29*(4), 273–287.

Nyarota, G. (2018). *The Graceless Fall of Robert Mugabe: The End of a Dictator's Reign.* Cape Town: Penguin Random House.

O' Docherty, M. (2016). *The Legacy of Robert Mugabe and the Zimbabwean African National Union-Patriotic-Front: A One Party State facilitating Dictatorship and Disregard for Human Rights.* Crystal Grove Books: North Carolina, Lulu Press Inc.

Onslow, S., & Plaut, M. (2018). *Robert Mugabe.* Johannesburg: Jacana Media.

Orwell, G. (1949). Reflections on Gandhi. *Partisan Review, 16*(1), 85–92.

Plato. (1952). The Seventh Letter. In *The Great Books* (J. Harward, Trans.). Chicago: Encyclopaedia Britannica. 7, pp. 387–391.

Plato. (1993). *Republic.* Oxford: Oxford University Press.

Potholm, C. P. (1979). *The Theory and Practice of African Politics.* New Jersey: Prentice-Hall Inc Publishers.

Power, S. (2008). How to Kill a Country: Turning a Breadbasket into a Basket Case in Ten Easy Steps-the Robert Mugabe Way. *Atlantic Monthly, 292*(5), 86–101.

Ranger, T. (1980). The Changing of the Old Guard: Robert Mugabe and the Revival of ZANU-PF. *Journal of Southern African Studies, 7*(1), 71–90.

Ranger, T. (2003). *The Historical Dimensions of Democracy and Human Rights in Zimbabwe. Volume 2: Nationalism, Democracy and Human Rights.* Harare: University of Zimbabwe Press.

Ranger, T. O. (1967). *Revolt in Southern Rhodesia, 1896-7: A Study in African Resistance.* London: Evanston Northwestern University Press.

Ranier, S. (1978). Fascist Politics as a Total Work of Art: Tendencies of Aesthetization of Political Life in National Socialism. *New German Critique, 14*(47), 48–60.

Rene Fullop-Miller. (1930). *The Power and the Secret of the Jesuits.* New York. The Viking Press.

Reno, W. (1998). *Warlord Politics and African States.* Boulder/London: Lynne Rienner Publishers.

Rogers, D. (2019). *Two Weeks in November: The Astonishing Untold Story of the Operation that Toppled Mugabe.* Jeppestown: Jonathan Ball Publishers.

Rotberg, R. I. (2010). Mugabe über alles: the tyranny of unity in Zimbabwe. *Foreign Affairs,* pp. 10–18.

Rupiya, M. (2005). Zimbabwe: Governance Through Military Operations. *African Security Studies, 14*(3), 116–118.

Sachikonye, L. (2011). *When a State Turns on Its Citizens: 60 Years of Violence in Zimbabwe*. Johannesburg: Jacana Media.

Sadomba, W. (2011). *War Veterans and Zimbabwe's Revolution: Challenging Neocolonialism and Settler International Capital*. Harare / Oxford: Weaver Press / James Currey.

Said, E. W. (1993). *Culture and Imperialism*. New York: Vintage Books.

Said, E. W. (1999). *Out of Place: A Memoir*. London: Granta Books.

Said, E. (2012). On Lost Causes. In *Reflections on Exile and other Literary and Cultural Essays*. London: Granta Books.

Sartre, J. (2001). *Colonialism and Neocolonialism*. London/New York: Routledge.

Saul, J. (2008). *Decolonisation and Empire: Contesting the Rhetoric and Reality of Resurbodination in Southern Africa and Beyond*. Johannesburg: Wits Press.

Saul, J. S., & Saunders, R. (2005). Mugabe, Gramsci and Zimbabwe at 25. *International Journal, 60*, 953–975.

Saunders, R. (2000). *Never the Same Again: Zimbabwe's Growth Towards Democracy*. Harare: Edwina Spicer Productions.

Scarnecchia, T. (2011). Rationalising Gukurahundi: Cold War and South African Foreign Relations with Zimbabwe, 1981–1983. *Kronos, 37*(1), 89–55.

Scarnecchia, T. (2014). Intransigent Diplomat: Robert Mugabe and His Western Diplomacy, 1963–1983. In S. Ndlovu-Gatsheni (Ed.), *Mugabeism?: History, Politics and Power in Zimbabwe*. New York: Palgrave Macmillan.

Schmitt, C. (1996). *The Concept of the Political*. London & Chicago: University of Chicago Press.

Schmitt, C. (2007). *The Concept of the Political*. London & Chicago: University of Chicago Press.

Schmitt, C. (2008). *The Concept of the Political: Expanded edition*. Chicago: University of Chicago Press.

Schopenhauer, A. (1909, 2012). *The world as will and representation*. Berlin: Courier Corporation.

Schramm, P. E. (Ed.). (1965). *Hitlers Tischegessprache im führehauptquartier, 1941–1942*. Stuttgart Germany: Seewald Verlag.

Scudder, C. W. (1972). Psychological Dimensions of Extremism. In E. West (Ed.), *Extremism Left and Right*. Michigan: Eerdmans Publishing Company.

Shamu, W. (2011). Mugabe is like Cremora: Shamu. *News Day*. Newsday.co.zw: Accessed 2 March 2019.

Sithole, S. (1979). On the Assassination of Herbert Chitepo and ZANU, 10 May 1976. In C. Nyangoni & G. Nyandoro (Eds.), *Zimbabwe Independence Movements: Select Documents*. London: Rex Collings.

Smith D., & Simpson C. (1981). *Mugabe Illustrated*. Salisbury: Pioneer Head.

Smith, D., Simpson, C., & Davies, I. (1981). *Mugabe*. London: Sphere Publishers.

Smith, I. (1997). *The Great Betrayal: The Memoirs of Africa's Most Controversial Leader*. London: Blake Publishing.

Snyder, T. (2017). *On Tyranny: Twenty Lessons for the Twentieth Century.* London: Bodley Head.

Stiff, P. (2000). *Cry Zimbabwe.* Alberton: Galago Publishing.

Stollman. (1978). In Rene Fullop-Miller (1930), *The Power and the Secret of the Jesuits.* New York. The Viking Press.

Strauss, J. C., & O'Brien, D. B. C. (2007). Introduction. In J. C. Strauss & D. B. C. O'Brien (Eds.), *Staging Politics.* London: IB Tauris.

Suresh, R. R. (2007). *Fit to Govern: The Native Intelligence of Thabo Mbeki.* Johannesburg: STE Publishers.

Tekere, E. (2007). *Edgar "2boy" Zivanai Tekere: A Life Time of Struggle.* Harare: SAPES Books.

Tendi, B-M. (2008). Patriotic History and Public Intellectuals Critical of Power. *Journal of Southern African Studies, 34*(2), 379–396.

Tendi, B.-M. (2011). Robert Mugabe and Toxicity: History and Context Matter. *Representation: Journal of Representative Democracy., 47*(3), 307–318.

Tendi, B.-M. (2013). Robert Mugabe's 2013 Presidential Election Campaign. *Journal of Southern African Studies, 39*(4), 963–970.

Tendi, B.-M. (2016). State Intelligence and the Politics of Zimbabwe's Presidential Succession. *African Affairs, 115*(459), 203–224.

Tendi, B-M. (2019). The Motivations and Dynamics of Zimbabwe's 2017 Military Coup. *African Affairs,* 1–29.

Thornycroft, P. (2003). Hitler Mugabe Launches Revenge Terror Attacks. *The Telegraph,* www.telegraph.co.uk: Accessed 6 April 2019.

Todd, G. J. (2007). *Through the Darkness: A Life in Zimbabwe.* Cape Town: Struik Publishers.

Tsvangirai, M. (2011). *At the Deep End.* London: Penguin.

Tucker, R. C. (1990). *Stalin in Power; The Revolution from Above, 1928–1941.* New York: Norton Publishers.

Vine, L. T. (1980). African Patrimonial Regimes in Comparative Perspective. *The Journal of Modern African Studies, 18*(4), 657–673.

Wa Africa, M. (2018). In R. Ndlovu (Ed.), *In the Jaws of the Crocodile: Emmerson Mnangagwa's Rise to Power.* Cape Town: Penguin Books.

Wa Thiongo, N. (1987). *Devil on the Cross.* Essex: African Writers Series: Heinemann.

Wa Thiongo, N. (2006). *The Wizard of the Crow.* London: Vintage Books.

Waddell, H. C. (1972). Common Features of Extremism. In E. West (Ed.), *Extremism Left and Right.* Michigan: Eerdmans Publishing Company.

Waite, R. G. L. (1977). *The Psychopathic God: Adolf Hitler.* New York: Basic Books.

Walsh, G. G. (1930). The Power and the Secret of the Jesuits by Rene Fulop-Miller, F.S. Flint and D.F. Tait. *The Catholic Historical Review, 16*(3), 338–340.

Wamba dia Wamba, E. (1996). Pan-Africanism, Democracy, Social Movements and Mass Struggles. *African Journal of Political Science, 1,* 1–133.

Wilber, K. (2017). *Trump and a Post-Truth World*. Colorado: Shambhala.

Woods, K. (2007). *The Kevin Woods Story. In the Shadow of Mugabe's Gallows*. Johannesburg: 30 Degrees South Publishers.

Wyk, V. J.-A. (2007). Political Leaders in Africa: Presidents, Patrons or Profiteers? *Occasional Paper Series: Accord, 2*(1), 2–38.

Zhuwawo, P. (2018). Patrick Zhuwawo Makes Shocking Revelations about Gukurahundi. *New Zimbabwe Vision*. Newzimbababwevision.com. Accessed 10 April 2019.

Zizek, S. (1989). *The Sublime Object of Ideology*. London: Phronesis.

Zizek, S. (1996). The Seven Veils of Paranoia, or, Why Does the Paranoiac Need Two Fathers? *Constellations, 3*(2), 139–156.

Zizek, S. (2001). What Can Lenin Tell Us About Freedom Today? *Rethinking Marxism, 13*(2), 1–9.

Zizek, S. (2003). Critical Response: I, a Symptom of What? *Critical Inquiry, 29*, 486–503.

Zizek, S. (2011). Three Notes on China: Past and Present. *Positions, 19*(3), 707–721.

Zizek, S. (2013). Some Bewildered Clarifications: A Response to Noam Chomsky. *International Journal of Zizek Studies, 7*(2), 1–8.

Zizek, S. (2015). *Trouble in Paradise: From the End of History to the End of Capitalism*. London: Penguin Books.

Zizek, S. (2016). *Against the Double Blackmail: Refugees, Terror and Other Troubles with the Neighbours*. London: Allen Lane: Penguin Books.

Zizek, S. (2017). *The Courage of Hopelessness: Chronicles of the Year of Living Dangerously*. London: Allen Lane: Penguin Books.

INDEX

A

Ablest strategists, 138
Abrahamic faiths, 91
Absolute power, 43, 46, 84, 143, 228, 235, 269, 281, 297
    achieved, 71
    corrupts, 198
Absolutism, 74, 134
    growing political, 71
Accorded star status, 245
Achebe, Chinua, 297, 322
Arrow of God, 118
Activists, 72, 125, 131, 308, 310
    committed human rights, 2
    respected human rights, 14
Aesthetics of vulgarity, 59
Affirmative necessity, 75
Africa, 2, 3, 7–10, 33–39, 67, 87–88, 94, 98–99, 146–148, 154–156, 160, 234, 280–281, 336–338
    new colonisers of, 160–161, 287
    postcolonial 44, 146, 148, 280
    post-independence, 37
African academy, 96

African ancestors and pre-colonial rulers, 205
African anti-imperialist leader, 68
African black masses, 4
African bourgeois class, 160
African bourgeois class of nationalist decolonizes, 161
African condition, 190
African continent, 2, 7
African continentalism, 323
African continental unity, 290
African cosmology, 166
African countries, 57, 154, 160, 337
African country, independent, 147
African despots, 78
African elder statesman, 263
African elite, 8, 160
African first ladies, gathered, 133
African freedom, 214
African heads, 133
African hero of unquestionable standing, 3
African identity, 156
African intellectualism, 190

© The Author(s) 2021
W. J. Mpofu, *Robert Mugabe and the Will to Power in an African Postcolony*, African Histories and Modernities, https://doi.org/10.1007/978-3-030-47879-7

Africanisation, 7
African leaders, 8, 12, 97, 100, 120,
    121, 146, 161, 192, 194, 215
  black, 4, 9
African liberation, 154, 216
  heroism, 3
  leaders, 207
  movements, 149
  struggle, 330
African liberator, 3
African National Congress, 254
African nationalism, 100, 149
  and Marxism, 95, 156
African nationalist, 97, 98, 149,
    160, 187
  consciousness, 8
  elite, 161
  produced, 154
  radical, 149
  rule, 100
  rulers, 97
African neo-traditionalism, 189
Africanness, 156
African norms, 258
African opponents, 240
African organisations, 155
African political decadence, 87
African political humanism, 166
African political leaders, 149
African political leadership
    traditions, 35
African political thought, 87
African political traditions, 35
African politicians, 187
  black, 186
African polities, 67, 255
African post-colonial, 99
African post-colonial attribute, 120
African postcolony, 33, 57, 67, 78, 85,
    96, 104, 212, 273, 280, 323–324
African post-independence, 8
  leaders, 4, 39

African pretentious middle class, 161
African pride, 258
African problem, 34
African ruler, 8
Africans, 3, 4, 16, 68, 87, 94,
    147–148, 156, 160, 165, 178
African state, independent, 149
African statesmanship, 336
African statesmen, 231
African subject, 156
African traditional fathers, 131
African tragic optimists, 4
African tyrants, 33, 35
African unity, 3, 290
African warrior tradition, 87
African writers, 3
Africa's cause, 37
Africa's heads, independent, 120
Africa's post-independence leaders, 9
Afrika, 333
Afroradicalism/Afro-radicalism, 98,
    118, 156–157, 216
Afro-radicalism claims, 156
Afro-radicals, 156
Agendas, 33, 94, 95, 138, 178,
    243, 257
  economic, 11
  high-minded historical, 36
  historical, 33
  imperial, 246
  social, 133
  vengeful, 240
Agriculture, 258, 260, 277
Allende, Salvador (President), 262
  Mugabe, 177
American foundational politics, 40
American political establishments, 175
American powers, 292
Americans, 40
Ancient Shona, 280
Anderson, Benedict, 157, 289, 293
Anglophiles, 159, 251

Anglo-Zimbabwe relations, 251
Anti-Christ, 73, 91, 199
Anti-colonial, 6, 9, 88, 205
  entitlement, 8
  ideologies, 8
Anti-colonial ego, 9
  denialist, 9
Anti-colonialism, 6–8, 10–11, 14, 65,
    88, 163, 187, 259, 336, 337
  confused, 7
  faulty, 163
  performed, 337
  vaunted, 255
Anti-colonialists, 8, 11, 336, 340
  black radical, 264
  die-hard, 6
Anti-Colonial Spectacles, 6
Anti-heroes, dangerous, 78
Anti-imperialism, 88, 337
  muscular, 2
  radical, 216
Anti-philosopher, 75
Anti-Semitism, 33, 140
Antithesis/anti-thesis, 100, 103, 254
Anti-ZANU-PF, 285
Apartheid, 160, 181, 258,
    264–265, 330
Apartheidic, 264
Apartheid machineries, 160
Apartheid regime, 254, 276
  racist South African, 330
Apartheid South Africa, 3, 5, 245,
    255, 275
Apartheid theorist, 279
Apostle of Satan, 244
Apostolic Faith Christian church, 319
Arab rulers, 68
Arab Summit, 68
Archaic phenomenon, 29
Arch-strategist, 93
Aristotle, 21, 191
Armageddon, 89

Armah, Ayi Kwei, 37
Armed struggle, 192, 195, 242–243
Armed takeover, 241, 242, 269
Army, 19, 80–82, 86, 207, 258,
    276–279, 287, 299,
    309–311, 323
  guerrilla, 80
  old Rhodesian, 323
  politicised, 329
  regular, 277
  respective liberation war, 269
  senior Rhodesian, 15
  unified, 279
Assassinations, 21, 54, 162, 219,
    311, 318
  critical, 34, 40
  dismissive, 231
  fittest, 95
  insane, 231
  political, 41, 142

B
Baghdad, 187
Beliefs, 26, 27, 29, 33–35, 121,
    122, 141–146, 163, 172,
    198–199, 202, 207–209,
    213, 266–267
  core, 145
  dangerous, 9
  heroes and heroism, 27
  ideological, 153
  opportunistic, 60
  optimistic, 26
  partisan, 268
  passionate, 219
  personal, 266
  political, 267
  tragic, 19
Benjamin, Walter, 234
Bhebhe, Ngwabi, 155, 288
Bible, 132

Biblical, 265, 268
  allusions, 283
  A bibliophile, 73
  Herod, 43
  proportions, 174
Biological Mugabe, 141
Biological warfare, 282
Bitterness, 54, 151, 153,
  245, 259–261
  personal, 151
Black empowerment, 99
Black Jesuses, 283
Black leaders, 7, 147, 192
  educated, 149
  well-spoken, 147
Black man, 249
Black man wants to be white, 249
Black market, 226, 324
Black marketeering, 41, 226–227, 320
Blackness, 186, 249, 251
Black politicians, 7, 146, 176
Black politics, 104
Blacks, 4, 12–15, 87, 252–253, 255,
  258–260, 263, 337, 340
  educated, 259
  hated, 263
Black Zimbabweans, 13–14,
  16–17, 340
Blair, Tony (British Prime Minister),
  156, 264
Blind faith, 26, 341
Blood diamonds, 324, 330
Blood enemies, 166
Bloodless rivalry, 88
Bloodletting, 62, 72, 83, 241
Blood lust, 277
Bloody, 58, 101, 323
  businesses, 86, 101
  consequences, 335
  heritage, 306
Blown, 76, 190, 216
Bludgeoning, heavy, 322

Blunders, 163, 204
Bokassa, Jean-Bedel, 293
Bourgeois classes, 160–161
  emergent, 160
  emerging African, 160
  new, 160
Brave decolonial liberator, 337
Brave spirit medium, 60
Bribe war-veterans, 83
Brigade, 251, 275–276
  mourned-Five, 282
  special, 300
Britain, 163, 176, 206–207, 217,
  245–246, 260–261, 264, 299
  Agreement, 244
  Christian missionary, 125
  colonisers, 161
  Empire, 255
  farmers, 234
  Governor, 241
  idea of, 260
  impressed black masses, 186
  politicians, 185, 251
  Prime Minister, 231, 286
  Rhodesians, 256
  Royal Family, 252
  White sensibility, 258
British Broadcasting Corporation
  (BBC), 264
Bulawayo, 126, 228, 273–274, 334
Bulloch & Morris, 191
Bureaucrat of death, 123
Bush, George, 246
Bush, George (Junior), 210

C
Caesar, Julius, 77, 285, 318
Cameroonian postcolony, 61, 227
Cannibalisation, 294–297
Cannibalism, 291, 293–294
  political, 293

Cannibalistic, 293
Carter, Jimmy (President), 146
Cartesianism, 207
Cartesian logic, 207
Cash, 60
    scarce, 38
Catholic Brotherhood, distinct, 141
Catholic priests, 128, 285
Catholics, 141, 149
Celebrating Mugabe's elevation, 229
Celebration, 43, 61, 65, 86, 93, 291,
        294, 327, 332, 334
    insane, 64, 77
    philosophical, 43
    public, 328
    spectacular, 46
    tyrant's obscene, 63
    vaunting, 62
Chauvinism and authoritarianism, 118
Chauvinists, 97–98
Chiwenga, General, 316, 325
Christ, 58, 72–73, 124, 144–145,
        200, 284
    Jesus, 258, 283
    political, 73
Christian religion, 285, 341
Christians, 71–73, 118, 141,
        144–145, 200
    real, 145
    true, 145
Christmas, 57
Citizens, 10, 32, 57–59, 98, 178, 229
    contented, 58
    White, 291
Citizenship, 212
Colonial, 7–10, 13, 34, 146, 148–150,
        158–159, 161, 216, 257–259,
        287, 336–340
    admired, 160
    acculturation, 251
    administration, 158, 340
    army, 258

authoritarianism, 161
civilisation, 338
class, 9
climate, 253
fundamentalism, 336
grudges, 340
history, 226
humiliation, 16
idea, 102
imagination, 166, 198
influence, 163
replaced, 9
Colonial domination, 105, 154, 166,
        192, 322
    reproduced, 337
Colonialism, 3–7, 9–11, 13–14,
        27–28, 32–35, 100, 105,
        120–121, 149, 154–155,
        159–164, 186–187, 205–206,
        213–216, 226, 258,
        285, 336–340
    administrative, 33, 69
    dethroned, 154
Colonialists, 6, 156, 188, 279, 287
    new, 98
    White, 7
Coloniality, 5–7, 9, 104, 106, 154, 156,
        162, 166, 336–337, 339, 341
    global, 158
    redefine, 166
    reproduced, 88
    survived, 339
Colonial politics, 3, 8, 85, 87,
        103–104, 161–162, 309, 315
Colonial rule, 7, 100, 159
Colonial sensibility, 161, 259
    internalising, 152
Colonial subjection, 228, 250
    enduring, 250
Colonial subjects, 249–250, 253, 258
    black, 250
    true, 35

Colonial violence, 10, 88, 121, 287
Colonies, 102, 105, 292, 307, 337
  former, 337
  settler, 176
Colonisers, 4, 9–11, 13, 33–35,
    87–88, 149, 158, 161, 186, 187,
    212, 213, 249–252, 256, 257,
    336, 339–340
  former, 13, 92, 104, 159, 250,
    256–257, 259
  new, 117, 158, 257
  new black, 4, 10
  settler imperialist, 249
  white, 149, 186, 188,
    250, 252–253
Colonising, 55, 163, 249
  colonial subject, 35, 150, 251, 341
Colonist, 205
Colonization, 160
Colonizers, 160
Colossal gatherings, 238
Commander-in-chief, 195
Congo, 320, 323, 324, 329, 330
Conquest and domination, 61–63, 68,
    86, 102, 243, 337
Constitution, 23, 40, 310, 329
Conviviality, spectacular, 308
Counter-revolutionaries, 300
Counter-threat, 317
Country, 1–3, 5–9, 22–25, 37–39,
    98–100, 147–148, 156–157,
    173–175, 212–214, 242–248,
    254–255, 269–271, 278,
    284–287, 297–300, 305–307,
    321–324, 331–334
Coup, 54, 134, 183–184, 194,
    198–200, 305–309, 312,
    314–315, 317, 318, 321, 322,
    325, 327–336
  real, 322
Coup d'état, 39, 274, 306, 319
Courageous confrontation, 331

Courts, 23, 45, 46, 60, 68, 107, 178,
    234, 310
  international criminal, 219
Crimes, 22, 53–56, 58, 84, 271,
    277–278, 285, 289, 293, 297,
    299, 313–314
Culture, 10–11, 13, 36, 38, 102, 118,
    161, 185, 201, 213, 214, 218

D
Dark chamber, 57
Dark covert capabilities, 21
Dark extremes, 183
Dark legacy decorates, 58
Death, 1, 3, 5, 21, 57–59, 74, 82,
    107, 175–177, 179, 180,
    182–183, 282–283,
    295, 324–325
  physical, 270, 293–294
  suspicious, 74
Death Mugabe, 175
  body, 180
Deception and cunning in politics, 92
Decision maker, 62
Declassified intelligence
    documents, 330
Decolonial, 3, 4, 6–7, 45–47, 100, 205
  critique, 250
Decolonial humanism, 153
Decoloniality, 6–7, 87, 158, 337, 339
Decolonisation, 33–35, 39–41, 78,
    147, 158, 243, 254, 339
Decolonise, 36
Decolonisers, 161, 339
Decolonising effort, 163
Decolonists, 32
Decolonization, 7
Deluded political prophets and
    messiahs, 200
Delusions, 9, 71, 74, 121, 128, 134,
    139, 172, 220, 233, 235

Democracy, 18, 29, 37, 92, 99, 156, 162, 165, 166, 176, 204, 335–336
Democratic activism, 69
Democratic Republic, 320, 322–323, 330
Democratic substitute, 232
Democratic theory, 29
Democratic thinking, 28
Democratisation, 48
Demonising, 204
Demons, 124, 264
  stubborn, 228
Denialism, 135, 210, 270, 285, 289, 296, 300, 325, 338
  denies, 135
  political, 9, 296
Denials, 106, 271, 308
Dependency complex, 256
Descartes, Rene, 207, 209, 285
Deserted mine-shafts, 282
Despotic mind, 74
Despotic strategies
Despotism, 62, 67, 78, 155, 203
  insane, 68
Despots, 43, 48, 55, 68, 74, 79, 85, 116, 123, 172, 178
Destitution, 175
Destruction, 175, 199, 267, 277
Detention, 104, 131, 192, 206
Dethrone, 3, 6, 34, 104
Dethronement, 226, 230, 327
Detractors, 138, 215
Devil, 4, 208–209
The devil incarnate, 138
Devilish, 209–210
  self-righteousness, 209
Devout participant, 141
Diabolic, 33, 91, 310
Dialogue, 29, 90, 97, 145, 249
Diamond, 37, 211, 321
Dictators, 3, 8, 13, 79, 177, 239, 253, 329, 333
  benevolent, 336

brutal, 34
fascist, 184
liberator to, 2
singular, 156
venal, 237
Dinyane Declaration, 319
Diplomacy, 205, 206
Diplomas, 146, 148
Diplomats, 130, 185, 192, 205–206
Disciples, 58, 284
Disciplinarians, strict, 141
Discipline, 56, 65, 75, 93, 140, 143, 145, 150, 151, 158, 162
  maintaining, 158
  physical, 129
  strict, 129
  strong, 145
  superior, 139
Disease, 21, 264, 281–282
  chronic, 21
  curable, 322
Disemboweling, 22
Disinvestment, 203
Disorder, 56, 232, 236–237, 296
  executive, 46
  political, 227
  radical, 236
Dissident menace, 275
Dissimulate, 237
Dissimulations, 25, 183, 206
Disunity, 157, 298–299
  national, 298
Divine, 130–131, 145, 172, 187, 199, 202, 229, 234, 266, 268
Divine anointing believed, 235
Divine anointment, 121, 172, 342
Divine appointee, 234
Divine appointment, 301
Divine wisdom, 121
Divinity, 73, 121, 198, 213, 230, 237, 262
Doctoral Degree, 324

Doctorates, 187, 209, 324–325
  honorary, 11
Doctrines, 99, 143, 156
  religious, 141
Dogmas, 99, 156, 267
Dogmatic inflexibility, 140
Domesticate, 67
Dominance Mugabe, 187
Domination, 42–43, 55–56, 61–68,
    72, 83–88, 90–92, 99, 102–105,
    107, 155, 189–190, 226, 315
Dominators, 28, 156, 157, 159
Domineering, 47
Dongo, Margaret, 82, 105, 130–131
Dongo's accusation, 131
DRC Congo, 323
DRC war, 211
DRC war and repeated political
    violence, 323
Dying civilisation, 339
Dyke, Lionel (Colonel), 282
Dzinashe Machingura, 25

E
Early childhood abandonment, 261
Early family life, 125
Earth, 10, 106, 142, 145, 153, 172,
    179, 181, 220, 286, 342
Earth Summit, 156
Eastern Europe, 177
Eccentric behaviour, 120
Eccentricities, 39, 119–120
Economic benefits, 211
Economic elites, 37, 212
Economic expediency, 177
Economic issues, 208
Economics 69, 144, 184, 208, 209
Economy, 10–11, 54, 55, 59, 83,
    242–243, 246, 297, 307, 321,
    323, 325
  collapsed, 188
  collapsing, 323

intimate, 130, 323
loot, 178
political, 156, 200, 322
Eden narratives, 198
Education, 72–73, 118, 120, 122,
    144, 146–153, 160, 161,
    186–190, 212, 215, 216,
    253, 254
  colonising, 149
  elevated, 250, 253
  finest, 189
  good, 187, 190
  grand, 251
  modern, 186–188
  political, 161, 288
  superior, 147–148, 163, 187
  university, 147
Egyptians, 59
Eichmann, Adolf Otto, 123, 209
Elections, 15, 36–37, 55, 82–83, 89,
    228–233, 246, 248, 268, 269,
    331, 334
  democratic Zimbabwean, 30
  disputed, 297, 329
  fair, 29, 47, 232, 331
  first, 22, 30
  first Zimbabwean, 76
  historical, 231
  parliamentary, 298
  presidential, 47, 157, 231, 299
  regular, 37
  rigging, 92
Electoral fraud, 15, 24, 92, 246
Electoral Fraudster, 229
Electoral outcomes, 338
Electoral victory, 24, 231, 246, 310
Enemies, 18–19, 26–27, 64, 69, 74,
    85, 88–89, 92–93, 98, 135–138,
    157, 164, 166, 182, 183, 191,
    199–200, 262, 267–268,
    271–272, 281
  country's, 299
  eternal, 99

fighting, 124
imaginary, 151
imagined, 269
new, 86, 157
real, 76, 98, 247
stubborn, 74
total, 89, 268
turn, 89
ultimate, 164, 268
white, 194
Engels, Friedrich, 149
Epistemic conditions, 272
Epistemicide, 275, 286
Epistemologies, 166
Escape, 78, 81–83, 124, 126, 130, 198,
    200, 311, 316, 334, 338, 339
Escapist tendencies, 81
Espouse, 72, 104, 197, 251
Essence, 3, 15, 18, 95, 183, 237,
    245, 259
Essentialist, 235
Eternity, 39, 120
Ethical abnegations, 144
Ethical practice, 89
Ethics, 90, 100, 103, 144, 207, 232
political, 93, 271
Ethnical dictatorship, authentic, 280
Euphoria, 11, 26–28, 40, 71, 174,
    248, 327–329, 332
black, 147
Eurocentric fundamentalisms, 165
Eurocentric modernity, 165
Europe, 69, 71, 75, 78, 131, 206,
    252, 260, 338
European colonizers, 160
European culture, 256
Evans, Sir Martin, 177
Evil, 3–5, 25–27, 29, 39–40, 64, 65,
    69–70, 77, 83–84, 87–88, 95,
    176–177, 181–182, 202–203,
    208–210, 244–246, 279–283,
    287–289, 334
appearance, 238

axis of, 101, 246
banality of, 270, 276–278, 282
debunking, 88
demon, 209
designed, 275
double, 83
enemies, 335
intentions, 276
isolating, 87
monster, 92
operation, 283
passions, 64
perpetuate, 283
personification of, 245, 284
political, 273
Excessive behaviour, 120
Execution, 194, 218, 257, 270, 276
unleash wanton, 219
Executive hooligan, 286
true, 212
Exhibitionism, 218
Exhibitionist, 134, 218
Exile, 150, 287, 291, 311, 316,
    319, 334
patriotic, 2
self-imposed, 313
short, 313
Existential deviation, 256
Exonerating, 301
Exoneration, 175
Expansion, 77, 237
Mugabe's education, 117
Exterminate, 299
Extermination, 300
Extra-legal operation, 271
Extremes, 30, 63, 80, 179, 282
Extremism, 77, 266

F
Faith, 58, 93, 132, 142, 182–183,
    187, 231, 319, 320
greatest, 140

Fake, 173, 187, 237, 245, 324
  doctors, 324
  generosity, 254
  identities, 198
  news, 339
  paradise, 198
  reality, 238
  religions, 178
Falls, Victoria, 273, 284
Family, 25, 27, 119, 122, 125–127,
    132, 133, 135, 137, 202, 203,
    233–234, 290, 293, 295
  Big dynasty, 7, 134, 290
  house, 134
  imaginary, 132
  life, 122, 125, 128, 233
  life invent, 125
  secret national, 234
  personal, 119
  unit, 135
Fanon, Frantz, 97, 154, 155, 157,
    160, 249–251, 259, 261, 280,
    281, 286, 290
Fascists, 75, 253
Fast Track Land Reform Programme,
    14, 216, 264, 299
Father, 119, 122, 123, 126–127,
    129–130, 132–133, 141, 175,
    256, 261, 295
  absent, 126, 129–131, 142
Fears, 12–15, 18–19, 41–43, 53–56,
    63–65, 80–83, 97–98, 100–101,
    119–126, 128, 172–173, 182,
    183, 208, 218–219, 226–228,
    232, 233
February Movement, 58
Femininity, 104–106
Feminisation, 106
Fetish, 31, 36, 118, 139, 148,
    187, 234
Fetishism, 342
  corrupt, 32
Fidelity, 336

Fifth Brigade, 28, 68, 269, 272,
    274–279, 283, 296
Fight, 6, 8, 34, 82, 84, 94, 151, 155,
    157, 159, 161, 195, 336–337
  bare-knuckled fist, 81
  bitter, 161
  colonialism, 10, 33–35, 100, 205, 315
  coloniality, 162
  domination, 32
  good, 82, 84
  monsters, 6
  monstrosities, 100
  negative, 6
  oppression, 316
  physical, 80
  positive, 6
  settler colonialism, 161
Fighters, 213, 226, 339
  black, 264
  nationalist liberation, 161
  supposed, 161
Fighting
  colonial domination, 33
  credentials, 82
  monstrosities, 339
  personality, 136
  political, 268
Fighting colonialism, 5, 9, 11
Fired Emmerson Mnangagwa, 313
Firing squad, 261
First February Movement, 236
First Lady, 133, 134
  learned, 134
  Mugabe, Grace, 8
First Secretary, 74
Flags, 94, 95, 99, 145, 240
  new, 4
Flatterers, 22, 55, 73, 125, 139,
    171–174, 178–179, 198, 220,
    239, 301
  artless, 139
  selfish, 173
Flatters, 60, 139

Flattery, 74, 139, 172, 220
  insane, 220
Flawed premises, 28
Flawed reality testing, 183
Force legitimacy, 85
Forces combined, 48
Force victory, 246
Foreign Affairs, 330
Foreign affairs trophy, 245
Foreign business moguls, 320
Foreign business underworld, 321
Foreign investors, 58, 226
Foreign minister, 246
Foreign office trophy, 163
Foreign personnel, 160
Formative conditioning, 233
Formative education, 141
Formative influence, 127
Formative site, 125
Formative years, 71, 127
Former guerrillas, 211, 305–308,
  312, 324
Former Rhodesians, 240, 256
Fragile anti-colonialism, 56
Fraud, 37, 39, 47, 48, 54, 60, 86,
  101–102, 226, 229, 337, 340
Fraudulent, 101, 338, 342
Freedom, 3, 4, 33–35, 39, 48, 95,
  117, 152–153, 255, 259,
  339, 341
  fighting, 33
  hard-won, 299
  human, 153
  pagan, 144
  political, 18
Freedom fighter, 2–7, 10, 12, 14–15,
  25, 26, 35, 75, 77, 180
Frelimo's distrust of Mugabe, 192
French origins, 141
Freud, Sigmund, 46
  death, 30
Freudian narcissist, 45
Freudians sense, 159

Fukuyama, Francis, 69
Fulop-Miller, Rene, 143
Fundamentalisms, 33, 63, 78, 118,
  163, 204, 254, 267
  indigenous, 165
  political, 89, 180–182
  postcolonial, 56
  religio-ideologico-political, 146
Fundamentalist, 22, 24, 67, 118, 227,
  262, 264–267, 301
  anti-modern, 165
  reduction, 249
  underside, 98
Funded opposition parties, 299
Funerals, 74, 150, 250, 266
  low key, 180

G
G40, 313
Gaddafi, Muammar, 68
  description, 68
Gallant anti-colonial, 94
Gallant fighter, 68
Gallant Pan-Africanist, 290
Gallant peace-maker, 92
Gallant warrior, 55, 191, 337
Gandhi, Mahatma, 181
Genocidal, 8, 98, 266, 271,
  277–279, 321
Genocide, 23, 24, 27, 29, 97–98,
  160, 210, 269–287,
  289, 294–297
Genocidists, 272
  tyrant, 44
Gerentocracy, 106
Gerrymandering, 103
Ghana, 3, 37, 38, 131–133,
  147–150, 186
Global North, 154
Global Politics, 118
Global South, 32–34, 46, 85,
  102–103, 154, 158, 178, 337

God, 20, 59, 106–108, 117–123,
    135–136, 141–144, 172,
    178–180, 206, 220, 229–231,
    233–235, 283–285,
    293, 341–342
Godfather, 53, 233, 316
    aging, 53
Godification, 114
Gospel, 17, 29, 220, 292
    political, 74
Government, 23, 25, 195,
    233–234, 236, 274, 276,
    293, 297–300,
    310–311, 313–314
    appointees, 248
    black, 138
    democratic, 45
    forces, 212
    minister, 271
    senior, 322
    totalitarian, 178
    transitional, 331
    western, 336
Governor, 32, 255
    care-taker, 255
Grace, Gucci, 133
Grandfather, 326
Grandiosity, 18, 21
    political, 4
Grand narratives, 39, 95
Great Zimbabwe, 205
Grim realities, 194
Grim understanding, 69
Guerrilla leader, 185,
    191–193, 196–197
Guerrilla movement, 162, 190, 191,
    194–196, 306, 311
    rogue, 311
Guerrillas, 38, 149, 159, 185,
    191–195, 210, 211, 218, 233,
    241, 257, 258, 268
    brave, 185

camps, 162, 193, 307
coerce, 193
legitimate, 195
thought, 194
war competencies, 192
Gukurahundi, 23, 97, 177, 269–271,
    274, 280, 283, 284, 294
Gukurahundi Genocide, 8, 22–24,
    97–98, 208, 267–275, 278–287,
    294–297, 309, 314,
    330–331, 334–335
    mass graves, 296
    post-independence, 162
Gullible audiences, 182
Gullible plebeians, 17
Guns, 54–56, 62, 76–77, 82–83, 85,
    194–195, 232–234, 308, 309,
    311–312, 323
    salute, 326

H
Hammurabi, 187
Harare, 59, 107, 145, 177, 228,
    245, 323
Harold-Barry, David, 321
Hate, 3, 54, 90, 104, 123, 126–128,
    248, 249, 260–267, 288
    political, 267
Head of Government, 74, 236, 281
Healers, traditional, 20
Hell, 10, 32, 59, 72, 78, 108, 146,
    208, 237, 257, 268
Heraclitus, 85
Herd, 81, 188–189
    boys, 81
    consciousness, 189
    instincts, 189
    national, 60
Heresy, 107, 342
Heretics, 75, 96, 220
Heritage, 24, 106, 232

Hero/heroes, 2, 11, 14–18, 27, 33, 63–64, 68–71, 78, 117, 180, 210, 214, 264, 291–294, 327, 329, 332, 335
Heroes Acre, 107, 108, 134, 180, 292–294
Heroes Day celebrations, 267
Heroism, 12–15, 17, 27, 68, 71, 181–182, 214, 215, 328, 331–332, 335
  black, 259
High Command, 193
  old ZANLA, 193
High Commissioner, 177
Higher Education, 184, 185, 230
High priest, 152
  political, 73
  true political, 267
  unquestionable, 188
Hill, Geoff, 136, 177
Historical political stalemate, 4
Historical reality, 31
Historical records, 274–275, 286
Historical scenario, 121
Historical site, 2
Historical task, 340
Historical travails, 75
History, 14–16, 26–28, 44, 63–64, 66, 76, 78–79, 84–85, 87, 118, 122, 157–158, 178–179, 184, 185, 275, 298–300, 323, 327, 328, 330–333
  concrete, 229
  conflicted, 240
  falsify, 298
  monopolise, 107
  Nietzsche, 87
  political, 118, 313
  produced, 122
  rewriting, 299
  traumatising, 121
  treacherous, 331

  true, 177
  true non-revolutionary, 288
  understandings, 64
  unfortunate, 176
Hitler, Adolf, 20, 21, 41–42, 75, 90, 123, 127, 184, 186, 197, 199–201, 209, 227, 237, 238, 277, 313
  Germany, 279
  mad, 22
  tenfold, 41
Hitler Mugabe, 75
Hitler of History, 22
HIV/AIDS, 21
Holland, Heidi, 77–78, 81–82, 104, 107, 117, 119, 126–132, 135–138, 141–147, 151, 152, 159–163, 171–172, 187, 199, 201–202, 04–206, 229–230, 243–247, 250, 252–254, 256–258, 260
Heidi, 26–27
Hollywood, 237
  and hell, 77
Holocaust, 270, 278
Homosexuals, 42, 265, 266
Hondo Yeminda, 307
Hooliganism, 310
  executive, 54, 236, 309
  true, 102
Hooligans, 10, 103
  unpolished political, 73
Hostage, 18, 34, 91, 118, 198, 285
Host guerrilla bases, 255
Hostility, 29, 139
  expected, 140
Human beings, 17, 26, 28–29, 47, 122, 125, 141, 159, 254, 259, 262
Humanisation, 39, 48, 72, 188, 341
Humanising, 175

Humanism, 47, 87, 90–91, 106
  critical, 103
  philosophy, 103
  Rhodesian colonialists, 340
Humanists, 32, 47, 104,
    203, 339–341
  true, 340
Humanist theory, 103
Humanity, 44, 164, 174, 180, 184–185,
    237, 239, 271–273, 277, 281, 289
  black, 18
  common, 253
Humanness, 256
Human rights, 99, 144, 176, 206,
    214, 265, 285
  abuses, 177
  lawyers, 328
Humble births, 120–121
Hunger, 55, 99, 120, 152, 182, 284
Hussein, Saddam, 19, 182–183, 187,
    191, 218
Hyperinflation, 34

I
Identity politics, 279, 320
Ideologies, 36, 67, 95–96, 98–100,
    118–120, 146, 153–158,
    272, 279
  and Utopia, 154
Ideologisation, 161, 228
Idi Amin, 3, 74, 217, 310
Idolatrous, 142, 209
Idolatry, 200, 292, 341
  political, 342
Idolisation, 26
  political, 342
Idolising, 142
Idols, 292, 341
  political, 342
Image of Mugabe, 210, 215, 294
Impeachment, 40–41

Imperviousness, 225
Imprisonment, 121, 150, 228,
    248, 256
Incarceration, 42
Incident, 37, 41, 82, 132, 250, 259,
    263, 282
  anecdotal, 250
  humiliating, 263
  lucky, 42
Independence, 4, 6, 7, 9–10, 13, 40,
    205–207, 212, 213, 215, 240,
    257–259, 261
  movement, 161
  political, 26, 336, 337, 340
  tyrants, 34
Indigenous, 234, 279
Individuals, 22–23, 25, 28, 79, 80,
    202, 204, 212, 214, 233, 237,
    320–323, 327–328
  ambitious, 44
  forceful, 22
  foreign, 320
  fragile, 182
  legitimate, 136
  opportunistic, 23
  rare, 120
  sick, 125
  well-intentioned, 163, 204
  white, 248
  why the paranoiac, 126
Indoctrination, 277
Inferiority, 129–130, 243, 251, 259
  constructed, 262
Informalisation, 54
Infrastructures, 7, 138, 159, 336
  dilapidated, 5
Ingqindi yegwala iyingozi, 81
Insane
  contradiction, 325
  ideas, 226, 227, 234
  imaginism, 229
  inability, 342

irrelevance, 232
Mugabe, Robert, 234
personage, 19
political lottery, 231
Insanities, 45, 55, 66–70, 74, 219,
     228, 229, 233–236, 282, 301
  political, 95, 177, 178, 219,
     227–229, 233–235
  pornographic philosophical, 79
  pure, 297
  true, 171, 233
Insecure chap, 25
Insecurity, 21, 68, 80, 81, 160, 182
  inordinate, 25
  insider, 334
  sector, 318
  system, 334
Inseparable twins, 232
Insider outsider, 217
Insiders, 99, 157, 283, 317, 318
  privileged, 317
  state security, 272
  trusted, 203, 319
Institutions, 26, 32, 40, 118, 201,
     203, 321, 322
  central democratic state, 45
  defend, 23
  defending, 178
  democratic, 69, 78, 329, 331
  international, 173
  productive, 150
  strong, 174
Insurrectionary tendencies, 242
Intellect, 206, 253
  average, 25
  combative, 138
  superior, 25
  an unhappy, 79
International musical celebrity, 134
International outcast, 214
International pressure, 76
International scales, 179

International solutions, 179
International standing, 273
International status, 68
International television, 310
International tourists, 273–274
Interregnum
  forbidding political, 4
  typical, 4
Invincibility, 9, 54, 184, 319
Irish legend and revolution, 207
Iscariot, Judas, 203

J
Jaws, 330, 332, 336
Jenkins, Martin, 64, 79, 95
Jerusalem, 209
Jesuit, 139–141, 143–145, 150, 207,
     228, 256
Jesuitical experience, 71
Jesuitisation, 139
Jesuitised, 141, 146
Jesuitised Mugabe, 200
Jesuitism, 139, 141, 143, 146
  unmasking, 143
Jesuit Mission, 141–143
Jesuit priests, 71, 123, 137, 139,
     141–142, 187
  radical, 141
  white, 249
Jesus, 139–141, 143, 283
Jesus Christ
  The Jewel of Africa, 246
Johnson, Samue, 99
Journalists, 1–2, 117, 120, 174–176,
     182, 184, 196–199, 210,
     212, 331–335
Judases, 72, 240, 319
Judiciary, 105, 310
Jurisprudence, 144, 328
Justice, 14, 41, 73, 94–96, 179,
     190–192, 195, 197, 284, 288

K

Kant, Immanuel, 164
Kaunda, Kenneth, 47, 103, 166, 194,
    207, 242, 294, 336–337
    commitment, 337
Kenyatta, Jomo, 149
Khama, Seretse, 294
Kidnappers, 273–275
Kidnapping, 273–275
Kidnapping of International
    Tourists, 273–274
Kim II Sung, 77
King of Kings of Africa, 68
King of the castle, 143
Kings of Africa, 68
Kissinger, Henry, 85
Knowledge, 72–73, 94, 118,
    128–129, 148, 186, 197, 270,
    273–274, 278, 285
Knowledgeability, 195
Kriger, Norma, 7

L

Lacanian narcissist, 163
Lacanian paranoiac, 45
Lacoste Faction, 307, 311
Lancaster House Agreement, 241
Land, 13–14, 58, 61, 94, 97–98, 156,
    157, 216, 217, 306, 307
    invasions, 208
    promised, 27–28, 31, 74,
        203–204, 228
    redistribution, 8
    sacred, 292
Language, 11, 24, 44–45, 77, 85–86,
    90–91, 94, 186,
    261–263, 265–266
    angry, 262
    deployed dehumanising, 262
Languaging, 261–268
    of Hate, 261–266

Large-scale corruption, 332
Large scale killings, 210
Large scale Mugabe, 188
Large scale violence, 188, 204, 270,
    283, 306
Large scale violent revenge, 271
Last days, 39
Latin America, 165
Law, 22, 26, 45, 46, 53–55, 58, 203,
    206, 208, 209, 212, 311, 315
    constitutional, 144
    dangerous dismissing, 76
Lawlessness, 227
    executive, 10, 22, 44, 105
Lawmaker, great, 187
Lawyers, 68, 331, 335
    vigilant, 328
Leaders, 7–8, 16–17, 26–27, 32–35,
    38–39, 86, 93–96, 116–124, 139,
    148–150, 155–156, 186, 191,
    192, 202–203,
    213–218, 280–281
    tyrannical, 99, 117, 158
Leadership, 35, 147–149, 151, 186,
    187, 191–193, 195, 200, 213,
    215, 216, 233, 310
Legacy, 14, 15, 25, 291, 295, 306,
    307, 310, 316, 323, 337, 342
Legitimacy, 160, 231, 234, 239
Legitimate forms, 29
Legitimates, 26
Legitimating, 89
Legitimation, 85, 146, 148, 149
Lesbians, 42, 265–266
Lesotho, 288
Lesser educated Morgan
    Tsvangirai, 187
Liberate, 32, 78, 104, 157, 165,
    239, 288, 295, 316,
    336, 338–340
    first, 341
Liberated country, 186

Liberating, 47, 103, 104, 130,
    321, 339–341
  light, 40
  terms, 154
Liberation, 6–8, 28–29, 32–34,
    39–40, 45–47, 67–73, 87–88,
    101–108, 123–124, 161–163,
    165–166, 204–205,
    336–337, 339–341
Liberation struggle, 7, 17, 94, 185,
    210, 213–215, 219, 255, 271, 281
  national, 214
Liberation war, 7, 88, 161, 190,
    213–214, 264
Liberties, 39, 66
License, 282–283
Life, 1, 36, 54, 61–63, 82, 87, 106,
    126–128, 136, 151, 163, 164,
    199, 203, 231–232, 268,
    294–296, 310–312,
    324–325, 337–339
Local indigenous practice, 165
Locations global, 210
Logic, 11, 24, 32, 90, 99, 290, 317
  inner, 61
  real, 317
Looting, 26, 37, 38, 58, 211, 227,
    310, 320, 324, 330
Lord Carrington's observation, 242
Loubiere, Jean-Baptiste, 141
Love, 12, 14, 15, 55, 76, 79, 94, 115,
    127–132, 138–139, 249–250,
    256, 260–261, 312
  affair, 133
Loyal, 20, 93, 107, 131, 313
  followers, 108
  sons, 316
  speaking x-ZANLA forces, 279
  subjects, 107
  water carrier, 313, 317
Loyalists, 116, 308, 334
  opportunistic, 199, 214

Loyalty, 96, 211, 308, 312–313
  enduring, 313
  fanatical ideological, 97, 279
Loyola, Saint Ignatius, 139–141, 143
Lucifer, 108, 207–209, 244
  biblical, 245
  treacherous, 228
  true, 207
Luciferic terms, 101
Lucky Asuelime, 3
Ludicrousness, 310
Lunacy, 95, 227, 233, 235
Lunatic, 235
  dangerous, 172, 220
  of one idea, 282
Lutheran, 71

M
Machel, Samora, 98, 191, 192,
    242–243, 247, 294
  signed, 242
Machiavelli, Niccolo, 5, 12, 48,
    61–65, 91–92, 102, 116, 121,
    124, 139, 159, 320, 331
Machiavellian, 93–95, 240
  leader, 124
  princes, 93–94
  science of power, 94
  sense Mugabe, 159
  true, 93
Machiavellianism, 67, 92–93
Mad Bob, 173, 183, 204, 220
Mad dictator, 177
Mad dog of the Middle East, 68
Madness Mugabe, 289
  moment of, 282
  perspectival, 342
Mafiadom, 316–318, 321
  exploitative, 321
Mafia family, 316–317
Mafia Godfather, 53

Magical, 58–61
Magician, 57–59, 64
    intoxicated, 59
Magnanimity, 91
Magnanimous, 230
Magnificence, 44, 66
    and prodigality, 244
Magniloquent sub-Churchilian
    cadence-betraying, 260
Mandela, Nelson, 42, 43, 152–153,
    164, 180, 181
Mannheim, Karl, 154
Manufacture arms, 86
Manufactured reality, 238, 298
Manufacturing, 272–273, 299
    popularity, 291
    reality, 300
Maosim, 189
Mao Zedong (Chairman), 56, 216
Mapoto, Albert (retired soldiers), 319
Marx, Karl, 96, 99, 122, 149, 184,
    258, 323
Marxism, 36, 95–96, 98, 156–158,
    189, 228
    and African nationalism, 149
    and nationalism, 96, 99, 156, 228
    rationalise, 258
Marxist, 96, 98, 100, 156, 158,
    205, 242
    beliefs, 139
    ideological formation, 158
    ideologies, 67, 98, 146, 154
    leaders, 11
Marxist-Leninist, 216
    discourse, 99
Massacres, 19, 24, 40, 57–58, 83, 96,
    98, 102, 182, 270, 273
    unleashed barbaric, 281
Mass graves, 5, 47, 58, 84, 180, 282,
    287, 306, 328
Mass killings, 286
Mass murder, 22, 31, 58, 227, 269

Mass protests, 299
Matabeleland, 6, 76, 126, 155, 177,
    212, 245, 251, 269, 270, 273,
    275, 278, 334
Mbembe, Achille, 3, 5, 10, 44, 56–67,
    98, 105, 116, 156–157, 239,
    243–245, 321, 324
    idea, 67
McGuiness, Mac, 138, 150, 257
    trusting, 257
Mckellen, Sir Ian, 27
Mclean, Sandra, 322
McMillan, Harold (British Prime
    Minister), 147
MDC-Alliance, 308–310
Mediocrity, 25, 322
Meditation, 42, 145
Meldrum, Andrew, 327
Melodious, new, 4
Mentality, 45, 157
    political, 137
Mentors, 136, 137, 141, 256, 313
    formative, 206
    political, 136
Mercy, 93, 138, 183, 242, 283, 311
Messiahs, 63–64, 69, 73–74, 128,
    148, 153, 172–174, 200,
    201, 204
    biblical, 128
    crucified, 164
    indispensable, 229
    saintly, 180
    true, 204, 319
Messianic, 73, 198–199, 244
Metanarrative
Metaphor, 115, 265, 323, 324, 341
    animal, 320
    living, 324, 337
    political, 131
Metaphysical, 58–60, 123, 124
    aspirations, 129
Mexico, 165

Militarisation, 54
Militarised junta, 311
Militarism, 206, 207, 209
Military, 5, 194, 211, 269, 277, 317, 329, 335
  bravado, 71
  coup, 134, 196, 230, 329
  faces, straight, 309
  fatigues, 131
Military junta, 124, 180, 290
  venal, 329
Militias, 19, 65, 80, 83, 172, 330
  personal, 277, 320
Mineral, rich, 37
Mines, 226, 227
  ransacking diamond, 226
Ministerial delegations, high-level, 60
Ministers, 37–38, 60, 73, 82, 105, 130, 131, 219, 226, 258, 260, 283, 319, 321
Missionary, 77, 181, 199
  collaborators, 160
  spirit, 73, 74, 77, 103, 142
  true political, 125
  trusted Catholic, 14
Mnangagwa, Emmerson (President), 19–21, 134, 174, 180, 282–285, 293, 307–324, 326, 328–335
  birth, 326
  bit hungry, 318
  characterised, 317
  of conspiring, 320
  cruelty, 323
Mnangagwa, Robert, 312, 320
Modern/colonial world, present, 34
Modernisation, 13, 155
Modernising mission, 88
Modernity, 9, 88, 148, 165, 206
  western, 166
Monarch, 199, 219, 235, 236
  big pre-colonial, 236
  medieval, 231

Monarchy, 236
  mythical, 236
Money, 37, 38, 107, 131, 181, 208, 248, 321
  big, 233
  printed, 83
  public, 38
Mono-maniac, 228
Monopolisation, 227
Monsters, 3, 10, 12, 26–30, 33–35, 43, 45, 171–176, 179–183, 196–199, 240–242, 244, 257
Monstrosity, 3, 6, 28, 30–31, 64, 173–175, 179, 182–183, 201–202, 244, 248, 331–333
Monstrous, 146, 173
  ego, 209
Monstrous philosophy, 146
  true, 146
Monumentalisation, 149
Morality, 62, 84, 101, 265
  dismisses, 62
  self-righteous, 265
Moral principles, 160
Moral registers, 30
Morbidities, 35
  political, 4, 33
Mortals, 122, 137, 183, 220, 230–231
  faulty, 183
  ordinary, 136
Mother, 38, 80–81, 119, 122–123, 126–130, 132–134, 136, 141–143, 176, 262
Mother figures, 132, 134
  materialist, 134
Mother of the nation, 132
Mother Teresa (saintly), 181
Movement for Democratic Change (MDC), 157, 228, 231, 232, 260, 266, 292, 296
Moyo, Gorden, 217

Moyo, Jonathan, 138, 139, 184, 199, 201, 205, 230, 305–307, 311–312, 323
Mozambique, 56, 131, 185, 191–193, 218, 233, 241–243, 307–308, 316, 319
Mozambique Mnangagwa, 319
Mpofu, Busani, 86, 218
Mugabe, Grace Marufu Ntombizodwa (wife), 132, 133, 173, 182, 183, 202, 220, 293, 307, 311, 314, 319
  corruption, 133
  fears, 183
Mugabe, Robert (President), 1–48, 56–108, 128–130, 133–135, 137–153, 155–166, 192, 193, 214, 226, 229–235, 237, 246–252, 280, 289, 305–342
  Afroradicalism, 99
  alerted, 319
Mugabe, Sally Hayfrod, 37, 131–133
Mugabe-centric narratives, 36
  beyond, 200
Mugabeism, 5–6, 215, 227, 306, 307, 313, 315, 325, 327, 333, 336, 338
  amplifying, 342
Mugabeist, 312
Mugabe regime, 316
  spree, 43
Mugabe's successors, 174, 327
  possessed, 325
Mugabe's violence, 84
  post-political inclinations, 26
Murder, 38, 210, 227, 271, 273–275, 311
  civilians, 311
  deliberate, 203
Murderers, 83, 272
  transforming, 79
Murderous, 106, 308
Music, 218, 289
Musician, true, 308

Muslims, 68
Mzilikazi, Great King, 326
Mzilikazi wa Africa, 333

N
Naiveté, 26, 29, 250
  post-political, 30, 64, 69
  white political, 14
Nameless enemies, 19
Narcissism, 136, 158, 233
Narcissist nihilist, 179, 218
  true, 218
Narcissist self-kissing, 46
Nation, 7, 16–18, 23–24, 38, 90–91, 96–101, 130–132, 157, 197, 228–229, 234, 279–281, 286–300, 320–323
National army, 211, 259, 274, 276, 320, 322–323, 329–330, 335
National assets, 217
National Democratic Party (NDP), 16, 186, 197
National emancipation, 148
National Heroes Acre, 9, 292
National holidays, 66, 106
Nationalism, 16, 36, 96, 99–100, 155–160, 228, 291
  claimed, 95
  cultural, 290
  degenerated, 97
  domineering, 155
  economic, 216
  exclusionary, 292
  gallant, 2, 216
  leftist, 118
  practiced, 291
  toxic, 157
Nationalism and Marxism, 36, 156–158
Nationalism's glorification, 155
Nationalist, 11, 63–64, 67, 95–98, 154, 157, 158, 161, 165, 205
Nationalists and Marxists in Africa, 100

National Shrine, 292
National Sports Stadium, 46
National struggle, collective, 214
National television, 264, 284
  screens, 244
National unity and reconciliation, 241
Nietzsche, Friedrich (*cont.*)
  escapes, 75
  essays, 73
  Harare, 66, 70
  peace, 87
  philosophical concept, 43, 48
  philosophical promise, 76
  philosophical thought, 73
  philosophy, 73
  triumphalist celebration, 43
  vaunting, 76
Nietzschean, 66, 124, 240
  idea, 67, 86
Nietzschean sense, 44
Nigeria, 248, 322
Nightmares, 18, 65, 123, 124, 204
  long, 18
  real, 229
Nihilism, 67, 75–78, 88, 95
  narcissist, 165, 179, 295, 299
  political, 87
  speculative, 75
Nihilist, 67, 92, 162, 235
Nkala, Enos (genocide), 270, 271, 282
Nkomo, Joshua Mqabuko, 15, 16,
    137, 138, 230–232, 263–264,
    268–283, 285–301
  argument, 273
  country, 212, 278
  departed, 295
  frame, 275
  honoured, 297
  name, 294
  punishing, 281
  supported, 279
  village, 296
  ZIPRA, 269–272, 275
ZIPRA dissidents, 272
ZIPRA in Zimbabwe, 275
Nkrumah, Kwame, 3, 39, 131, 147,
    148, 207
  potential, 147
Nkrumahism, 189
Nobility, 230, 262
Norman, Andrew, 27, 71, 75, 137,
    145, 148, 192, 203, 206, 242,
    245–246, 248, 251, 255, 281, 296
Norman, Denis, 260
Nyarota, Geoff, 9, 11, 37, 39,
    173–177, 179, 192, 199, 307
  use, 176
Nyerere, Julius (Presidents), 194, 207,
    231, 241, 242, 246, 263, 294
Nyerereism, 189

O
Obsessed love, 42
Occupational hazards, real, 54
Occidentalizing, 291
O'Doherty, 226
Olympics of power and violence, 320
Olympics of revenge, 56
One-party state, 23–24, 90–92, 276,
    277, 291
  defacto, 24
  Snyder, 24
  strong, 23
Opponents, 62–64, 74, 81–83,
    99–101, 126, 127, 164, 171,
    172, 183, 186–187, 200, 220,
    262–265, 293–294, 338
  disciplining, 66
  eternal, 308
  fearless, 175
  frighten, 76
  legitimate, 199
  overcoming, 64
  radical, 255
  real, 82

Opponents of Mugabe, 127, 175
Opportune circumstances, 42
Opportunism, 22, 93, 260, 288, 291
  calculated, 103
  political, 175, 301, 329
  true, 212
Opportunists, 23, 133–134, 178, 205,
    214, 215
  power monger, 210
  practiced, 211
Opposition, 23–24, 27, 74, 75, 83,
    85, 162, 165, 190, 228–232,
    246, 248, 328
  ZAPU, 24
Opposition Movement, 157, 260
Oppress, 166, 244, 259, 289, 340
Oppressing, 65
Oppression, 45, 104, 107, 159, 208,
    214, 244, 279, 288
Oppressive machinery, 257
Oppressive regimes, 321
Oppressors, 28, 103–104, 152–153,
    165, 249, 259, 316, 339–342
  admired, 75
  former, 259
  new, 117
  new colonial, 10
  present, 44
Orations, 74, 186
  grandiose, 311
  graveside, 74
Orator, 197
  fire-eating, 193
Organisations, 10, 12, 23, 28, 34,
    140, 184, 196, 212
  criminal, 233
  dangerous terrorist, 273
Organised Evil, 281–287
Over-Presence, 127
Overthrow, 19, 54, 67, 80, 134, 205,
    230, 243, 274, 328
Overthrown, 164, 195, 231, 314–315
Overthrow of Mugabe, 54, 239

P
Pagan ethos, 40
Paganism, 145
  political, 144
Pagans, 72, 144
Pan-African hero, 94
Pan-Africanism, 36, 95, 98,
    189–190, 216
  dramatisations of liberation
    heroism, 2
  envisage, 190
Pan-Africanist ideals, 217
Pan-Africanist liberation movements
    and intellectualism, 190
Pan-Africanist writers, 205
Pan-African liberation, 57
Pan-African nationalism, 145
Pan-African nationalists, 145
Pan-African redemptive ideology, 63
  forgiveness, 14
  pastures, 73
Pan-African solidarity and African
    continentalism, 323
Paradigm, 7, 85–87, 103, 105
  aggressive, 91
  political, 46–47, 158
Paradisal, 12, 30, 289
  era, 210
Paradise, 29, 204, 257
  fool's, 9
Paradox, 77, 183, 234, 239, 293, 306,
    312, 319, 321, 324, 339
  cruel, 83, 289
  historical, 337
  painful, 228
  political, 78
  true Machiavellian, 55
Paranoia, 42, 126, 163, 204,
    233, 280–282
  national, 98
  the seven veils of, 127
Paranoiac, 45, 126, 163
Parents Day event, 319

Parirenyatwa, Samuel, 294
Parliament, 23, 58, 178, 258,
    308, 329
Parliamentarians, 258, 322
Partisan army, 277
    special, 276
Partners, 267
    intimate, 42
Partnership, 318
Part of Mugabe, 213, 250, 273, 315
Partriachal, 105
Party, 22–25, 37–38, 74, 103, 138,
    139, 194, 228–230, 246–248,
    274–275, 278–280, 286–301,
    305–307, 319
    old, 306
Party ZANU-PF, 267
Patriarchal, 106, 118, 131
Patriarchy, 104–107, 132
    exploitative, 105
Patrimonial regimes, 36
Patriotic front, 138
    united, 263
Patriotism, 16, 99, 157, 212, 292–293
    observed, 99
Patriots, 99, 157, 293, 300
Patronage, 211
    political, 133
Patrons and profiteers, 37
Paul Moorcraft records, 263
Peace, 8, 11–12, 14, 17–18, 29, 86,
    90–94, 163, 164, 240–242,
    297–299, 296–299
    dramatise, 92
    perpetual, 164
    sang, 242
    short, 86
Pentecostal, 172
PF-ZAPU, 299
    swallow, 291
Philosophical energy, 65
Philosophical formation, 119, 124, 154

Philosophical inquiry, 156
Philosophical inspiration, 103
Philosophically Mugabe, 217
Philosophical method, 79
Philosophical musings, 122
Philosophical negation, 75
Philosophical paradox, 78
Philosophical personality, 119, 125
Philosophical practice, new, 75
Philosophical sensibility, 117, 125
Philosophical stupidity, 8
Philosophic kingship, 35
Philosophy, 61–62, 70, 75, 77, 79,
    102–104, 107, 144–147, 200,
    201, 207, 209
    anti-philosophical, 76
    contradicted, 75
    decolonial, 46
    faked, 156
    humanist, 100
    intellectual, 141
    of liberation, 47, 67, 85,
        102–104, 165
    nihilistic, 46
    political, 25–26, 45–46, 104, 146,
        207, 215
    revolutionary, 218
    stubborn, 146
Phobias, 117, 233, 249, 263
Pinochet, Augusto, 19, 127, 141, 148,
    186, 241, 262
    attack, 271
Plagiarised copy, 187
Plagiarism, 148, 243
Plato, 18, 122, 198, 229
Plaut, Martin, 7, 99, 198, 210, 211
Police, 19, 32, 65, 80–81, 172, 258,
    270, 273, 309, 334
    commanders, 309
    officers, 187, 321
    senior, 324
    state, 104, 204

Policeman, former, 257
Political ambitions, 75, 134, 229,
   276, 326
   direct, 134
   untampered, 101
Political animalism, 320
Political animals, 2, 17, 30, 131, 135,
   191, 198, 220
Political communication, 90
   weaponised, 300, 306
Political communicators, 139, 311
Political competitors, 293, 295
Political conditioning, 213
Political conditions, 119, 208
Political conduct, 201
Political confidence, 149
Political connivance, 276
Political contestations, 62
Political context, 87
Political contracts, 285
Political controversies, 185
Political credential, 151
Political culture, 22, 23, 155,
   161–162, 213–214, 220, 306,
   307, 310, 314, 316, 337, 338
   national, 79
Political curriculum vitae, 114
Political deeds, 101
Political demands, 89
Political dispensations, 26
Political drive, 64–66
   spirited, 100
Political/economic structures, 158
Political effect, 101
Political effort, 148
Political enemies, 20–21, 90, 97, 127,
   160, 164, 172, 199, 220,
   264, 266
Political entrepreneurs, 31
Political establishment, 85
   present militarised, 342
Political events, 307

Political expediency, 217
Political experiment, 328
Political extortion, 298
Political extremists, 22, 262
   true, 267
Political factor, doubtful, 191
Political followership, 16
   political forces, 236
Political fortunes, 196–197
Political friendships, 138
Political fundamentalist, 27, 41,
   262, 266
   true, 181, 268
Political gamesmanship, 138
Political gangsterism, 316
Political genealogy, 320
Political generalisations, 87
Political gladiator, 136
Political glory, 193
   true, 180
Political goals, 235, 280
   opportunistic, 298
Political handler, 312
Political hooliganism, 44
   Mugabe, 105
   normalised, 79
Political humanism, 104
   critical, 103
Political ideas, 36, 48, 149, 163, 185,
   199, 227, 307–308
   simplistic, 189
Political ideologies, 11, 95
   principled, 207–208
Political image, 291, 293
   personal, 291
Political imagination, 48, 179, 264
   hateful, 266
   self-serving, 99
Political indoctrination staff, 277
Political insanity re-evaluates, 235
Political interests, 12, 72, 306
   personal, 14, 321

Political intrigue, 1
Political kind, 179
Political leaders, 7–8, 95, 96, 103,
    104, 118–120, 122, 148–150,
    152, 159, 195, 198, 341
  cast, 328
  produced, 161
  turning, 341
  young, 122
Political leadership, 4, 78, 120, 123,
    132, 186
  entered, 205
Political legacy, 44, 56, 306, 310, 312,
    337, 338
  great, 78
Political legitimation, 161
  international, 159
Political machinery, 214
Political manure, 41
Political marketing, 307
  good, 294
  personal, 213
Political martyrdom, 67
Political mechanisms, 78
Political messiah, 72, 164, 174,
    213, 293
  enigmatic, 175
  true, 193
Political methodology, 311
Political mindsets, 161
Political moderation, 46
Political monsters, 177, 182, 241
  studied, 27
Political movements, 161, 194
  modern, 306
Political noises, right, 162–163
Political nutrition, 293–294
Political office, 127, 151, 229,
    306–309, 320, 325
Political opinions, 121, 147, 266
Political opponents, 26, 30, 71–72,
    85, 89–91, 150–152, 165, 262,
    265, 267–268, 277–278, 280

Political opportunity, 138
Political opposition, 19, 23–24, 27,
    29, 228–229, 264, 266, 269,
    270, 277–278, 329–331
Political order, 140, 154
  new, 5, 10
Political orientation, 277
Political parties, 23–24, 41, 80, 98,
    228, 231–233, 287, 291,
    297–300, 308, 313
Political passions, 146, 155, 158, 227,
    278, 282
  neo-traditional, 118
Political pathology, 87
Political performances, 45, 98, 255,
    262, 270
  illicit, 44
  public, 74, 152
  spectacular, 2
Political persuasions, 162, 245
Political Philosophy of
    Mugabeism, 215
Political phrases, 306
Political politeness, true, 294
Political positions, 179, 218, 321
Political power, 5, 32, 44, 60, 80, 86,
    108, 148, 172, 281, 288
  personal, 300
Political practice, 77, 215
  anti-political, 77
Political principles, clear, 207
Political problems, 15, 85, 131, 196
  typical, 179
Political production, 87, 117,
    124, 158
  spectacular, 179
Political projects, 29
Political pursuits, 131
Political reactions, 122
Political realities, 30, 98
Political reason, 18
Political record, 33
Political reformers, 341

Political relations, 177, 212
  managed, 34
Political relationship, 312
  special, 315, 319
Political religion, 172, 183, 292
  personalised, 137
Political rivalry, intense, 266
Political rivals, 5, 273
  dead, 297
Political ruminations, 48, 122
Political rupture, 239
Political sanitation, 279
Political scapegoats, 48
Political scenario, 39
Political self-righteousness, 268
Political settlements, 29
Political settlement testament, 242
Political silliness, 59, 228
Political size, 250
Political somnambulism, 318
Political strategists, 306
Political strategy, 136
  poor, 336
Political support, 177, 217, 247, 255
  personal, 293
Political system, 7, 10, 31, 35, 36,
    159-, 176–177, 201, 212,
    308, 339
Political tantrums, 171
Political tendencies, 8
Political theory, 30
Political thinker, 95, 96, 131, 138,
    159, 162, 216
  reasoned, 215
Political thought, 38–40, 66, 70, 90,
    93, 100, 103, 158, 164, 200,
    201, 203, 337, 338
  corrupted, 32
Political treasure, 134
Political understanding, 64
Political universe, 228, 235, 240
  unconscious, 238

Political values, 235
Political vauntings, 76
Political violence, 24, 26, 27, 54–56,
    101, 102, 210, 213, 281, 309,
    311, 313, 335, 338
  deploying, 92
  large-scale, 314
  Mnangagwa, 314
Political wellness and wisdom for
    leaders, 183
Political wing, 193
Political wisdom, 188, 229, 243, 245
  important, 101
Political world, 235, 312
  dry real, 200
Politicians, 22, 26–30, 32, 39–41, 74,
    90–92, 100–101, 164, 195–196,
    210–212, 307–309, 320–321,
    324–325, 329–331, 335–336
  anti-political, 75
Politicidal, 89
Politicking, 314
  learned, 311
Politics, 26–29, 31–32, 39–41, 46–48,
    62, 67, 75, 85–94, 97–98,
    100–107, 135, 164–166,
    184–187, 209, 277–279,
    305–308, 311–313, 327–328
Polity, 54–55, 84, 175, 228, 242, 297,
    321, 324
  decaying, 325
Pollutants, 97–98, 264, 308
  disposable, 279
Pontificate, 74, 134, 293
Pontificating, 293
Popular politicians, 334
Populations, 2, 3, 5, 10, 12, 14–16,
    57, 58, 69, 70, 265, 269,
    271, 328
  black, 15
  civilian, 76, 283
  clobber, 23

dominated, 316
hypnotised, 17
lesbian, 265
mislead, 185
national, 55, 322
suffering, 133
unarmed, 42
Populism, 189, 280
cheap, 189
political, 188
simplistic, 189
Populist methodologies, 280
Populist reason, 189–190, 236, 243
Pornographic, 79
Pornography, 61–62
Portraits, 219, 236, 237
Portray, 34, 57, 274, 279, 280, 293
bribes, 37
national Heroes Acre, 73
ZAPU, 274
Post-colonial/postcolonial, 120, 121, 250, 316
authenticity, 165
codes, 146
cult, 155
practice, 6
Postcolony/posctolonies, 3, 34, 53–108, 120, 121, 316–321, 323–325, 327–329
Postcoup, 327
Post-independence, 35, 120
era, 12, 161–162
immature, 255
Post-Mugabe, 327
Post-Mugabe Zimbabwe, 315, 325, 332
Post-political anticolonial mistake, spectacular, 11
Post-political belief, dangerous, 27
Post-political blunder, 30, 240
first, 329
Post-political climates, 28, 33, 71

Post-political excitements, 26, 327, 328
Post-political immaturity, 30
Post-political inclinations, 334
Post-political innocence and naiveté, 26
Post-politicalism, 30
Post-political limits, 69
Post-political mistake, 29, 176
tragic, 26, 328
Post-political performances, 14
Post-political puzzle, 333
Post-political readings, 64
Post-political tendencies, 327
Post-political understandings, 26
Post-political worship of leaders, 174
Post-politics, 26, 29, 89, 212, 334
tragic, 328
Post-Traumatic Stress Disorder, 225
Power, Samantha, 5
Power, 7–10, 32–36, 40–48, 58–95, 97–108, 116–128, 142–152, 155–165, 171–174, 186–191, 195–202, 210–213, 215–220, 241–254, 281–291, 316–323, 331–333, 336–342
Powerlessness, 39, 42, 55, 106, 120, 172, 339
Pragmatism, 48, 243
political, 243
Pre-colonial rulers, 205
Predecessor, 333
Pre-destination, 121, 149, 198, 199
believed, 163
Predetermine, 154
Predicament, 31
egocentric, 204, 227
Predictable tragedy, 202, 204
Predictions, 39, 139, 325
Prejudice, 68, 97, 153
Presentations and representations of Mugabe, 210

Presidency, 35, 175, 211, 230, 269, 307, 335
  party's, 193
President, 8, 9, 16, 19, 55, 59–61, 229–230, 269, 274, 300, 309, 313, 314, 317
  apartheid South African, 160
  co-vice, 291
  executive, 235
  fallen, 25
  first, 40
  flying, 232
  former, 315
  friends, 41
  grandfather, 326
  mafia, 323
President Mugabe, 313, 317
President of Mozambique, 192
Prime Minister, 120, 192, 284
  bespectacled black, 4
Prime Time, 264
Princes, 55, 61–63, 65, 91–93, 139, 208–209
  born, 65
  exhorted, 92
  new, 65
  cunning, 240
  true, 208
  true drama, 186
Prison, 37, 106, 131, 150–153, 198–200, 227, 233, 255–256, 335, 341
Promised land naiveté, 27
Promises, 12, 63, 70–71, 77–78, 80, 92, 93, 124, 180, 331–332
  ambitious philosophical, 66
  carried, 180, 203
  mesmerising, 12
  post-political, 71
  soothing, 241
Propaganda, 48, 94, 248, 251, 273, 293
  cheap, 178

Propagandist, 181
Propensities, 216–217, 300, 340
  self-eating, 114
Property, 107, 156, 208, 298
  personal, 165
Property rights, 244
Prophecy, 128, 139, 141, 172, 187, 205–207, 326
  false, 178
  old, 327
  self-fulfilling, 237
Prophetic, 73, 74, 244
Prophets, 185, 290, 325
  charismatic, 199
  enterprising, 60
  false, 213
  judgement day, 267
  political, 186
Protesting injustices, 315
Pseudo-religiosity, 266
Pseudo-struggles, 163, 339
Psychoanalysis, 30, 45, 233
Psychoanalysts, 12, 116, 117, 122
Psychoanalytical efforts, 45
Psychological conditioning, 30, 117
Psychological woundedness, 127
Psychopathological level, 249
Psychopathology, 125

Q
Qualification, 150
  coveted doctoral, 325
Queen, 11, 134, 163, 189, 245, 251, 286
Quelimane, 192
Questions central, 159
  important, 123, 332
  national, 287
  political, 180
  stubborn, 181, 332
  stubborn historical, 334
Quiet ruthlessly, 271

R
Race, 25, 48, 97, 244–246, 280, 281,
     287, 290
  political, 20
  pure German, 227
Race-based policies, 16
Racism, 6–8, 68, 97, 216, 247–248,
     278–279, 290, 291, 340
  invoking, 260
Racist, 9, 14, 67, 154, 249, 251,
     254, 255, 259, 263,
     264, 279
  animosities, 340
  apartheid regime, 160, 255
Radicalism, 259
  black, 255
Rape, 22, 58, 106, 275, 281, 311,
     322, 340
Reagan, Ronald, 68
Rebellions, 157, 342
Rebuking Nelson Mandela, 258
Recolonisation, 255
Reconciliation, 11, 13–15, 17–19,
     23–24, 27–29, 90–94,
     240–245, 247–250
  dramatise, 250
  human, 265
  national, 248
  performances of, 248, 276
  performed, 245
  post-political, 14
  retracting, 340
Reconciliation policy, 6, 340
  national, 248
Reconciliation rhetoric, 11
  lyrical, 241, 340
Reconciling, 261
Reconstitution, 235
Reconstruction, 235
Regionalism, 281, 290
Regionalist, 278–279
Rehumanisation, 107
  mutual, 259
Rehumanising value, 104

Reigns, 186, 209, 324
Relationship, 122, 135, 138, 240,
     249, 250, 312, 314
  faulty, 183
  instrumental, 226
  personal, 312
  special, 313, 318, 319, 334
Relatives, 107, 279, 283
Religion, 56, 59–61, 74, 77, 116,
     123, 140, 144, 284, 287, 292
Religiosity, 265
  strong, 123
Religious activities, 141
Religious background, 72
Religious beliefs, 123, 141, 181
  attacked, 73
Religious conditions, 123
Religious congregation, 199
Religious crusaders, 266
Religious kind, 231
Removal of Mugabe, 274, 305, 308,
     322, 329, 338
Remythologise, 239
Replacing Mugabe, 274, 320
Representations of Mugabe, 210
Republic of corruption, 37
Resurrection, 153, 287, 305–308
  stubborn, 34
Retirement, 182, 219, 226
Retribalization, 7
Revenge, 19, 56, 66, 80, 104, 153,
     240–244, 271, 272
  black, 13, 71
  intention to, 240–246
  nihilist, 241
Reverberated long distances, 265
Revisionist reconstructions, 271
Revocation of Reconciliation, 247–249
Revolution, 26, 33, 38, 40, 94, 306,
     310, 312, 314, 320, 327–328
  brave, 115
  long awaited, 331
  real, 327
  the vanguard of the, 194

Revolutionaries, 99, 228, 288, 312, 341
  bible, 149
  ideas, 217
  messianism, 74
  party, 300
  principles, 217
  socialist, 180
  struggle, 23
  unquestionable, 229
  unwavering, 213
Revolution that lost its way, 336
Rhetoric, 11, 17–19, 22–24, 36, 48,
    61, 65, 177, 227
  good political, 29
  official, 22
  performed, 11
  performed mesmerising, 14
Rhetorical force, 16
Rhodesia, 3–5, 131, 137, 147–149,
    192, 198, 252–253, 255, 272, 279
Rhodesian colonialism, 6, 241
  replacing, 315–316
Rhodesians, 27, 71, 176–177, 185,
    204, 241–242, 251, 269,
    274, 340
  assassins, 319
  black, 185, 186, 189, 213
  colonial, 258
  propaganda, 251
Roberts Suresh, Ronald, 198
Romantic, 177
  imaginists, 204
  ruthless, 177, 183
Rotberg, Robert, 91
Rule, 23–24, 34–35, 39–41, 58, 86,
    88, 100–101, 119–120, 124,
    150–151, 159–161, 175–176,
    179–180, 199–200, 226–228,
    245–246, 266, 323
Ruled Lucca, 116
Ruler, 57–61, 63, 65, 67, 74, 84, 86,
    88, 105, 115

Ruler of Aburiria, 57–58
Rural Housing, 319
Russian communism, 162
Rusty fascist ideas, 310
Ruthlessness, 271

S
Sacred tenets, 289
Sacrifices, 7, 103, 182, 242, 299
  demanded, 188
  friends, 138
  human, 67
  Zambia, 337
Sadat, Anwar (Cairo), 59
Samora Machel and Frelimo, 192
Samora Machel of Mozambique,
    191, 241
Saudi King, 68
Saul, John, 34, 93
Scandalisation, 102
Scandal, true, 322
Scarcity, 147, 197
Scholars, 1–2, 26–27, 30–32, 43,
    44, 93, 131–132, 176,
    178–179, 184–186,
    194–198, 200,
    210–211, 240–241
  escaped, 333
  fascinated, 120
  journalists, 36, 54, 182, 196–198,
    210, 212, 242, 269
Scholarship, 29, 41, 103
  political, 31
School, 7, 63, 117, 126, 136–137,
    141, 150–152, 162, 288
School children, 46, 213, 239, 296
  hapless, 173
Schooling activities, 282
Schooling, lower, 233
Secessionist movements, 155
  produced, 287

Secretary/secretaries, 133, 139, 194, 323
Secretary General, 230
Secrets, 26, 143–144, 160, 235, 286
  agreement, 276
  high, 118
  security services, 19
  service, 80
Secular ideologies, 146
Security, 22, 81, 159, 160, 232, 318–319, 330, 334
  colonial administration's, 159
Sekeramayi, Sydney, 283
Selective amnesia, 299
Self-absorption, 136
Self-belief, 200
  political, 200
Self-believing, 68
Self-celebration, 200, 320
Self-confessed adventure seekers, 2
Self-confidence, little, 174
Self-consciousness, 145
Self-constitution, 237
Self-defeating behaviour, 218
  his, 194
Self-denial, 188
Self-denialism, 188
Self-determination, 94
Self-discipline, 143
Selfishness, 136
Self-loving, 55, 212, 234
Self-promotion, 213
Self-reflection, 68
Self-sacrificing missionaries, 140
Self-sacrificing zealot, 181
Self-worship, 145, 200, 233
Self-worshipping, 55, 234
  narcissist, 212
Sell-outs/sellouts, 86, 149, 157, 228, 300
Semi-religious temperament, 146
Semi-urban sanitation, 264

Sermon, 284
Settler colonialism, 163, 287, 328, 336
  white, 3–4, 185
Settlers, 68, 159, 234
  white, 104, 160, 248
Sex, 20
Sexual morals, 21
Sexual perverts, 265
Shona, 269–270, 278–280
  babies, 279
  tribe, 97, 280
  word, 97
Shona-recruited Fifth-Brigade, 279
Shrine, 60, 180, 292–295
Simulacrum, 238
  pure, 238
Sinners, 71–72, 108, 165, 199, 220, 227–228, 267, 268, 292, 341
  lost, 200
  misguided, 229
Sins, 13, 74, 107, 126, 129, 267
  gravest, 38
  monumental, 335
Sissy, 80, 106, 137, 193–194, 219
Sisters, 59, 186, 255, 262
  twin, 38
Sithole, Ndabaningi, 19, 25, 136, 192, 230–231, 287, 288
  replacing, 193
Sober analysis, 176
Sober thought, 271
Social behaviour, 233
Social contract, 29
Socialisation, 125, 145
  early, 228
Socialism, 99, 155
Societies, 21–22, 24, 26–28, 33, 34, 87, 90, 117, 122–123, 136, 139–144, 178
  civil, 329
  sick, 125

Soldiers, 185, 187, 191, 192, 195–196, 211, 269–270, 283, 284, 308–309, 311, 319–321, 323, 332–333, 335
  hug, 308
  hundred, 319
  shot, 309
  true, 195
  trusted, 226
Soldiery, 318, 329
Sons, 117, 121–124, 126, 128, 132, 279, 284, 312, 314, 318, 326, 332
Sophistication, 248
Sorcerers, 318, 320
  competing, 318
Sorcery, 19–21, 297, 316
  order of, 238
  political, 293, 294, 296, 301
Soul of the nation, 291
Souls, 73, 150, 259, 293
  black, 256
  common, 60, 231
  fragile, 172
  humiliated old, 54
  lost, 199
  wounded, 127, 269
South Africa, 160, 180, 208, 254, 255, 264, 313, 316, 322, 325, 332
  neighbouring, 254
South African, 14, 72, 208, 248, 276, 322, 330
  celebrated, 333
  controversial, 180
  liberation movement, 330
  transition, 166
South African Defence Forces, 330
South African Department of Foreign Affairs, 330
South African Transport and Allied Workers Union (SATAWU), 41

Southern Africa, 71, 162, 246, 337
Southern African, 330
Southern part, 326
Southern Zimbabwe, 70, 283
Sovereignty, 41, 94, 337
  national, 290
Soviet totalitarianisms, 48
Spell, 17, 92, 117, 136, 198, 316, 325
Spheres of influence, 154
Spice Girls, 133
Spirited campaigns, 96
Spirited drive, 91, 226, 282, 337
Spirited efforts, 34
Spirited passion, 43
Spirit mediums, 60
Spiritual debts, 132
Spirituality, 60
Squander, 77, 248
Squandering, 332
Stalin, Joseph, 21, 75, 78, 148, 182, 184, 186, 190–191, 237
  Great Terror, 271
Stalinism, 189
Stalinist, 46, 74, 236
Starvation, 116, 203, 282
  deliberate, 281
State House, 38, 250
State institutions, 7
  captured, 318
Stateless nations and nationless states, 100
Statement, 182–183, 256, 283, 334
  patriotic, 157
State Mugabe, 136
  one-party, 23
States, 10–11, 33–35, 65–66, 119, 124, 130, 133, 241–243, 245, 275–276, 280, 283
  agents, 272
  banquet, 80
  commandist, 155
  custody, 334

Statesman, 240, 243
  great African, 3
  magnanimous, 240
Statesmanship, 245
Statesmen, 265
  dead, 292
  shrewdest, 140
Station, 251, 252
  private, 65
Staunch supporters-erstwhile ZANLA
  guerillas, 281
Steal attention, 42
Stigmatisation, suffered, 96
Stock, 92, 306, 327
  house of, 225
  political, 7
Stones, 9, 310
Stooges, 300
Storied dalliances, 88
Story, 1, 16, 125, 211, 230, 312, 317,
  323, 326
  historical, 202
Stratagems, 20, 103
Strategist, 148
  calculating, 334
Streets, 308, 311, 329, 332–333
  pot-holed, 59
Students Representative Council, 15
Sub-human behaviour, 265
Subject, 3, 21, 30, 40, 64, 70,
  200–201, 276, 280, 283, 286
  authentic national, 157
  black, 253
  colonising, 67
  paranoiac, 126
  penetrable, 106
  personal, 165
  slippery, 70
Subjectivity, 32
  political, 46
Submissions, 88, 105
Sub-nations, 155

Subordination, 155, 186
Substance true, 145
  unknown, 263
Substitutes, 89
Substitute, true, 141
Substitution, 89–90
Suburban parishes, 285
Succession puzzle, 329
Successor, 43, 184, 211, 226,
  312, 325
  ambitious, 327
  aspiring, 185
  dutiful, 293
  loathed, 134
  potential, 199
Such has not come, 151
Such-pseudo-religiosity, 145
Suffering black masses, 206
Sugar diabetes, 21
Suicide, 185, 200
  committed, 335
Superiority, 64, 151, 185, 253, 259, 285
  imagined, 61
  invented, 262
  political, 186–187
  sense of, 149, 186
  unarguable, 249
Super-powers benefitted handsomely,
  global, 322
Superstitions, 121, 145
Superstitious, 183
Supervised curfews, 282
Supporters, 55, 57, 106, 171–173,
  175, 179, 180, 183, 185,
  187–189, 219–220, 262, 264,
  270, 271
  actuality Mugabe's, 172
  dissident, 283
  opportunistic, 173
  of ZAPU, 231
Survival, 81, 84, 95, 150, 217, 233
  political, 105

Survivalism, 335
Sycophancy machinery, 133
Sycophants, 22, 55, 139, 172, 178,
    239, 301, 342
  opportunistic, 198
Symbiotic, 122, 212
Symbolism, 250, 289, 291
  religious, 74
Symbols, 76, 82, 233, 238, 289–292,
    294, 296, 341
  election, 76
  international, 214
  personal, 62, 82
Sympathisers, 271
Systematic Cruelty and Organised
    Evil, 281–287
Systemic dispensation, 66
Systemic factors, 200–201
Systems, 11, 23, 31, 33–35, 100–101,
    158–160, 201, 248, 249, 252,
    334, 337–338, 342

T
Takawira, Leopold, 294
Takoradi, 147
Talismans, 151, 234
Tanks, 59, 308, 309, 311
  armoured, 307
Tanzania, 246, 255, 289
Tanzania and Samora Machel of
    Mozambique, 241
Tattered human rights record, 297
Teachers, 141, 142, 147–148, 152,
    188, 201, 218
  contented, 205
  educated school, 174
  expatriate, 147
  fellow, 136
  superior, 143
Teachings, 141, 143
  expatriate, 131
  religious, 141

Tekere, Eddie, 82
Tekere, Edgar, 25, 82, 104,
    137, 191–193
  admonished, 193
Televised presentation, 310
Television, prime-time, 308
Television viewers, 244
Temporary Measures, 258
Temptation, 3, 33, 64, 80, 213
  post-political, 327, 333
  real, 80
  resist modernist, 87
  totalitarian, 181
  true, 252
Tendi, Blessing-Miles, 19–21, 54, 63,
    71, 77, 204, 238, 265, 268,
    290, 326
  key informant, 20
Tentacles, 285
  political, 285
Terrified tycoons, 227
Terrifying, 8, 19, 281
  personages, 80, 117
Territory, 82
Terror, 5, 15, 31, 40, 81, 84, 174,
    180, 273, 281, 283
Terrorisation, 231
Terrorism, 30–31, 77, 161
Terrorists, 272
  armed, 274
Testimony, 207
Theft, 58, 211, 275
  epical, 227
Theorists, 61, 85, 90, 117
  democratic, 29
Thief/thieves, 18, 181, 317
  dedicated, 272
Thinkers, 15, 89, 122, 125, 187, 206
  cerebral, 72
  compromised, 89
  individual, 207
  post-political, 269
  principled, 206

superior, 188
supreme, 209
trusted, 329
Thinking, 27–29, 31–32, 40, 61,
    88–90, 176, 185, 197, 271,
    290, 312
  anti-political, 28
  hard, 33
  independent, 25
  optimistic, 69
  philosophical, 72
  political, 69, 322
  positive, 80
  post-political, 28
  simplistic colonialist, 14
  superior, 152
  tragic, 40
  vigilant pessimistic, 28
  white, 13–14
Third World, 165–166
  wa Thiongo, Ngugi, 17, 57
Thompson, Colin, 212
Threats, 54, 62, 63, 76, 171, 197,
    218, 242, 317, 320
  corrupt, 246
  deploy, 217
  distributing, 165
  obscene, 218
  public, 309
  simulate, 272
  smallest, 286
  true death, 74
Togarira, Nomatter, 59
Tongoogara, Josia Magama, 192, 193
Totalitarianism, 43
  origins of, 48
Totalitarians, 74, 76
Totality, 266, 280
Totems, 317, 320
Tourists, 273–274
  foreign, 275
Toxic circle, 104

Toxic ideology, 97
Toxic individual smuggle, 180
Toxicity, 96, 161, 166
Toxic nationalist ideological push, 98
Toxic passions, 119
Traditions, 59–61, 238, 281, 291,
    315, 337
  lawless, 77
  long, 81
  political, 35, 162
Tragedy, 7, 11, 39, 44, 64, 67,
    202–204, 261, 323,
    325, 327–329
  capital, 104
  cardinal, 192
  historical, 70
  human, 79
  joint, 315
  postpolitical, 329
  produced, 203
  true, 203, 207
Tragi-comedies/tragicomedy, 39,
    55–57, 59
Tragi-comic idiocies, 116
Tragic contradiction, 77
Tragic effects, 214
Tragic expression, 281
Tragic figure, 68, 124, 202–203
Tragic formulation, 47
Tragic proportions, 100–101
Train, 31, 173, 238, 330
Traitors, 27, 59, 68, 72, 86, 100, 157,
    180, 203, 214, 300
  true, 8, 205, 281
Transformation, 69, 179, 214
Transformer, 341
Transition, 2, 166
  military assisted, 329
Transportation, 282
Trappings, 27, 166, 198, 290
  corrupting, 71
  innocent, 29

Treachery, 11, 39, 160, 207, 228, 328
Treatise, 22, 25
Tribalism, 6, 8, 97, 212, 278–281,
    287, 290, 291, 337
  deployed, 279, 280
  excluded, 97
  mobilised, 99
  opportunistic, 287
Tribalist, 154, 155, 279
  agendas, 278
  mind, 279
  project, 278
Tribal oligarchy, 290
Tribal rivalries, 287
Tribal sentiments, 299
Tribes, 19, 32, 97–98, 155,
    212, 279–281
  minority, 98
Tribulations, 121, 193, 327
Trickery, 193, 338, 339
  tired, 292
Troubled family backgrounds
Troublesome, 286
Truism, 250, 289
  dry, 311
Trump, Donald, 178
Trust, 124, 203, 233, 256
  Soames, 256
Trusted disciple, 204
Trusted Emmerson Mnangangwa, 230
Trusted friend, 145
Trusted hand, 313, 315, 328
Trusted Kant, 164
Trusting Mugabe, 14
Truth, 94–95, 162–164, 175–179,
    184–185, 190, 197, 200, 201,
    209, 234–235, 237,
    243, 274–275
Tsholotsho, 319
Tsvangirai, Morgan, 19, 196, 231,
    260, 296–297
Turn antagonism, 29
Turn weaponising, 119

Tutelage, 123
  strong religious, 71
Tyrannical, 15, 23, 24, 36, 74, 91,
    126, 132, 152, 153, 162
  ego, 60, 175
  framework, 119
  kind, 143
  motives, 215
  regimes, 178
  sensibility, 145
  vaunt, 68
Tyranny, 21–22, 26–27, 31,
    35–37, 43–44, 61–63, 67,
    69, 70, 77, 80, 88, 91, 98,
    100–101, 116, 155,
    177–179, 328
  captive audience, 94
  caricatures, 57
  celebrating artless, 44
  compresses, 20
  durability of, 325
  endured, 328
  fertilized, 41
  forces, 94
  inaugurated diabolic, 26
  legacy of, 313, 320
  of Mugabe, 227, 328
  normalising, 78
  nourishes, 178
  opponents, 20
  outposts of, 101, 315
  perfected, 181
  popularity, 22
  sacrifices, 73
  studies essentialise, 78
  true, 5
  venal, 295, 322
Tyrants, 2–3, 17–22, 24, 35, 36, 38,
    41–43, 56–69, 73–75, 83–84, 92,
    93, 101–103, 115–117, 122–123,
    177–179, 182–184,
    196–197, 202–204
  blind, 59

deluded, 325
fallen, 66, 293, 325
feared, 83
good, 23, 318
individual, 36, 184
mistaking, 25
new, 327
normalise, 24
nurture, 27
postcolonial, 59
potential, 69
ranting, 129
true, 41, 197

U
Ultra-nationalism, 291
Ulu in Chinua Achebe's *Arrow of God*, 118
Umdala Wethu Gala, 291
Umzingwane District, 298
Understanding of Mugabe, 203
United Kingdom (UK), 177, 241, 252
United Nations, 3, 324
    report, 22
United States, 211, 246
Unity, 23, 27, 90–92, 138, 155, 162, 240, 263, 290, 291, 295–300
    great, 91
    ideological, 23
    multi-racial, 23
    political, 91, 297
    simulating, 240
Unity Accord, 285–286, 291
Unity Pact, 270
Universities/university, 15, 74, 148, 149, 151, 152, 236, 311, 324, 325
    briefcase, 187, 324
    college, 152
    western, 11
Utter self-indulgence, 143

V
Vatican, 181
Vengeance, 18, 42, 153, 275
    true, 242
Veterans, 7, 214–215
    angry, 2
    true war, 82
Vice-Presidency, 319
Vice-president, 15, 20, 270, 274
    appointed, 270
Victims, 57, 88, 106, 116–117, 182–183, 200, 208, 210, 219, 282–284, 289, 296–298, 301
    angry, 153, 296
    bribe, 296
    burned, 282
    clobbered, 178
    former, 92
Victories, 12, 26, 29, 82, 121, 181, 231, 246, 310, 335, 338
    disputed electoral, 310
    inevitable, 230
    manipulated, 231
    political, 281, 338
Villagers, 63, 279, 296
    murdering, 309
    villages harassing, 309
Villages, 275
    pretending, 309
    remote, 63
Villains, 68–69, 117, 214
    cartoon, 175
    true, 215
Vine, 36
Violence, 15, 43–45, 47, 76–77, 83–90, 93–94, 101–103, 155, 157–158, 213–214, 218–219, 231–234, 267–271, 281–288, 314–316, 321–322
    applying, 219
    biblical, 271
    degrees in, 56, 84, 155, 209, 215
    delivered, 70, 203

Violence (*cont.*)
  denormalise, 102
  deployed sexual, 106
  diabolic, 14
  discharged, 56
Violent, 29–30, 95, 101, 152, 155,
    158, 161, 279, 281, 291, 297
  attacks, 270
  colonial, 214
  coup, 262
  coward, 92
  dispute, 42
  drive, 64
  elimination, 268
  ghosts, 3
  guerrilla movement, 213
  history, 138
  ideology, 99
  impunity, 10
  instincts, 119
  kind, 291
  legacy, 314
  measures, 119
  operation, 86
  passion, 293
Violent crimes, 190, 218
  committed, 219
Virgin conception, 128
Vivid dramatisation, 250
Volcanic temper mirrors, 79
Voters, 82, 127, 228, 231
  coerce, 92
Votes, 22, 24, 62, 67, 217, 228,
    230–232, 258, 260
  electoral, 62
  free, 248
  wasted, 24, 232
Voting, 228, 247, 248, 298
Vulgarity, 263, 322
Vulnerability, 42–43, 47, 54, 79–81,
    84, 116, 119, 127, 172, 180
  inner, 213
  social, 42
Vulnerable personages, 318

W
Walls, Peter (General), 30, 231, 258
Walsh, Gerald Groveland, 141
Wamba Dia Wamba, Ernest, 57
War, 48, 70–71, 76, 82, 85–90,
    102, 105–107, 191–194,
    262, 268, 315–316,
    322, 323
  acceptability, 101
  against, 86
  arts of, 65, 90
  civil, 269, 275
  cold, 69, 86, 177
  dispense, 87, 194
  elevates, 62
  enacted, 90
  engineer, 86
  erects, 86
  expensive, 71
  final, 89
  gruelling, 67
  guerrilla, 6, 191, 192, 268
  hot, 86
  injuries, 83
  liking, 62
  machine, 81–83, 193, 226
  machinery, 80
  Nelson Maldonado-Torres, 105
  new, 86
  paradigm of, 85–89, 103
  path, 165
  prisoner, 82
  questioned Mugabe's, 82
  symbolised, 90
  total, 240
  ultimate, 88
  valorisation of, 92–94
War credentials, 196
  believed liberation, 307
Warlords, 55, 62, 101, 323–324
  true, 227
Warrior-Grandfather, 326
Warrior kings, 35
Warriors, 34, 82, 85, 176

Warrior tradition, 35, 85, 87–88
  domineering, 87
War-time friends, 134
War veterans, 82–83, 310
  feared, 134
War Vets, 310
Weakling, 80, 84
  angry, 80
Weakness, 2, 55, 65, 79–81, 84, 116,
    119, 123, 172, 261, 340
  defeating, 2
  fear of, 2, 55, 261, 325
  human, 87
  physical, 80, 129
  racial, 79
Wealth, 133, 226, 287
  amass, 226, 323
  amassed massive personal, 38
Weaponisation, 311
Weaponise, 106, 251
Weapons, 16, 41, 42, 72, 90, 93,
    117–119, 152, 172, 186,
    194, 274
Well-argued conclusion, 132
Western capitals, 11
Western civilisation, 187–189, 338
Western cynicism, 178
Western education, 215
  achieved, 215
  acquired, 160
Westerners, 254
  civilised, 254
Western nations, 299
Western neocolonialism, 32
White population, 17, 23, 29, 198,
    217, 242–243, 247–248, 254,
    258, 260
  suspicious, 11
Whites, 12–15, 104, 204, 205, 240,
    242–245, 247–248, 250–253,
    256–257, 259–261
  accommodating, 258
  appointed, 258
  expectations, 14

exploiters, 241
farmers, 246, 286
journalists, 27
racist bigot, 264
racist selfishness, 14
securocratic machinery, 257
Zimbabweans, 13, 17, 176, 243,
    247, 299
Widows, 57
  angry, 287
Wife/wives, 105, 123, 126, 131, 134,
    180, 206, 210–211, 226, 256,
    290, 307–308, 325
  abandoned, 128
  first, 37
  subdued, 105
  vicar's, 263
Wikileaks cables, 323
Wilber, Ken, 178, 179, 184, 197, 218,
    220, 342
Wilde, Oscar, 31
Willems, Wendy, 290, 294
Witchcraft, 19–21, 57, 293, 316, 322
  organisation, 316
  political, 316–317
  practising, 21
  purposes, 21, 293
Wizard, 21, 57, 293
Woman, 99, 126, 132, 183, 341
  deeply spiritual, 335
  pious, 132
  powerless young, 60
  unhappy, 130
Women, 22, 99, 105–107, 157, 188,
    279, 283, 288, 293,
    310–311, 315
  ambitious, 134
  despised, 105
  docile, 219
  pregnant, 22, 296
  rapeable, 106
  raped, 106
  raping, 309
  servile, 105

World, 1–3, 13, 16–17, 27–29, 41–43,
    66–69, 79, 84–88, 139–142,
    162–165, 172–175, 177–179,
    201–203, 214–216, 227–231,
    237–238, 245–248, 261–265
  extreme, 41
  gloomy, 44
  imaginary, 139
  impressionable, 73
  indigenous, 156
  insane, 289
  modern, 43, 85, 87, 197
  normal, 324
  opinion, 273
  order, 179
  phenomenon, 78
  politics, 87
  post-political, 179
  problem, 34, 87
  real, 9, 114, 139, 163, 172, 173,
    198, 204, 209, 220, 229,
    231, 235
  of reality, 213, 232
  religion, 143
World system, 36
  imperial, 175
  modern colonial, 86, 177
Worldwide acceptance, 91
Worship, 55, 62, 105, 107, 173, 174,
    180, 182–183, 200, 236, 292
Worshippers, 197
  self-serving, 178
Wrong model, 88
  political, 338

Y
Younger days, 311
Youths, 3, 106, 116, 180, 213, 326
  troubled, 123
Yue Jiang, 41

Z
Zambezi, 337
Zambia, 47, 103, 208, 255, 336, 337
Zambians, 208, 336
  prisons, 193
ZANU-PF supporters, 174, 189
  organised, 270
ZANU-PF Women's League, 290
Zapatistas, 165
Zapatista struggle, 165
ZAPU, 230, 231, 268–278,
    281–287, 291, 294,
    298–299
  bandits, 275
  crashing, 243
  leadership, 282
  party, 268–269
  and ZIPRA dissidents, 276
  and ZIPRA fighters, 273
ZANU-PF axe, 162
Zarathustra, 57, 77, 84, 150
ZDF, 329
Zhuwawo, Patrick (Former minister),
    274, 307, 311
Zimbabwe, 2–5, 12, 21–23, 27–29,
    34–39, 155–158, 175–177,
    201–205, 209–213, 243–246,
    256–258, 269–272, 279–282,
    286–294, 300–301,
    308–338, 341–342
  amounts, 339
  argument, 322
  betrayal of, 203
  betrayed, 180, 203
  border areas, 324
  capitalist, 71
  collapse of, 202
  colonise, 331
  cost, 26
  coup overtook, 307
  darkest hour, 177

dark history of political violence and
    public insecurity, 335
descent, 34
destabilise, 275
entertained, 197
enveloped, 309, 328
espoused reduced, 105
fix, 333
haunted, 61
history, 288, 332, 335
postcolonial, 14
post-independence, 27, 151, 162,
    313, 336
power in, 15, 174, 217, 226, 227,
    255, 306, 331, 333
ruled, 5, 34
ZAPU and Nkomo's ZIPRA
    dissidents, 272
Zimbabwe African National
    Union, 288
Zimbabwe African Regional Union
    (ZARU), 288
Zimbabwe African Tribal Union
    (ZATU), 288
masquerading, 288
Zimbabwean African National Union
    (ZANU), 136, 138, 193, 230,
    270, 275, 288, 297, 298
armies, 194
axe, 268
formed, 288
idea, 194, 233
party and government, 297
ZANU-loyal military formation, 279
Zimbabwean African National
    Union-Patrioti Front
    (ZANU-PF), 25, 193, 194, 196,
    226–227, 232, 233, 270–275,
    277–278, 280, 285–287,
    296–298, 300, 311–313
Zimbabwean history, 94, 106
studied, 216

Zimbabwean liberation, 264
movement, 192, 287, 311
Mugabe, 5
Zimbabwean liberation struggle, 10,
    191, 213–214
and shed Mugabe, 213
Zimbabwean National Army, 329
Zimbabweans, 2–5, 16–17, 23–24,
    27–28, 38–40, 46–47, 69–71,
    157, 173–175, 208–209,
    212–213, 234, 236, 298–300,
    308–313, 325–332, 335–337,
    341, 342
Mugabe, 3
multitudes, 59, 295
nation, 290, 291
nationalism, 157
nationalist leaders, 5
politics, 20, 125, 270, 277, 313,
    321, 341
polity, 228
poor, 133
population, 20, 26
postcolony, 5–6, 14–15, 55–57,
    63–64, 66–67, 71,
    90–92, 101, 103–104,
    226–227, 320–324,
    327–328, 337
postcolony Mugabe, 10, 37, 65, 73
post-independence government, 176
Zimbabwe Defence Forces, 310
Zimbabwe for Zimbabweans, 291
Zimbabwe Military Intelligence, 316
Zimbabwe Mnangagwa, 323
Zimbabwe Mugabe, 23, 32, 54–55,
    102, 266, 338, 340
Zimbabwe National Army
    Brigade, 280
Zimbabwe National Attack
    Forces, 312
Zimbabwe National Defence
    Forces, 312

Zimbabwe National People's Army
    (ZANLA), 158, 162, 192, 269,
    274, 287, 299
  camps, 193
  guerrilla army, 192
  guerrilla camps, 56
  guerrilla commander, 192
  guerrillas, 131, 192
  guerrillas in Mozambique, 242
Zimbabwe News, 195
Zimbabwe People's Army (ZIPA),
    193, 268
Zimbabwe's independence, 2, 6, 8,
    159, 258
  David Smith, 212

Mnangagwa, 319
Mugabe, 240, 269
Zimbabwe the past is the
    future, 321
Zionism, 282
  aggressive, 33
ZIPRA, 269–277, 281, 287, 299
  army, 274
  cadres, 274, 276
  discredit, 274
Zombification, mutual, 59, 245
Zombifying, 59
Zvimba, 134, 180, 293
Zvino ballpoint pen icharwisana, 83
Zvobgo, Eddison, 194, 195, 263

CPSIA information can be obtained
at www.ICGtesting.com
Printed in the USA
LVHW080542020822
724957LV00004B/203